# MAOH
## JUVENILE REMIX

STORY AND ART BY
MEGUMI OSUGA

ORIGINAL STORY BY
KOTARO ISAKA

D1440064

(From Goethe's "Erlking")

"My son, wherefore seek'st thou thy face thus to hide?"

"Look, father, the Erlking is close by our side! Dost thou see not the Erlking, with crown and with train?"

"My son, 'tis the mist rising over the plain."

"My father, my father, and dost thou not hear the words that the Erlking now breathes in mine ear?"

"Be calm, dearest child, thy fancy deceives; the wind is sighing through withering leaves."

"My father, my father, and dost thou not see, how the Erlking is showing his daughters to me?"

"My darling, my darling, I see it aright, 'tis the aged grey willows deceiving thy sight."

"My father, my father, he seizes me fast, for sorely the Erlking has hurt me at last."

# CONTENTS

# Chapter 58 Nightlight

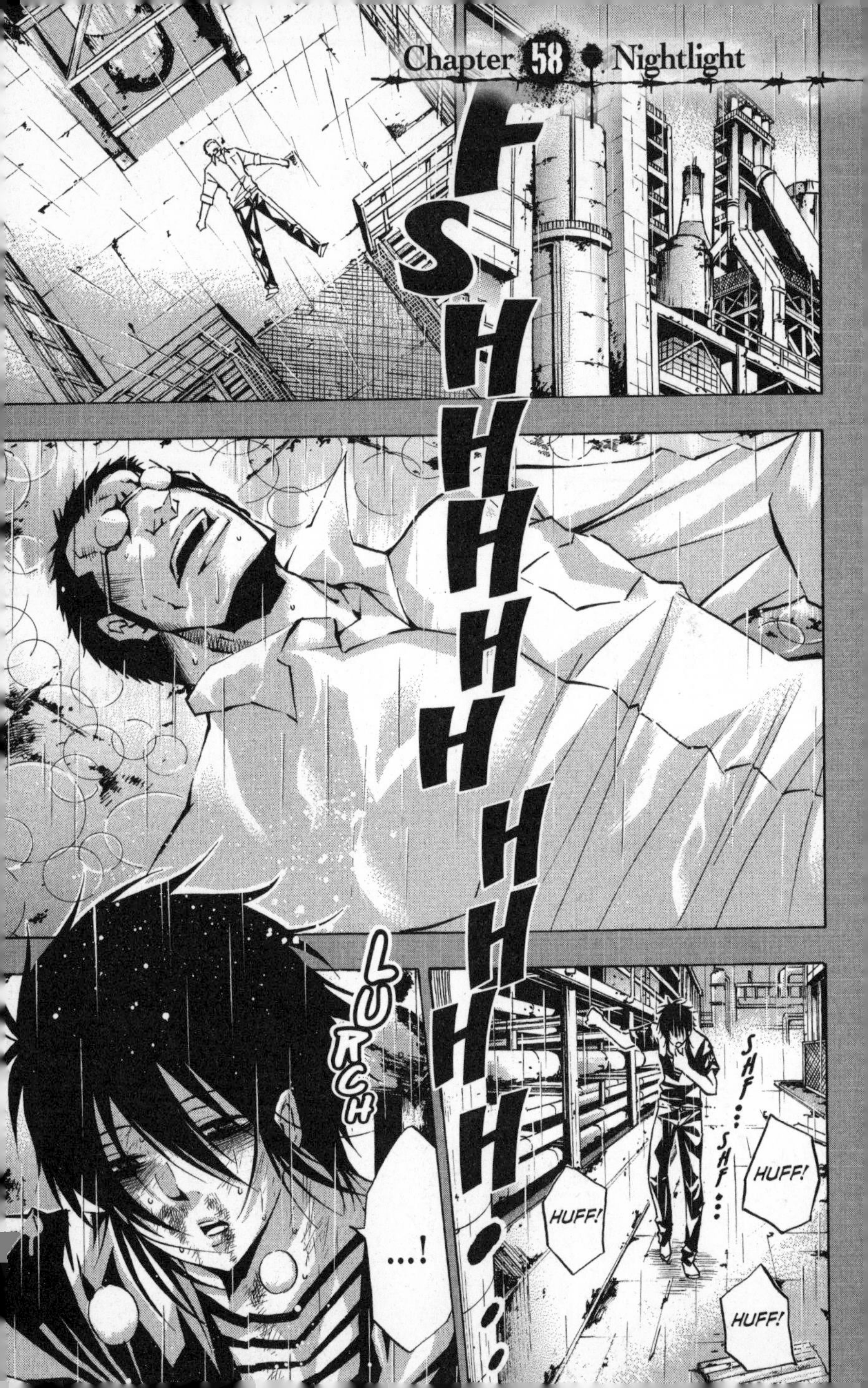
FSHHHHHHHHHHH...
SHF... SHF...
HUFF!
HUFF!
HUFF!
LURCH
...!

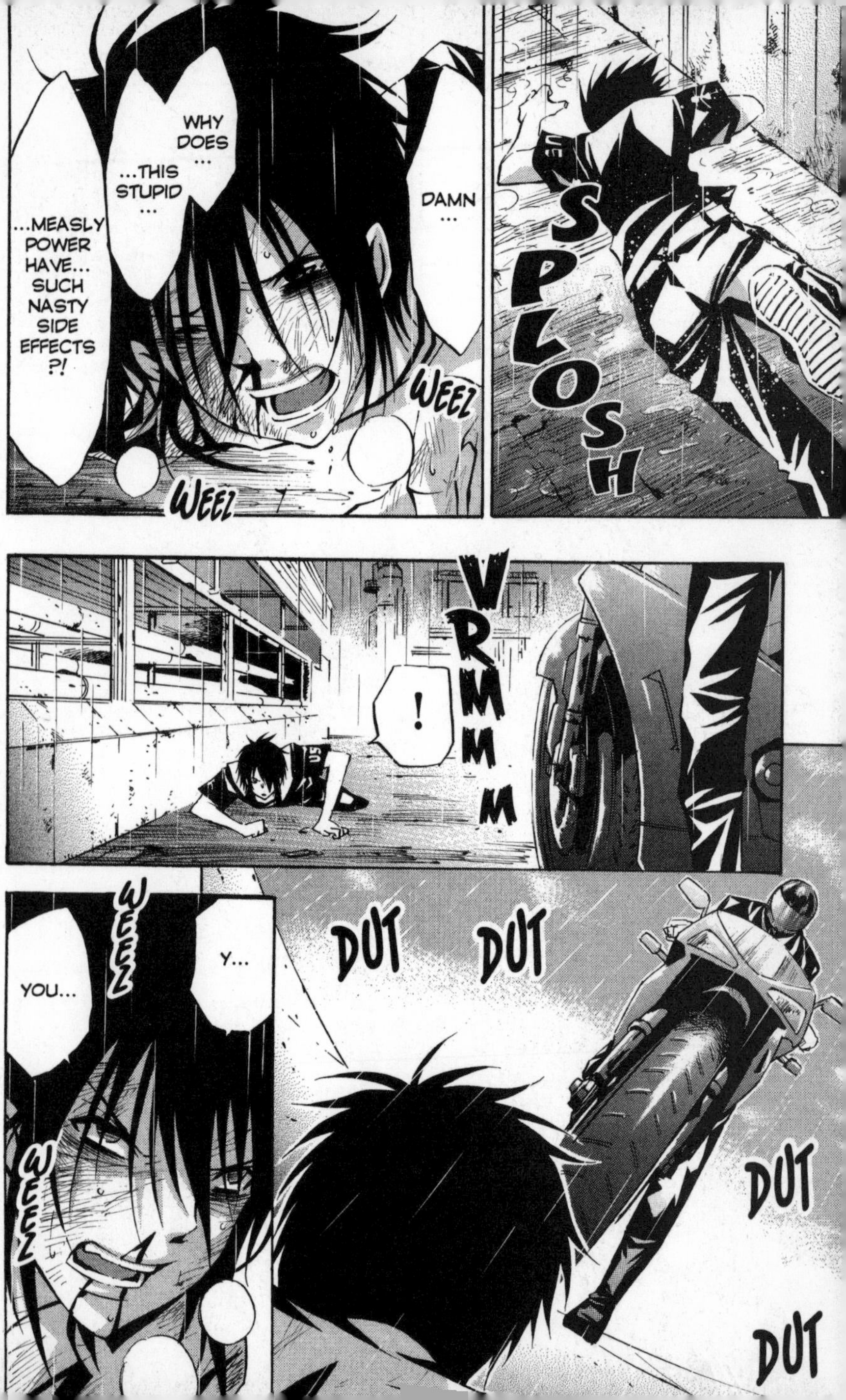
SPLOSH
DAMN...
WHY DOES...
...THIS STUPID...
...MEASLY POWER HAVE... SUCH NASTY SIDE EFFECTS?!
WEEZ
WEEZ
VRMMMM
!
DUT
DUT
DUT
DUT
Y...
YOU...
WEEZ
WEEZ

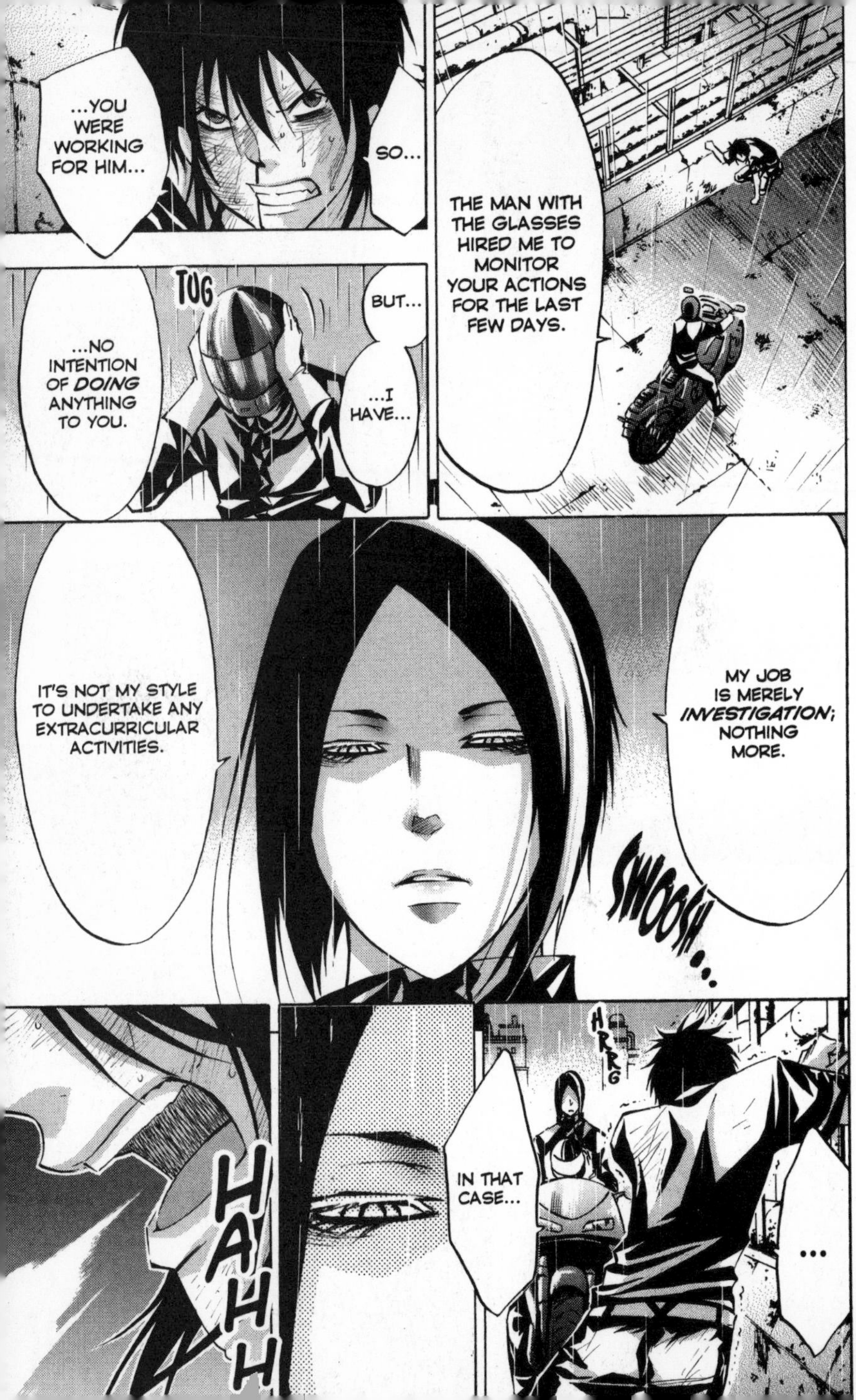
THE MAN WITH THE GLASSES HIRED ME TO MONITOR YOUR ACTIONS FOR THE LAST FEW DAYS.
SO...
...YOU WERE WORKING FOR HIM...
TUG
BUT...
...I HAVE...
...NO INTENTION OF *DOING* ANYTHING TO YOU.
MY JOB IS MERELY *INVESTIGATION*; NOTHING MORE.
IT'S NOT MY STYLE TO UNDERTAKE ANY EXTRACURRICULAR ACTIVITIES.
SWOOSH...
...
HRRRG
IN THAT CASE...
HAHHH

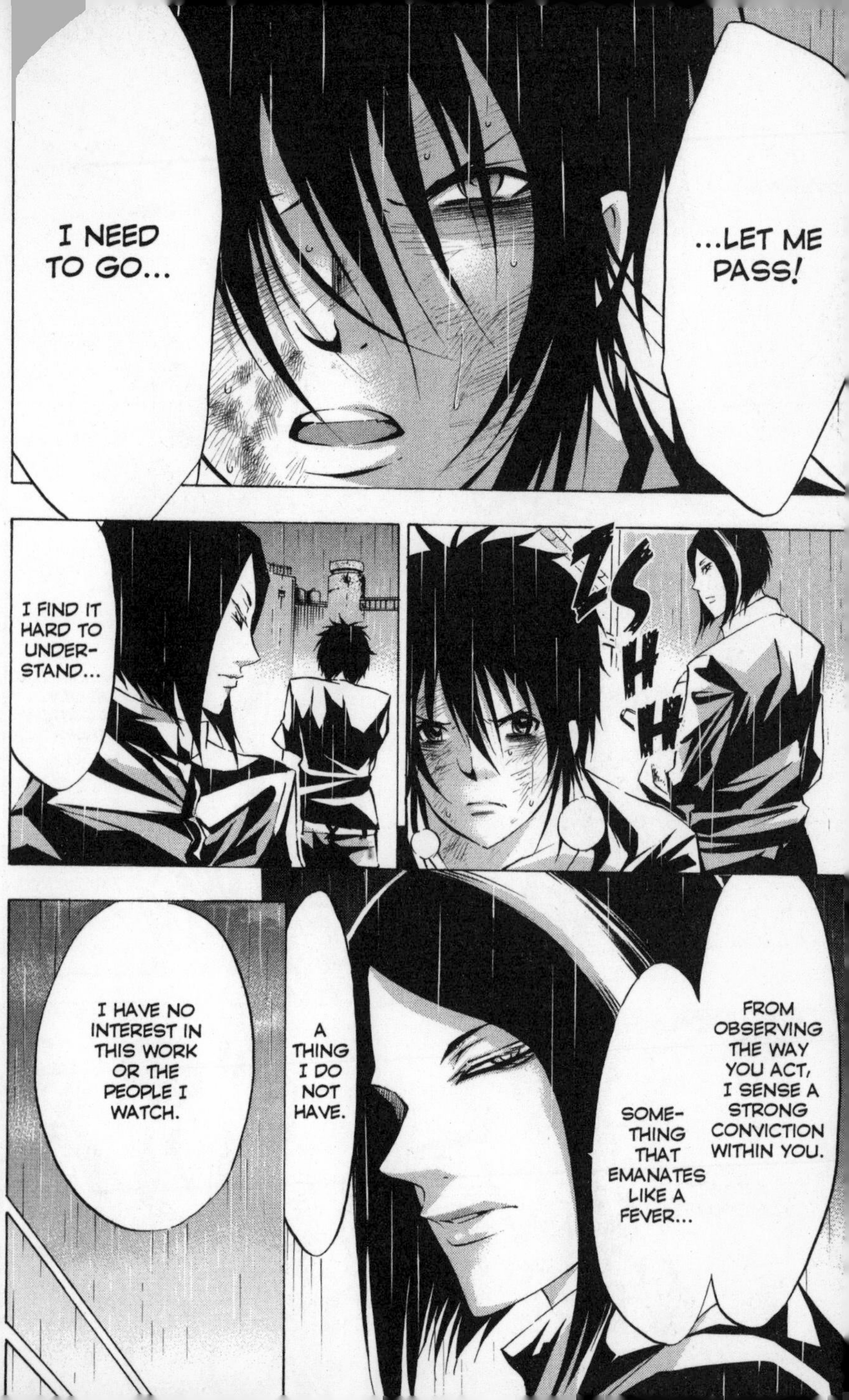
...LET ME PASS!
I NEED TO GO...
ZSHHH
I FIND IT HARD TO UNDERSTAND...
FROM OBSERVING THE WAY YOU ACT, I SENSE A STRONG CONVICTION WITHIN YOU.
SOMETHING THAT EMANATES LIKE A FEVER...
A THING I DO NOT HAVE.
I HAVE NO INTEREST IN THIS WORK OR THE PEOPLE I WATCH.

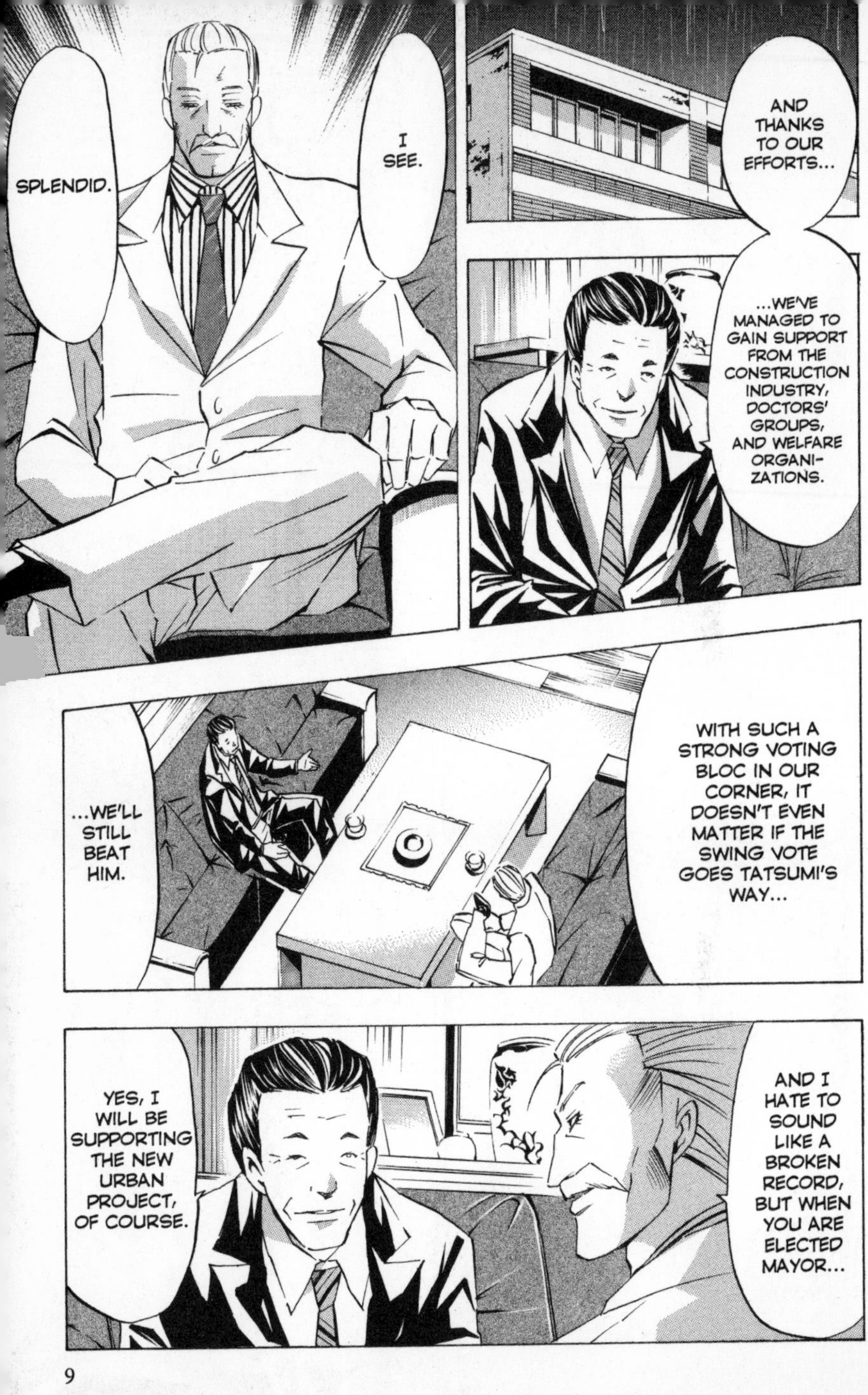
AND THANKS TO OUR EFFORTS...
...WE'VE MANAGED TO GAIN SUPPORT FROM THE CONSTRUCTION INDUSTRY, DOCTORS' GROUPS, AND WELFARE ORGANI-ZATIONS.
I SEE.
SPLENDID.
WITH SUCH A STRONG VOTING BLOC IN OUR CORNER, IT DOESN'T EVEN MATTER IF THE SWING VOTE GOES TATSUMI'S WAY...
...WE'LL STILL BEAT HIM.
AND I HATE TO SOUND LIKE A BROKEN RECORD, BUT WHEN YOU ARE ELECTED MAYOR...
YES, I WILL BE SUPPORTING THE NEW URBAN PROJECT, OF COURSE.

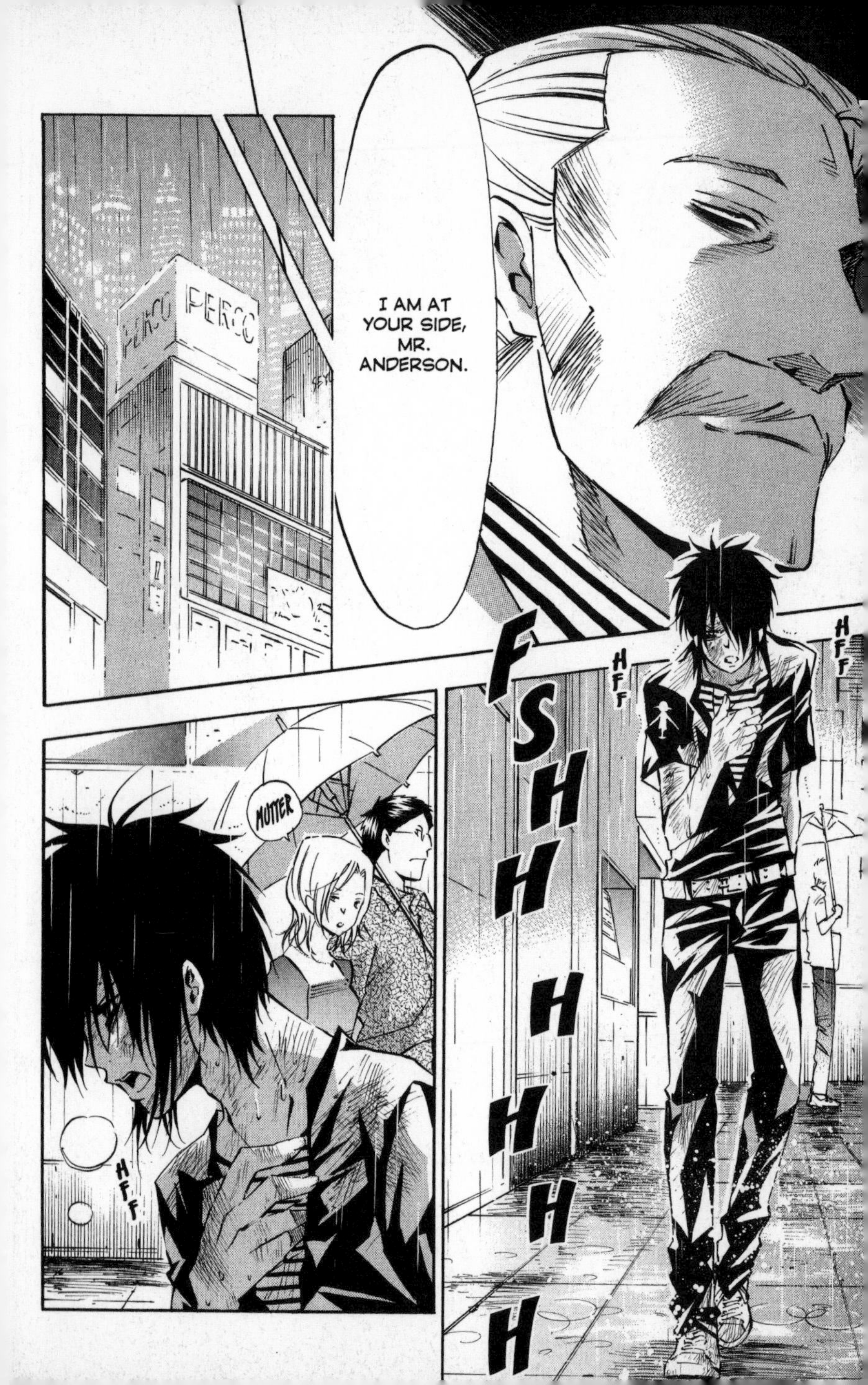
I AM AT YOUR SIDE, MR. ANDERSON.
PERCO
HFF
HFF
FSHHHHHHH
MUTTER
HFF

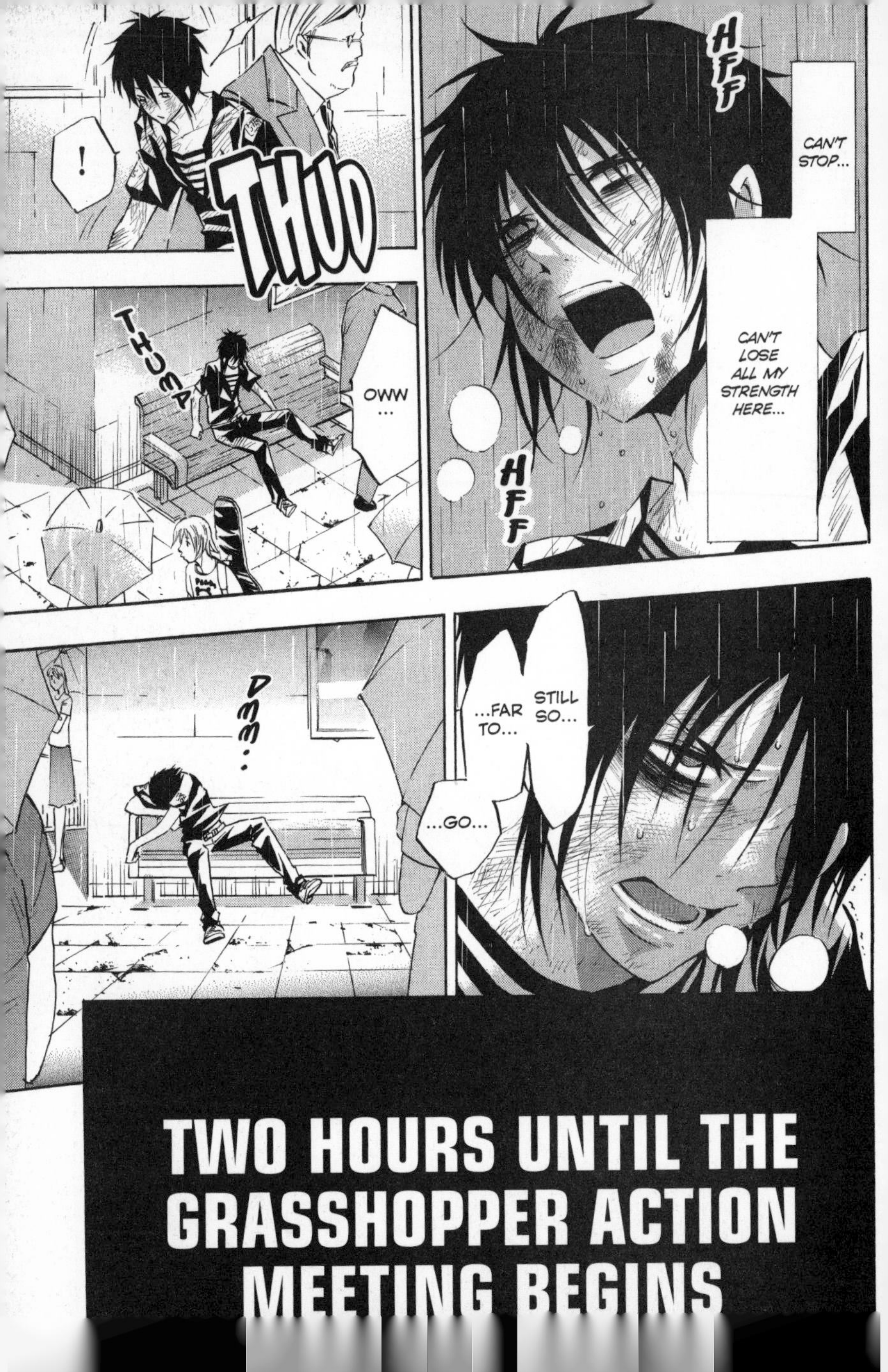
HFF
CAN'T STOP...
CAN'T LOSE ALL MY STRENGTH HERE...
HFF
!
THUD
THUMP
OWW...
STILL SO...
...FAR TO...
...GO...
DMM..
TWO HOURS UNTIL THE GRASSHOPPER ACTION MEETING BEGINS

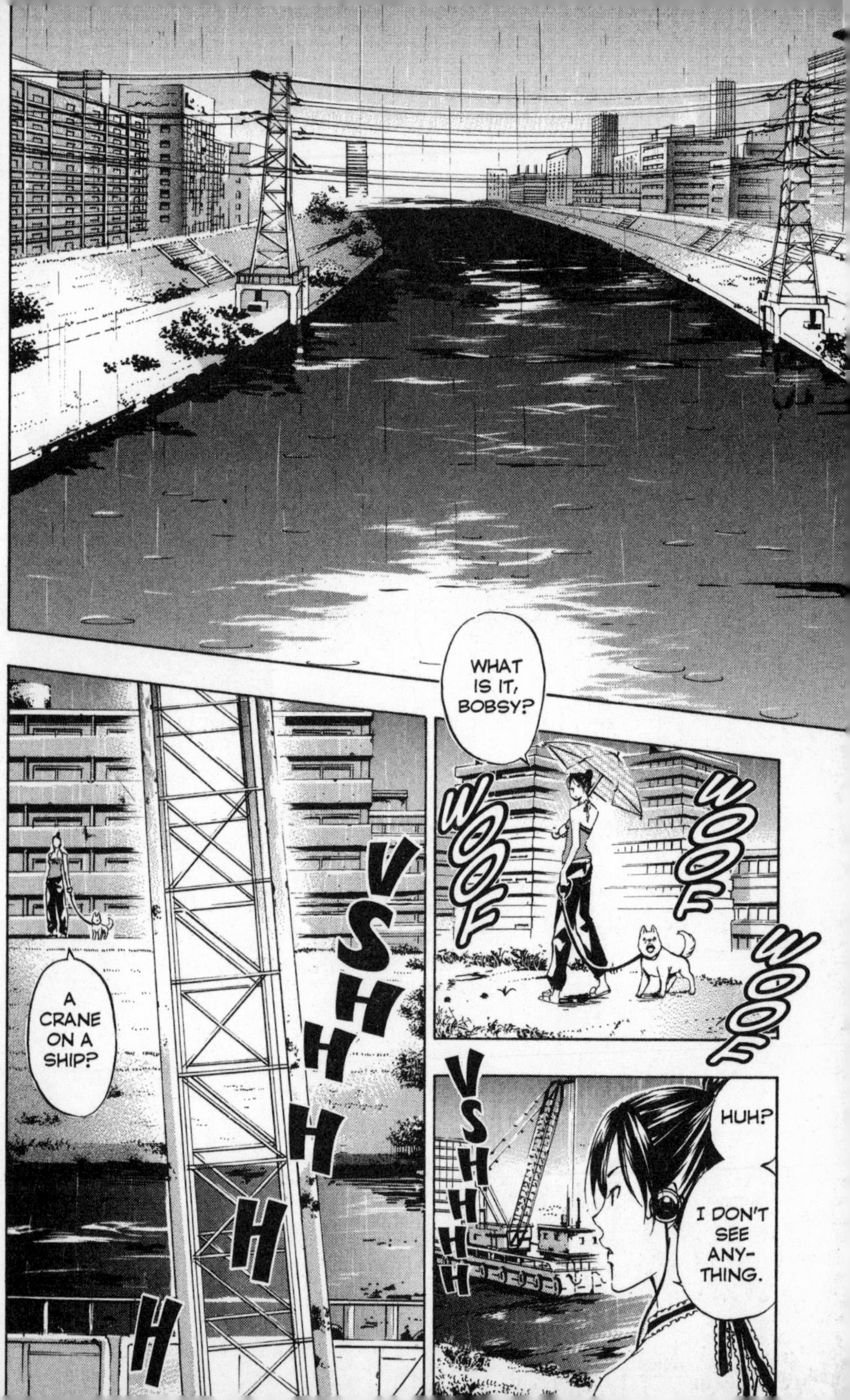
WHAT IS IT, BOBSY?
WOOF
WOOF
WOOF
HUH?
I DON'T SEE ANY-THING.
VSHHHHH
A CRANE ON A SHIP?
VSHHHHHH

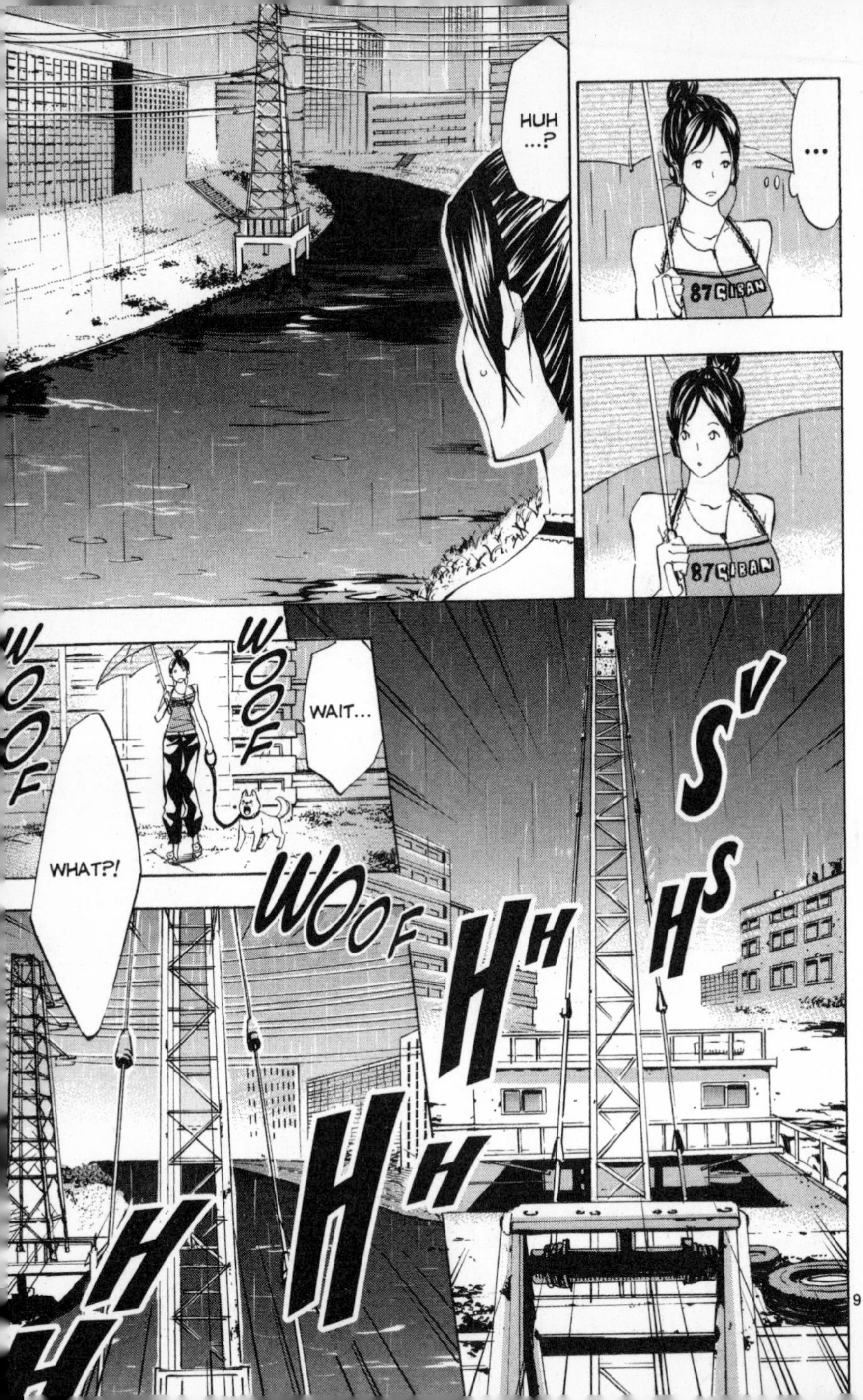
...
HUH ...?
WAIT...
WOOF
WOOF
WHAT?!
WOOF

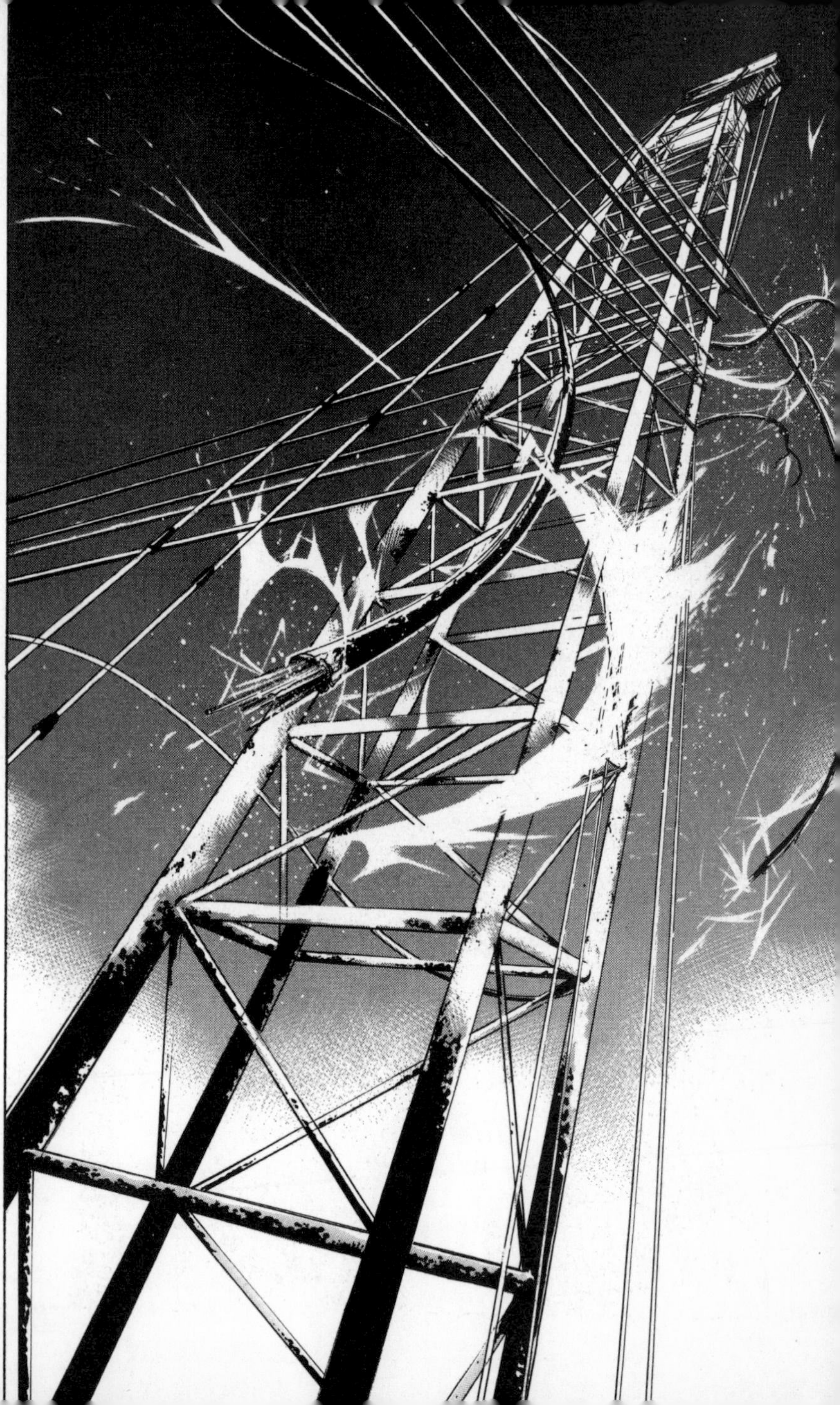

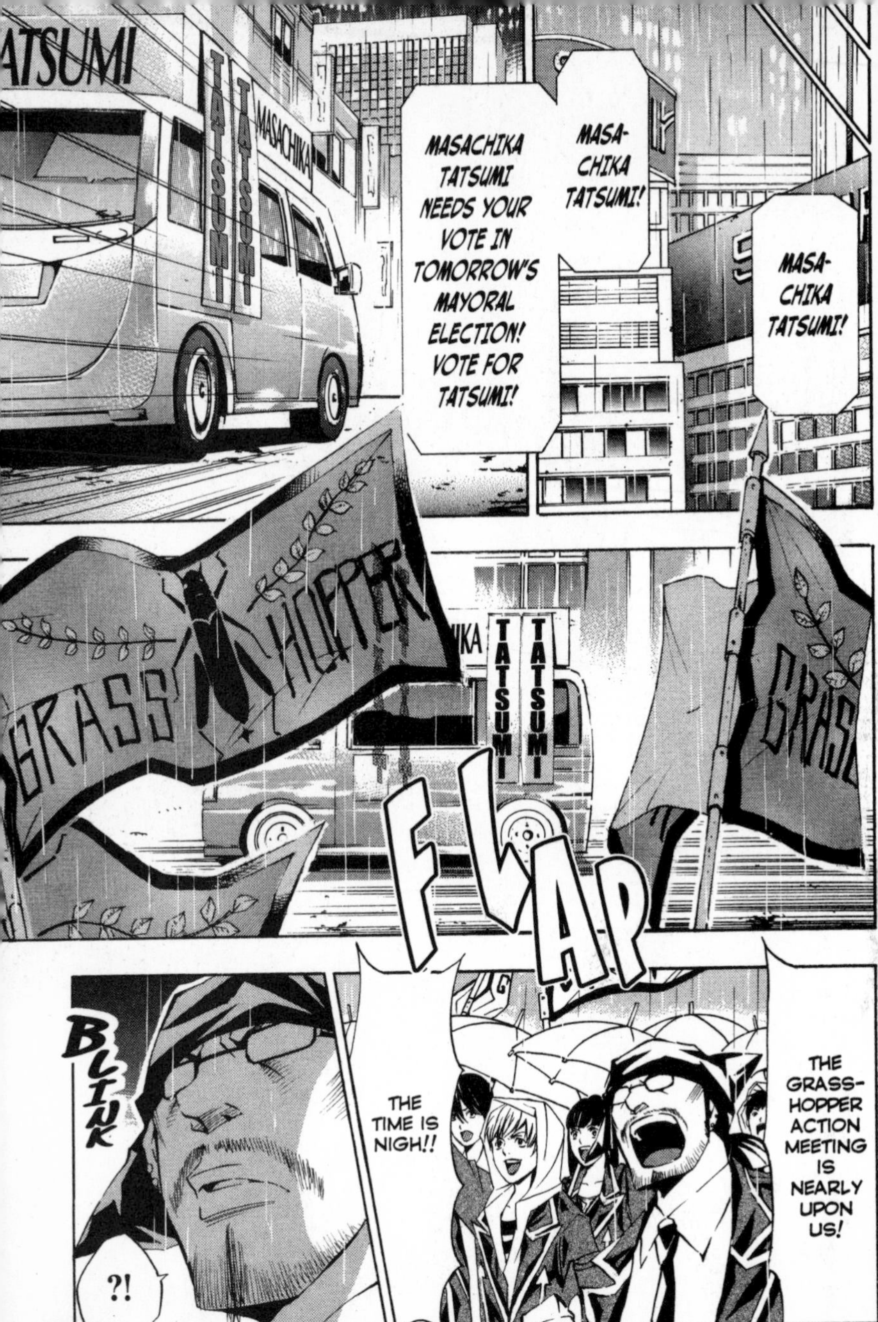
MASA-CHIKA TATSUMI!
MASA-CHIKA TATSUMI!
MASACHIKA TATSUMI NEEDS YOUR VOTE IN TOMORROW'S MAYORAL ELECTION! VOTE FOR TATSUMI!
TATSUMI
MASACHIKA
TATSUMI
TATSUMI
GRASS HOPPER
TATSUMI
TATSUMI
FLAP
THE GRASS-HOPPER ACTION MEETING IS NEARLY UPON US!
THE TIME IS NIGH!!
BLINK
?!

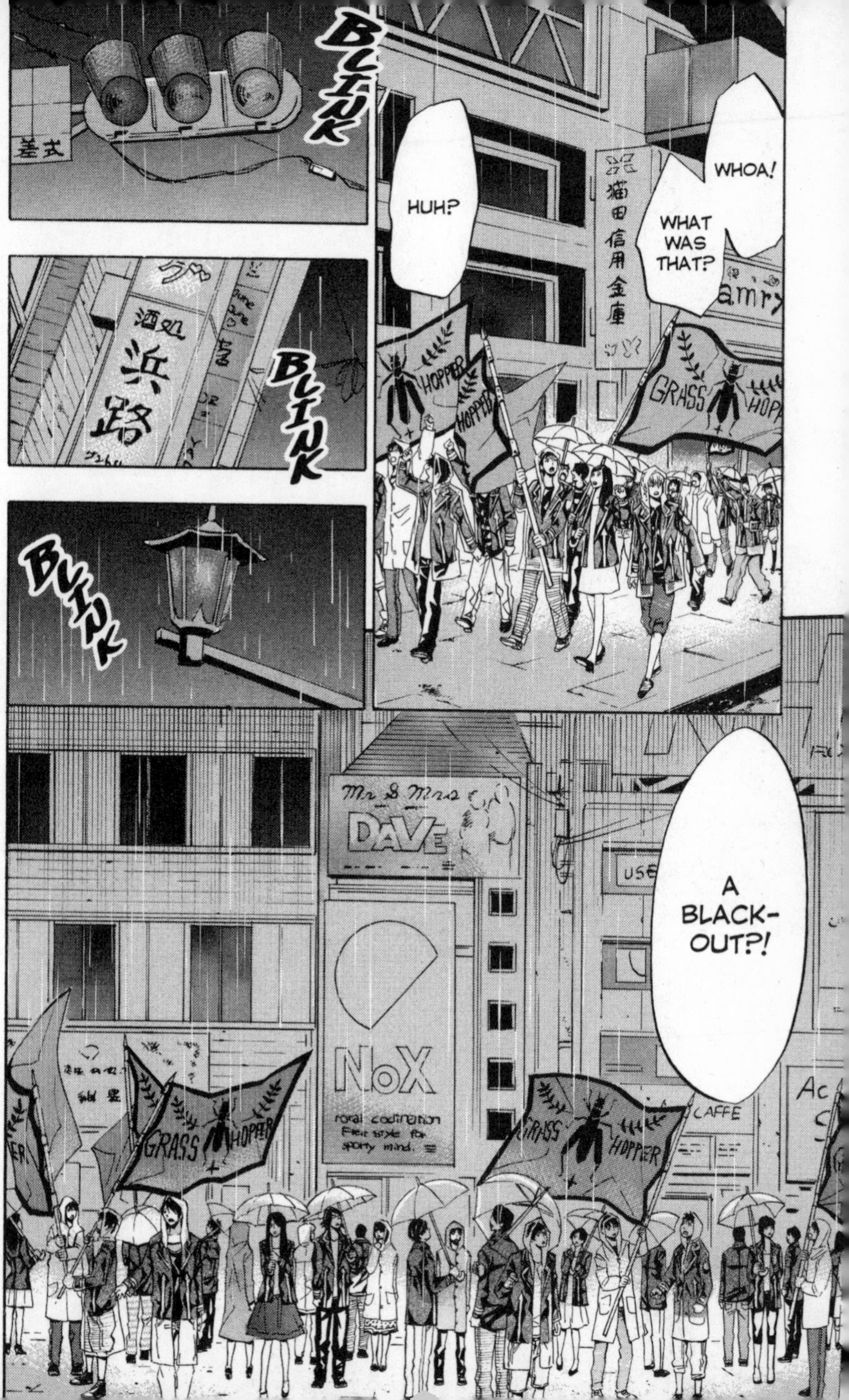
WHOA!
WHAT WAS THAT?
HUH?
GRASS HOPPER
BLINK
BLINK
BLINK
A BLACK-OUT?!
DAVE
NoX
CAFFE
GRASS HOPPER

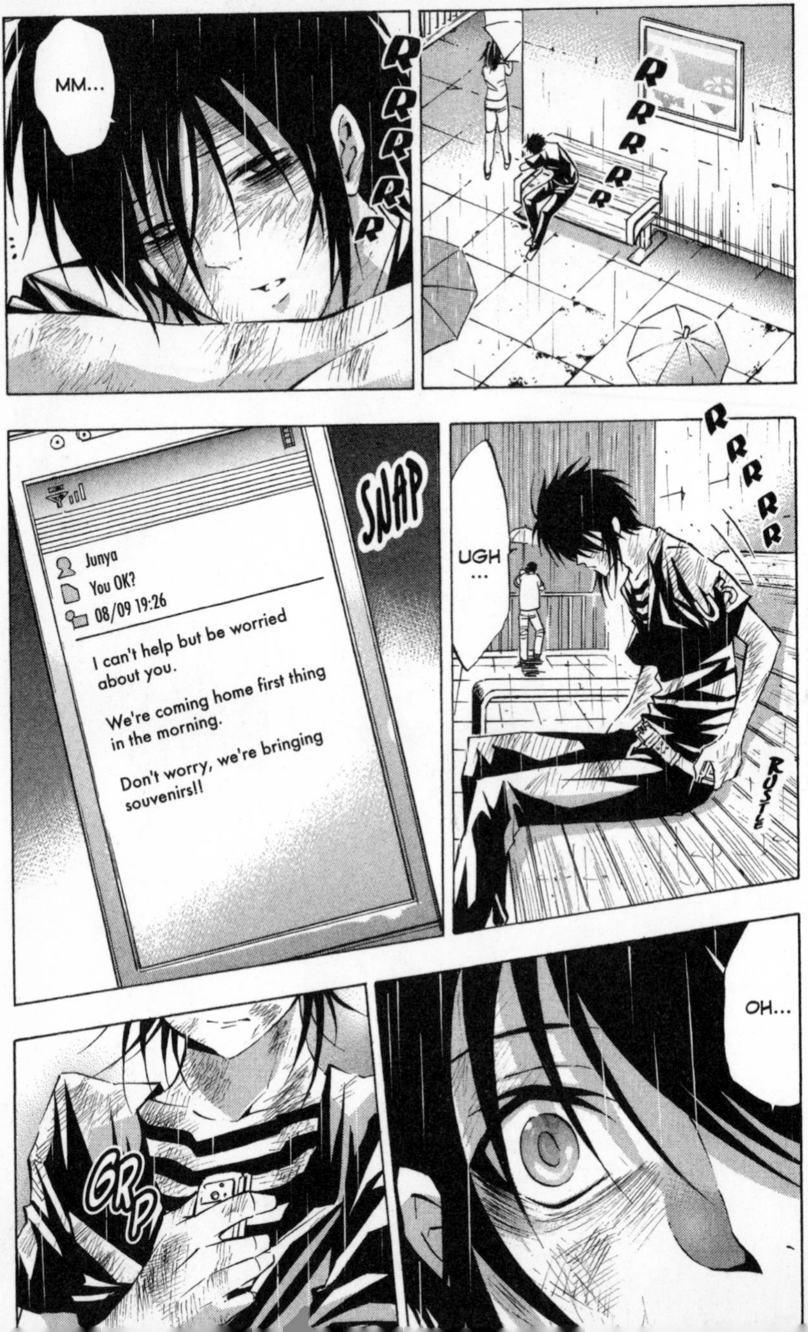
RRRRR
MM...
RRRRRR
RRRRR
UGH...
RUSTLE
SNAP
Junya
You OK?
08/09 19:26
I can't help but be worried about you.
We're coming home first thing in the morning.
Don't worry, we're bringing souvenirs!!
OH...
GRP

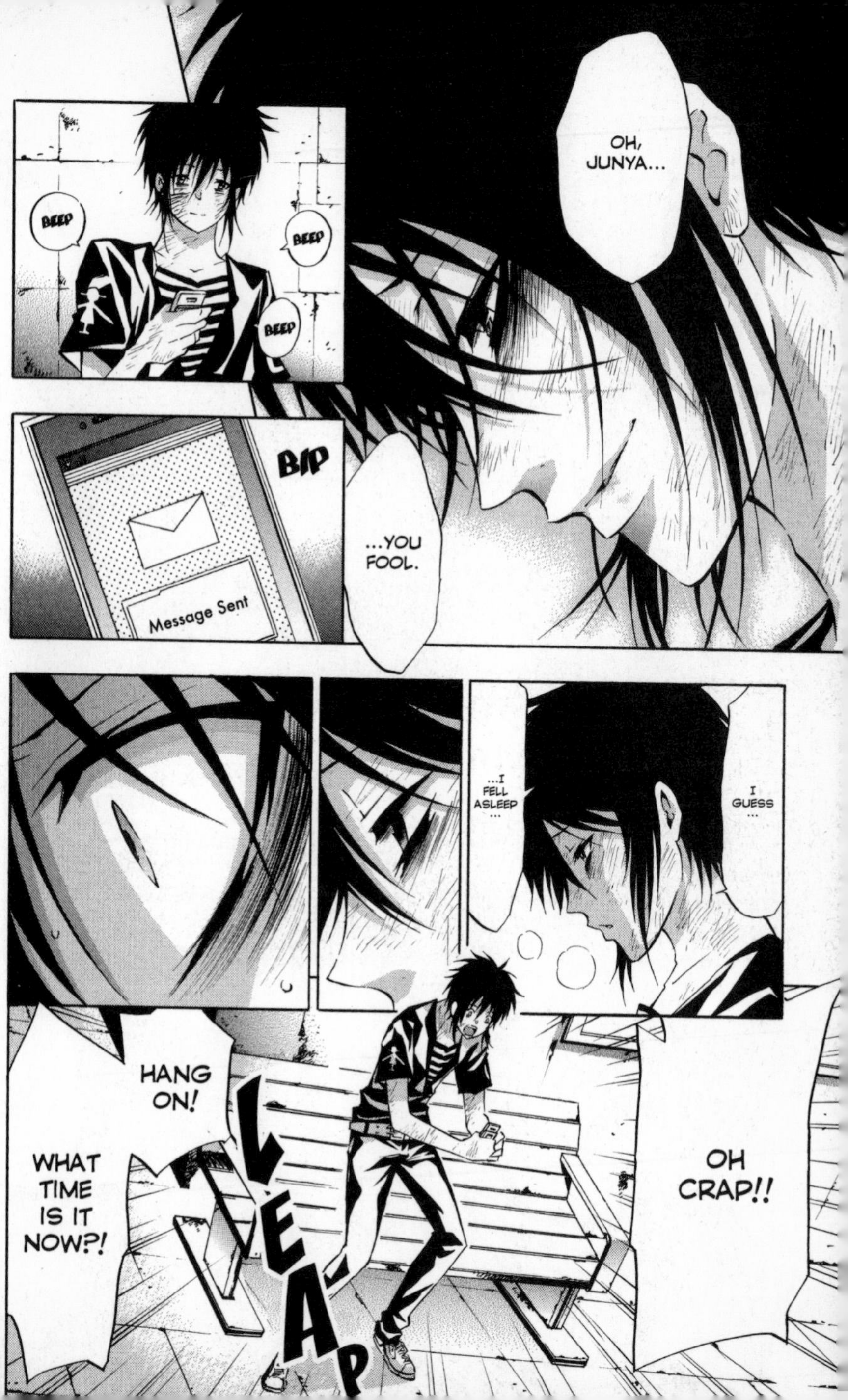
OH, JUNYA...
...YOU FOOL.
BEEP
BEEP
BEEP
BIP
Message Sent
I GUESS ...
...I FELL ASLEEP ...
OH CRAP!!
HANG ON!
LEAP
WHAT TIME IS IT NOW?!

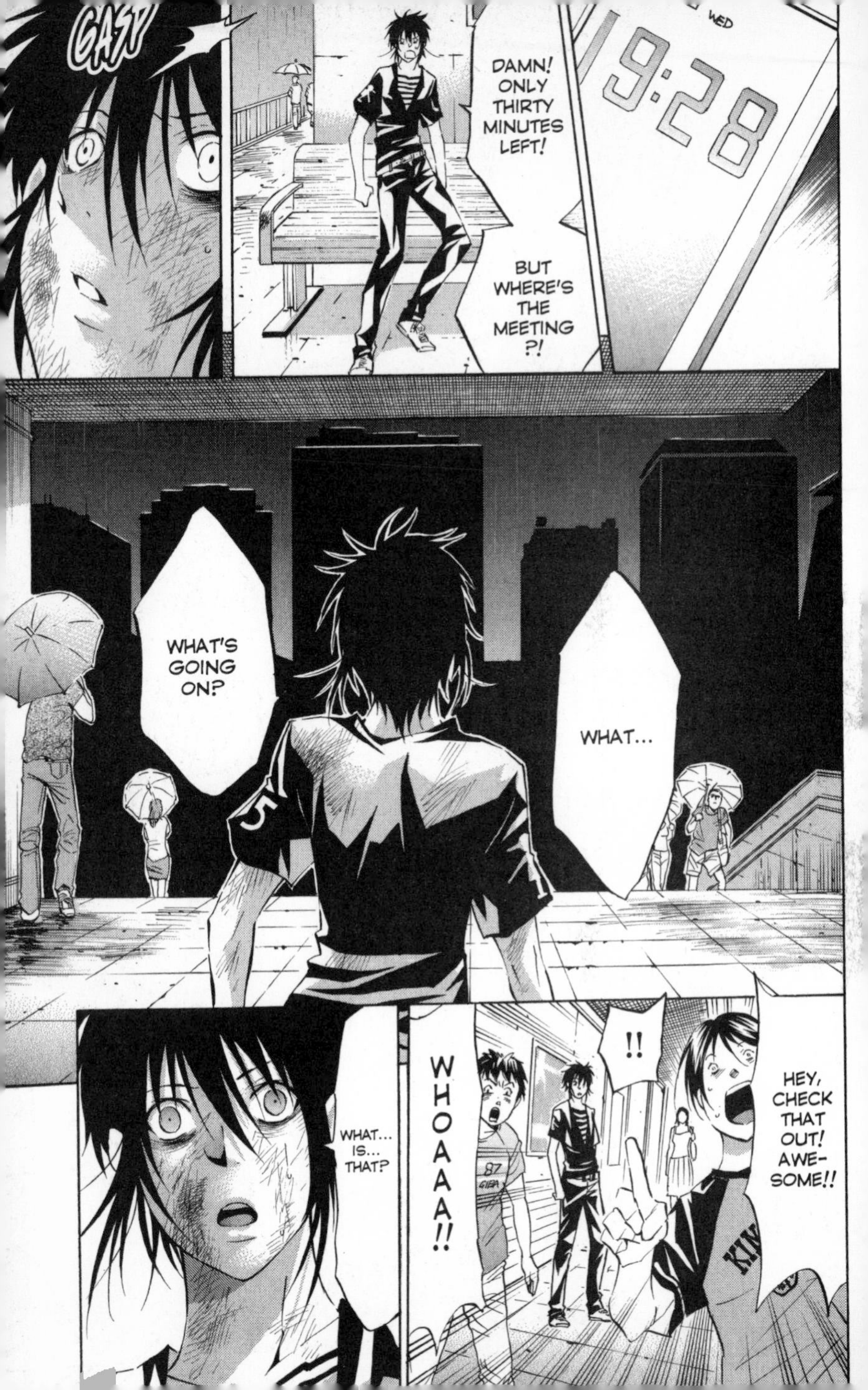
WED
19:28
DAMN! ONLY THIRTY MINUTES LEFT!
BUT WHERE'S THE MEETING ?!
GASP
WHAT...
WHAT'S GOING ON?
HEY, CHECK THAT OUT! AWE-SOME!!
!!
WHOAAA!!
WHAT... IS... THAT?

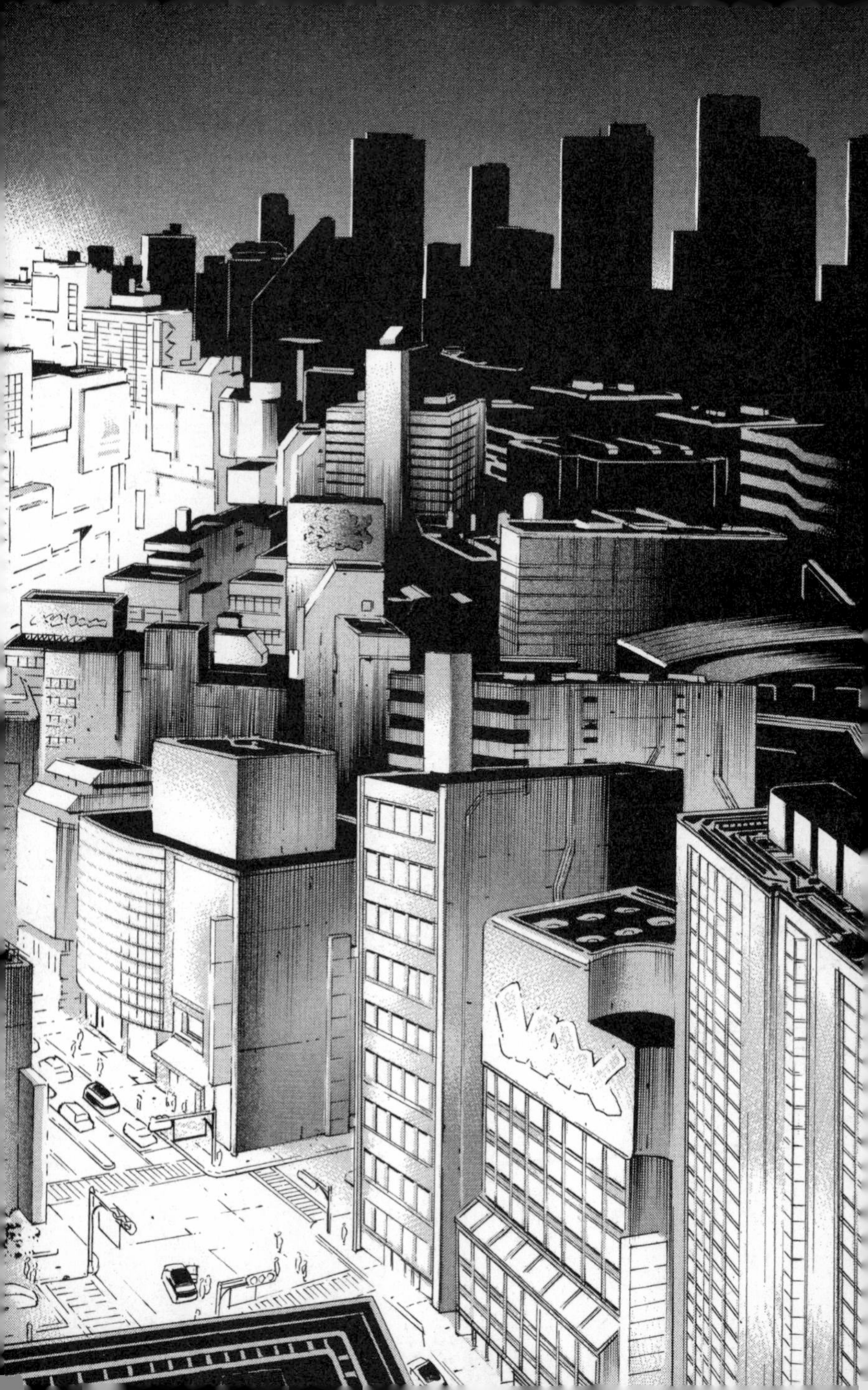

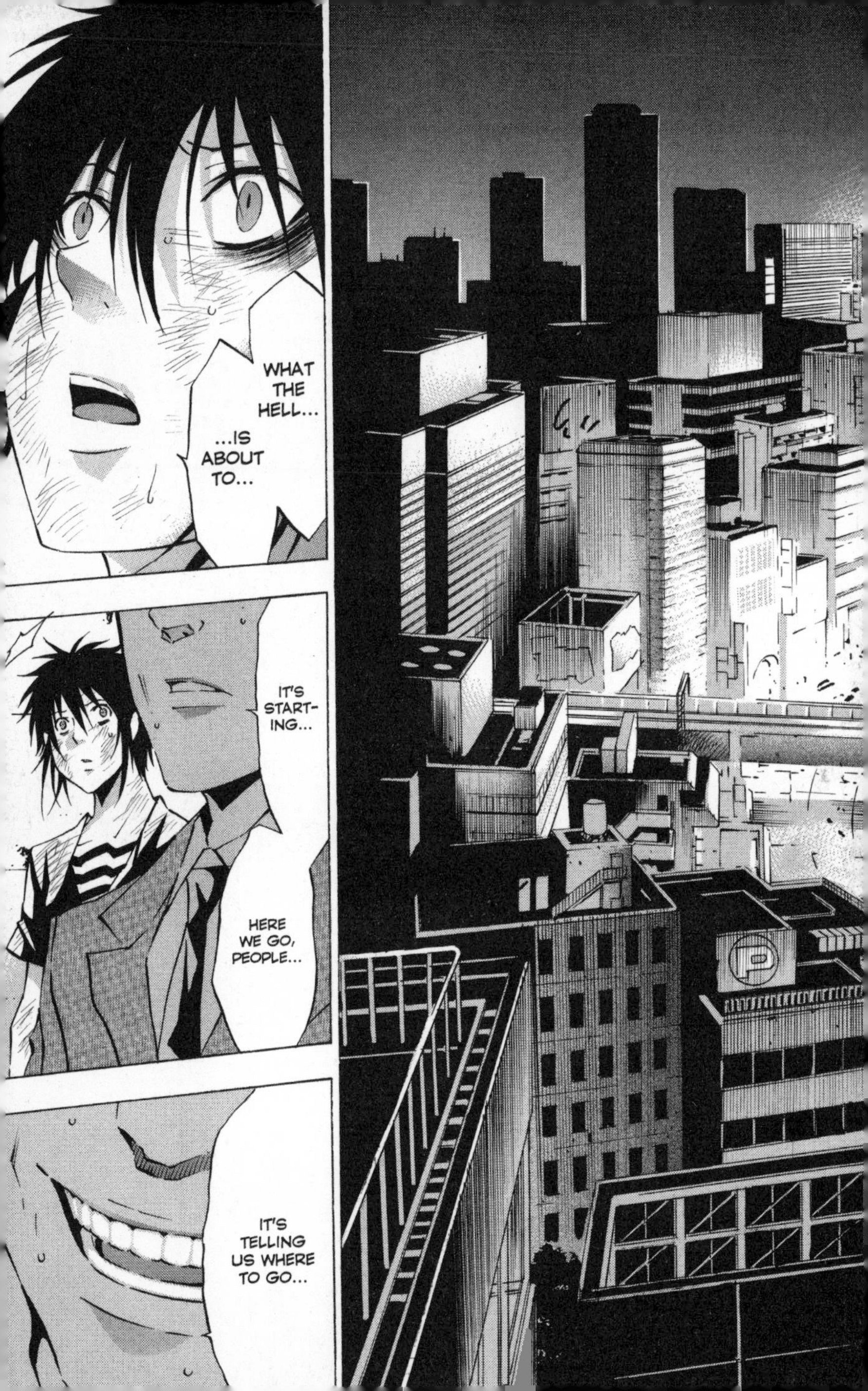
WHAT THE HELL...
...IS ABOUT TO...
IT'S START-ING...
HERE WE GO, PEOPLE...
IT'S TELLING US WHERE TO GO...

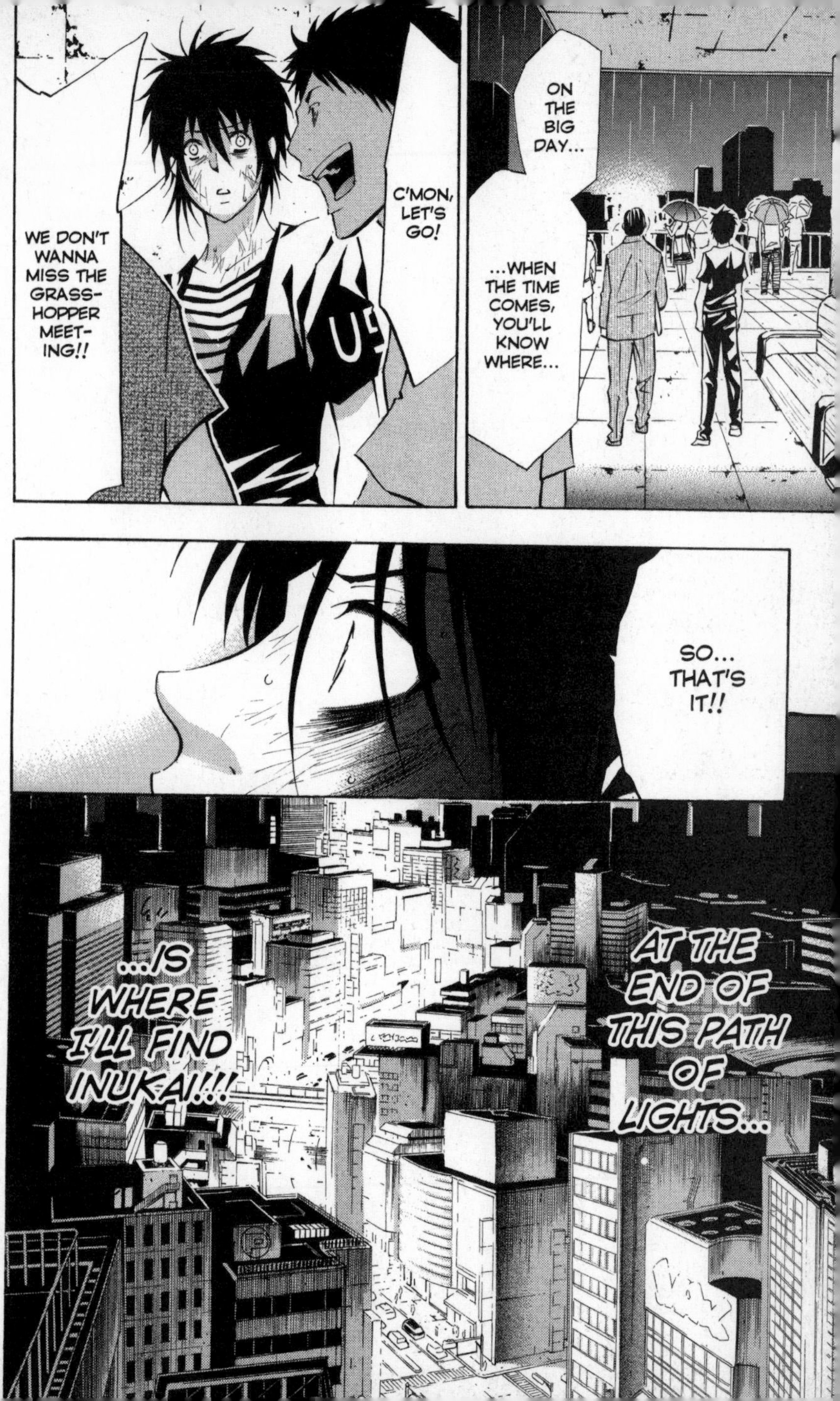
ON THE BIG DAY...
...WHEN THE TIME COMES, YOU'LL KNOW WHERE...
C'MON, LET'S GO!
WE DON'T WANNA MISS THE GRASS-HOPPER MEET-ING!!
SO... THAT'S IT!!
AT THE END OF THIS PATH OF LIGHTS...
...IS WHERE I'LL FIND INUKAI!!!

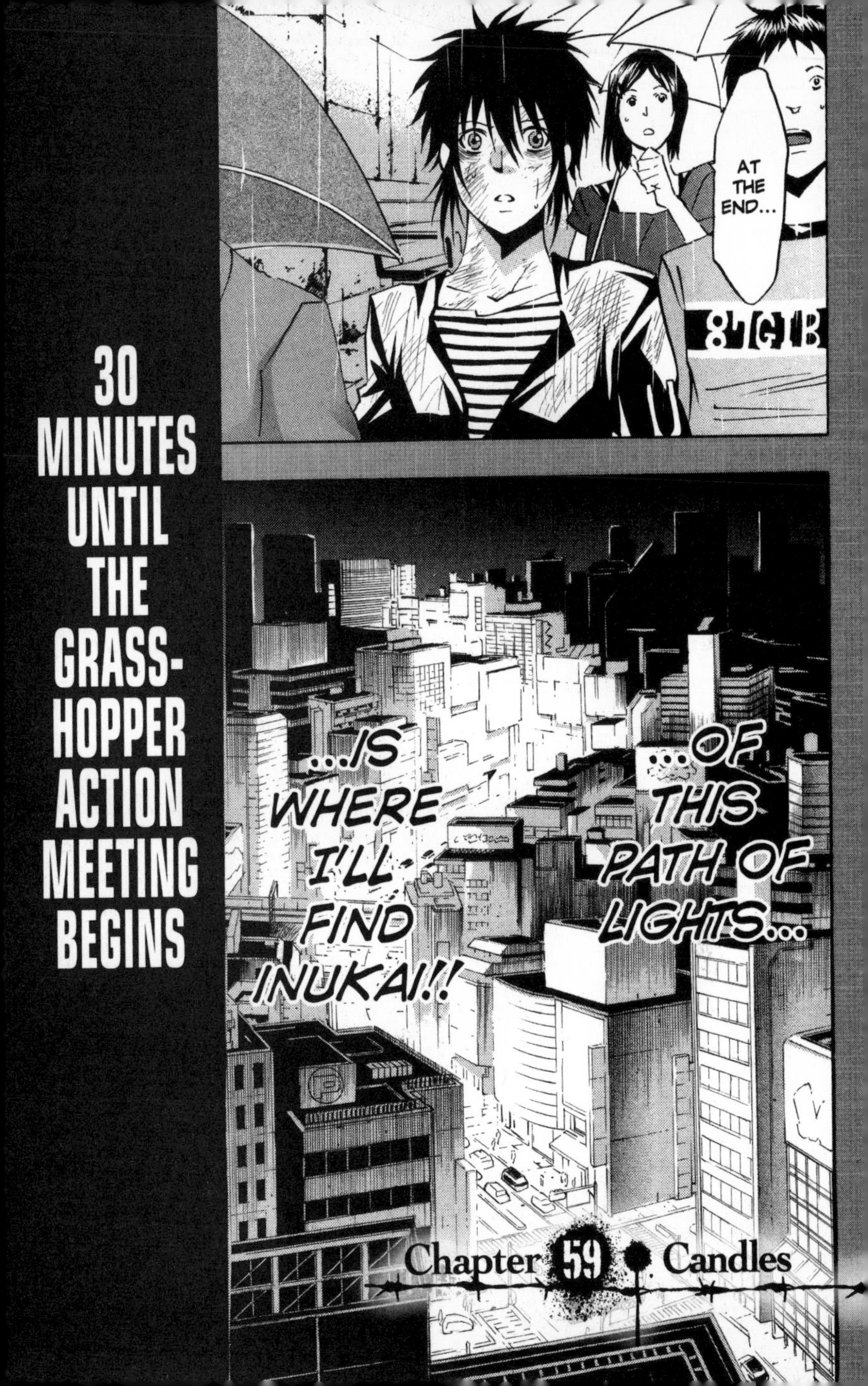
AT THE END...
...OF THIS PATH OF LIGHTS...
...IS WHERE I'LL FIND INUKAI!!
Chapter 59 Candles
30 MINUTES UNTIL THE GRASS-HOPPER ACTION MEETING BEGINS

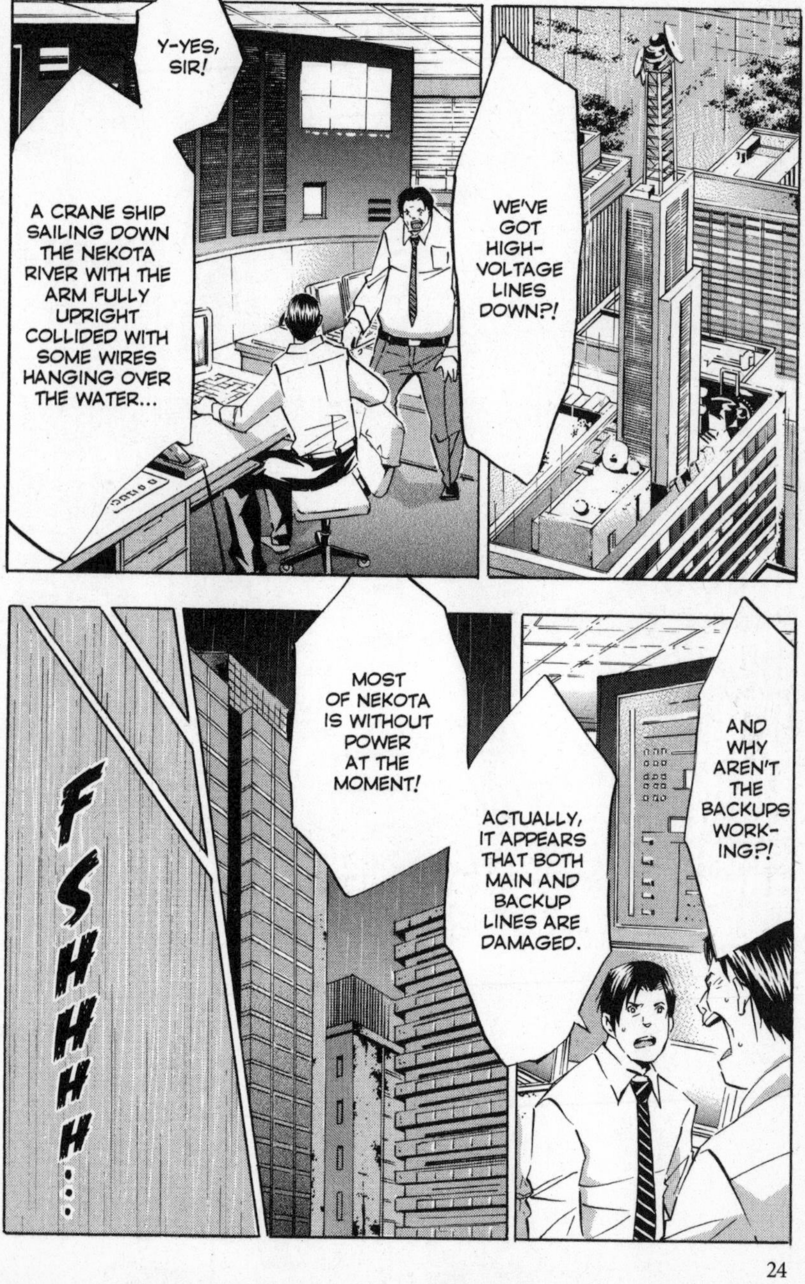
WE'VE GOT HIGH-VOLTAGE LINES DOWN?!
Y-YES, SIR!
A CRANE SHIP SAILING DOWN THE NEKOTA RIVER WITH THE ARM FULLY UPRIGHT COLLIDED WITH SOME WIRES HANGING OVER THE WATER...
AND WHY AREN'T THE BACKUPS WORKING?!
ACTUALLY, IT APPEARS THAT BOTH MAIN AND BACKUP LINES ARE DAMAGED.
MOST OF NEKOTA IS WITHOUT POWER AT THE MOMENT!
FSHHHHH...

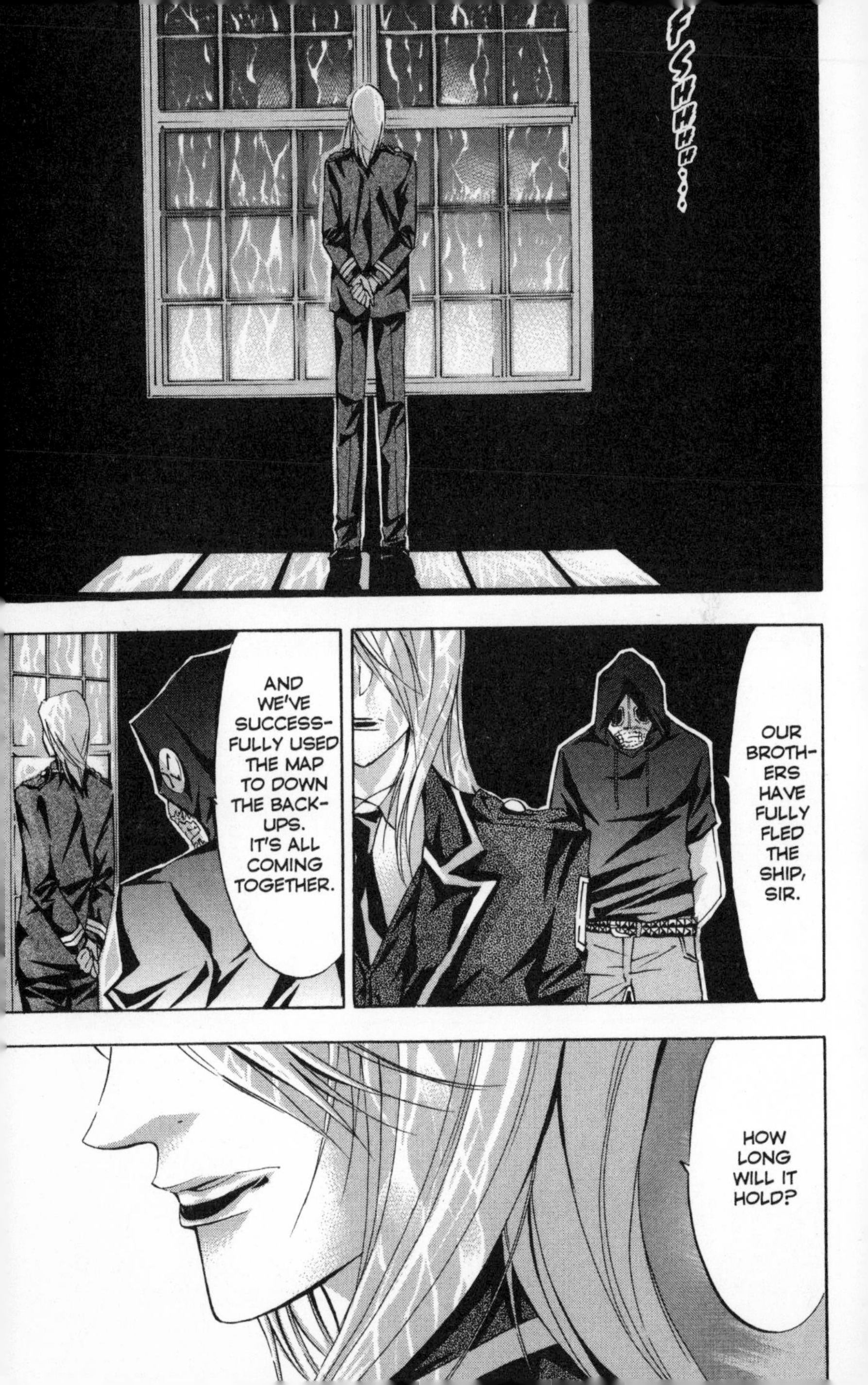
FSHHHH...
OUR BROTH-ERS HAVE FULLY FLED THE SHIP, SIR.
AND WE'VE SUCCESS-FULLY USED THE MAP TO DOWN THE BACK-UPS. IT'S ALL COMING TOGETHER.
HOW LONG WILL IT HOLD?

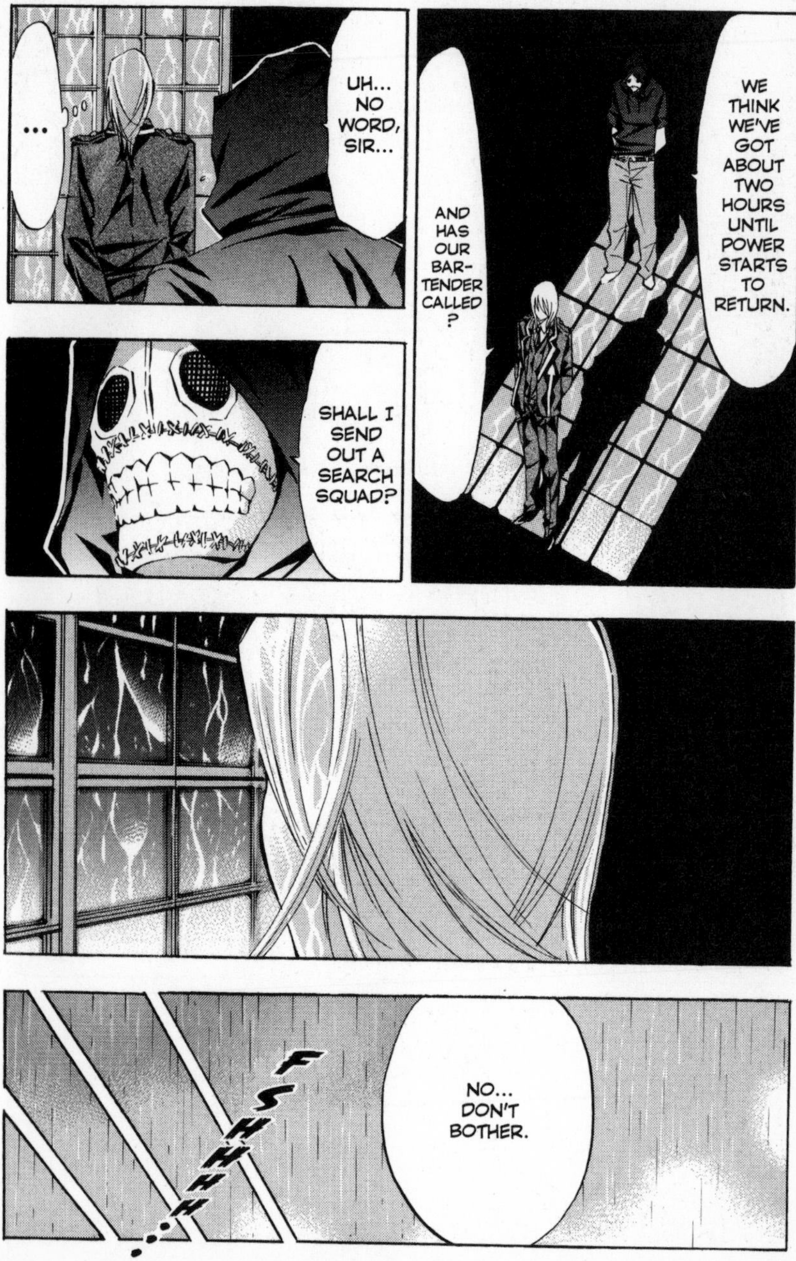
WE THINK WE'VE GOT ABOUT TWO HOURS UNTIL POWER STARTS TO RETURN.
AND HAS OUR BARTENDER CALLED?
UH... NO WORD, SIR...
...
SHALL I SEND OUT A SEARCH SQUAD?
NO... DON'T BOTHER.
FSHHHH...

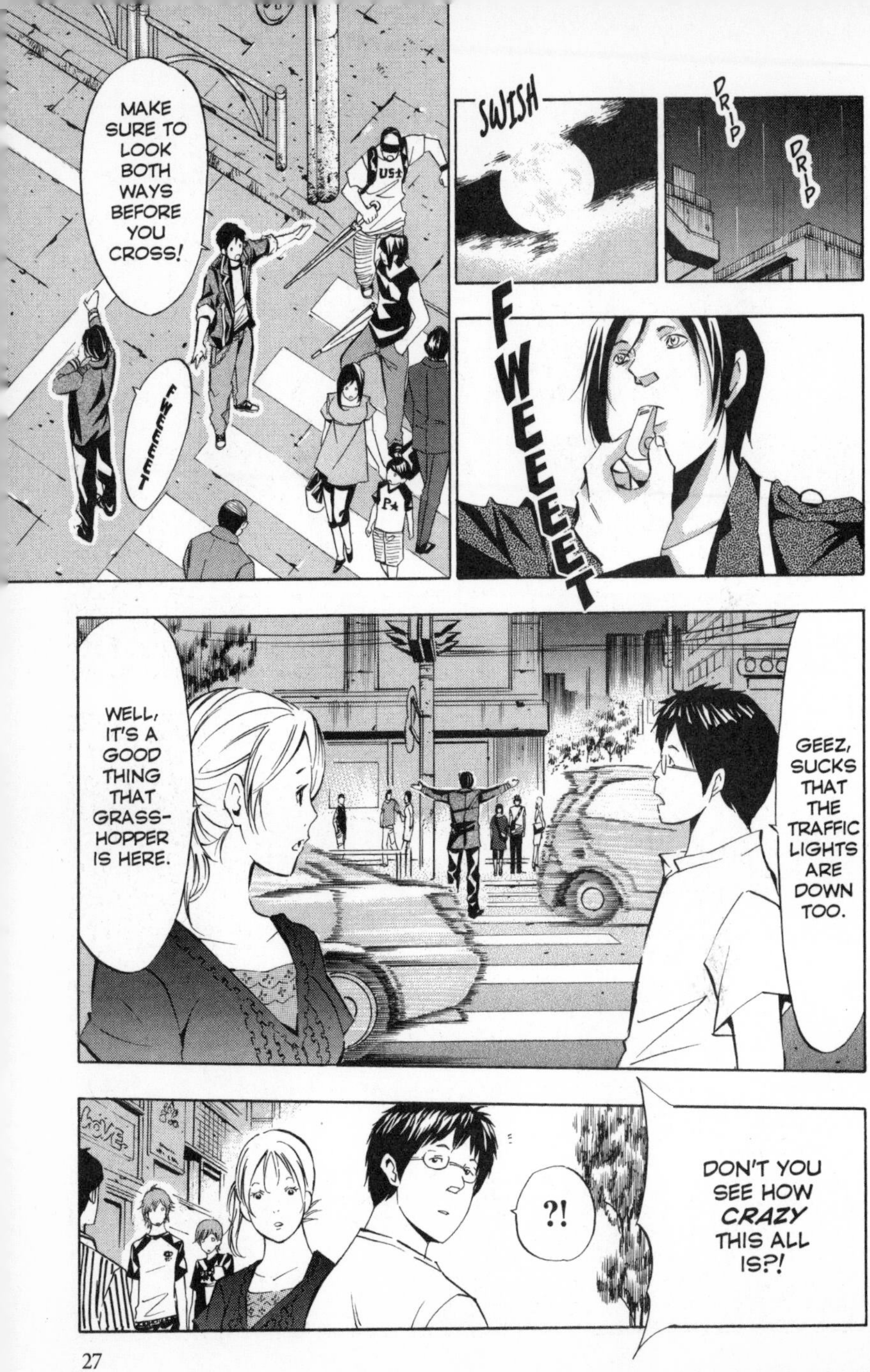
DRIP
DRIP
SWISH
FWEEEEET
MAKE SURE TO LOOK BOTH WAYS BEFORE YOU CROSS!
FWEEEET
GEEZ, SUCKS THAT THE TRAFFIC LIGHTS ARE DOWN TOO.
WELL, IT'S A GOOD THING THAT GRASS-HOPPER IS HERE.
DON'T YOU SEE HOW *CRAZY* THIS ALL IS?!
?!

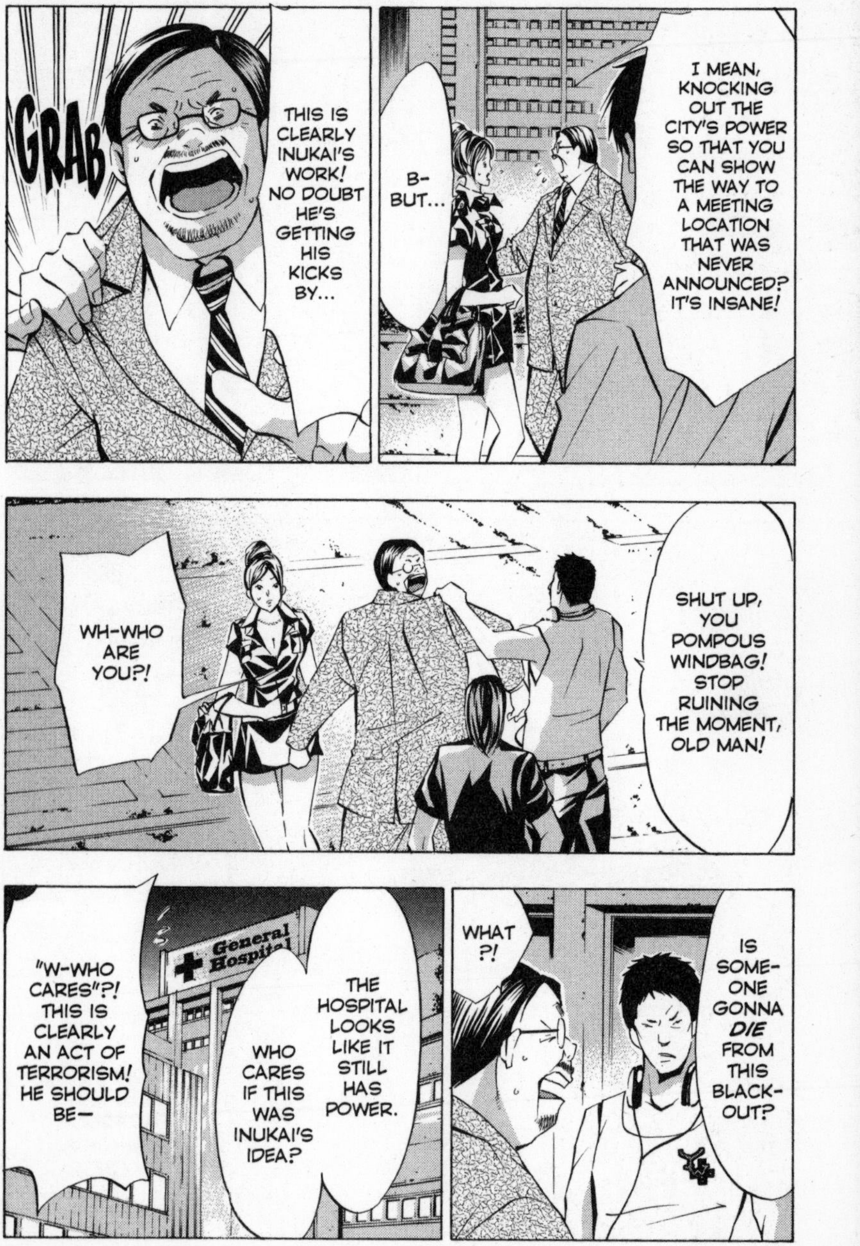
I MEAN, KNOCKING OUT THE CITY'S POWER SO THAT YOU CAN SHOW THE WAY TO A MEETING LOCATION THAT WAS NEVER ANNOUNCED? IT'S INSANE!
B-BUT...
THIS IS CLEARLY INUKAI'S WORK! NO DOUBT HE'S GETTING HIS KICKS BY...
GRAB
SHUT UP, YOU POMPOUS WINDBAG! STOP RUINING THE MOMENT, OLD MAN!
WH-WHO ARE YOU?!
IS SOME-ONE GONNA DIE FROM THIS BLACK-OUT?
WHAT?!
THE HOSPITAL LOOKS LIKE IT STILL HAS POWER.
WHO CARES IF THIS WAS INUKAI'S IDEA?
General Hospital
"W-WHO CARES"?! THIS IS CLEARLY AN ACT OF TERRORISM! HE SHOULD BE—

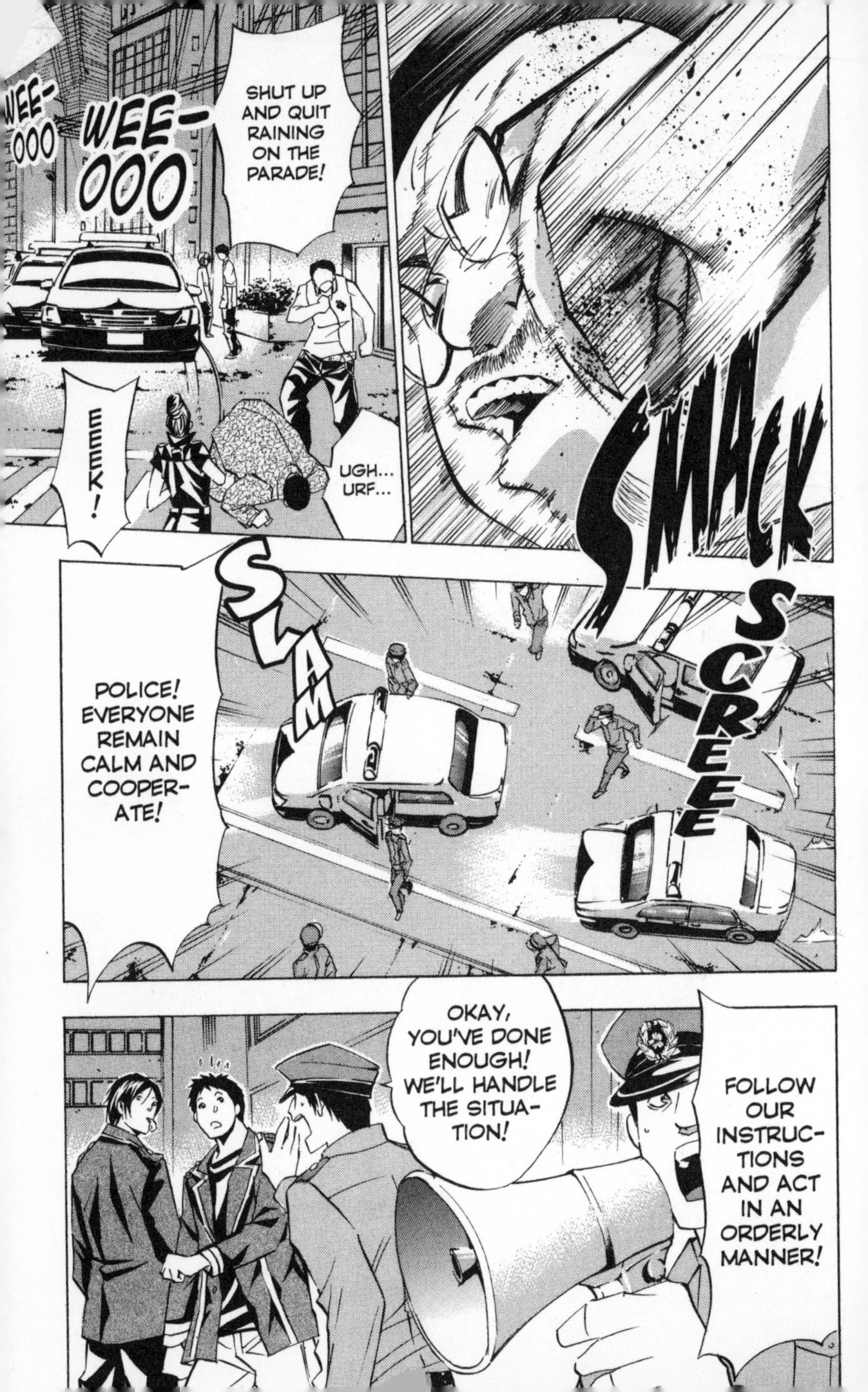
SMACK
SHUT UP AND QUIT RAINING ON THE PARADE!
WEE-OOO
WEE-OOO
UGH... URF...
EEEK!
SCREEE
SLAM
POLICE! EVERYONE REMAIN CALM AND COOPER-ATE!
FOLLOW OUR INSTRUC-TIONS AND ACT IN AN ORDERLY MANNER!
OKAY, YOU'VE DONE ENOUGH! WE'LL HANDLE THE SITUA-TION!

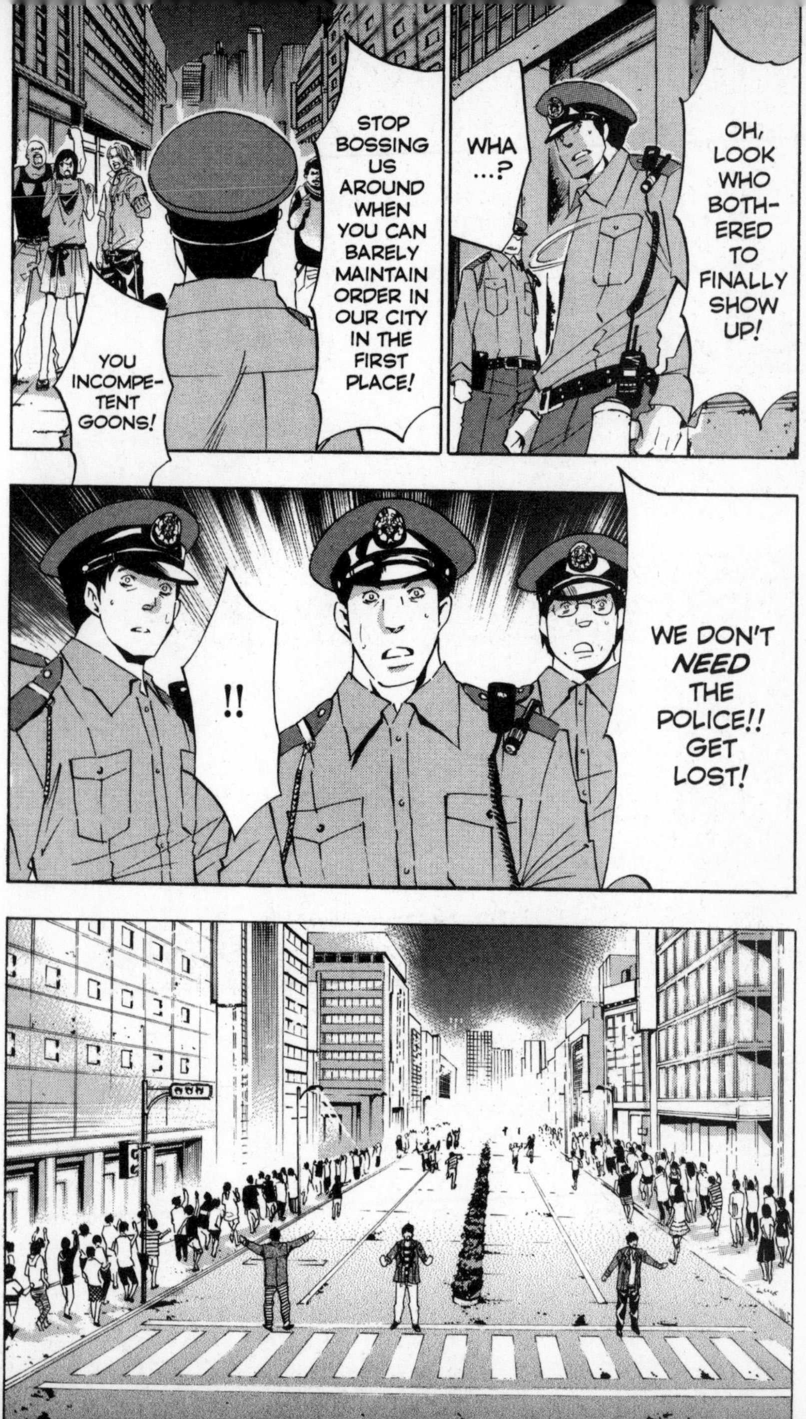
OH, LOOK WHO BOTH-ERED TO FINALLY SHOW UP!
WHA ...?
STOP BOSSING US AROUND WHEN YOU CAN BARELY MAINTAIN ORDER IN OUR CITY IN THE FIRST PLACE!
YOU INCOMPE-TENT GOONS!
WE DON'T *NEED* THE POLICE!! GET LOST!
!!

RED_EVELOPMENT
DISTRICT AHEA
NO TRESPASSING

HUFF!

HUFF!

HURRY, WE'VE ONLY GOT TEN MIN- UTES!

!

UGH...

WEEZ

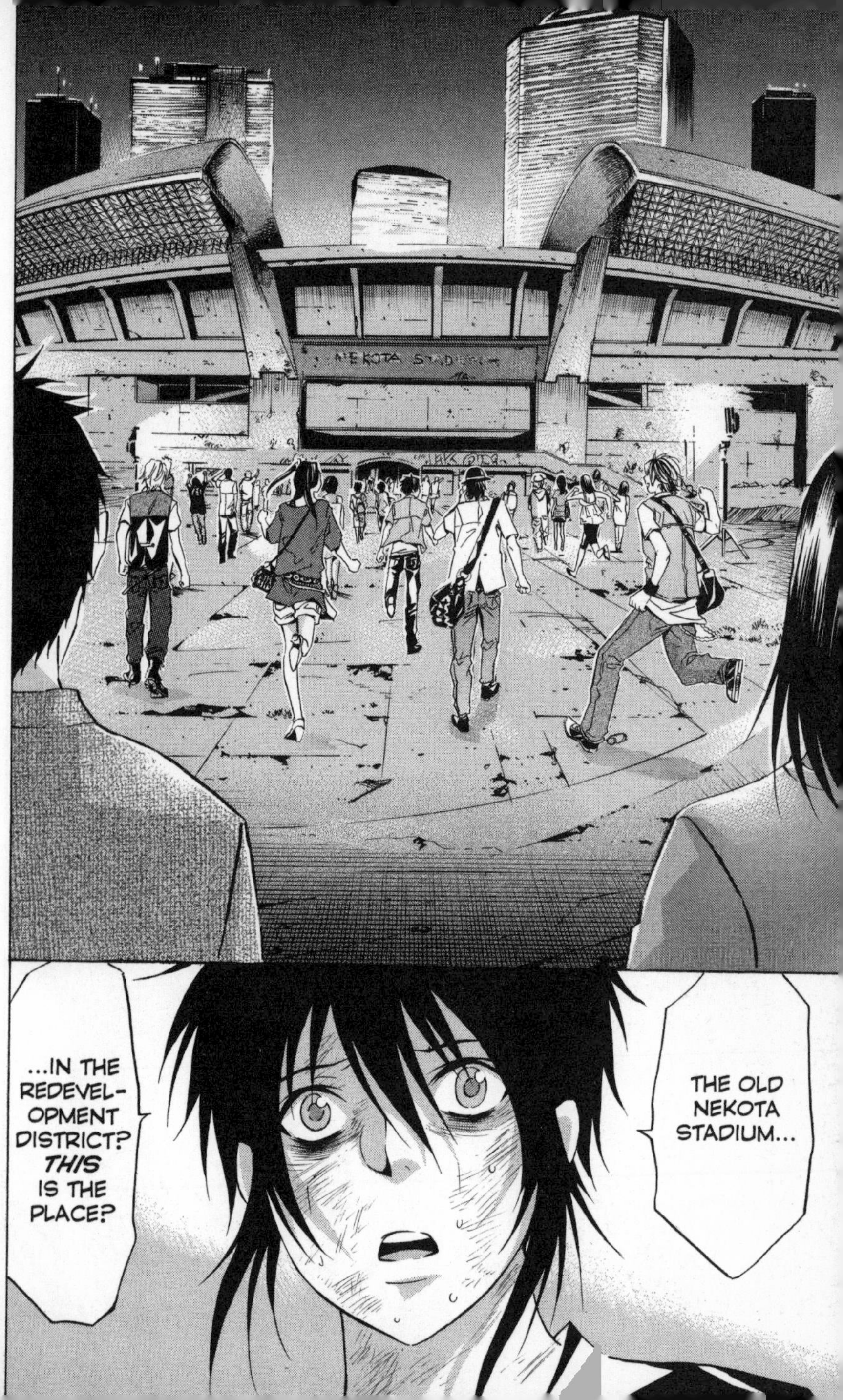
THE OLD NEKOTA STADIUM...
...IN THE REDEVEL-OPMENT DISTRICT? *THIS* IS THE PLACE?

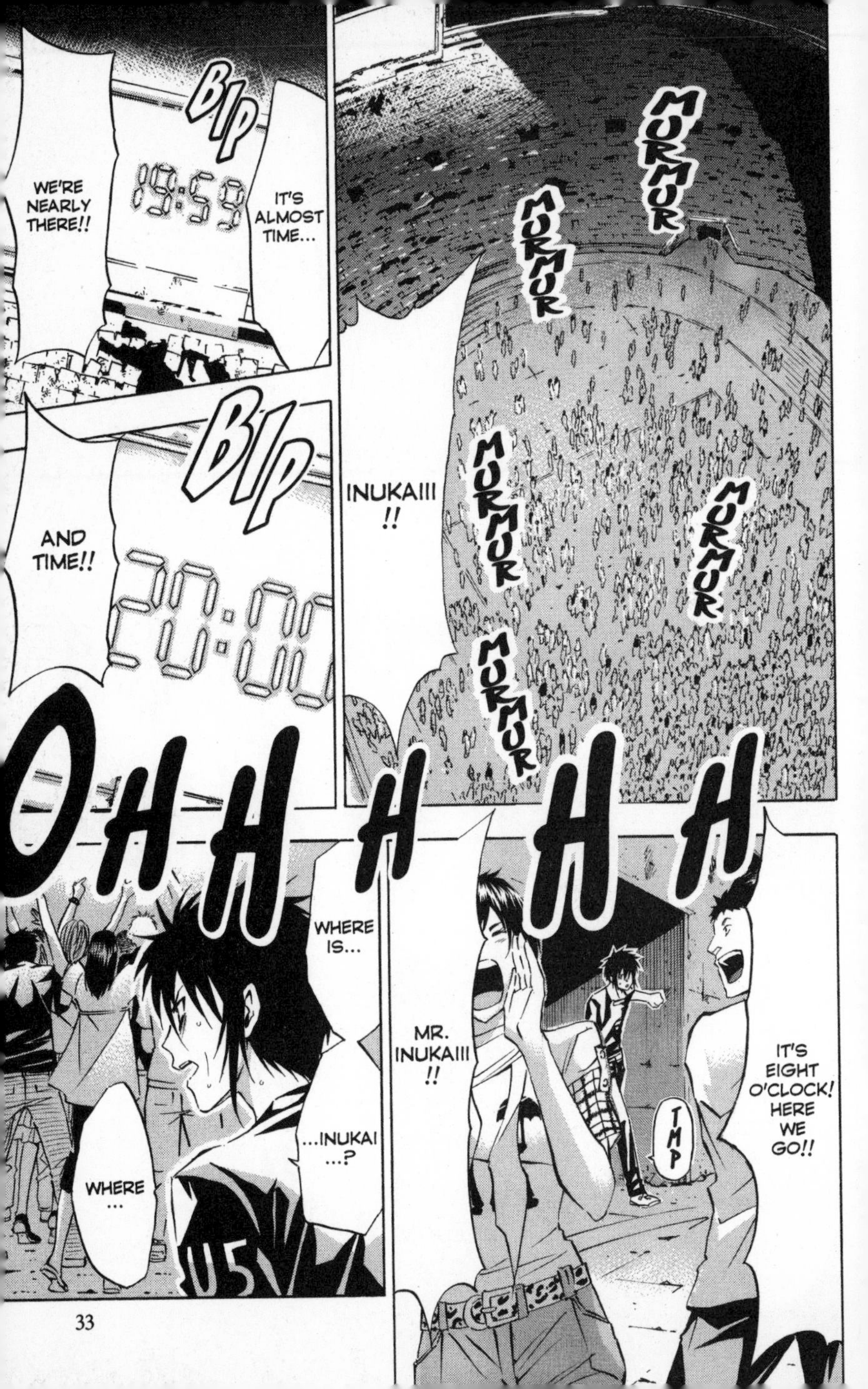
MURMUR
MURMUR
MURMUR
MURMUR
MURMUR
INUKAIII!!
BIP
IT'S ALMOST TIME...
19:59
WE'RE NEARLY THERE!!
BIP
AND TIME!!
20:00
OHHHHHH
IT'S EIGHT O'CLOCK! HERE WE GO!!
TMP
MR. INUKAIII!!
WHERE IS...
...INUKAI...?
WHERE...
U5

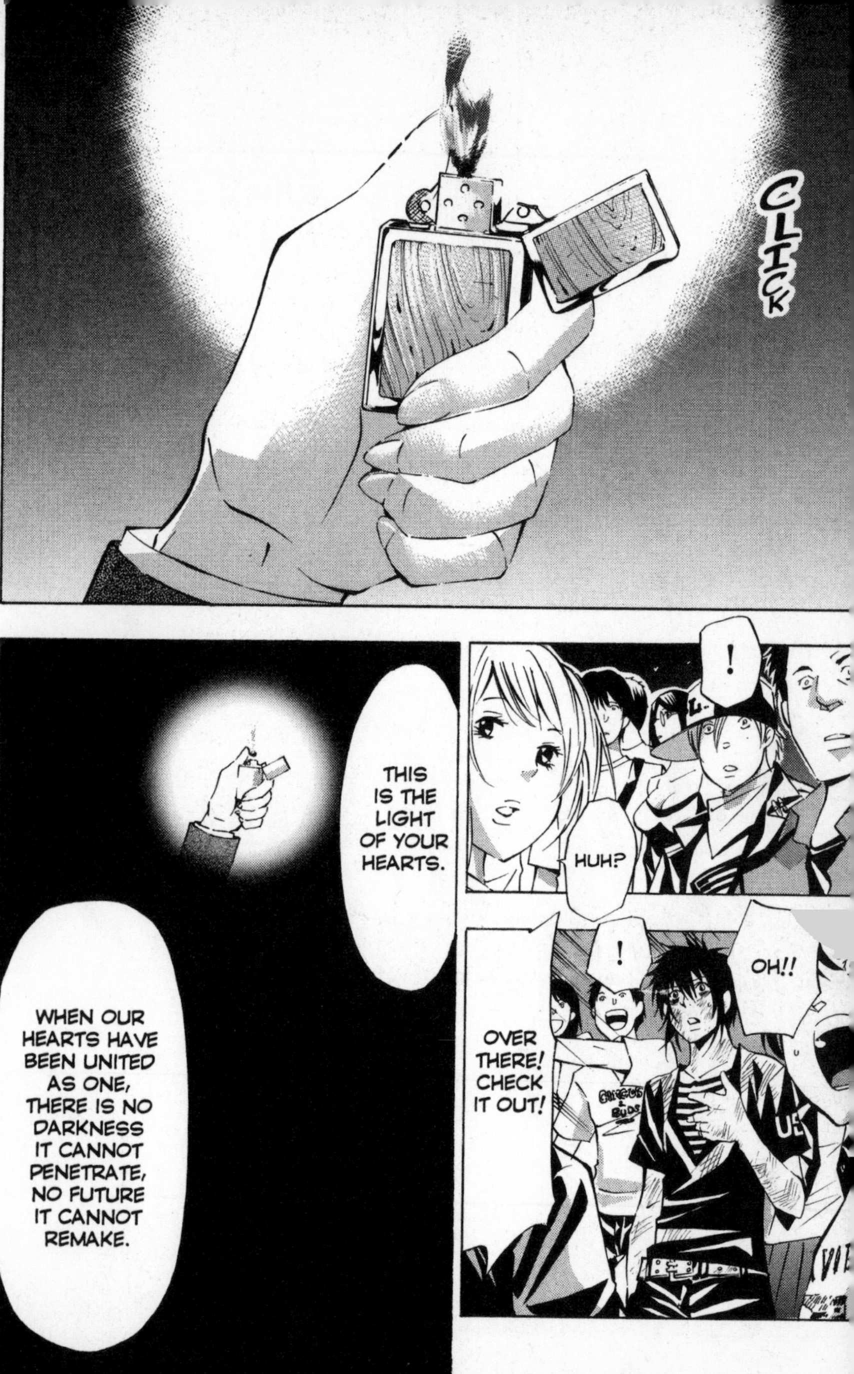
CLICK
!
HUH?
OH!!
!
OVER THERE! CHECK IT OUT!
THIS IS THE LIGHT OF YOUR HEARTS.
WHEN OUR HEARTS HAVE BEEN UNITED AS ONE, THERE IS NO DARKNESS IT CANNOT PENETRATE, NO FUTURE IT CANNOT REMAKE.

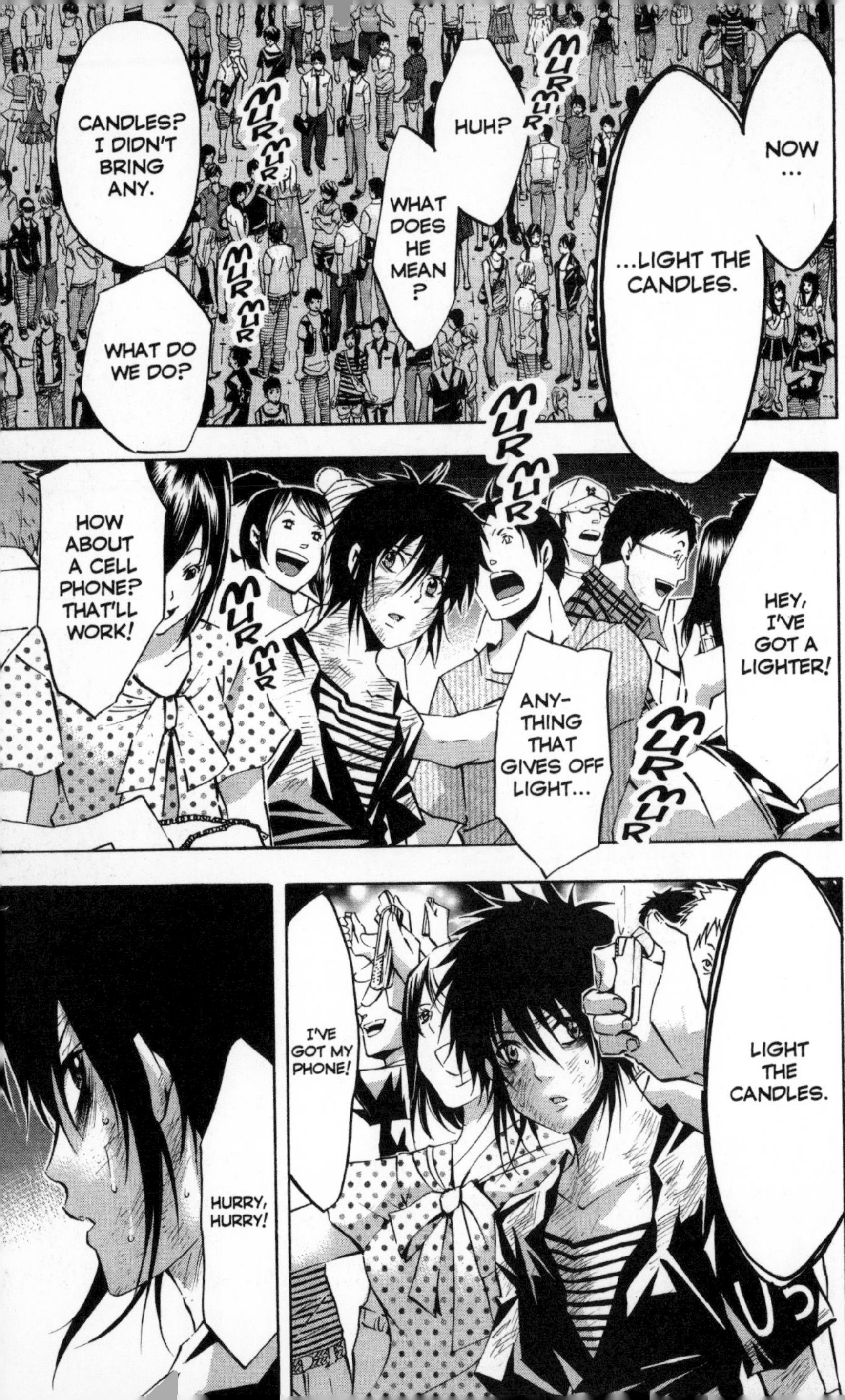
NOW ...
...LIGHT THE CANDLES.
MURMUR
HUH?
WHAT DOES HE MEAN?
MURMUR
CANDLES? I DIDN'T BRING ANY.
MURMUR
WHAT DO WE DO?
MURMUR
HEY, I'VE GOT A LIGHTER!
MURMUR
ANYTHING THAT GIVES OFF LIGHT...
MURMUR
HOW ABOUT A CELL PHONE? THAT'LL WORK!
LIGHT THE CANDLES.
I'VE GOT MY PHONE!
HURRY, HURRY!

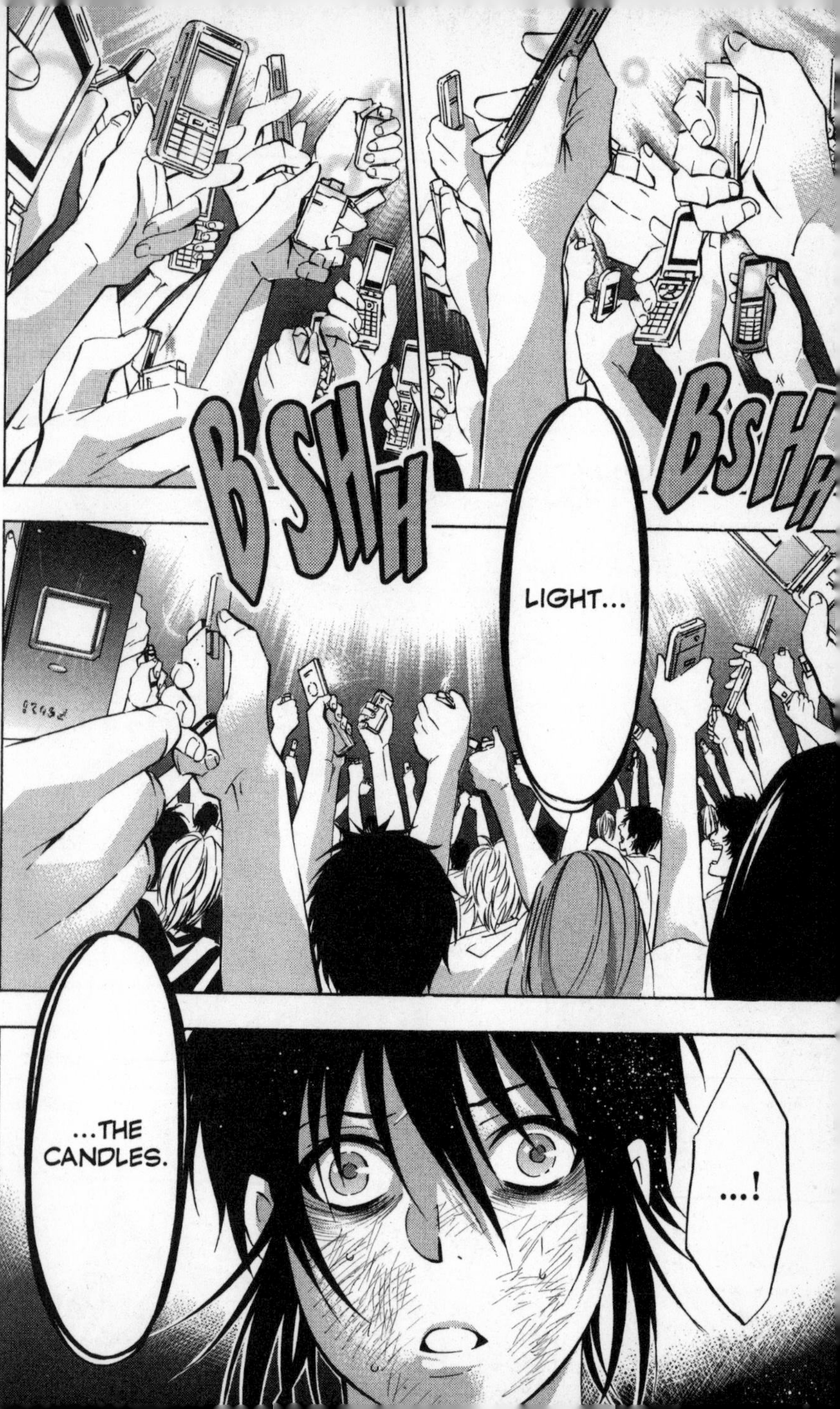
BSHH
BSHH
LIGHT...
...THE CANDLES.
...!

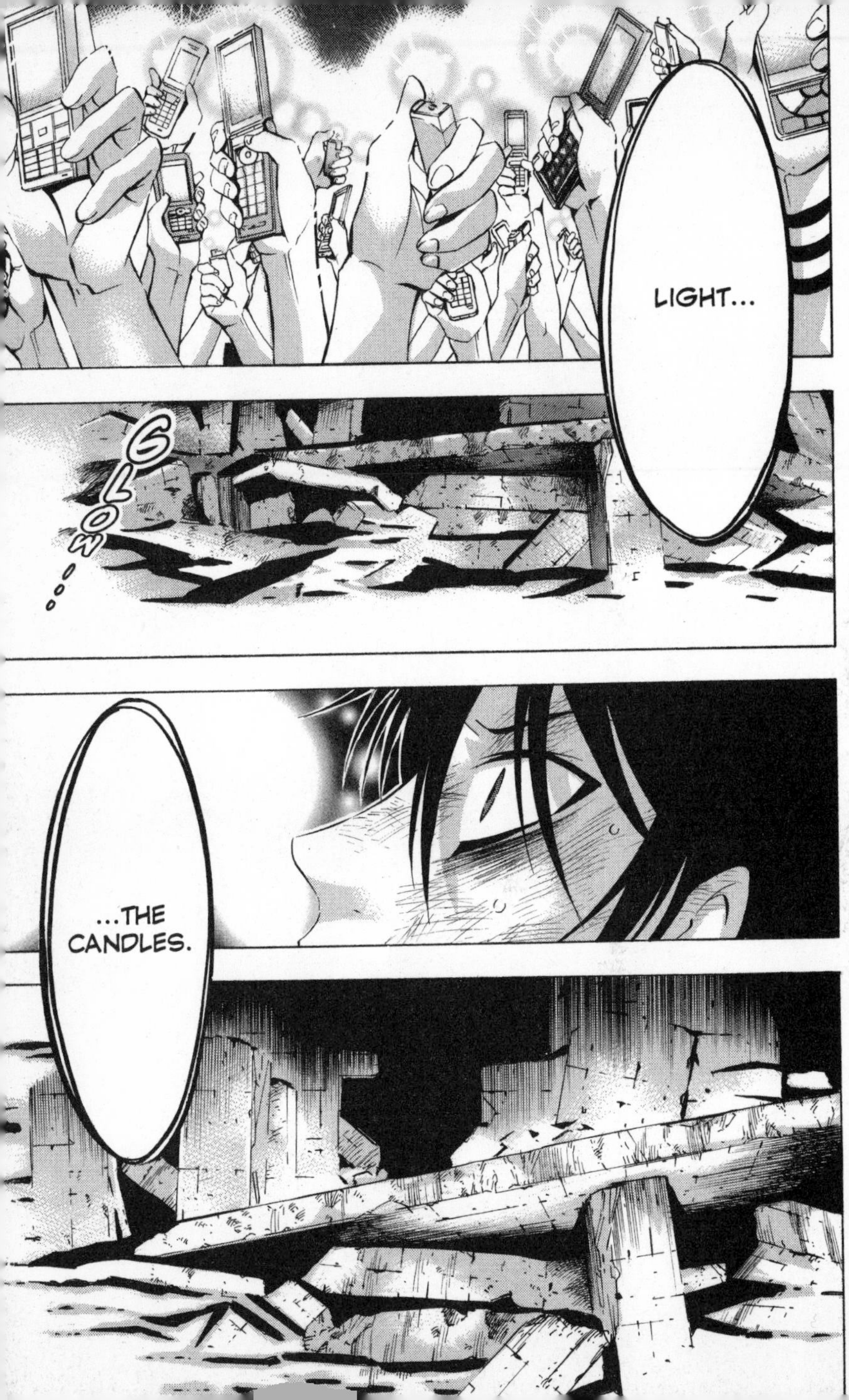
LIGHT...
GLOW...
...THE CANDLES.

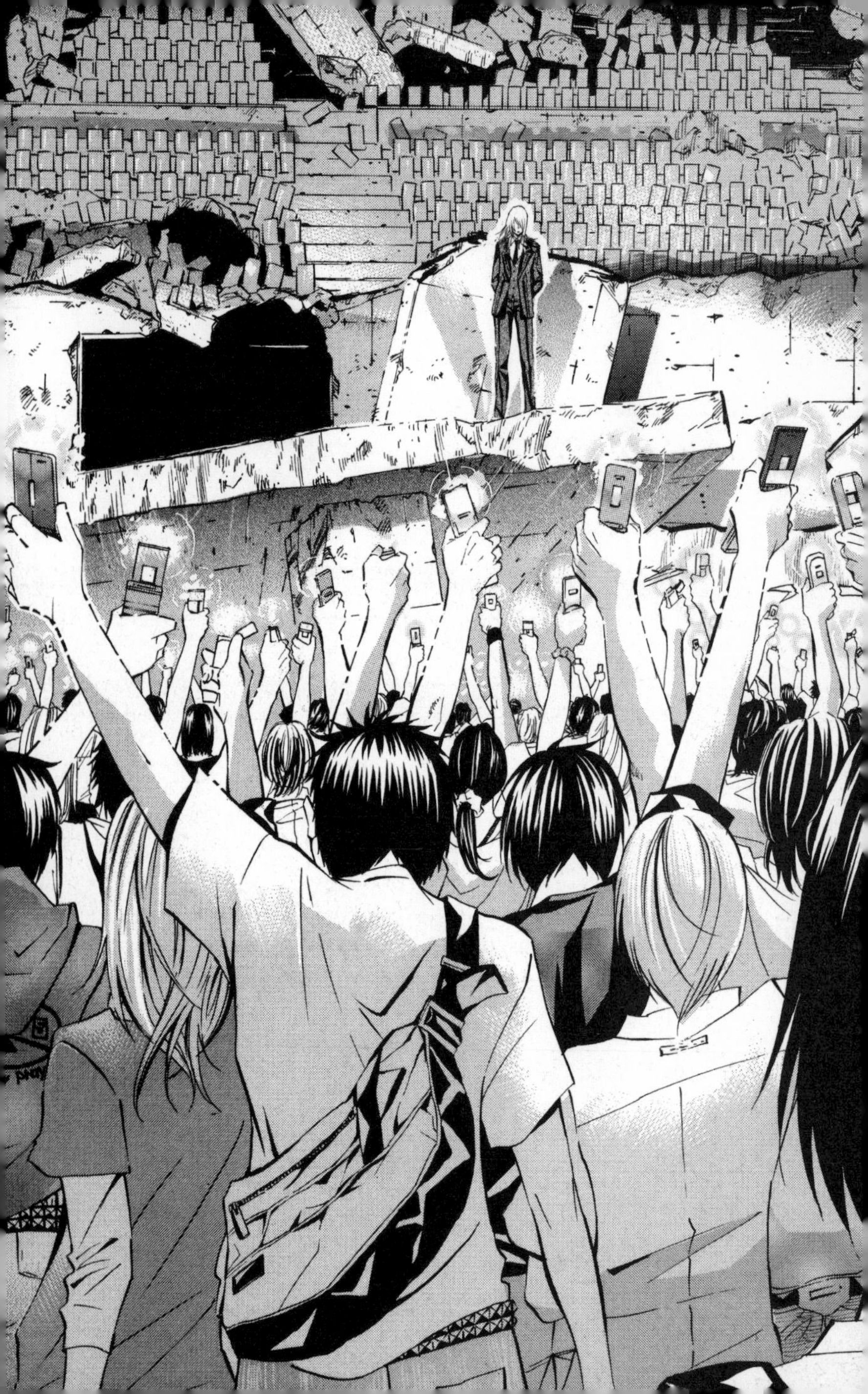

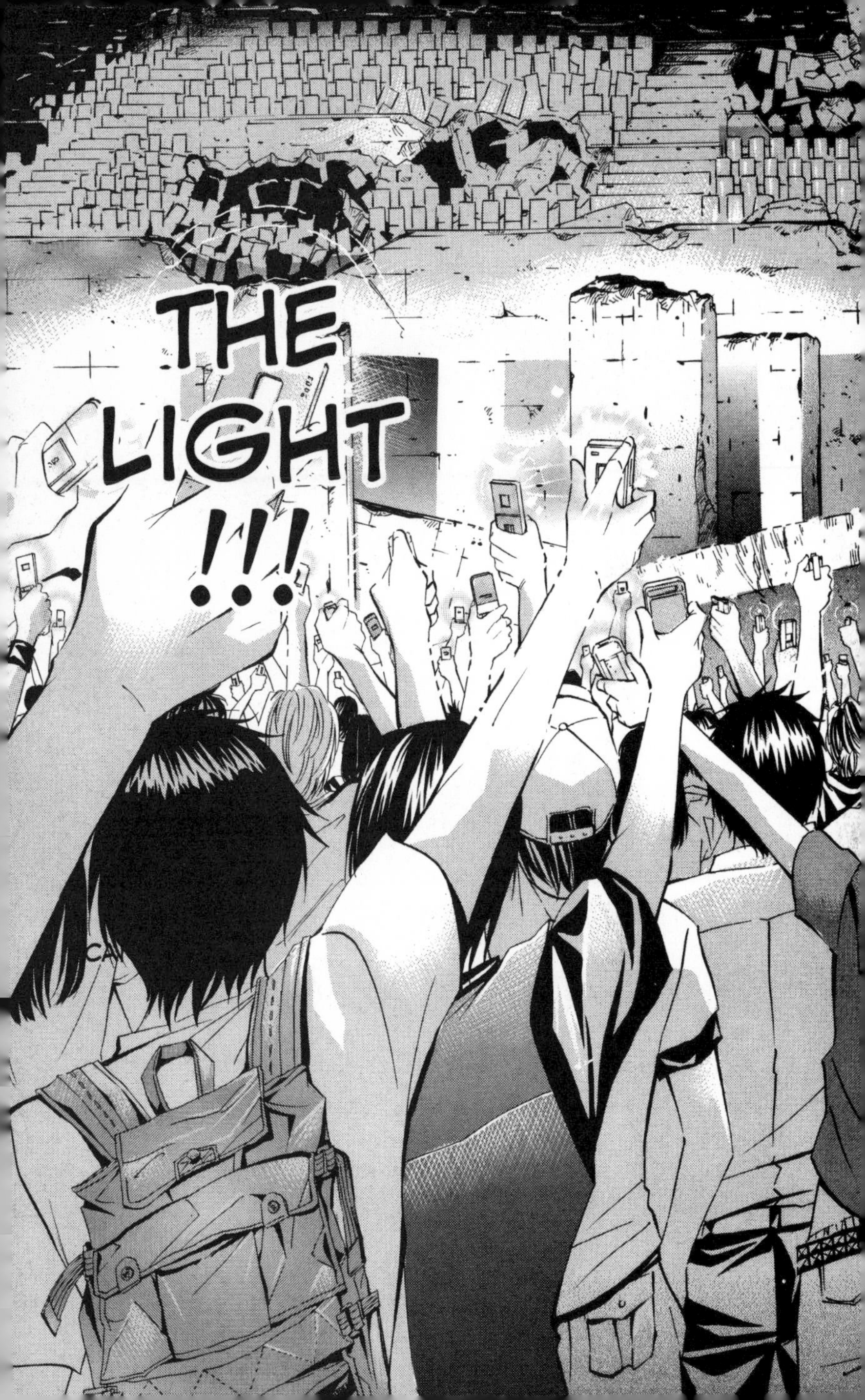
THE LIGHT !!!

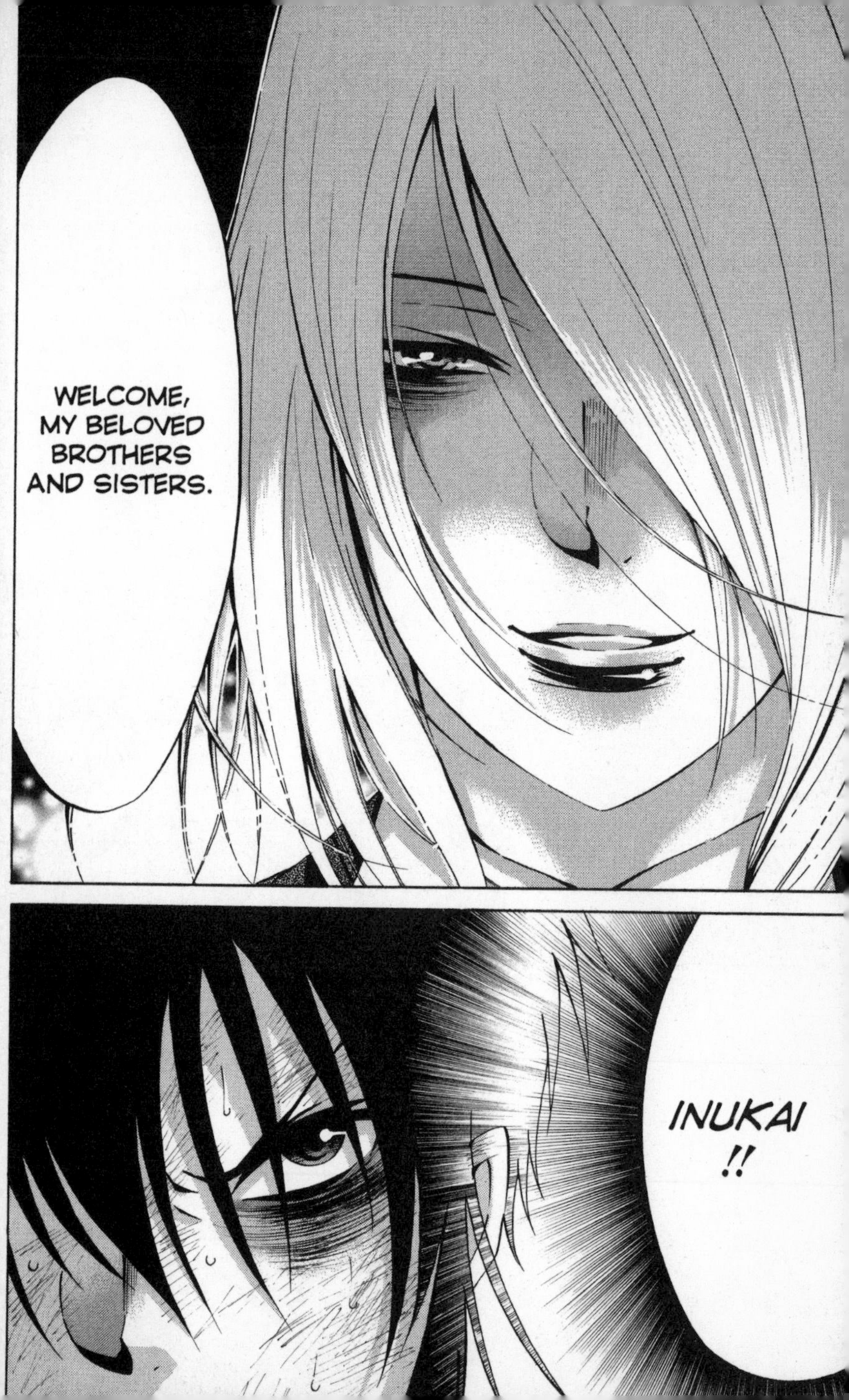
WELCOME, MY BELOVED BROTHERS AND SISTERS.
INUKAI !!

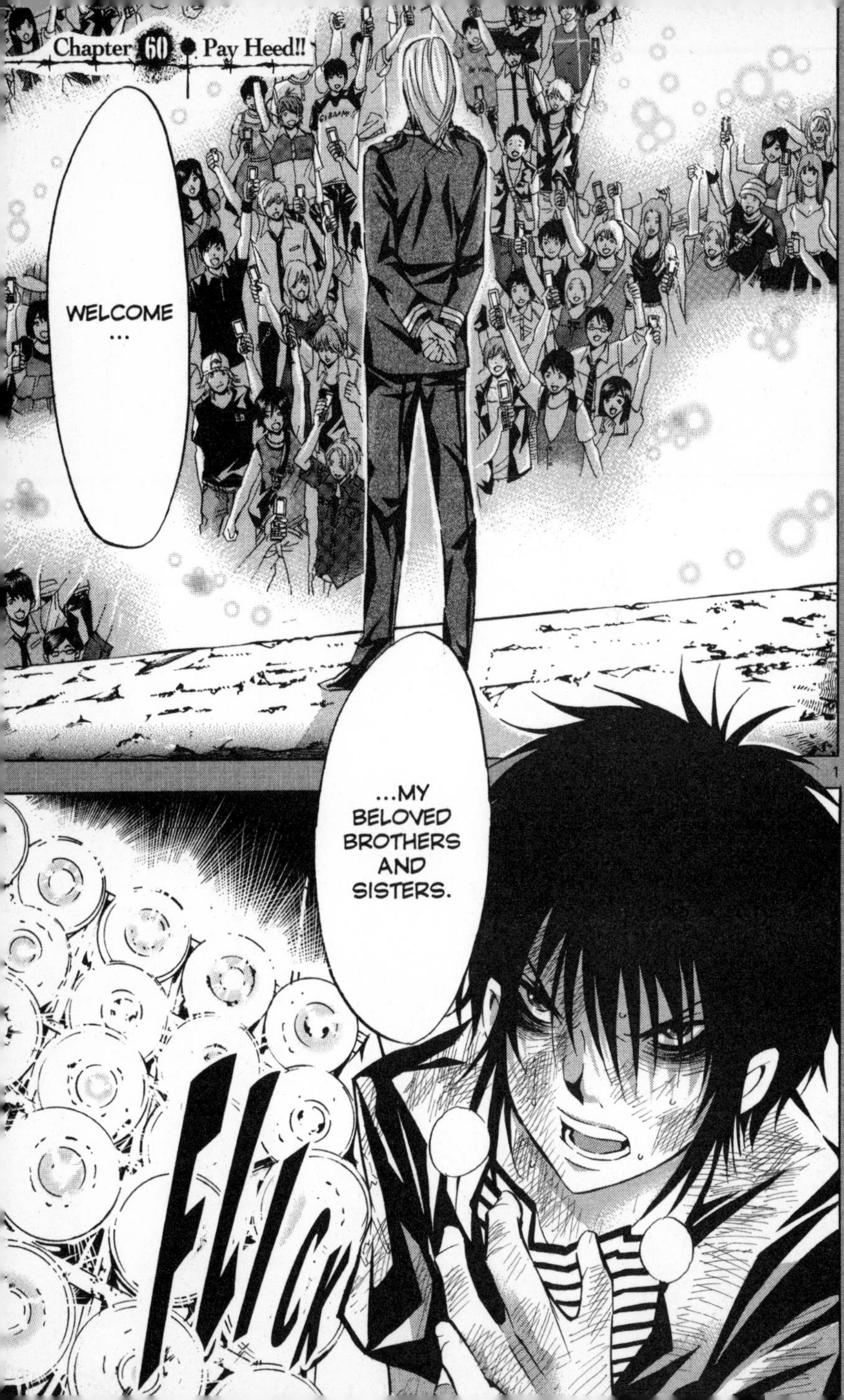
Chapter 60 Pay Heed!!
WELCOME ...
...MY BELOVED BROTHERS AND SISTERS.
1

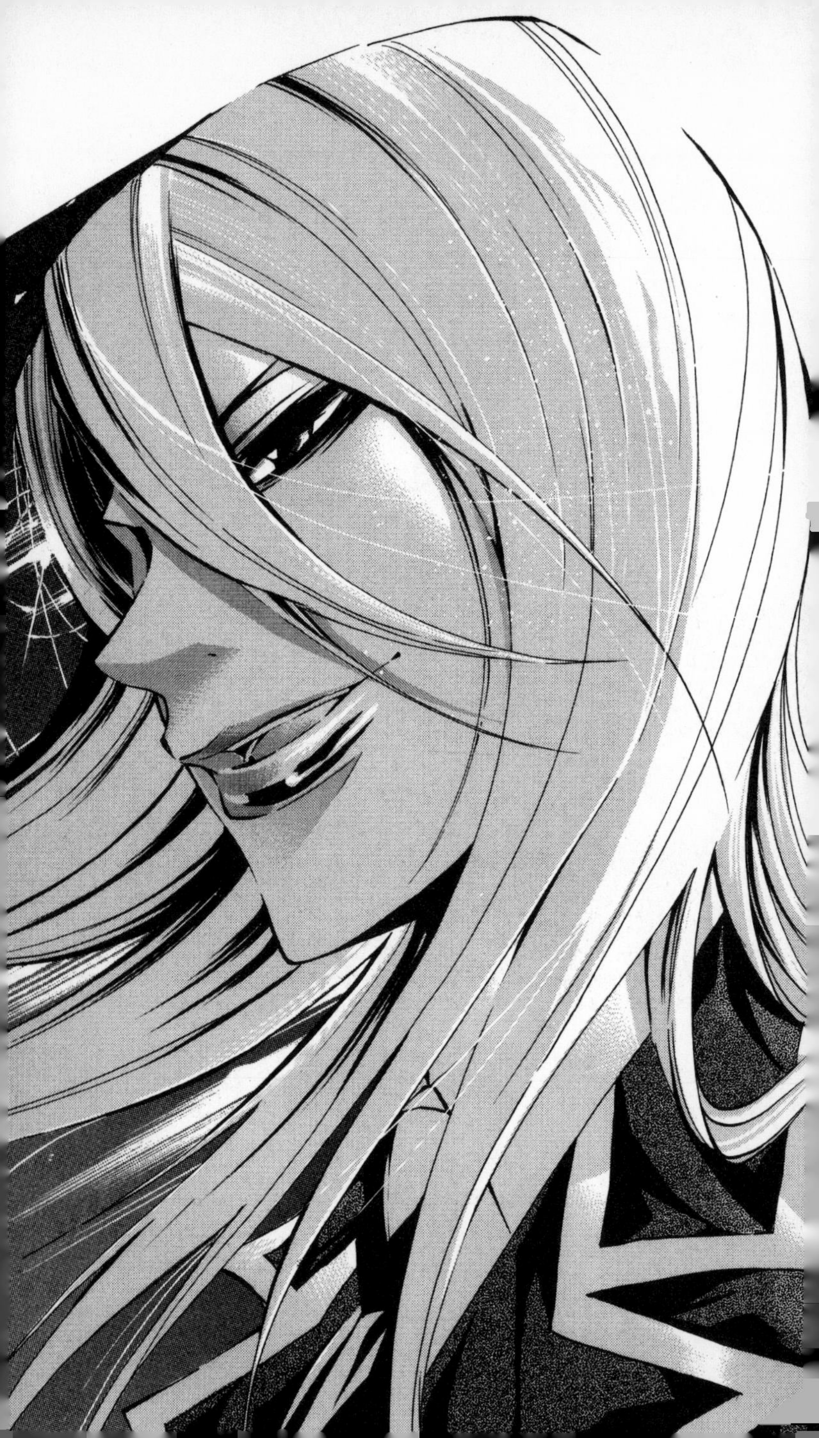

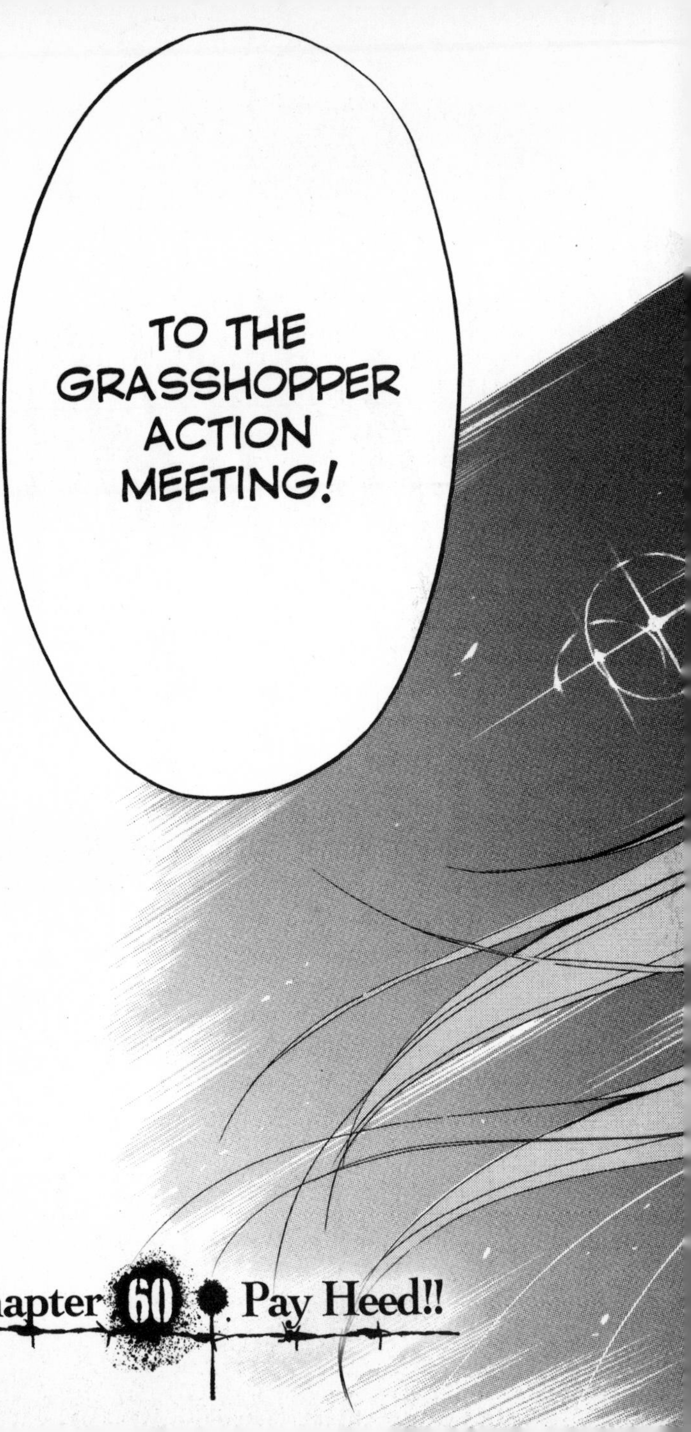
TO THE GRASSHOPPER ACTION MEETING!

# Chapter 60 Pay Heed!!

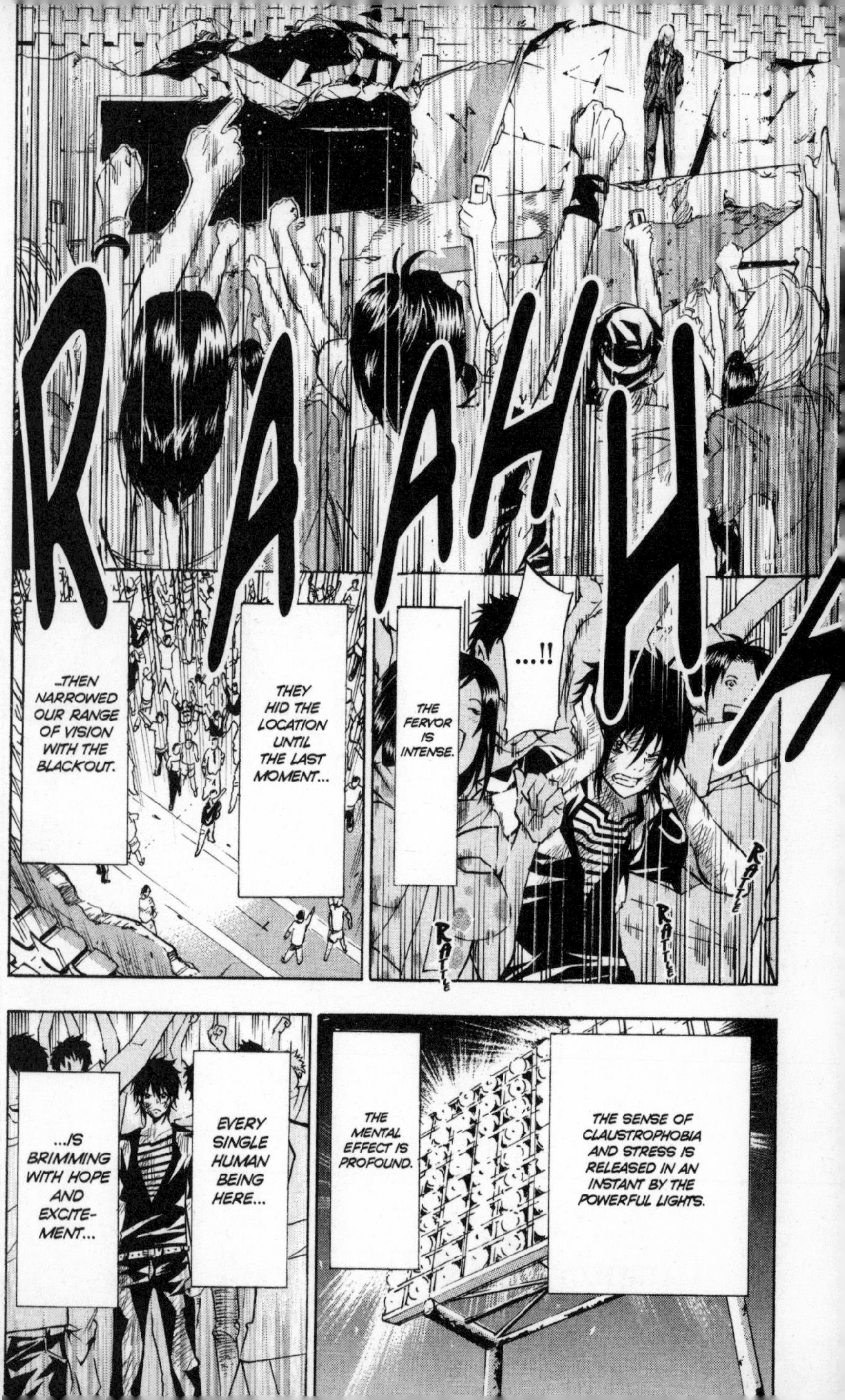
RAAHH
...!!
THE FERVOR IS INTENSE.
RATTLE
RATTLE
RATTLE
THEY HID THE LOCATION UNTIL THE LAST MOMENT...
...THEN NARROWED OUR RANGE OF VISION WITH THE BLACKOUT.
THE SENSE OF CLAUSTROPHOBIA AND STRESS IS RELEASED IN AN INSTANT BY THE POWERFUL LIGHTS.
THE MENTAL EFFECT IS PROFOUND.
EVERY SINGLE HUMAN BEING HERE...
...IS BRIMMING WITH HOPE AND EXCITE-MENT...

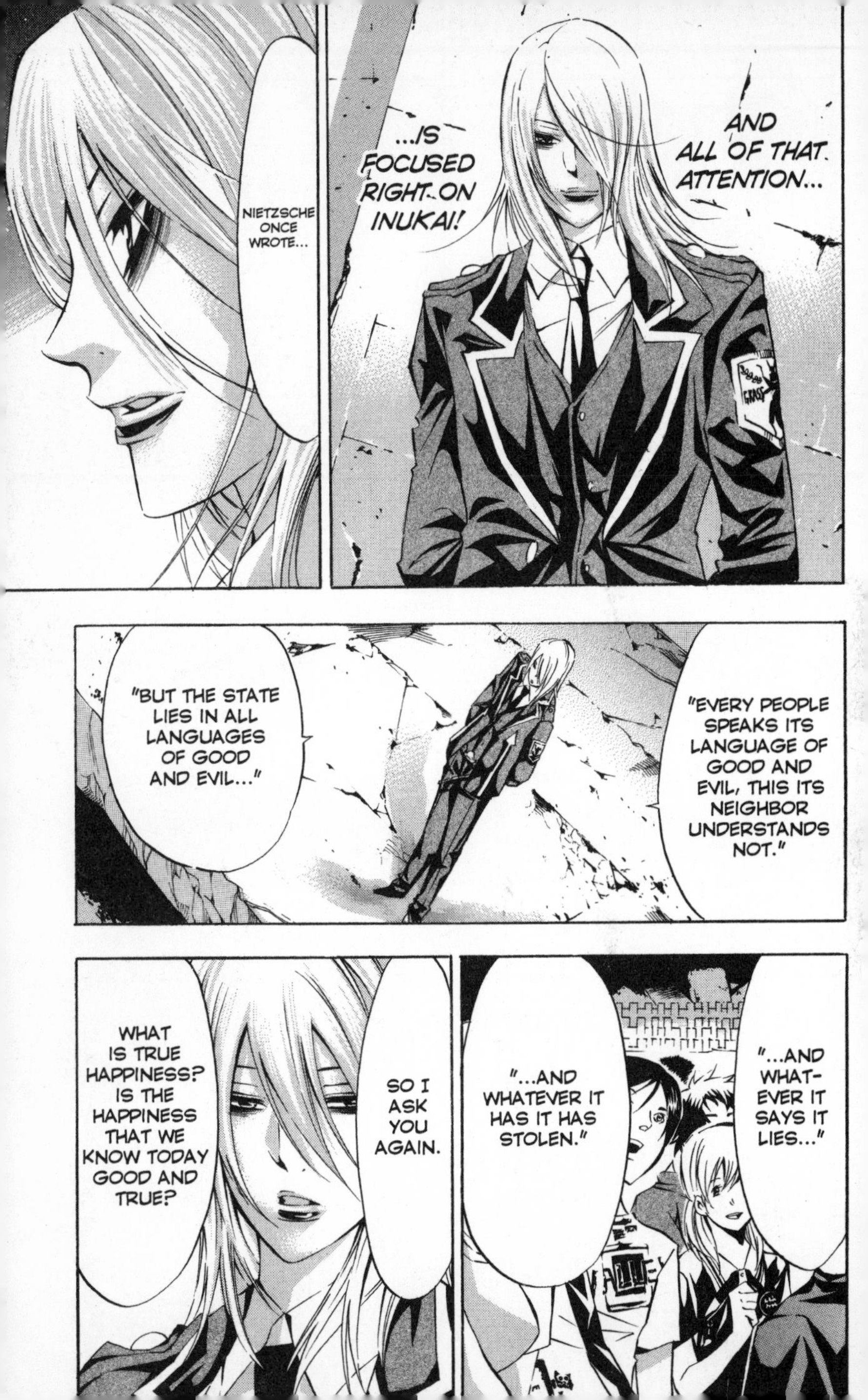

AND ALL OF THAT ATTENTION...
...IS FOCUSED RIGHT ON INUKAI!
NIETZSCHE ONCE WROTE...
"EVERY PEOPLE SPEAKS ITS LANGUAGE OF GOOD AND EVIL, THIS ITS NEIGHBOR UNDERSTANDS NOT."
"BUT THE STATE LIES IN ALL LANGUAGES OF GOOD AND EVIL..."
"...AND WHATEVER IT SAYS IT LIES..."
"...AND WHATEVER IT HAS IT HAS STOLEN."
SO I ASK YOU AGAIN.
WHAT IS TRUE HAPPINESS? IS THE HAPPINESS THAT WE KNOW TODAY GOOD AND TRUE?

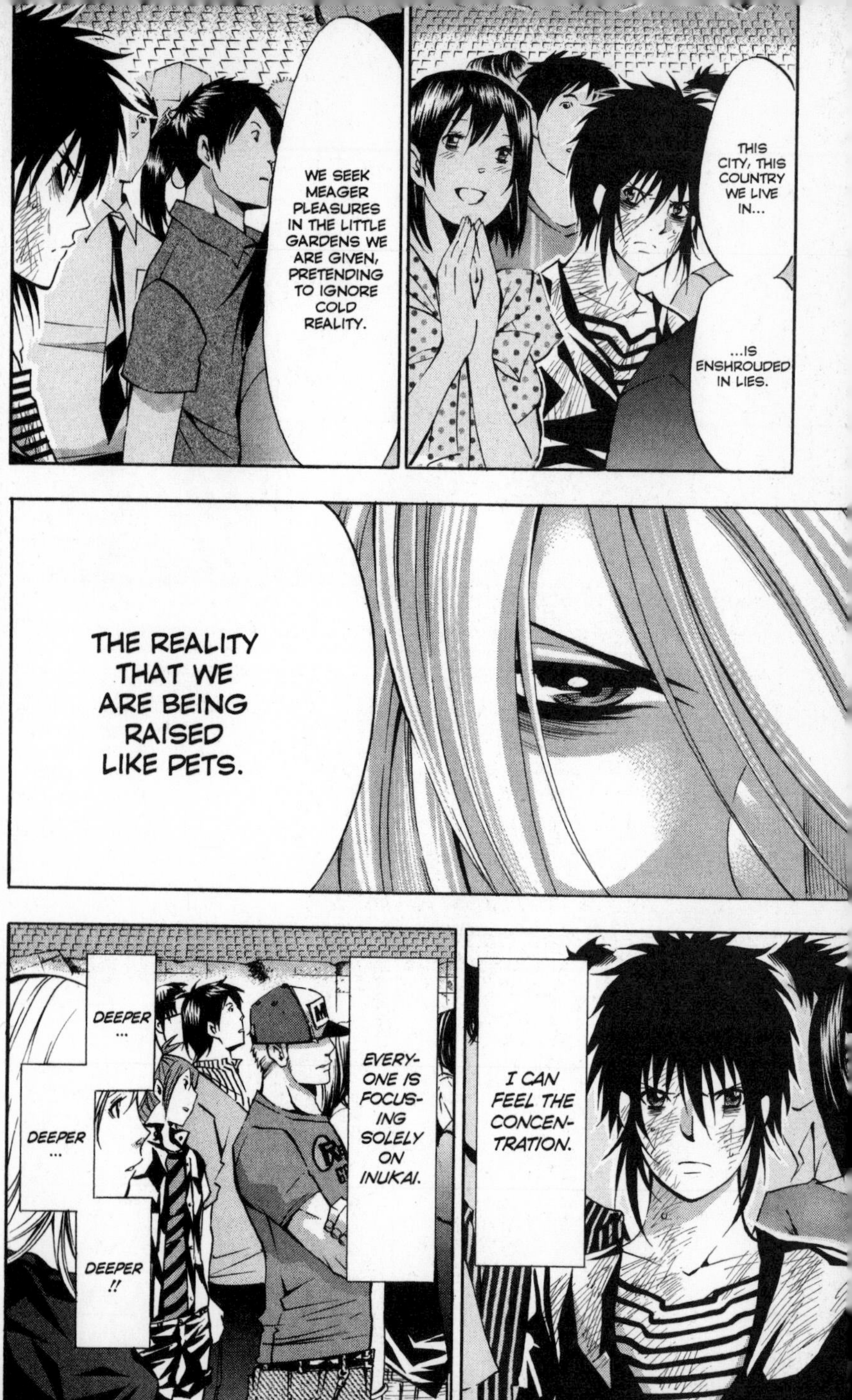
THIS CITY, THIS COUNTRY WE LIVE IN...
...IS ENSHROUDED IN LIES.
WE SEEK MEAGER PLEASURES IN THE LITTLE GARDENS WE ARE GIVEN, PRETENDING TO IGNORE COLD REALITY.
THE REALITY THAT WE ARE BEING RAISED LIKE PETS.
I CAN FEEL THE CONCENTRATION.
EVERYONE IS FOCUSING SOLELY ON INUKAI.
DEEPER...
DEEPER...
DEEPER!!

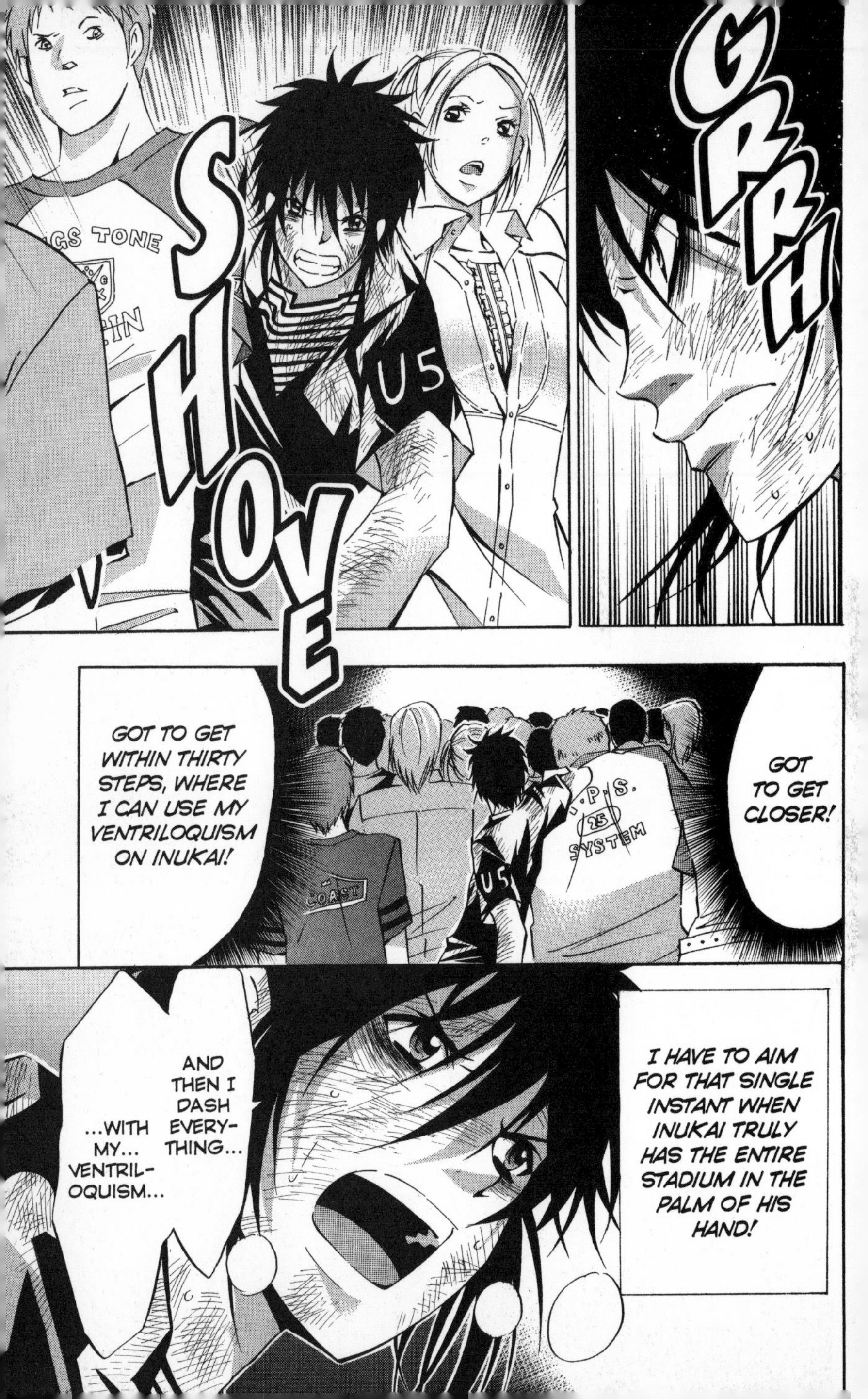
GRRH
SHOVE
GS TONE
GOT TO GET CLOSER!
GOT TO GET WITHIN THIRTY STEPS, WHERE I CAN USE MY VENTRILOQUISM ON INUKAI!
I HAVE TO AIM FOR THAT SINGLE INSTANT WHEN INUKAI TRULY HAS THE ENTIRE STADIUM IN THE PALM OF HIS HAND!
AND THEN I DASH EVERY-THING...
...WITH MY... VENTRIL-OQUISM...

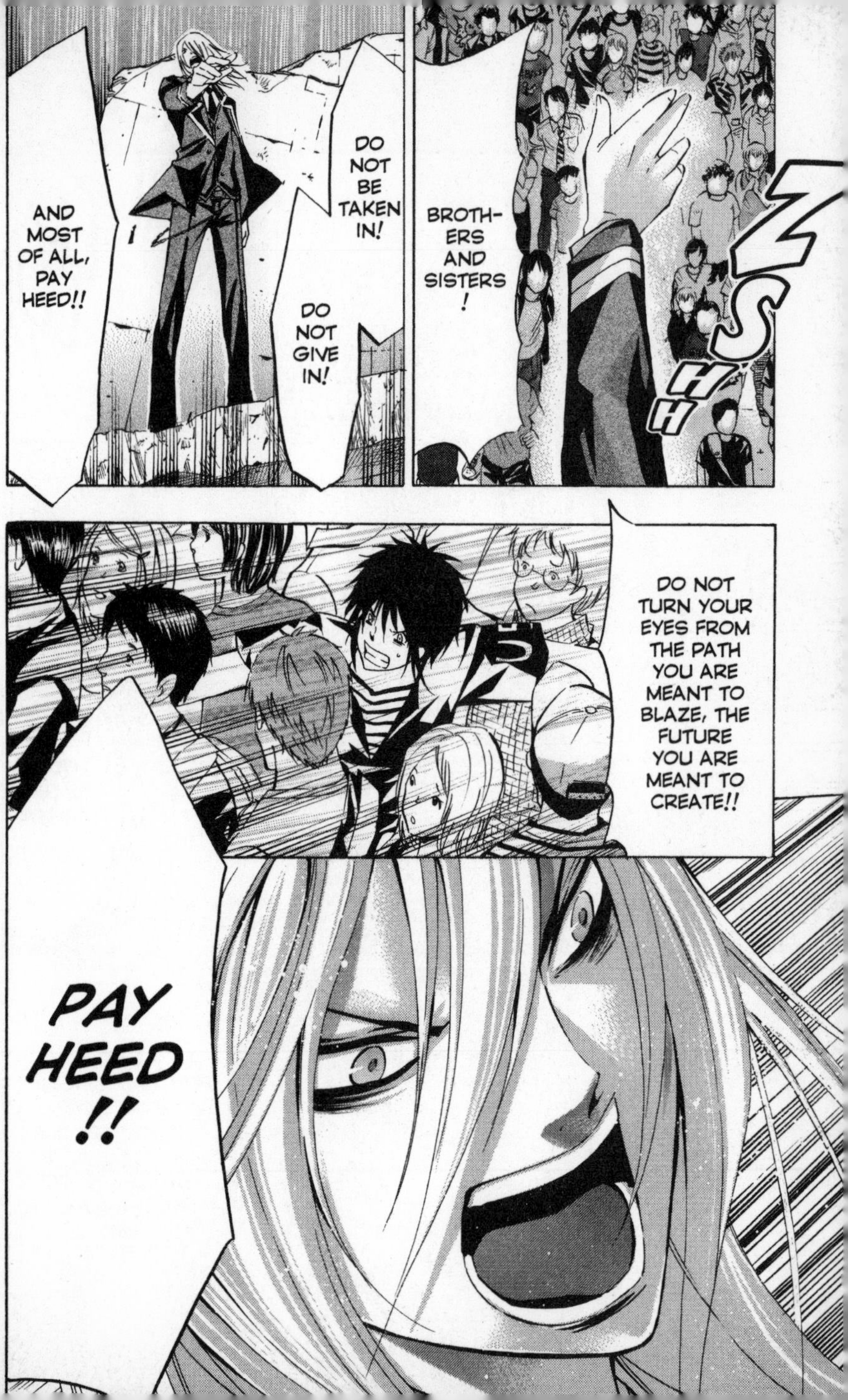

BROTHERS AND SISTERS!
ZSHH
DO NOT BE TAKEN IN!
DO NOT GIVE IN!
AND MOST OF ALL, PAY HEED!!
DO NOT TURN YOUR EYES FROM THE PATH YOU ARE MEANT TO BLAZE, THE FUTURE YOU ARE MEANT TO CREATE!!
PAY HEED!!

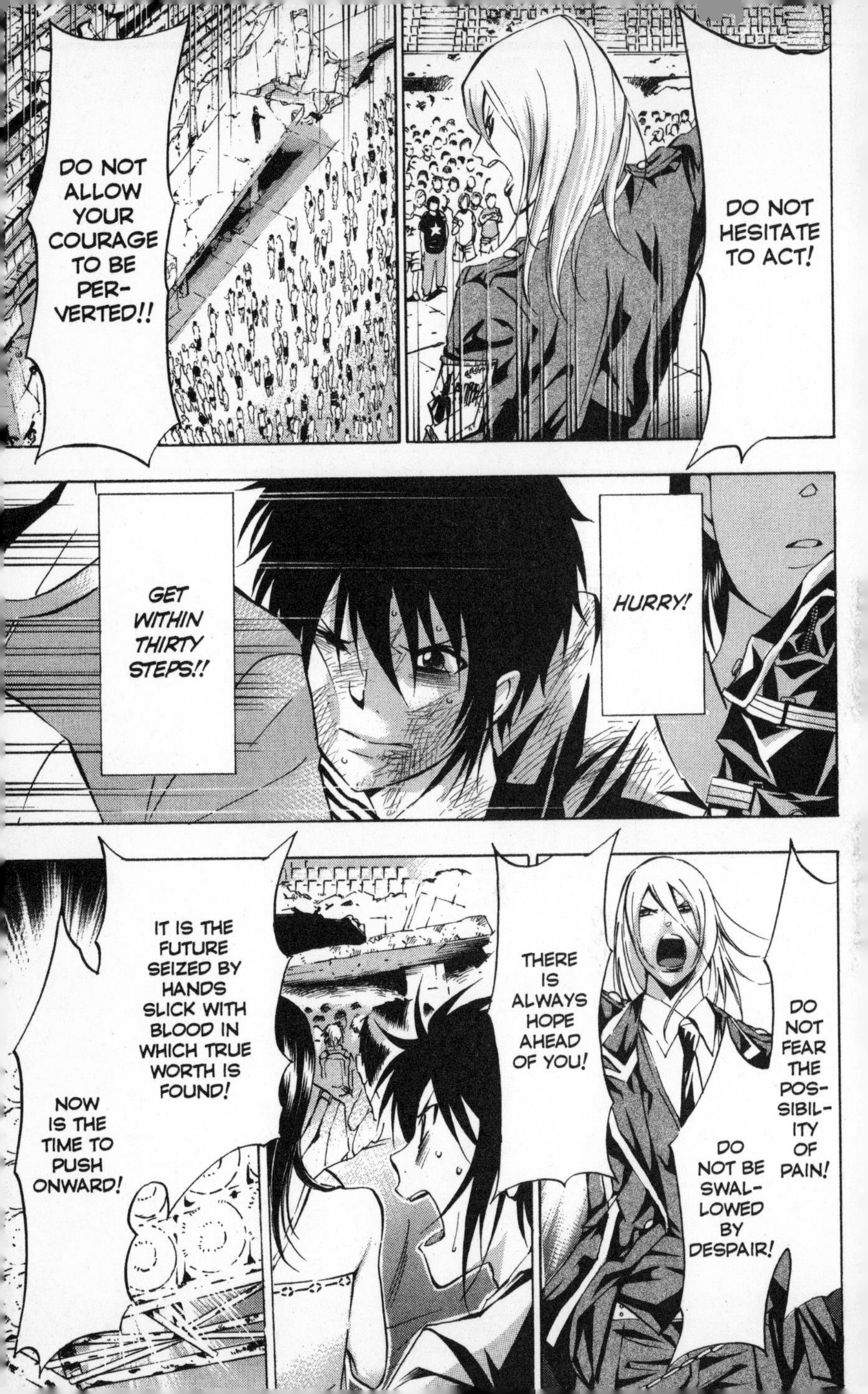
DO NOT HESITATE TO ACT!
DO NOT ALLOW YOUR COURAGE TO BE PERVERTED!!
HURRY!
GET WITHIN THIRTY STEPS!!
DO NOT FEAR THE POSSIBILITY OF PAIN!
DO NOT BE SWALLOWED BY DESPAIR!
THERE IS ALWAYS HOPE AHEAD OF YOU!
IT IS THE FUTURE SEIZED BY HANDS SLICK WITH BLOOD IN WHICH TRUE WORTH IS FOUND!
NOW IS THE TIME TO PUSH ONWARD!

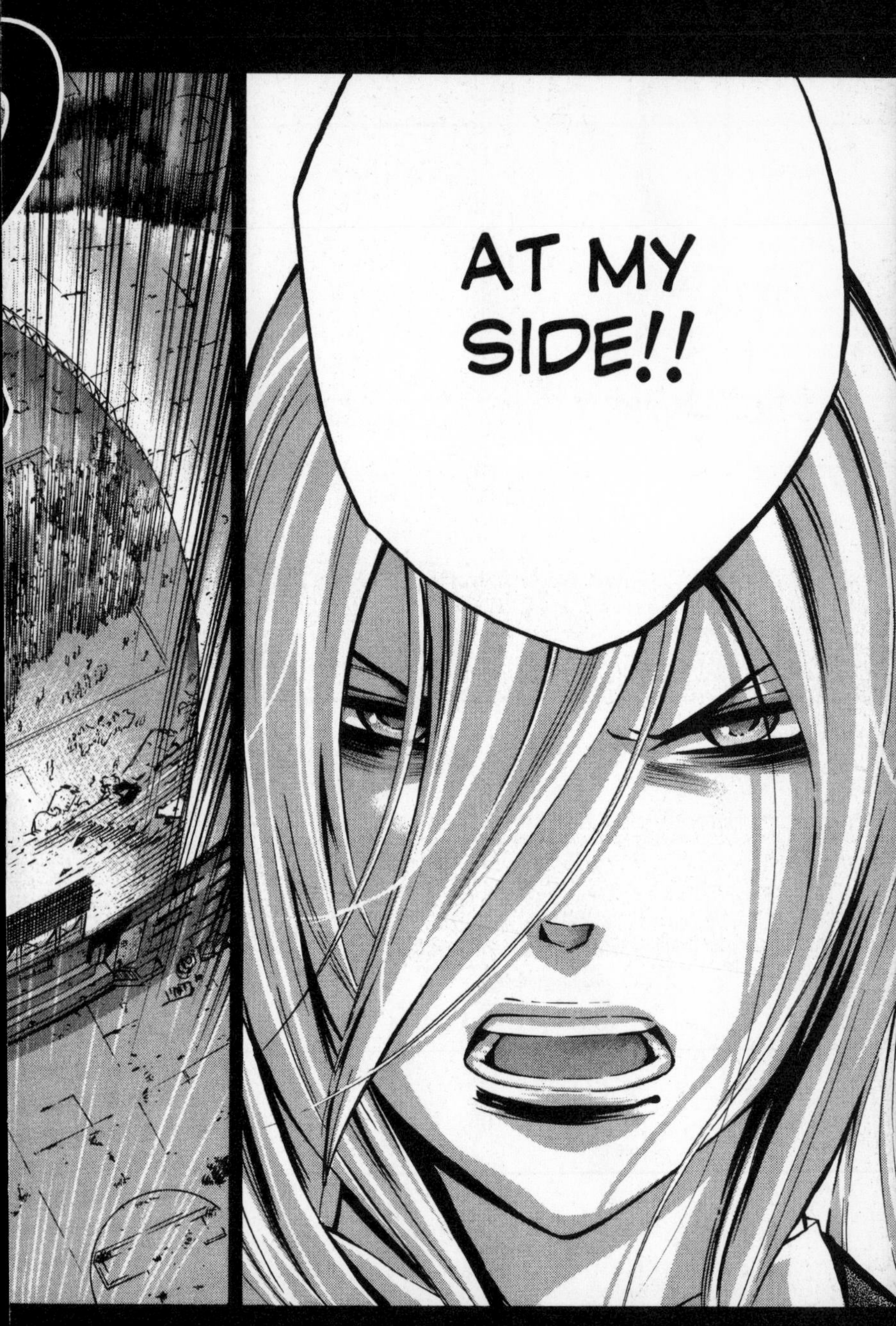
AT MY SIDE!!

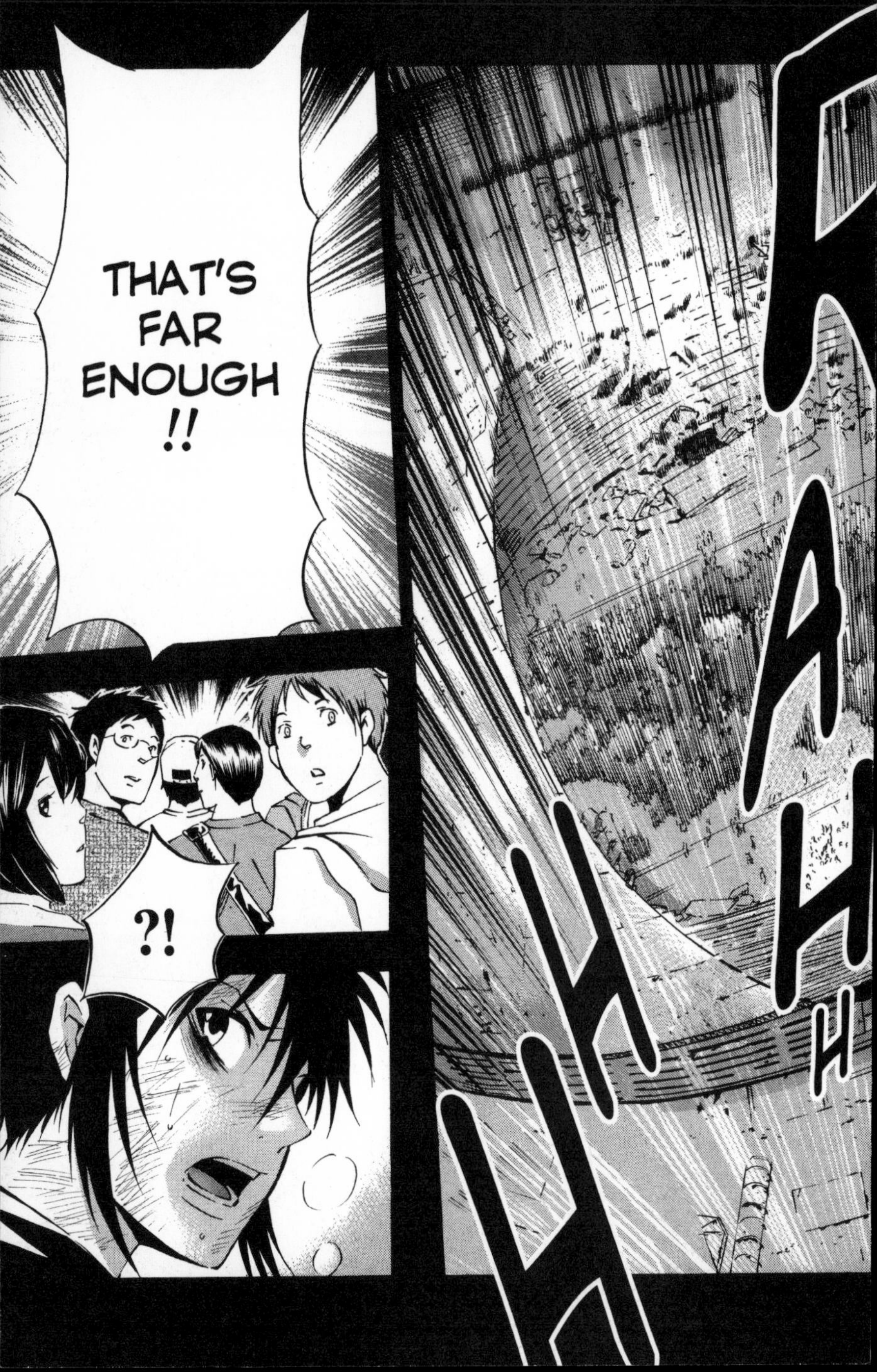
THAT'S FAR ENOUGH !!
?!

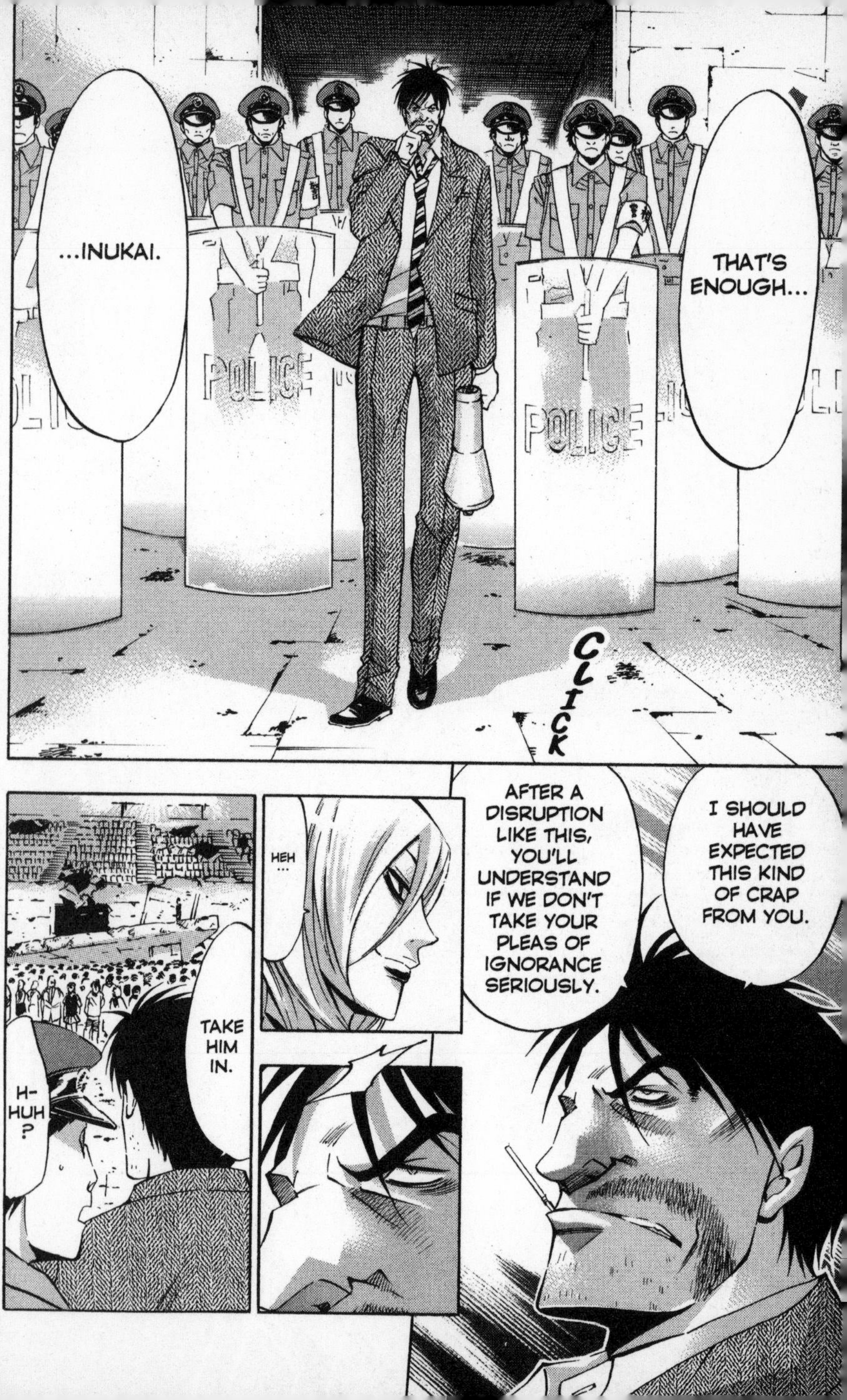
THAT'S ENOUGH...
...INUKAI.
CLICK
I SHOULD HAVE EXPECTED THIS KIND OF CRAP FROM YOU.
AFTER A DISRUPTION LIKE THIS, YOU'LL UNDERSTAND IF WE DON'T TAKE YOUR PLEAS OF IGNORANCE SERIOUSLY.
HEH ...
TAKE HIM IN.
H-HUH?

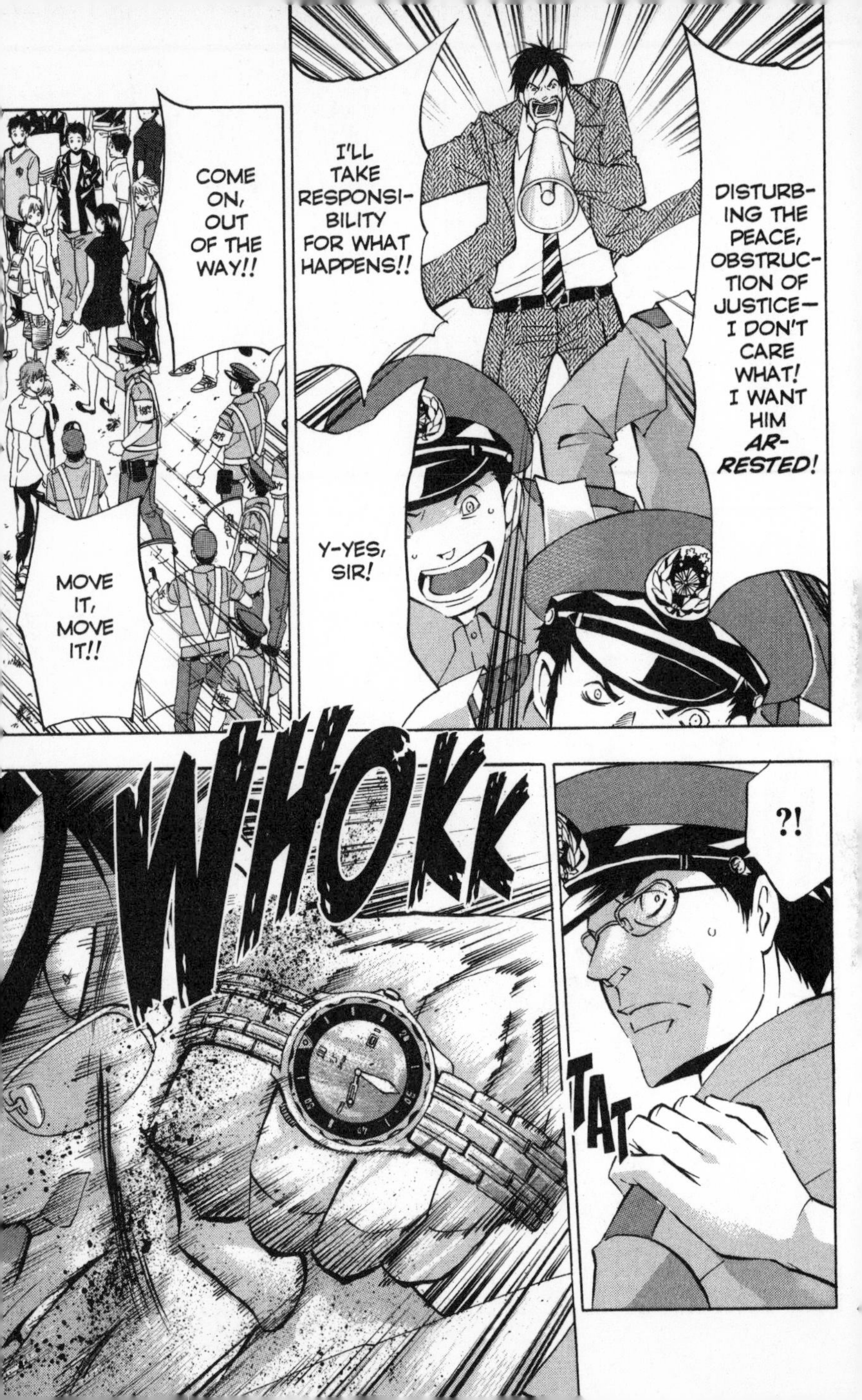
DISTURBING THE PEACE, OBSTRUCTION OF JUSTICE— I DON'T CARE WHAT! I WANT HIM *ARRESTED*!
I'LL TAKE RESPONSIBILITY FOR WHAT HAPPENS!!
Y-YES, SIR!
COME ON, OUT OF THE WAY!!
MOVE IT, MOVE IT!!
?!
TAT
WHOKK

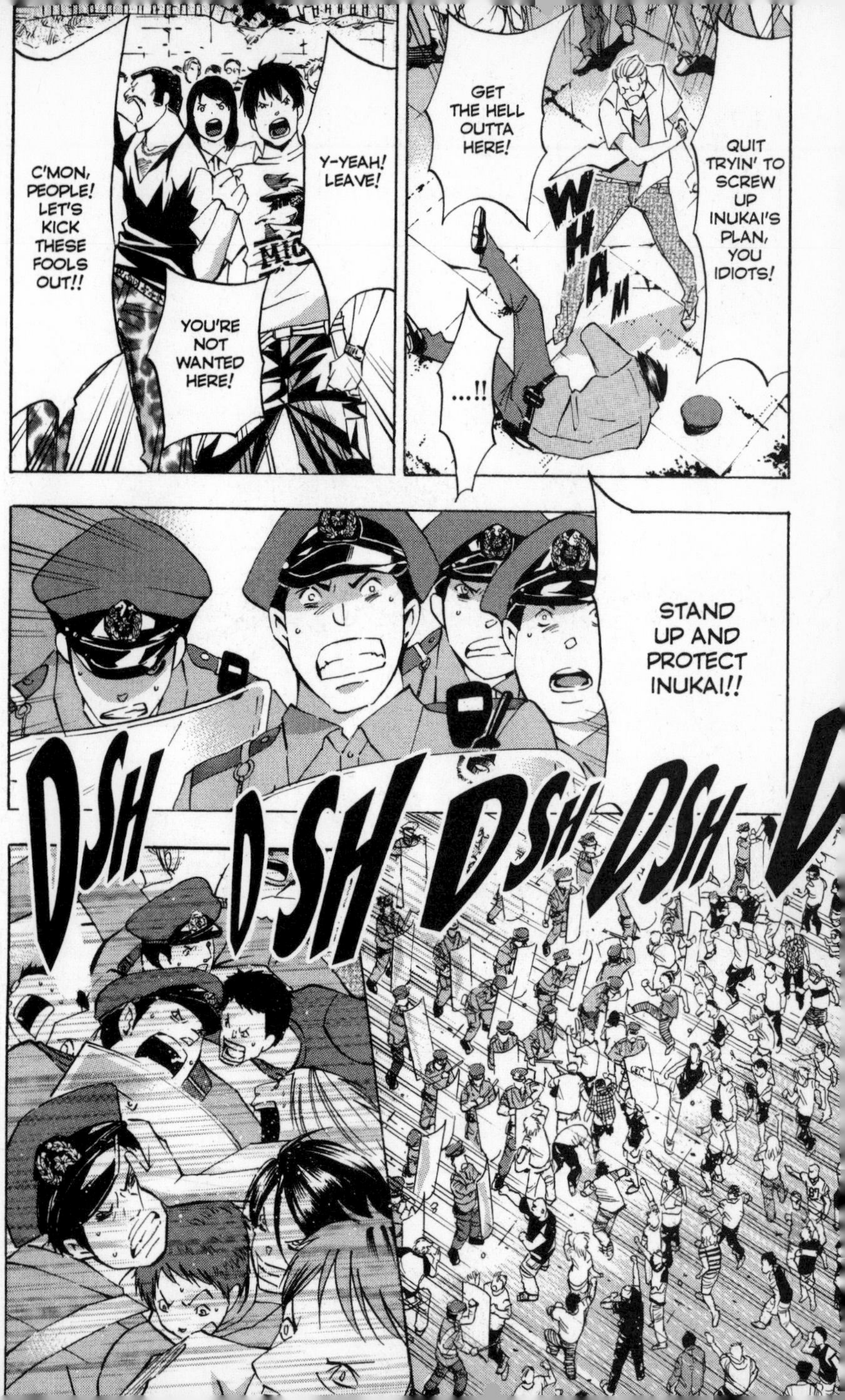
QUIT TRYIN' TO SCREW UP INUKAI'S PLAN, YOU IDIOTS!
GET THE HELL OUTTA HERE!
WHAM
...!!
Y-YEAH! LEAVE!
C'MON, PEOPLE! LET'S KICK THESE FOOLS OUT!!
YOU'RE NOT WANTED HERE!
STAND UP AND PROTECT INUKAI!!
DSH DSH DSH DSH DSH

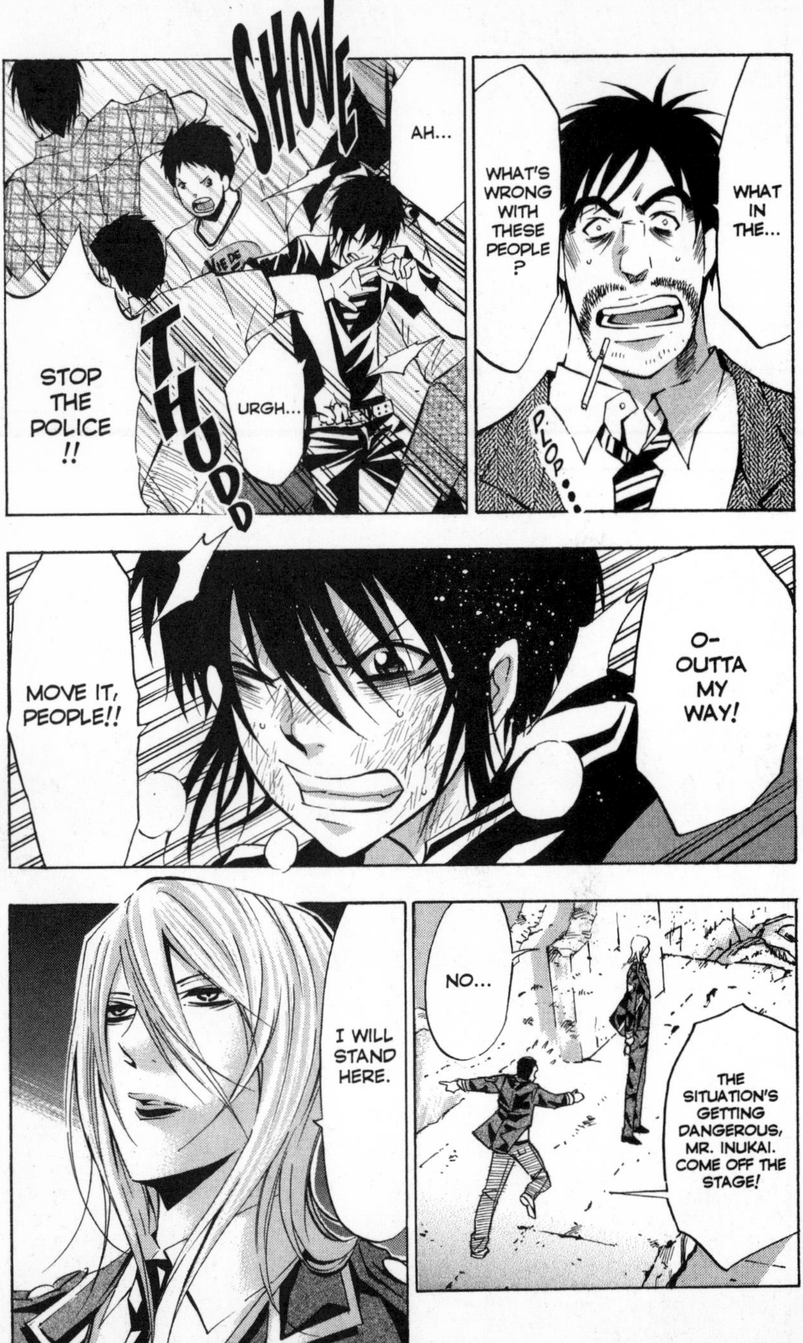
WHAT IN THE...
WHAT'S WRONG WITH THESE PEOPLE?
PLOP...
AH...
SHOVE
URGH...
THUDD
STOP THE POLICE!!
O-OUTTA MY WAY!
MOVE IT, PEOPLE!!
THE SITUATION'S GETTING DANGEROUS, MR. INUKAI. COME OFF THE STAGE!
NO...
I WILL STAND HERE.

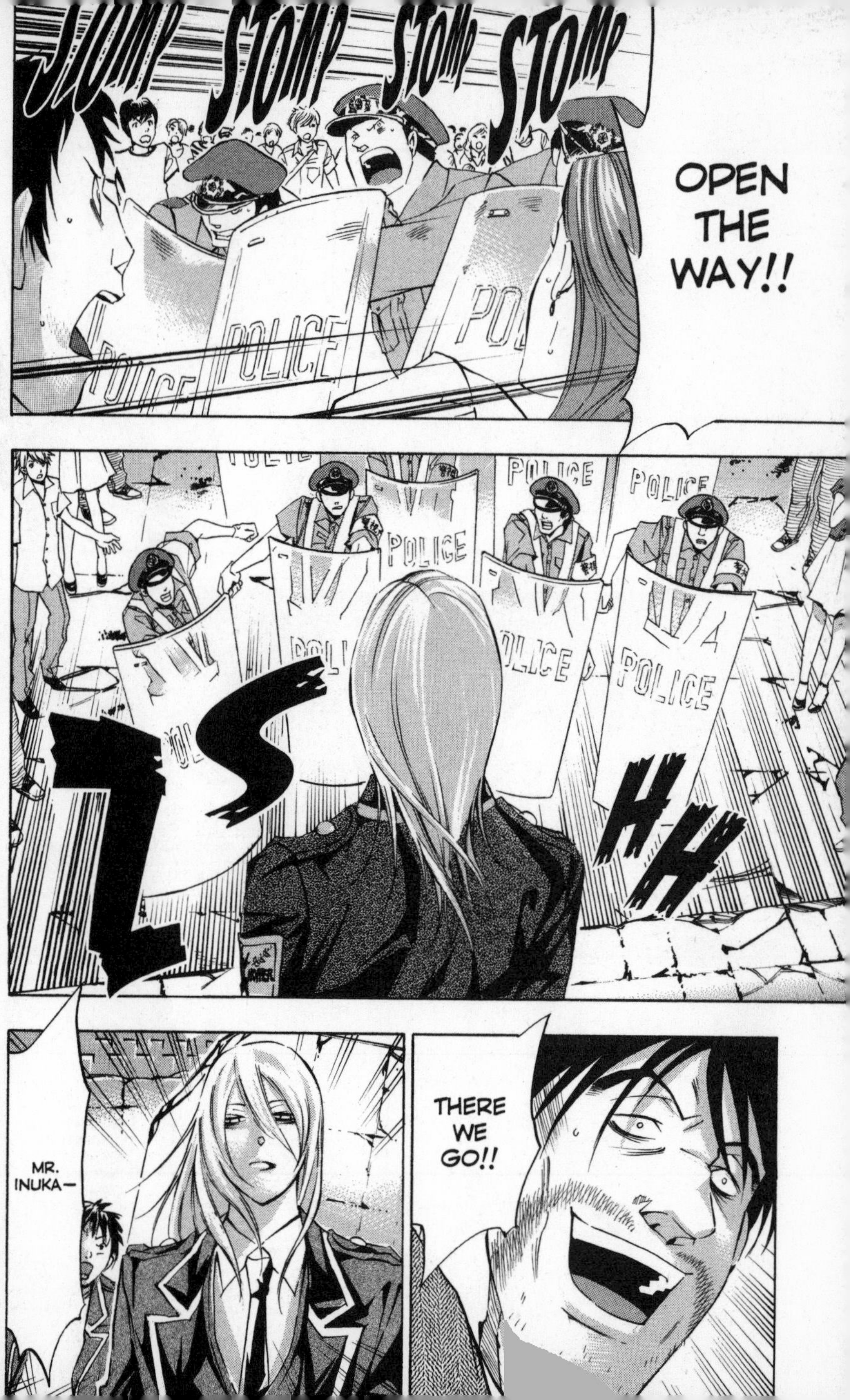
STOMP STOMP STOMP STOMP
OPEN THE WAY!!
THERE WE GO!!
MR. INUKA—

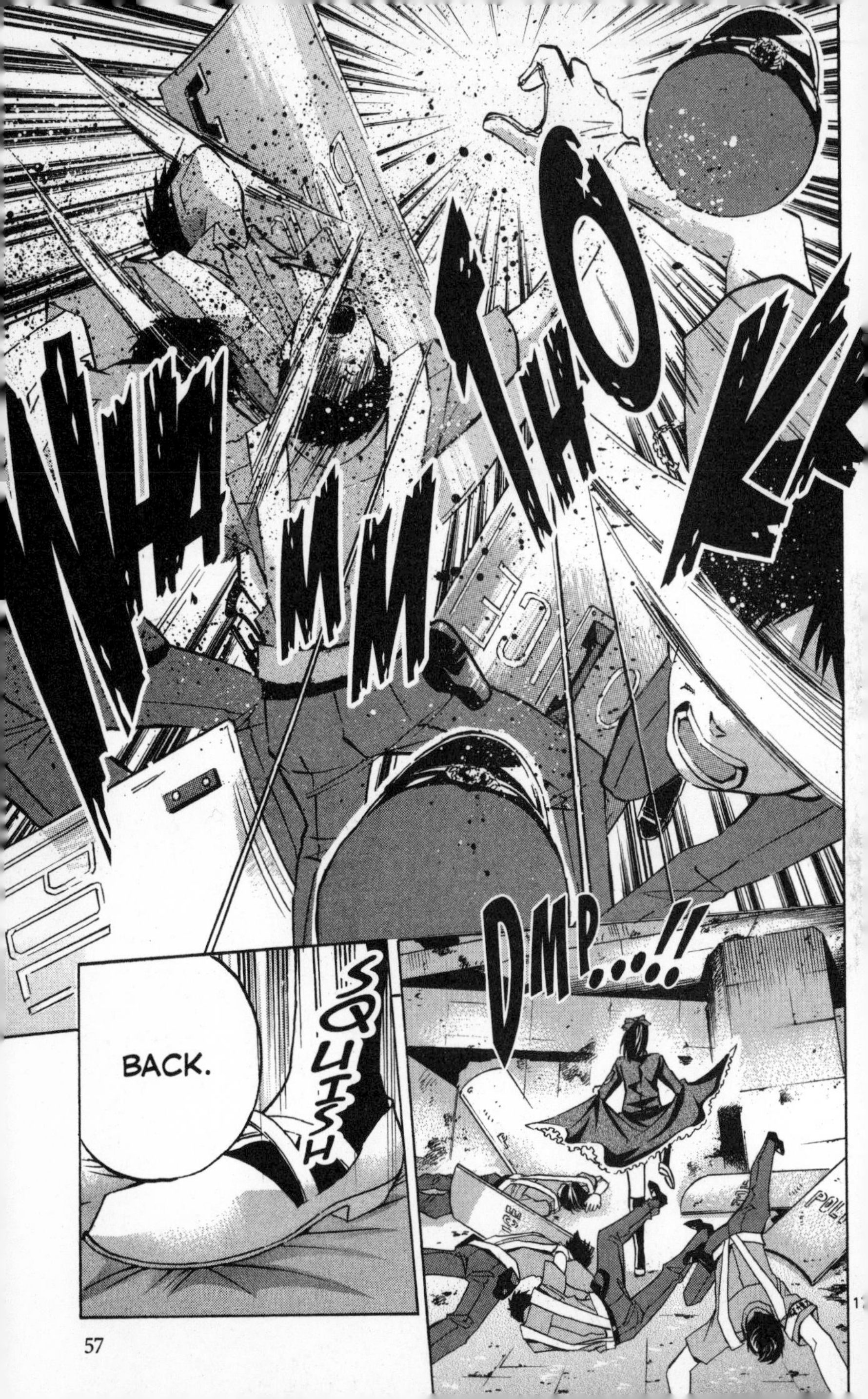
WHAMMM THOK
DMP...!!
SQUISH
BACK.

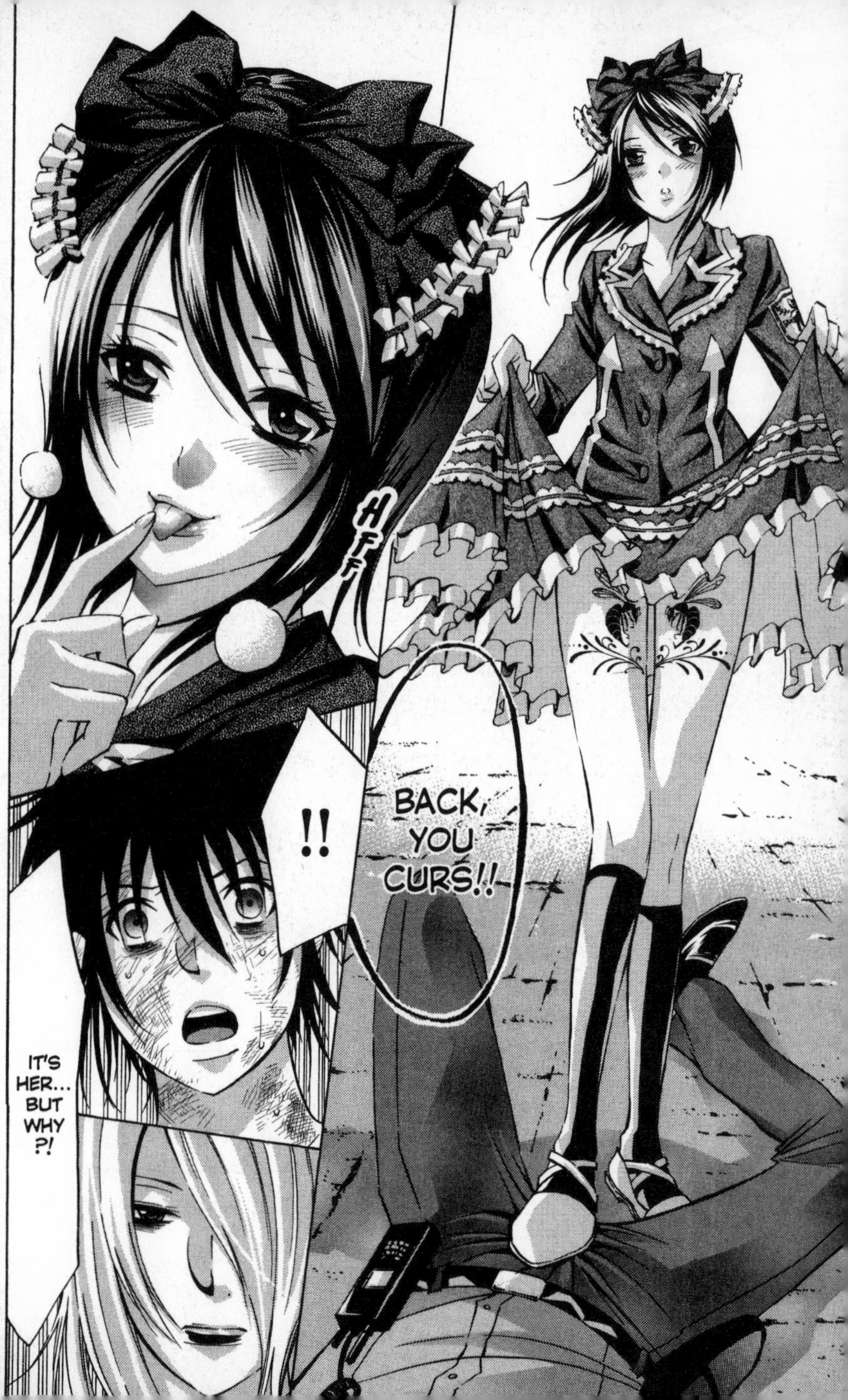
BACK, YOU CURS!!
HFF
!!
IT'S HER... BUT WHY?!

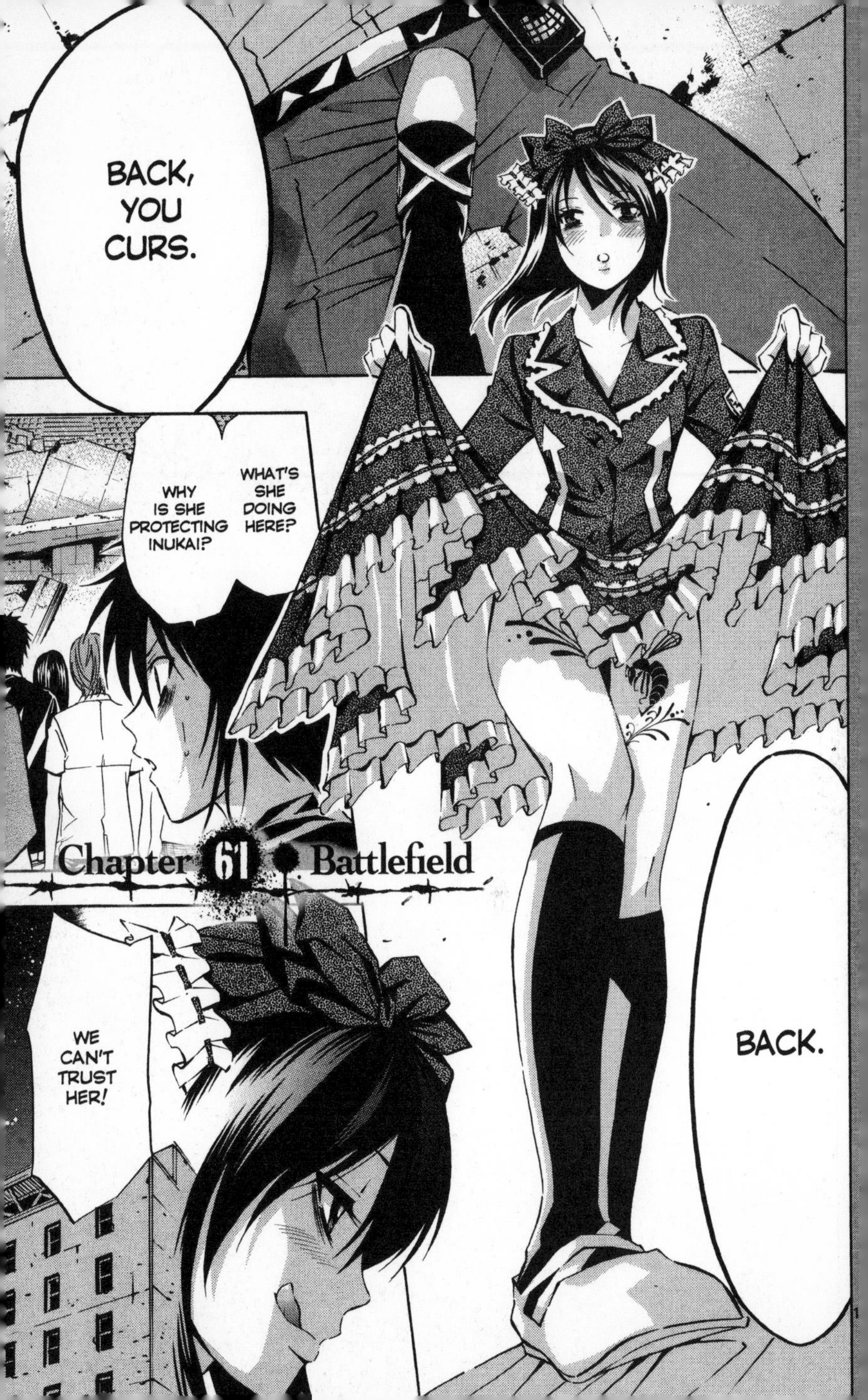
BACK, YOU CURS.
WHAT'S SHE DOING HERE?
WHY IS SHE PROTECTING INUKAI?
Chapter 61 Battlefield
BACK.
WE CAN'T TRUST HER!

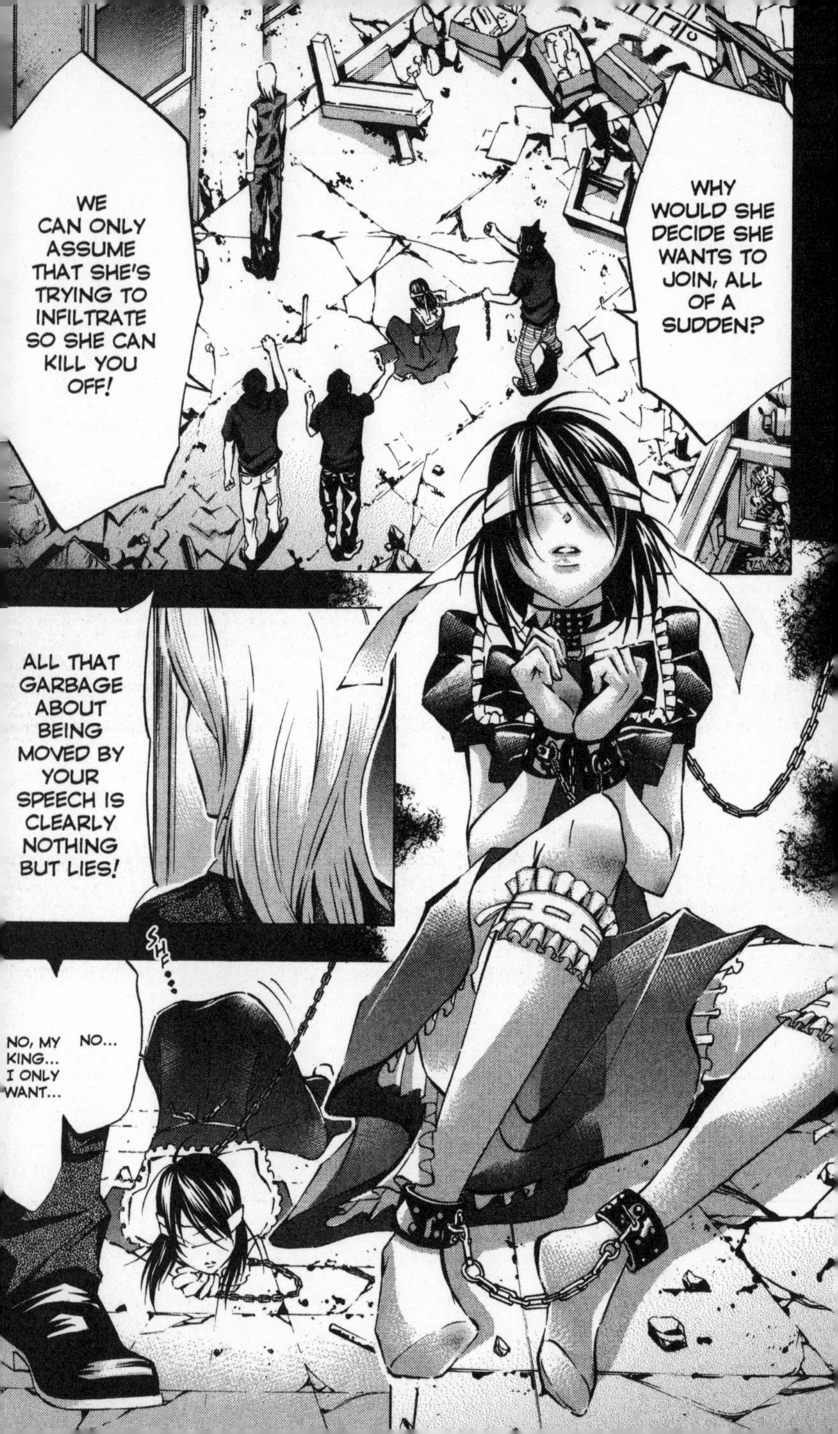
WHY WOULD SHE DECIDE SHE WANTS TO JOIN, ALL OF A SUDDEN?
WE CAN ONLY ASSUME THAT SHE'S TRYING TO INFILTRATE SO SHE CAN KILL YOU OFF!
ALL THAT GARBAGE ABOUT BEING MOVED BY YOUR SPEECH IS CLEARLY NOTHING BUT LIES!
SHF...
NO...
NO, MY KING... I ONLY WANT...

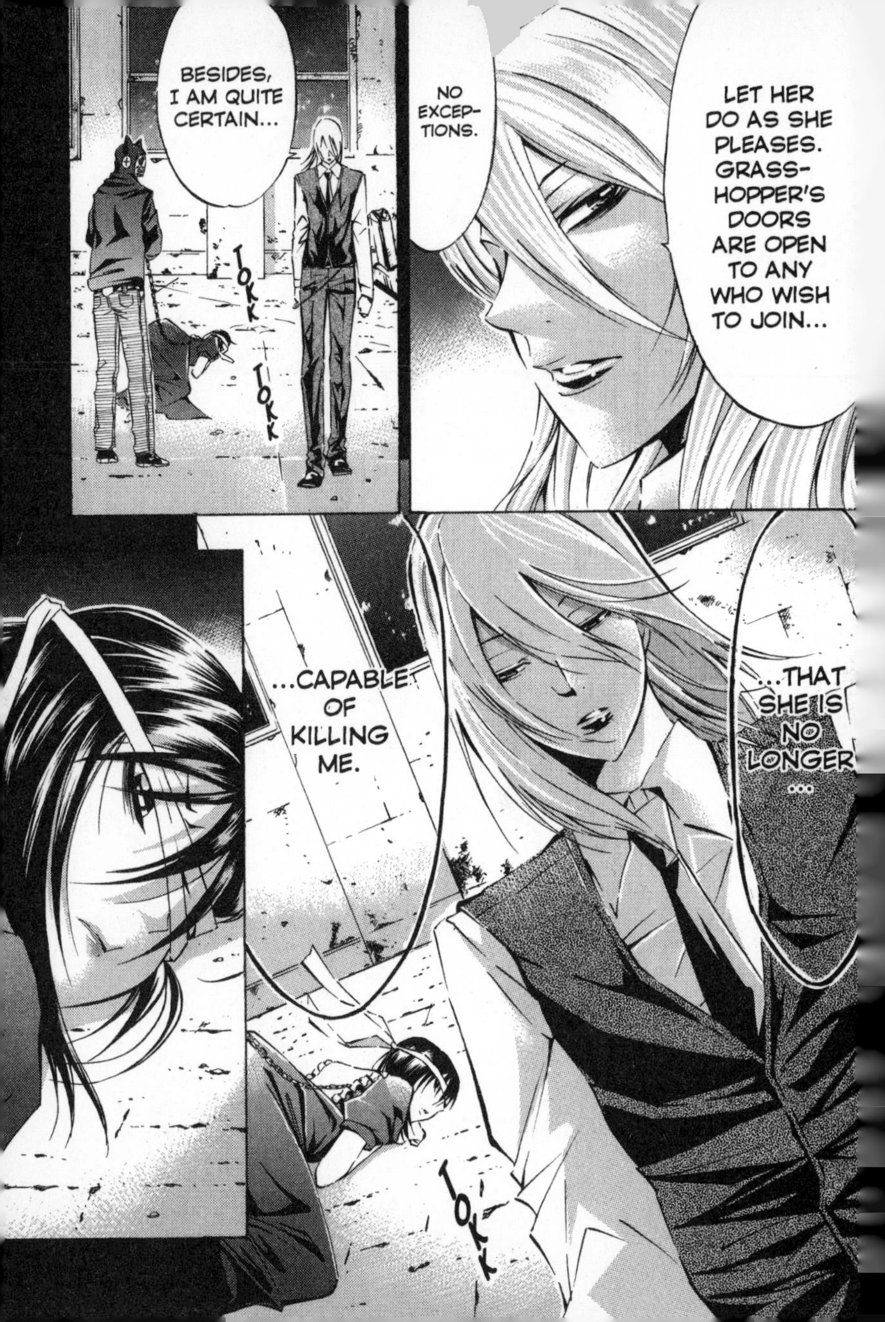
LET HER DO AS SHE PLEASES. GRASSHOPPER'S DOORS ARE OPEN TO ANY WHO WISH TO JOIN...
NO EXCEPTIONS.
BESIDES, I AM QUITE CERTAIN...
TOKK
TOKK
TOKK
...THAT SHE IS NO LONGER...
...CAPABLE OF KILLING ME.
TOKK

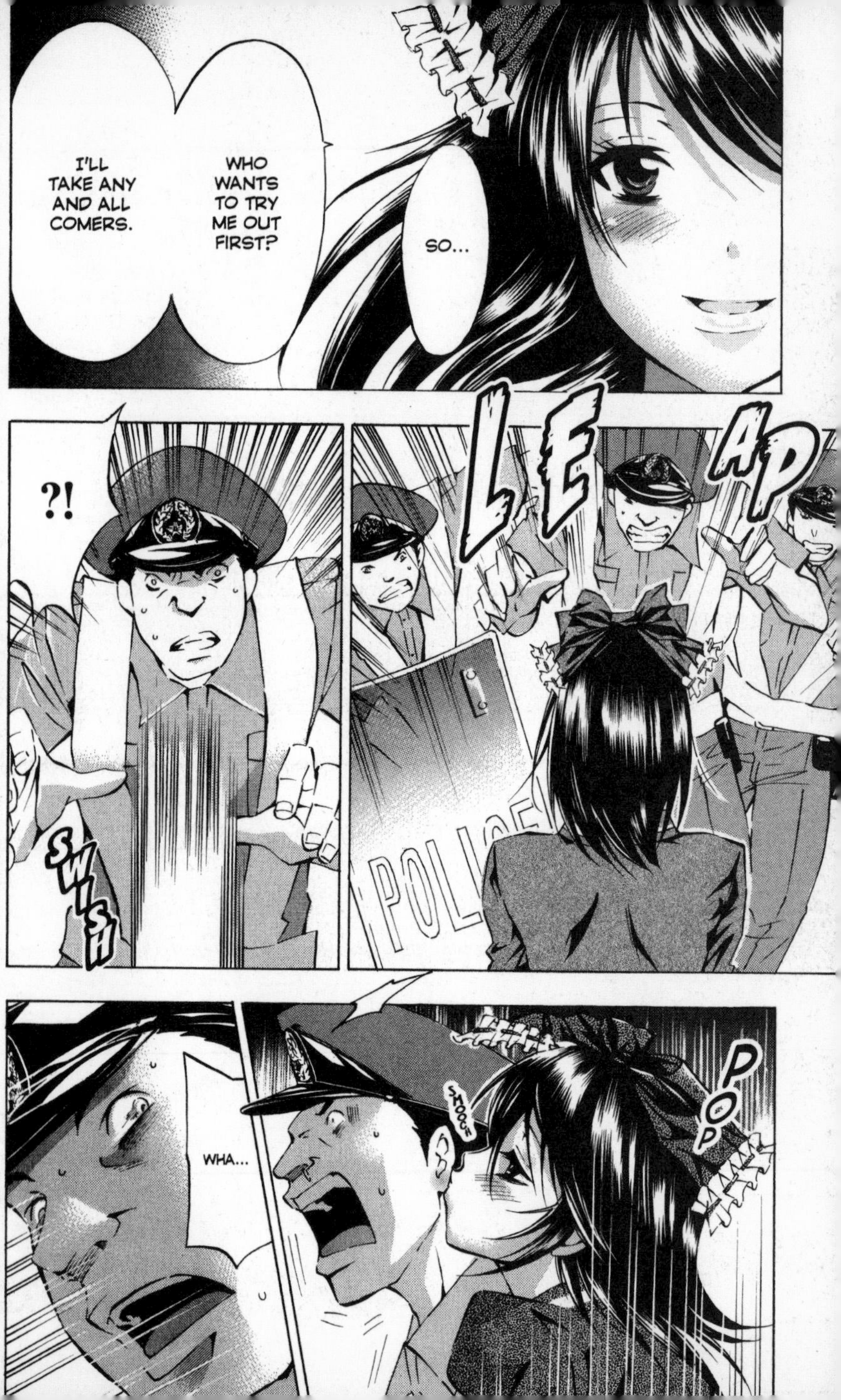
SO...
WHO WANTS TO TRY ME OUT FIRST?
I'LL TAKE ANY AND ALL COMERS.
LEAP
POLICE
?!
SWISH
POP
SMOOCH
WHA...

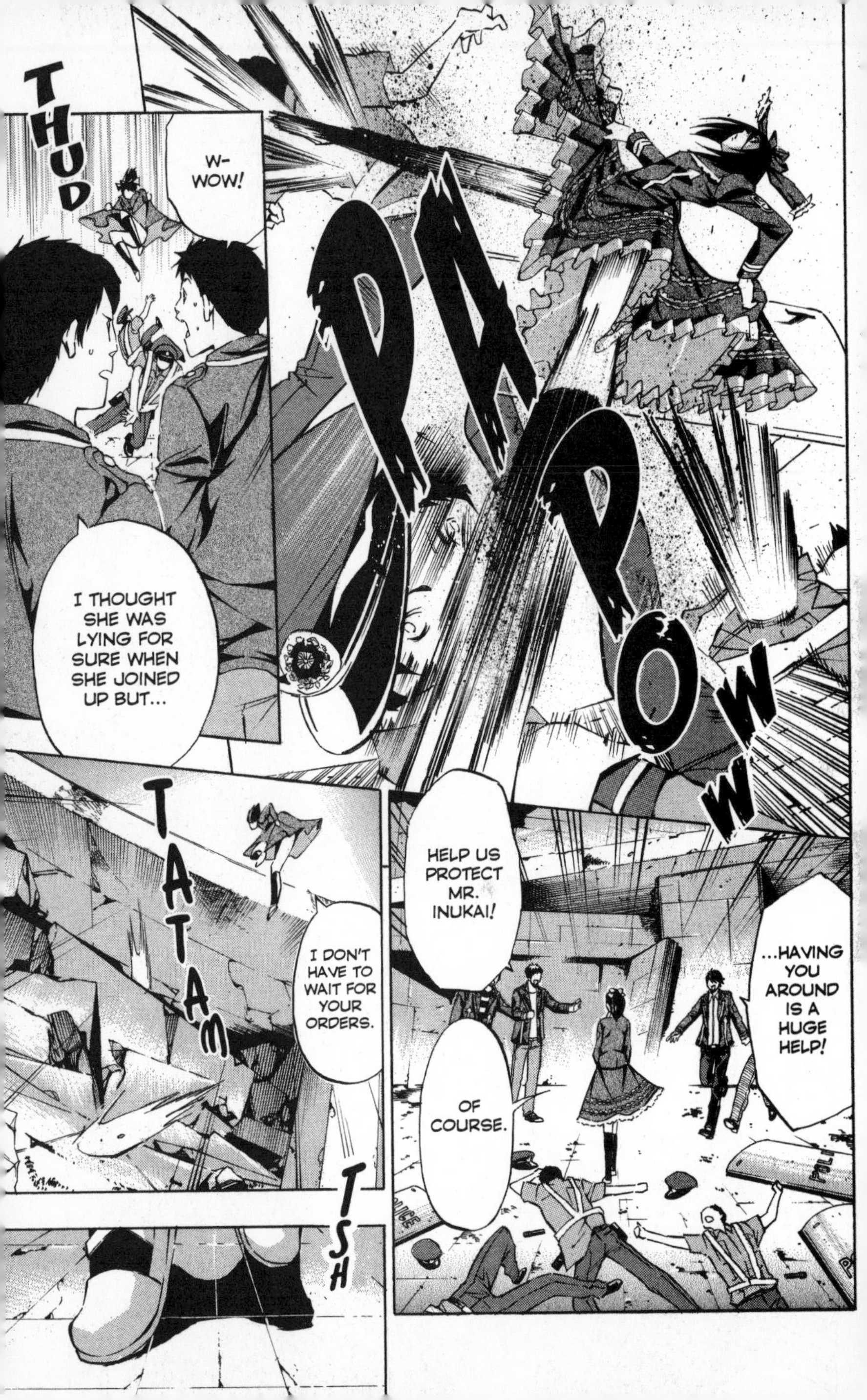
PAPOWW
THUD
W-WOW!
I THOUGHT SHE WAS LYING FOR SURE WHEN SHE JOINED UP BUT...
HELP US PROTECT MR. INUKAI!
...HAVING YOU AROUND IS A HUGE HELP!
OF COURSE.
TATAM
I DON'T HAVE TO WAIT FOR YOUR ORDERS.
TSH

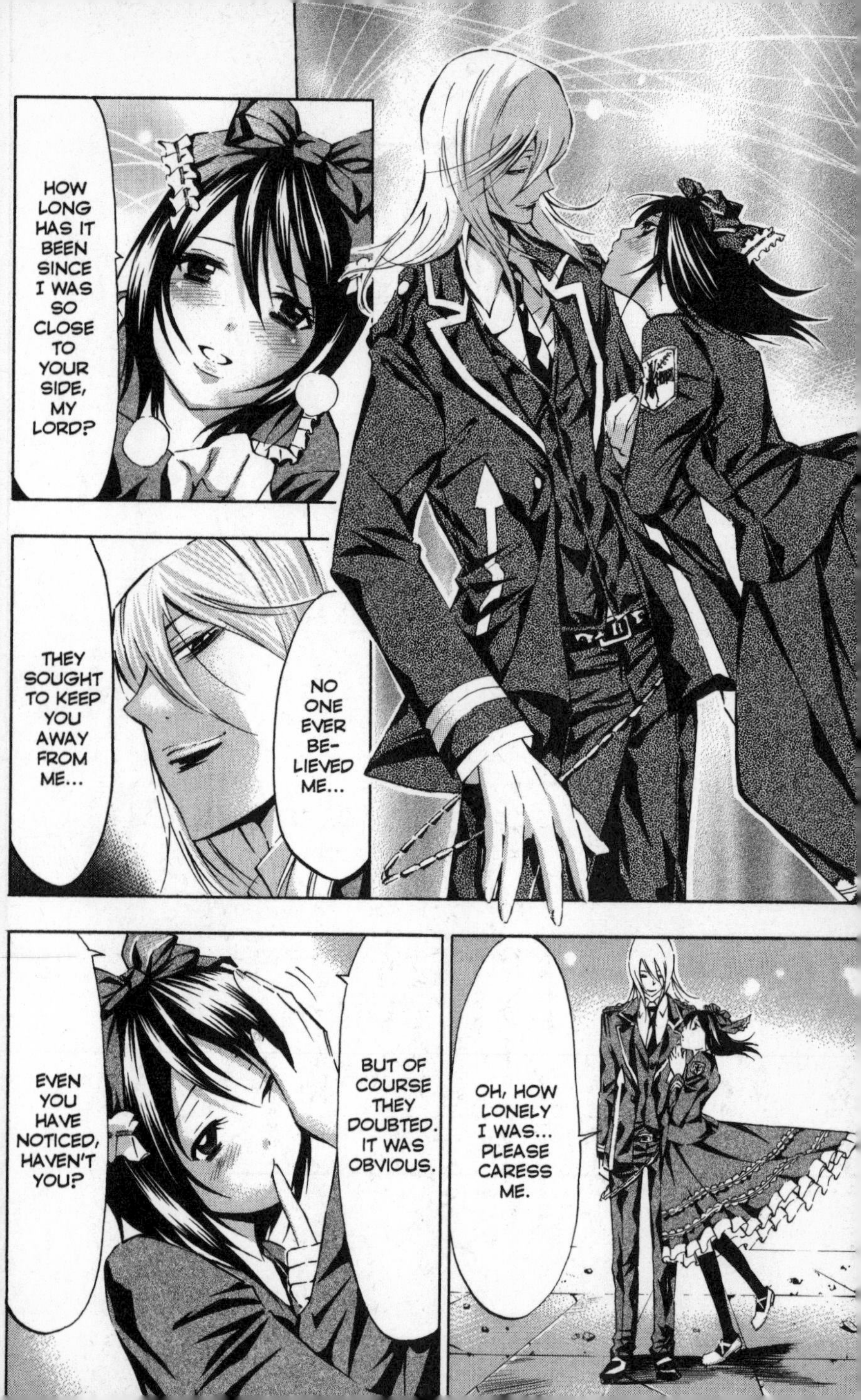
HOW LONG HAS IT BEEN SINCE I WAS SO CLOSE TO YOUR SIDE, MY LORD?
NO ONE EVER BE-LIEVED ME...
THEY SOUGHT TO KEEP YOU AWAY FROM ME...
OH, HOW LONELY I WAS... PLEASE CARESS ME.
BUT OF COURSE THEY DOUBTED. IT WAS OBVIOUS.
EVEN YOU HAVE NOTICED, HAVEN'T YOU?

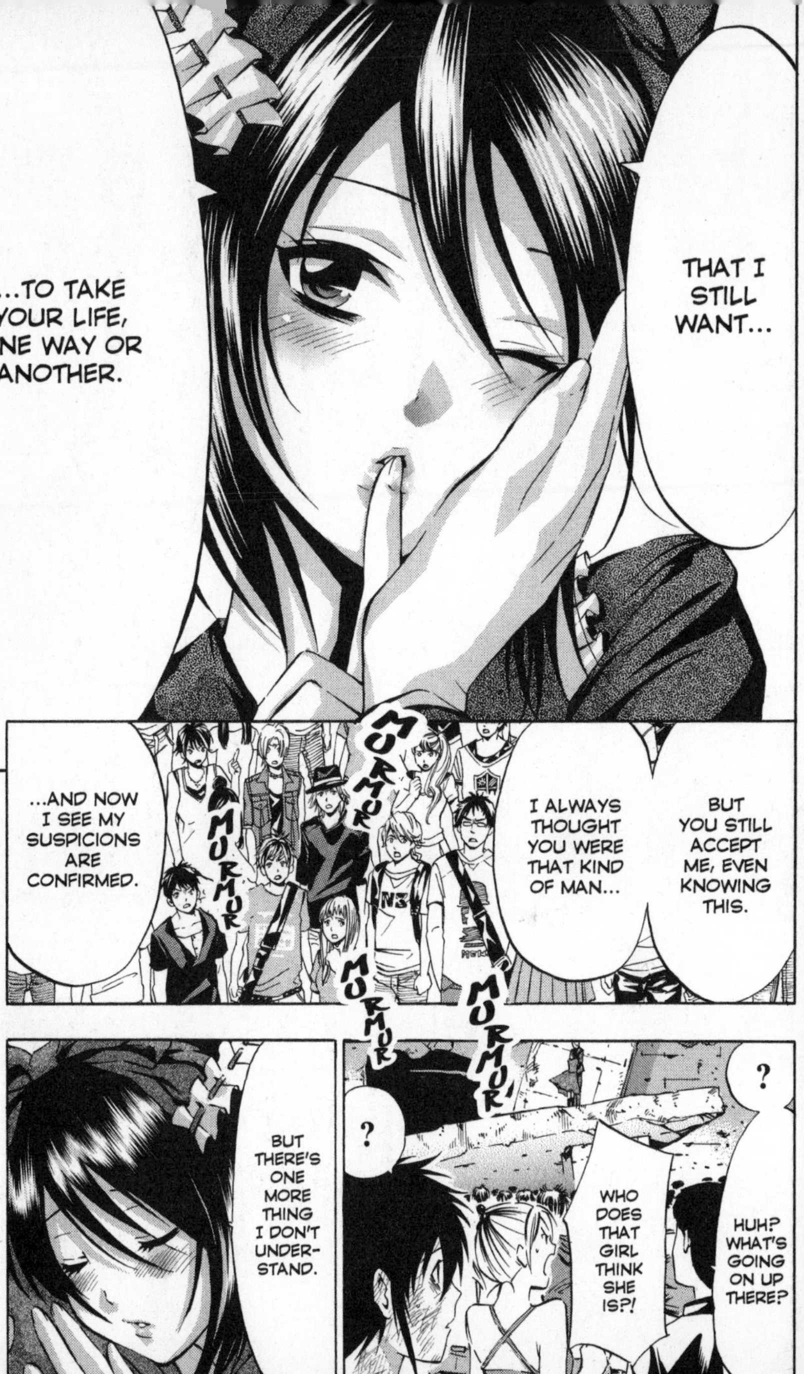
THAT I STILL WANT...
...TO TAKE YOUR LIFE, ONE WAY OR ANOTHER.
BUT YOU STILL ACCEPT ME, EVEN KNOWING THIS.
I ALWAYS THOUGHT YOU WERE THAT KIND OF MAN...
MURMUR MURMUR
...AND NOW I SEE MY SUSPICIONS ARE CONFIRMED.
MURMUR MURMUR
?
HUH? WHAT'S GOING ON UP THERE?
WHO DOES THAT GIRL THINK SHE IS?!
?
BUT THERE'S ONE MORE THING I DON'T UNDER-STAND.

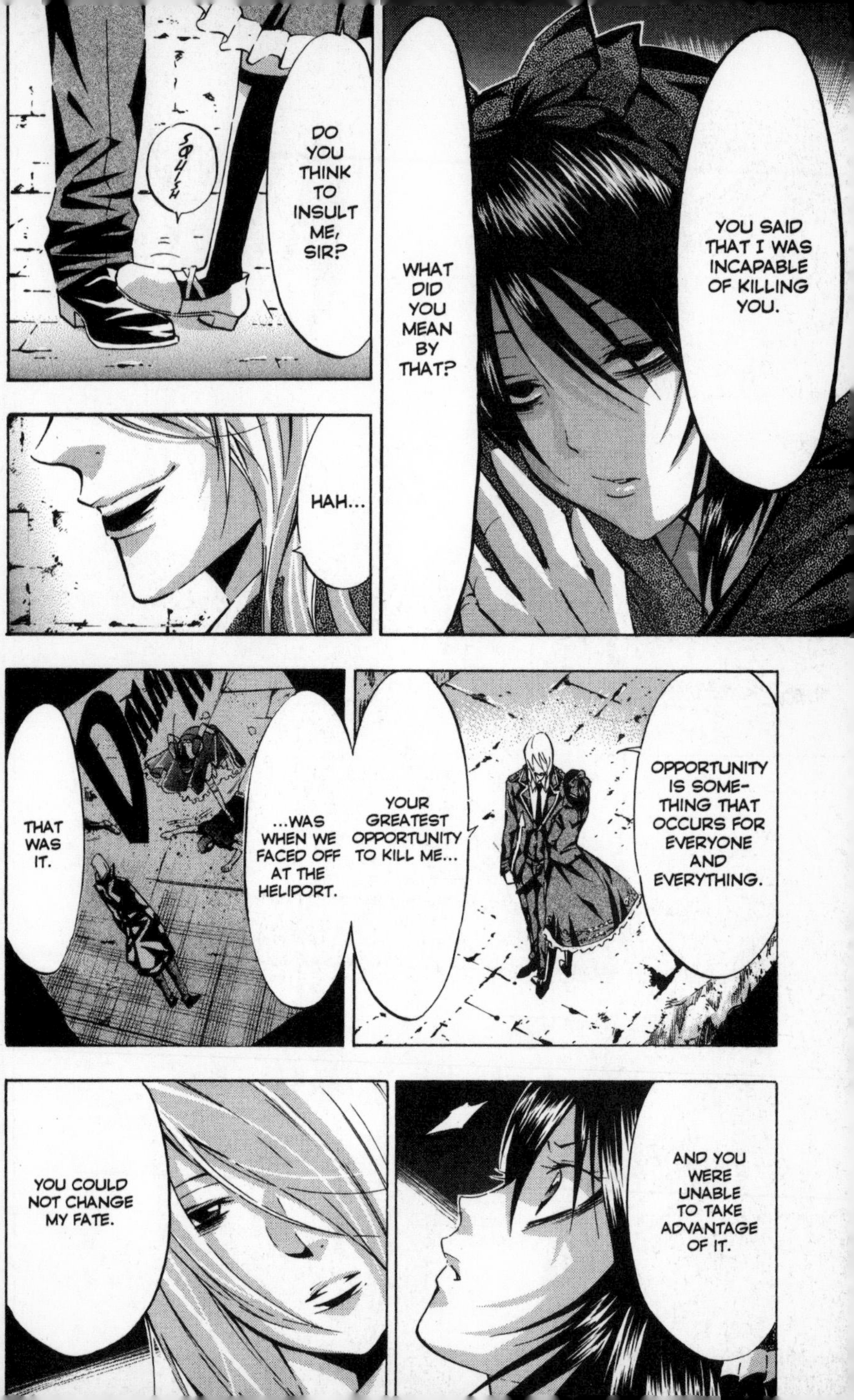
YOU SAID THAT I WAS INCAPABLE OF KILLING YOU.
WHAT DID YOU MEAN BY THAT?
DO YOU THINK TO INSULT ME, SIR?
SQUISH
HAH...
OPPORTUNITY IS SOME-THING THAT OCCURS FOR EVERYONE AND EVERYTHING.
YOUR GREATEST OPPORTUNITY TO KILL ME...
...WAS WHEN WE FACED OFF AT THE HELIPORT.
THAT WAS IT.
AND YOU WERE UNABLE TO TAKE ADVANTAGE OF IT.
YOU COULD NOT CHANGE MY FATE.

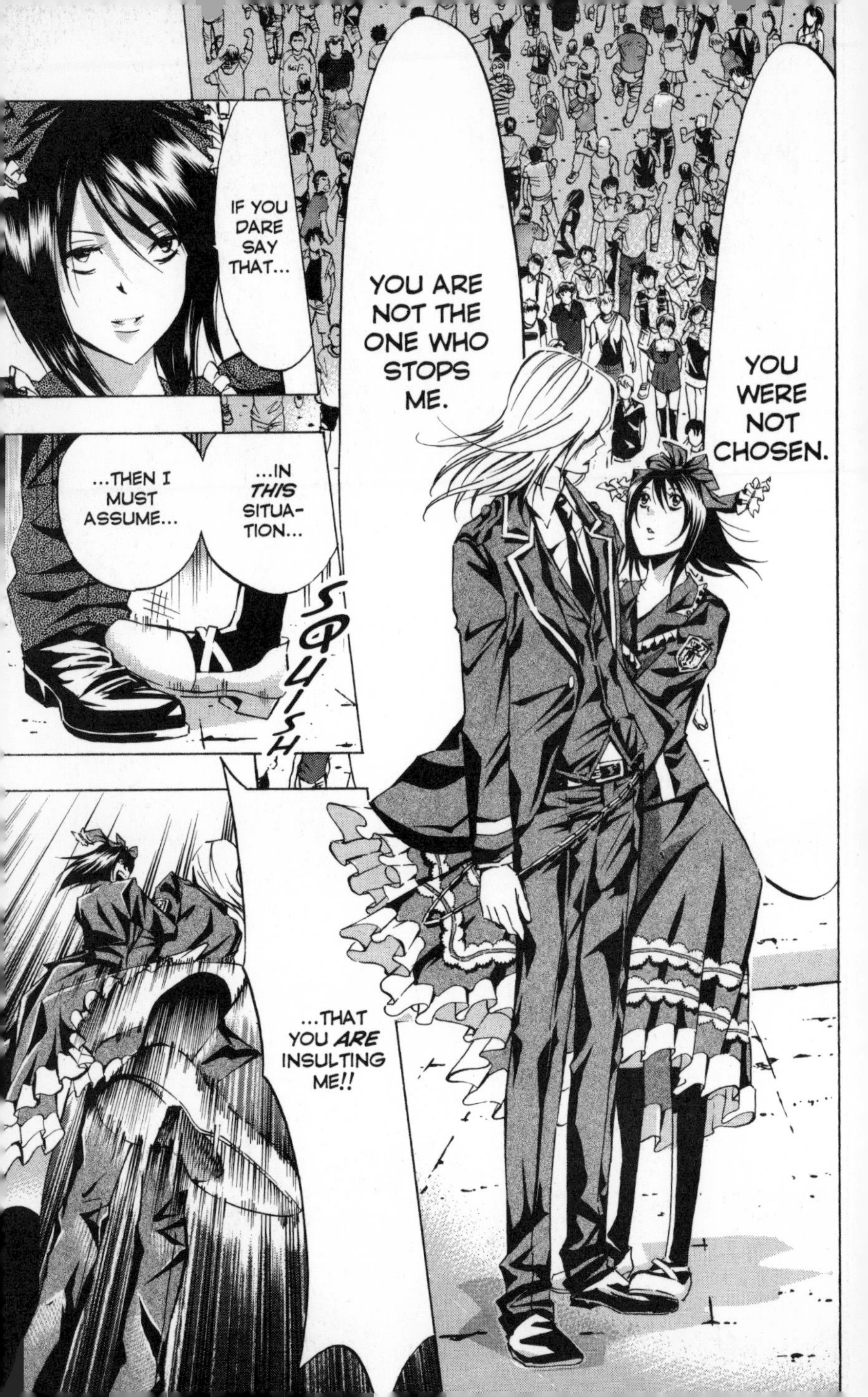
YOU WERE NOT CHOSEN.
YOU ARE NOT THE ONE WHO STOPS ME.
IF YOU DARE SAY THAT...
...IN *THIS* SITUATION...
...THEN I MUST ASSUME...
SQUISH
...THAT YOU *ARE* INSULTING ME!!

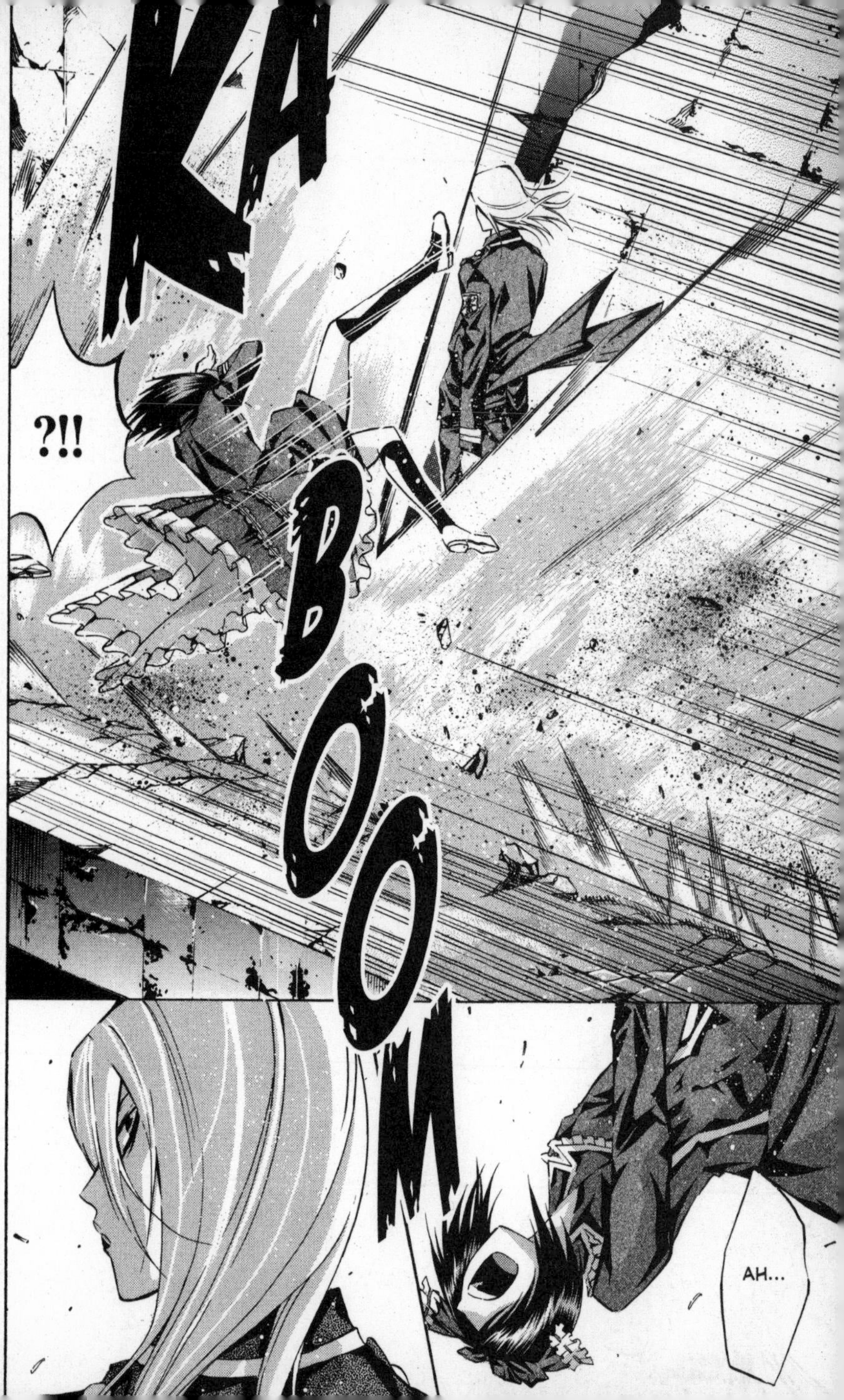
KA
BOOM
?!!
AH...

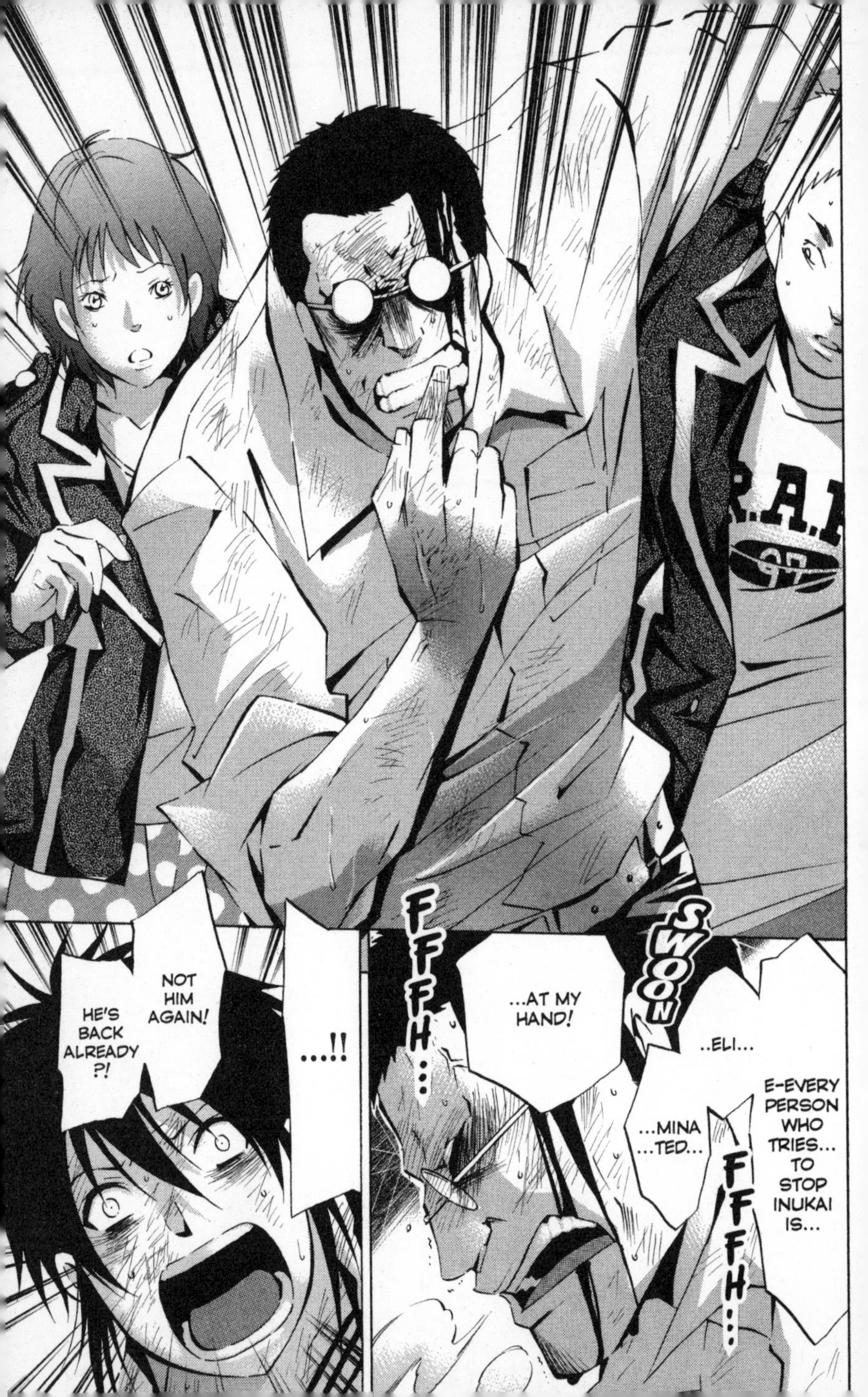
SWOON
E-EVERY PERSON WHO TRIES... TO STOP INUKAI IS...
..ELI...
...MINA ...TED...
FFFH...
...AT MY HAND!
FFFH...
...!!
NOT HIM AGAIN!
HE'S BACK ALREADY?!

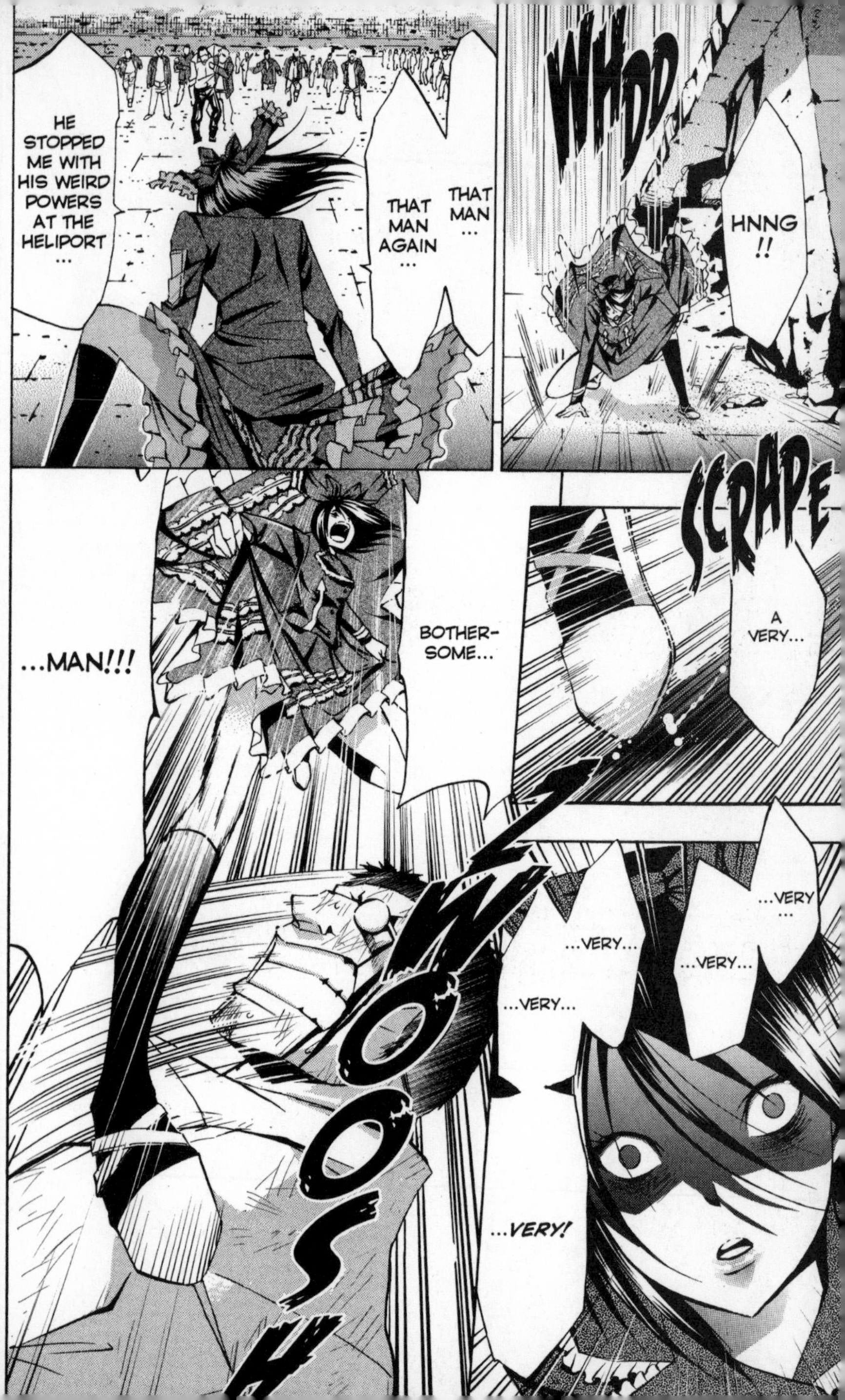

WHDD
HNNG !!
THAT MAN ...
THAT MAN AGAIN ...
HE STOPPED ME WITH HIS WEIRD POWERS AT THE HELIPORT ...
SCRAPE
A VERY...
...VERY ...
...VERY...
...VERY...
...VERY...
...VERY!
BOTHER-SOME...
...MAN!!!
WOOSH

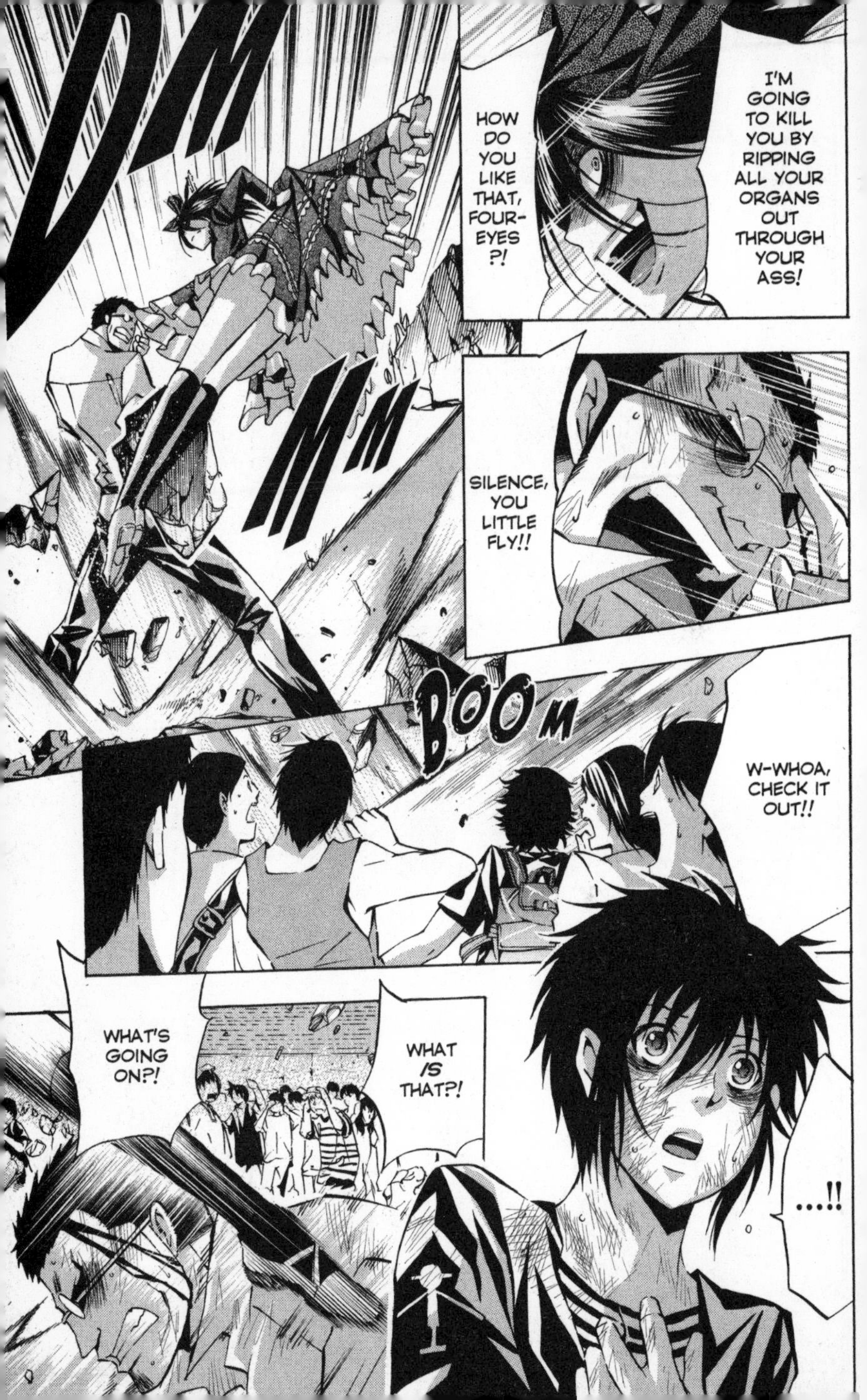
I'M GOING TO KILL YOU BY RIPPING ALL YOUR ORGANS OUT THROUGH YOUR ASS!
HOW DO YOU LIKE THAT, FOUR-EYES?!
SILENCE, YOU LITTLE FLY!!
BOOM
W-WHOA, CHECK IT OUT!!
...!!
WHAT IS THAT?!
WHAT'S GOING ON?!

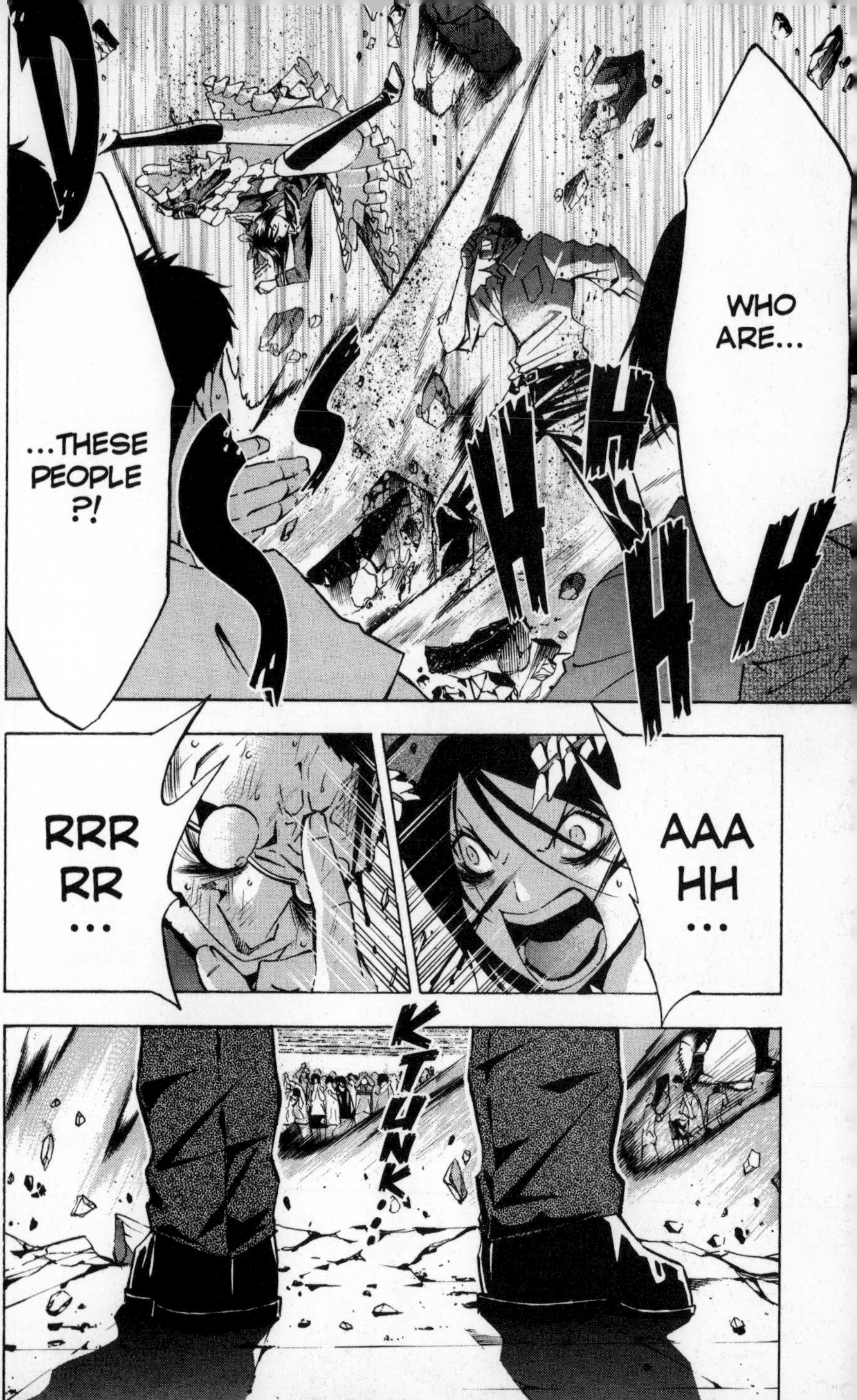
WHO ARE...
...THESE PEOPLE?!
AAAHH...
RRRRR...
KTUNK

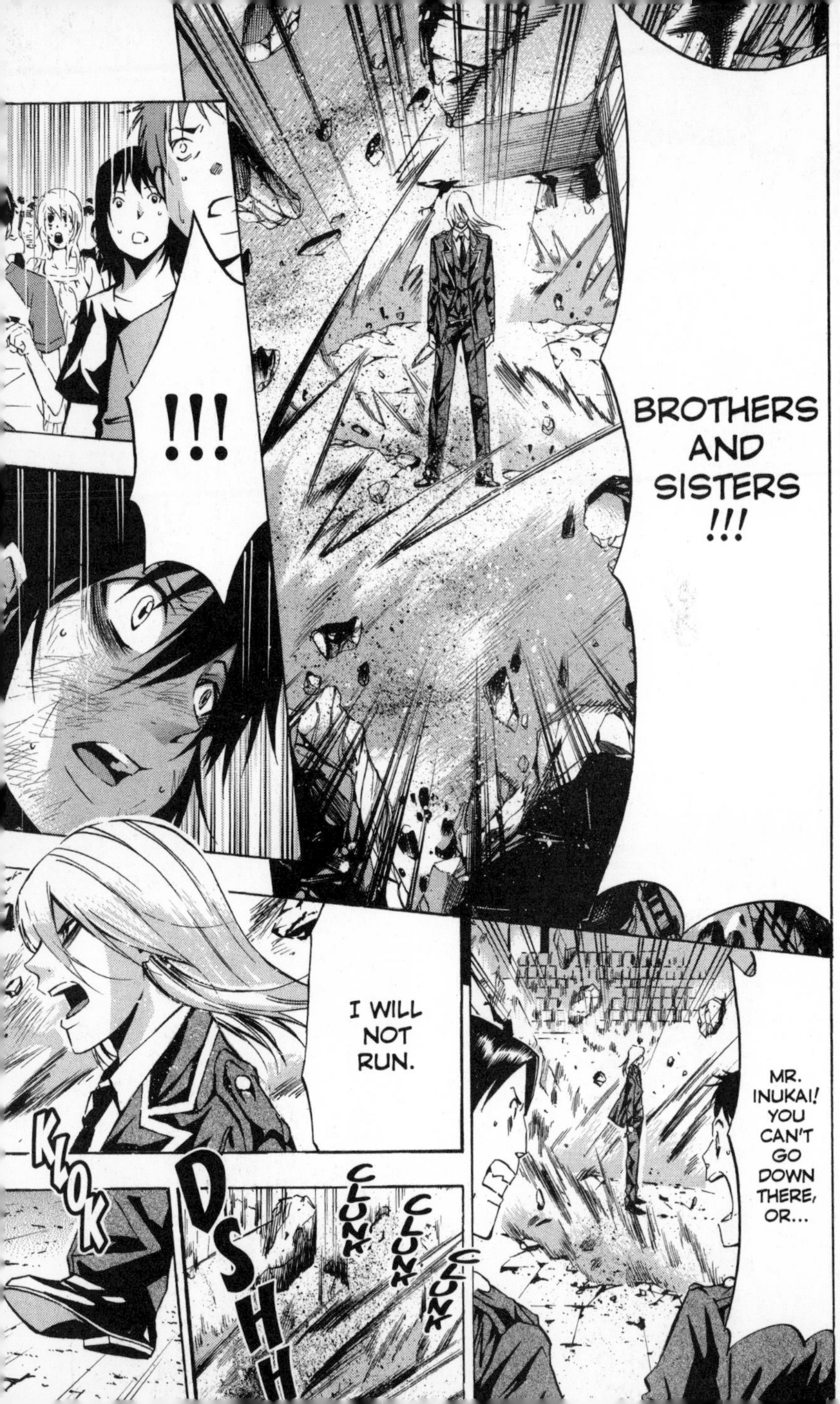
BROTHERS AND SISTERS!!!
!!!
MR. INUKAI! YOU CAN'T GO DOWN THERE, OR...
I WILL NOT RUN.
CLUNK
CLUNK
CLUNK
DSHHH
KLOK

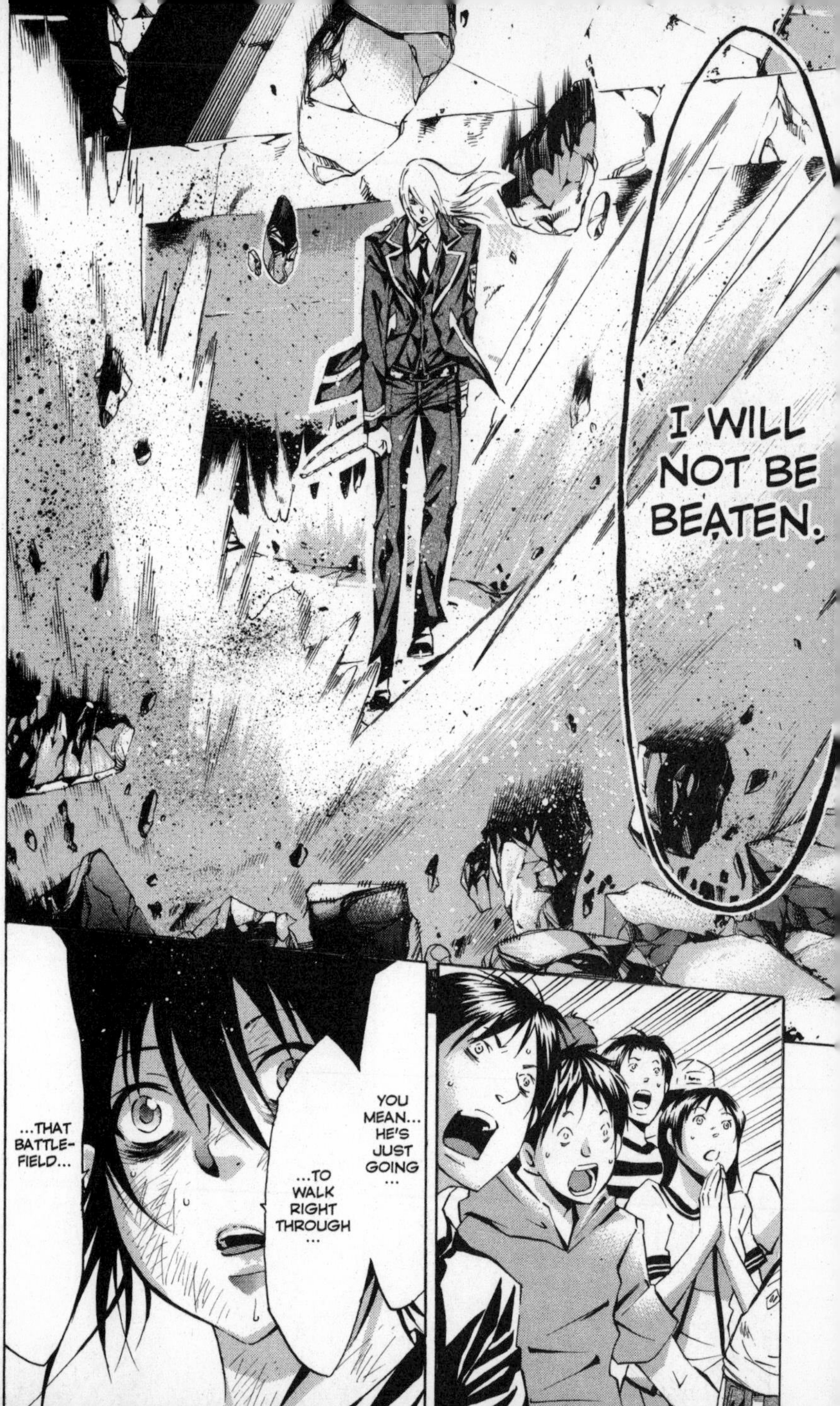
I WILL NOT BE BEATEN.
YOU MEAN... HE'S JUST GOING...
...TO WALK RIGHT THROUGH...
...THAT BATTLE-FIELD...

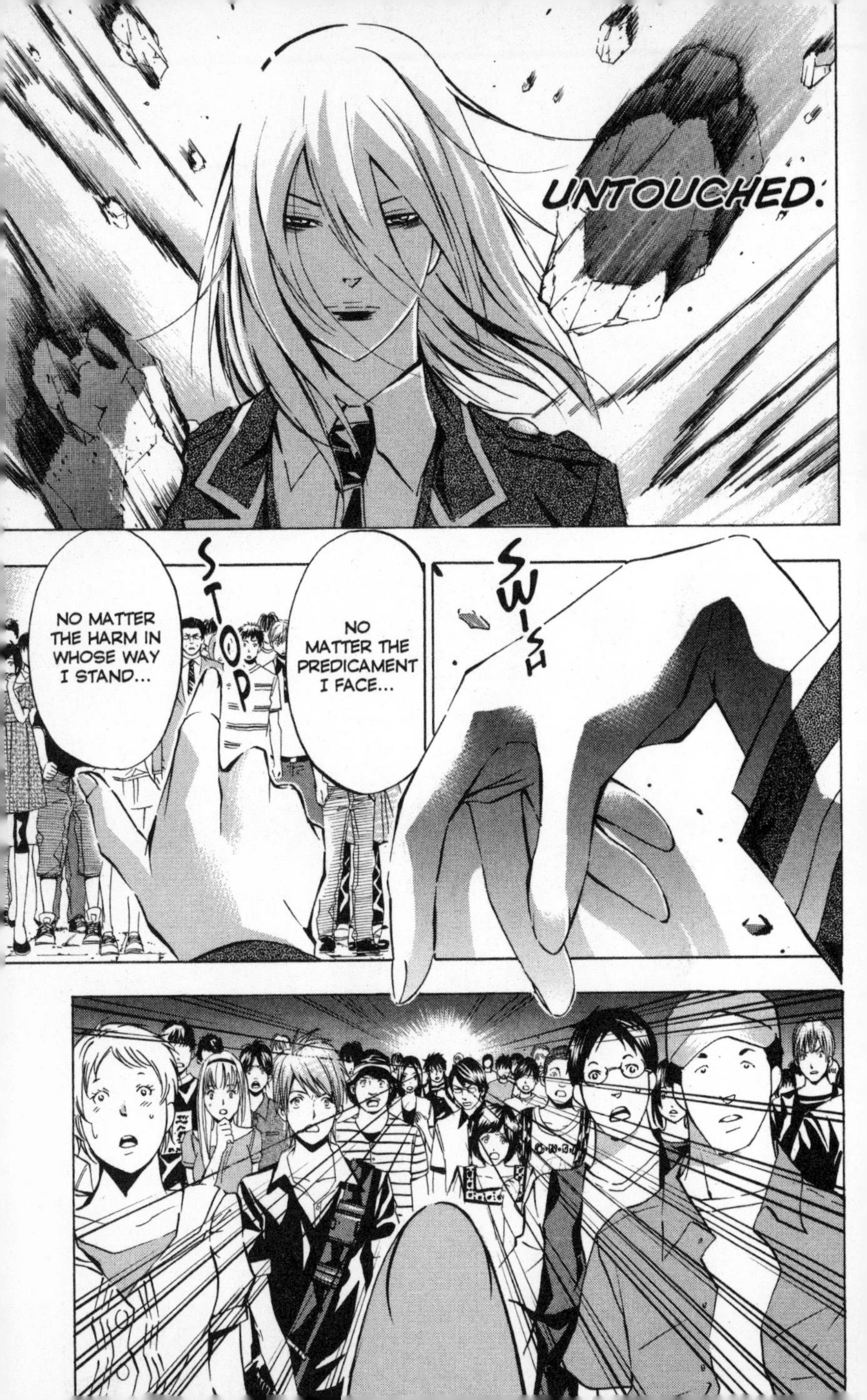
UNTOUCHED.
SWISH
NO MATTER THE PREDICAMENT I FACE...
STOP
NO MATTER THE HARM IN WHOSE WAY I STAND...

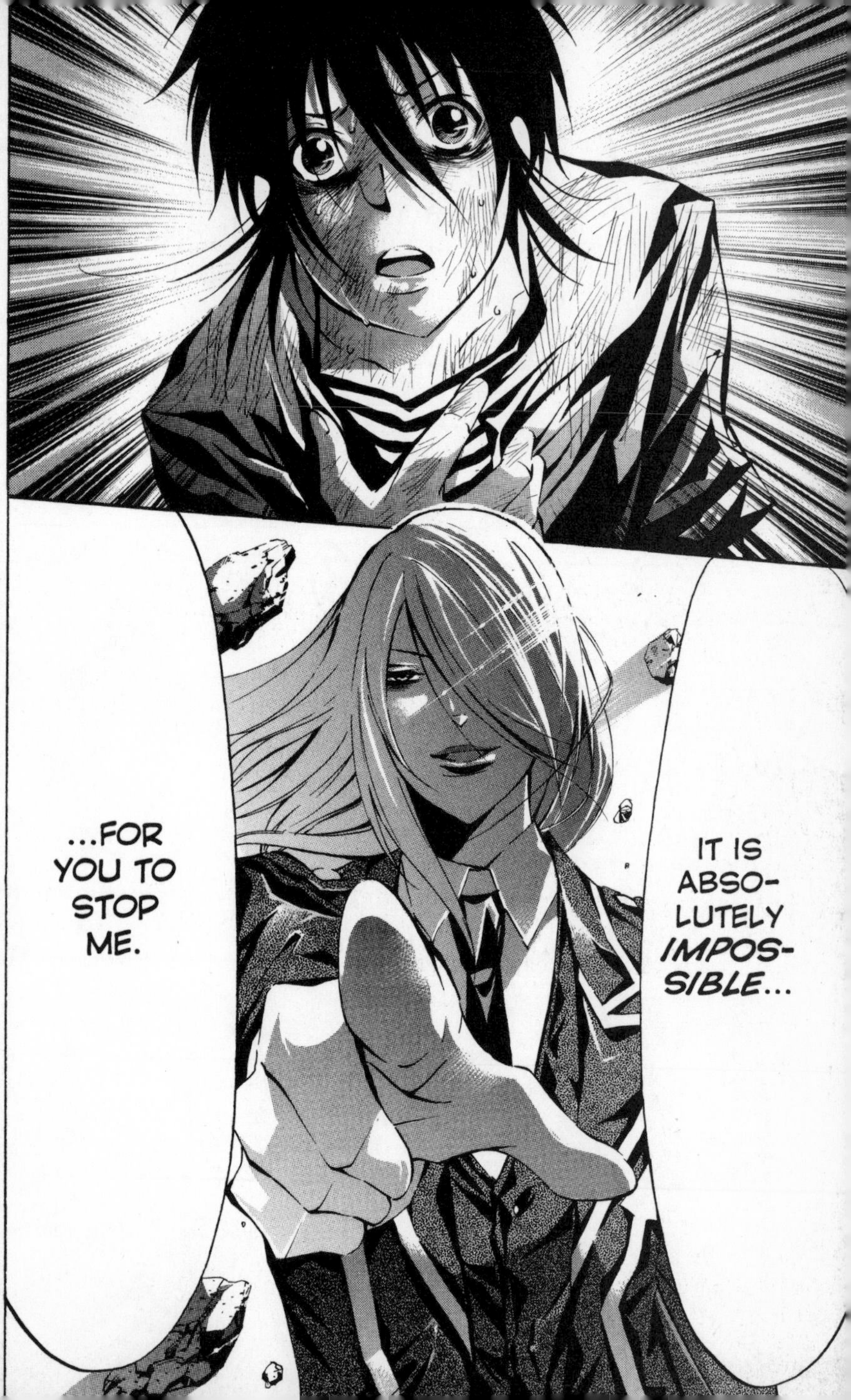
IT IS ABSO-LUTELY *IMPOS-SIBLE*...
...FOR YOU TO STOP ME.

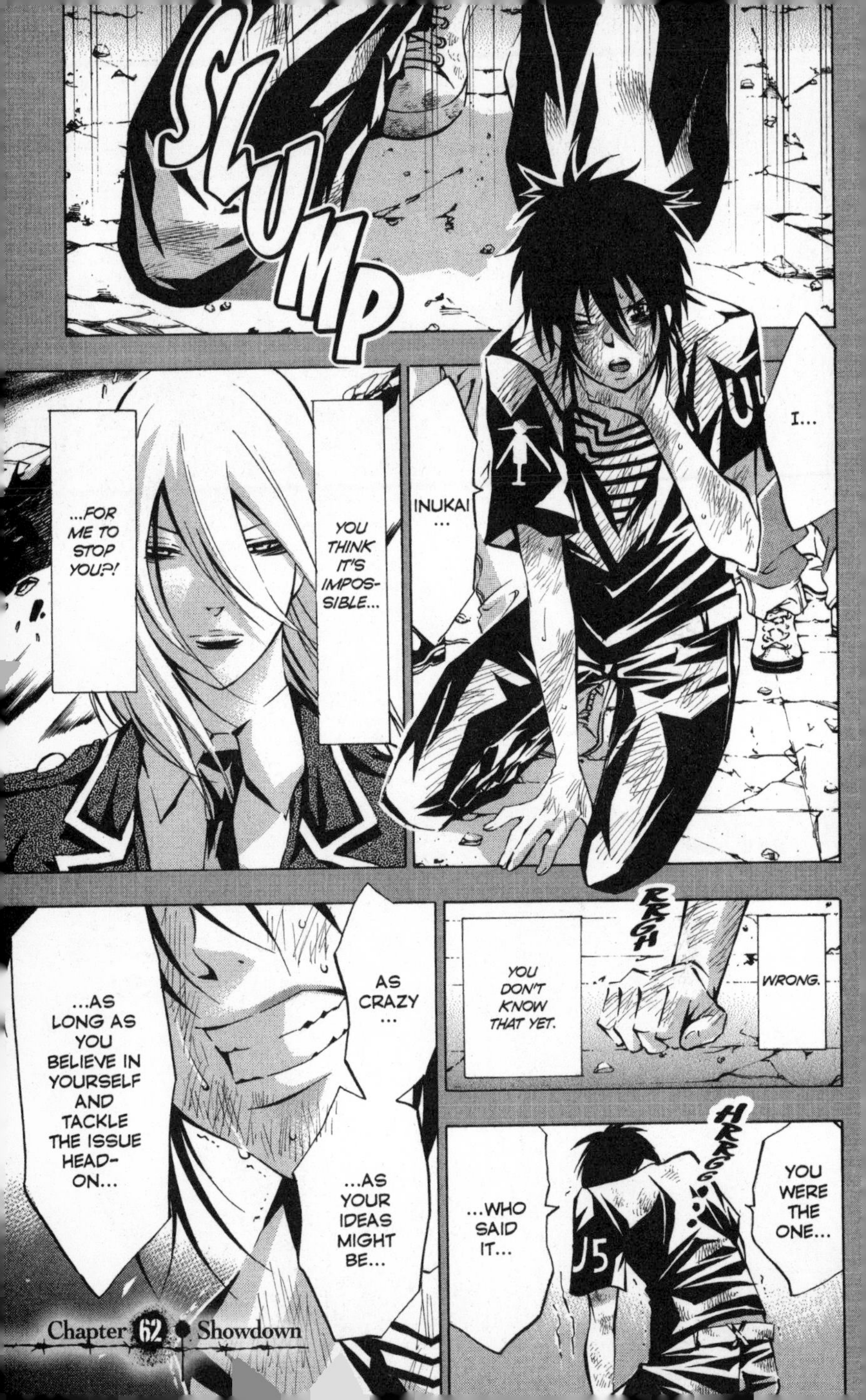
SLUMP
I...
INUKAI...
YOU THINK IT'S IMPOSSIBLE...
...FOR ME TO STOP YOU?!
RRGH
WRONG.
YOU DON'T KNOW THAT YET.
HRRGG
YOU WERE THE ONE...
...WHO SAID IT...
AS CRAZY...
...AS YOUR IDEAS MIGHT BE...
...AS LONG AS YOU BELIEVE IN YOURSELF AND TACKLE THE ISSUE HEAD-ON...
Chapter 62 Showdown

# Chapter 62 Showdown

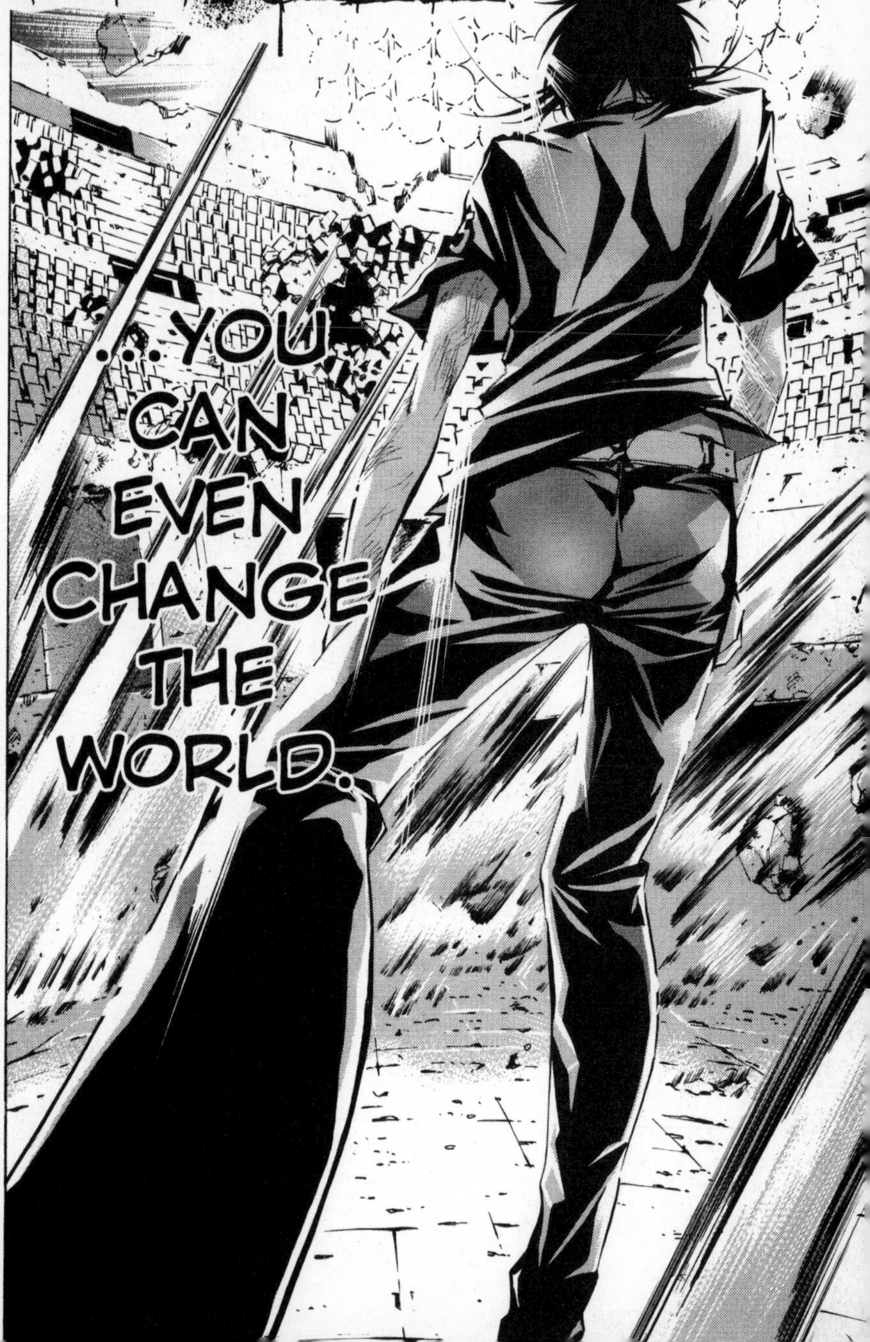
...YOU CAN EVEN CHANGE THE WORLD.

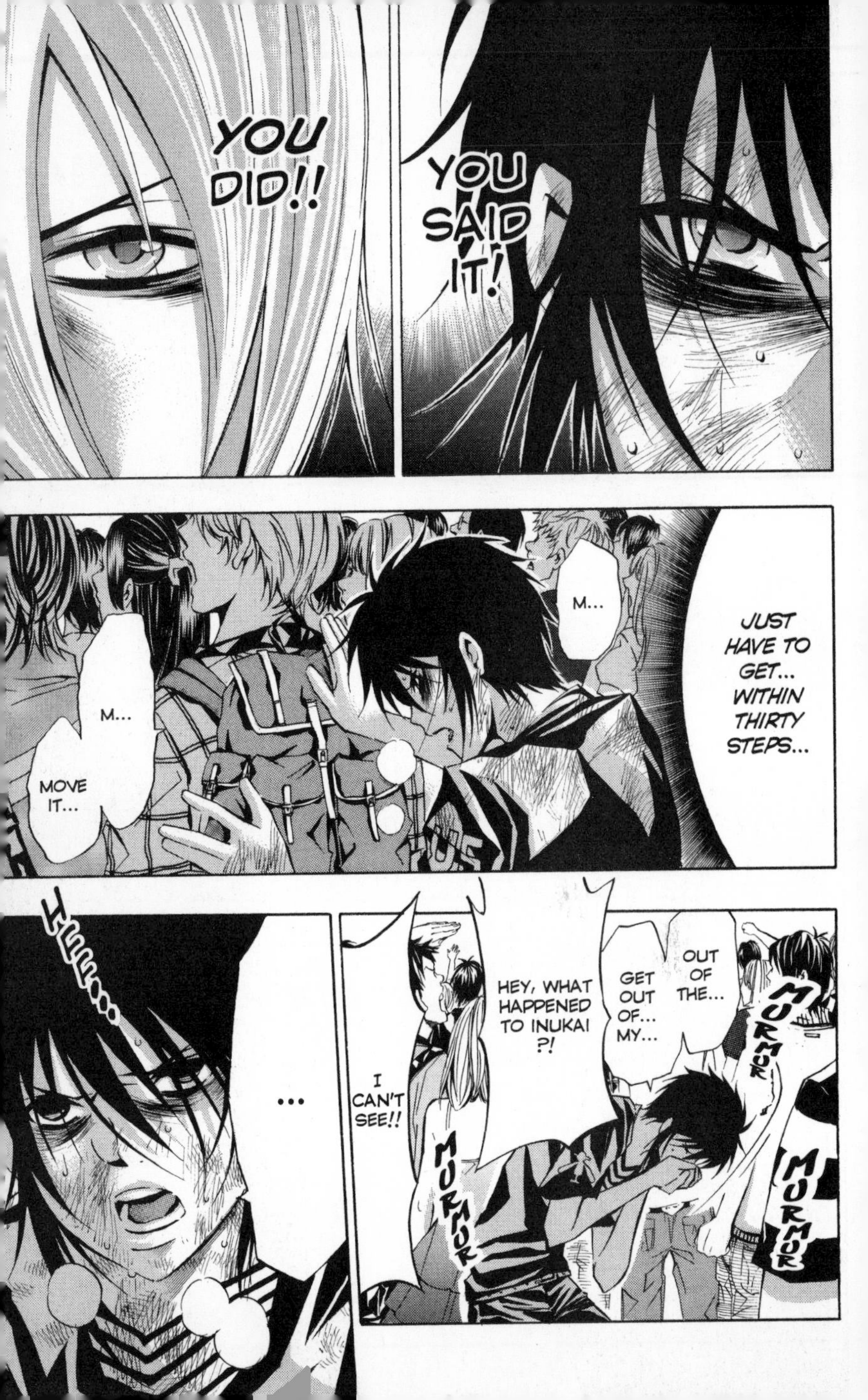
YOU SAID IT!
YOU DID!!
JUST HAVE TO GET... WITHIN THIRTY STEPS...
M...
M...
MOVE IT...
OUT OF THE...
GET OUT OF... MY...
HEY, WHAT HAPPENED TO INUKAI ?!
MURMUR
MURMUR
I CAN'T SEE!!
MURMUR
HEEE...
...

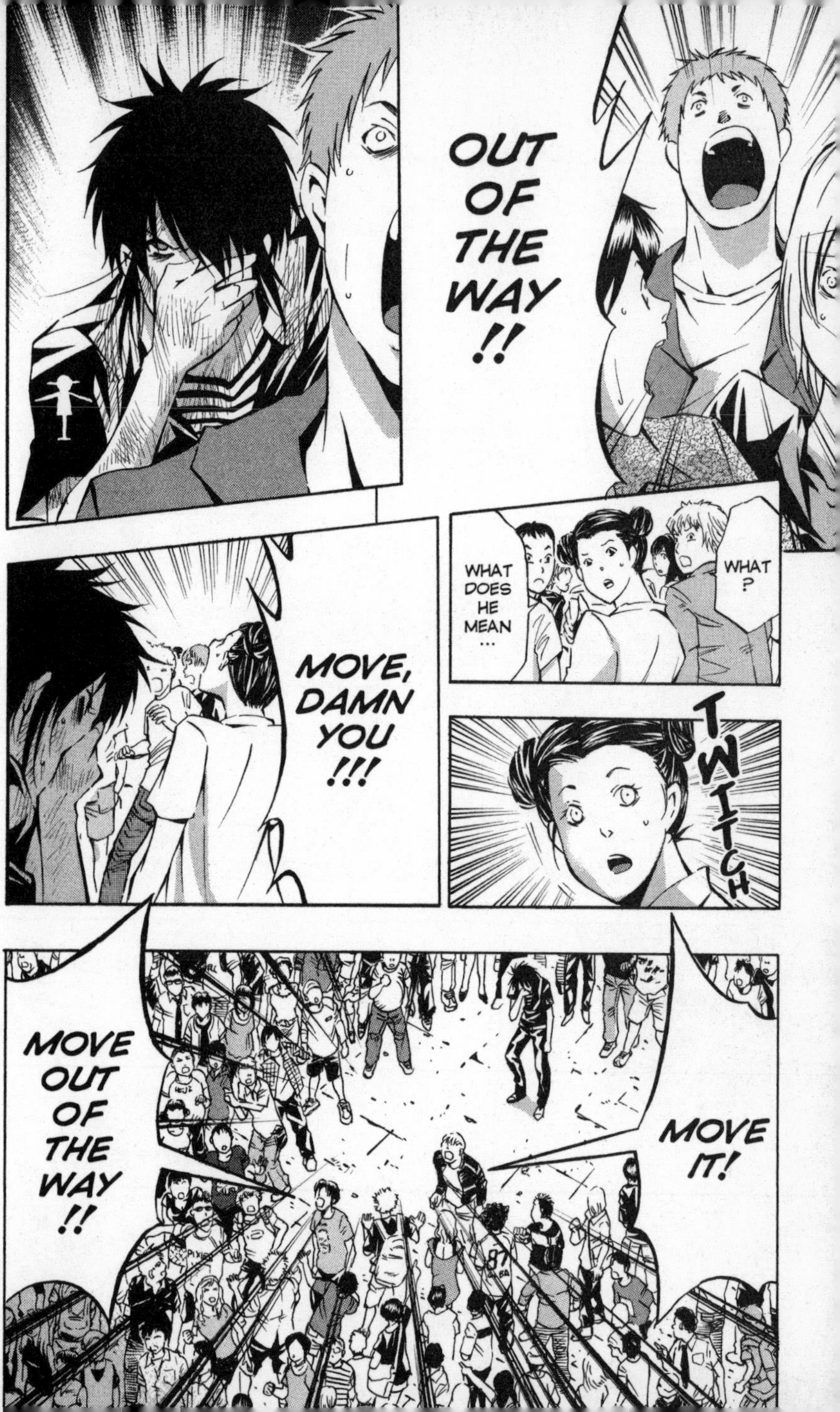
OUT OF THE WAY!!
WHAT?
WHAT DOES HE MEAN...
TWITCH
MOVE, DAMN YOU!!!
MOVE IT!
MOVE OUT OF THE WAY!!

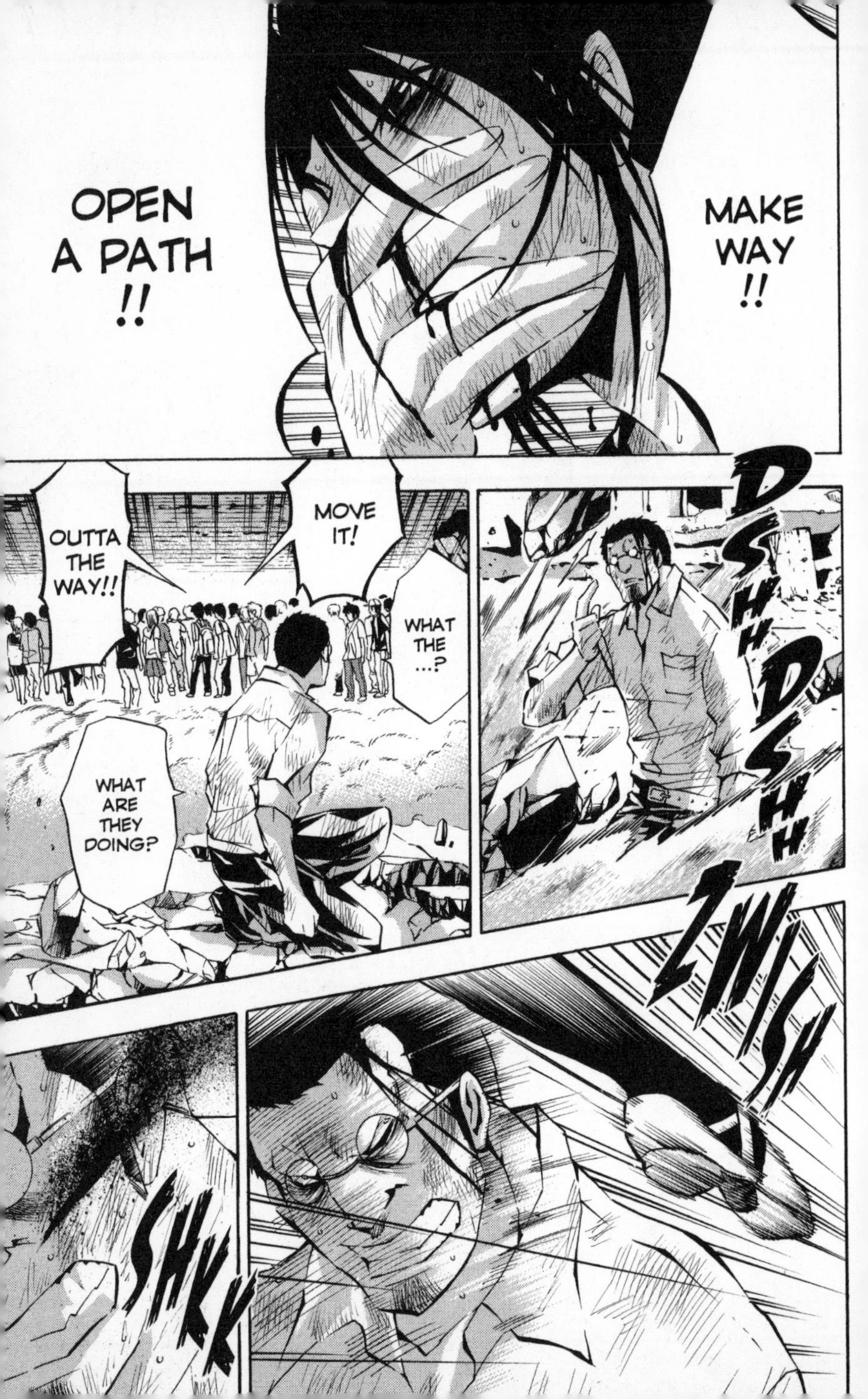

MAKE WAY!!
OPEN A PATH!!
DSHH
DSHH
MOVE IT!
OUTTA THE WAY!!
WHAT THE ...?
WHAT ARE THEY DOING?
ZWISH
SHKK

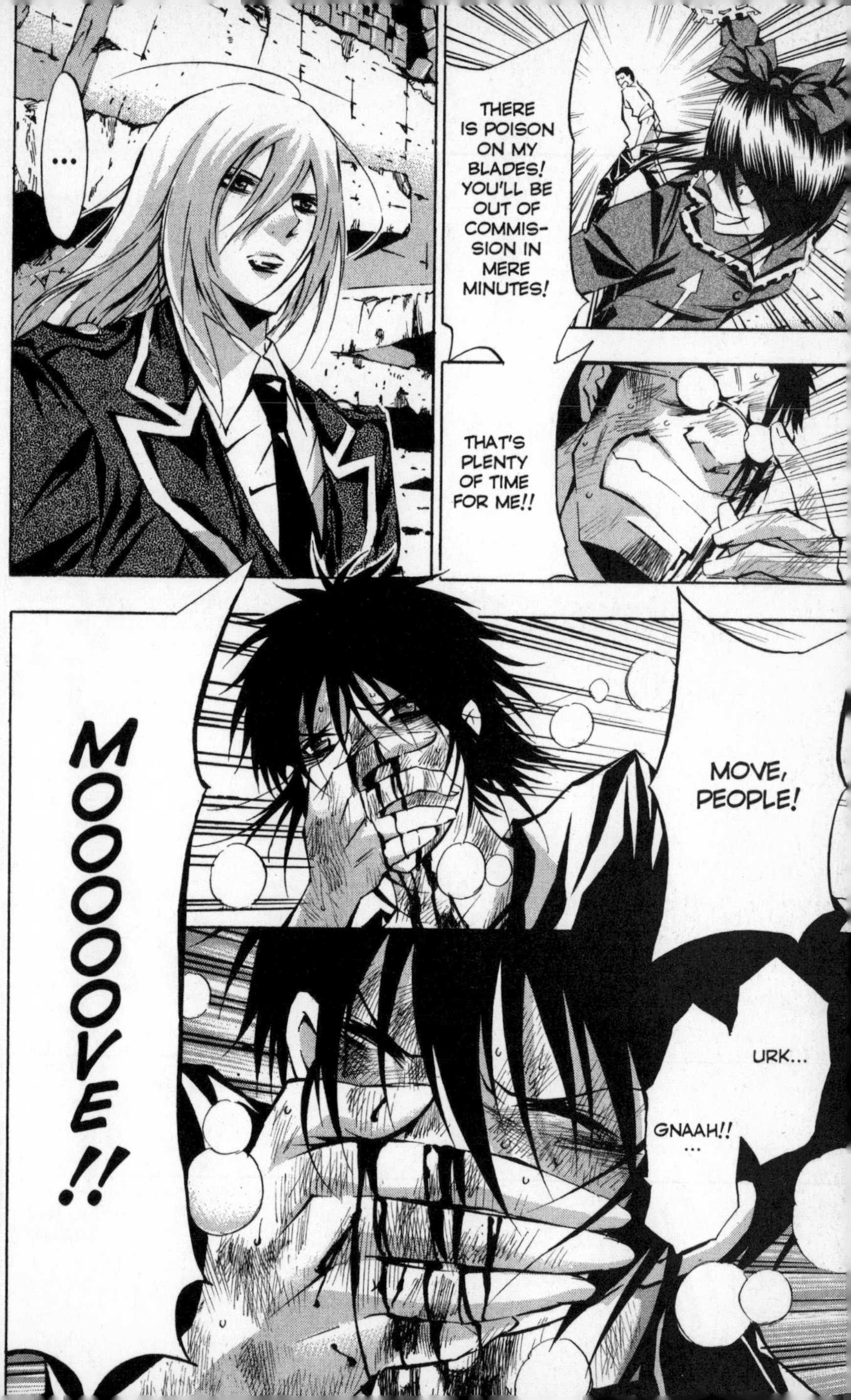

THERE IS POISON ON MY BLADES! YOU'LL BE OUT OF COMMISSION IN MERE MINUTES!
THAT'S PLENTY OF TIME FOR ME!!
...
MOVE, PEOPLE!
MOOOOOOOVE!!
URK...
GNAAH!!
...

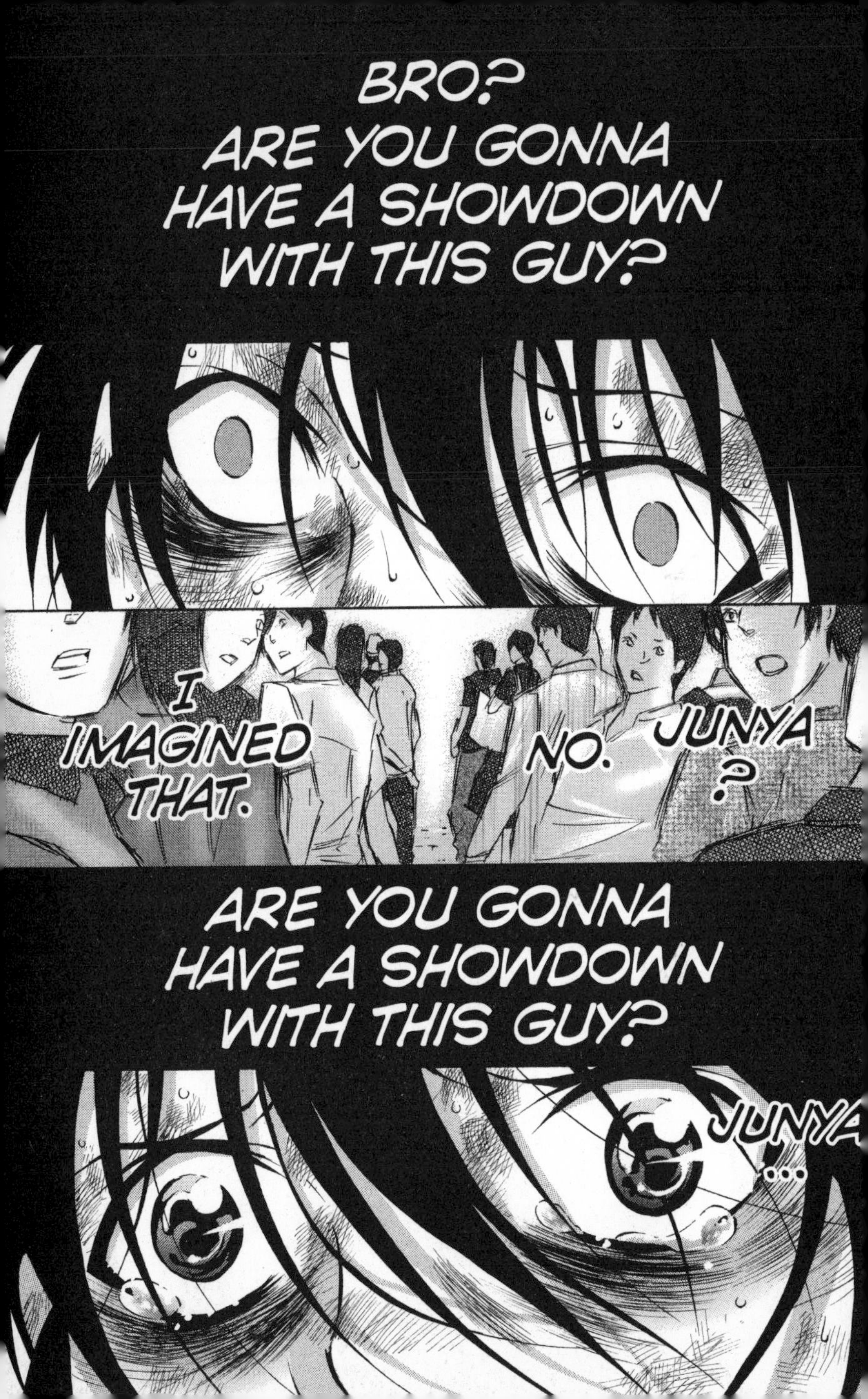
BRO? ARE YOU GONNA HAVE A SHOWDOWN WITH THIS GUY?
JUNYA?
NO.
I IMAGINED THAT.
ARE YOU GONNA HAVE A SHOWDOWN WITH THIS GUY?
JUNYA...

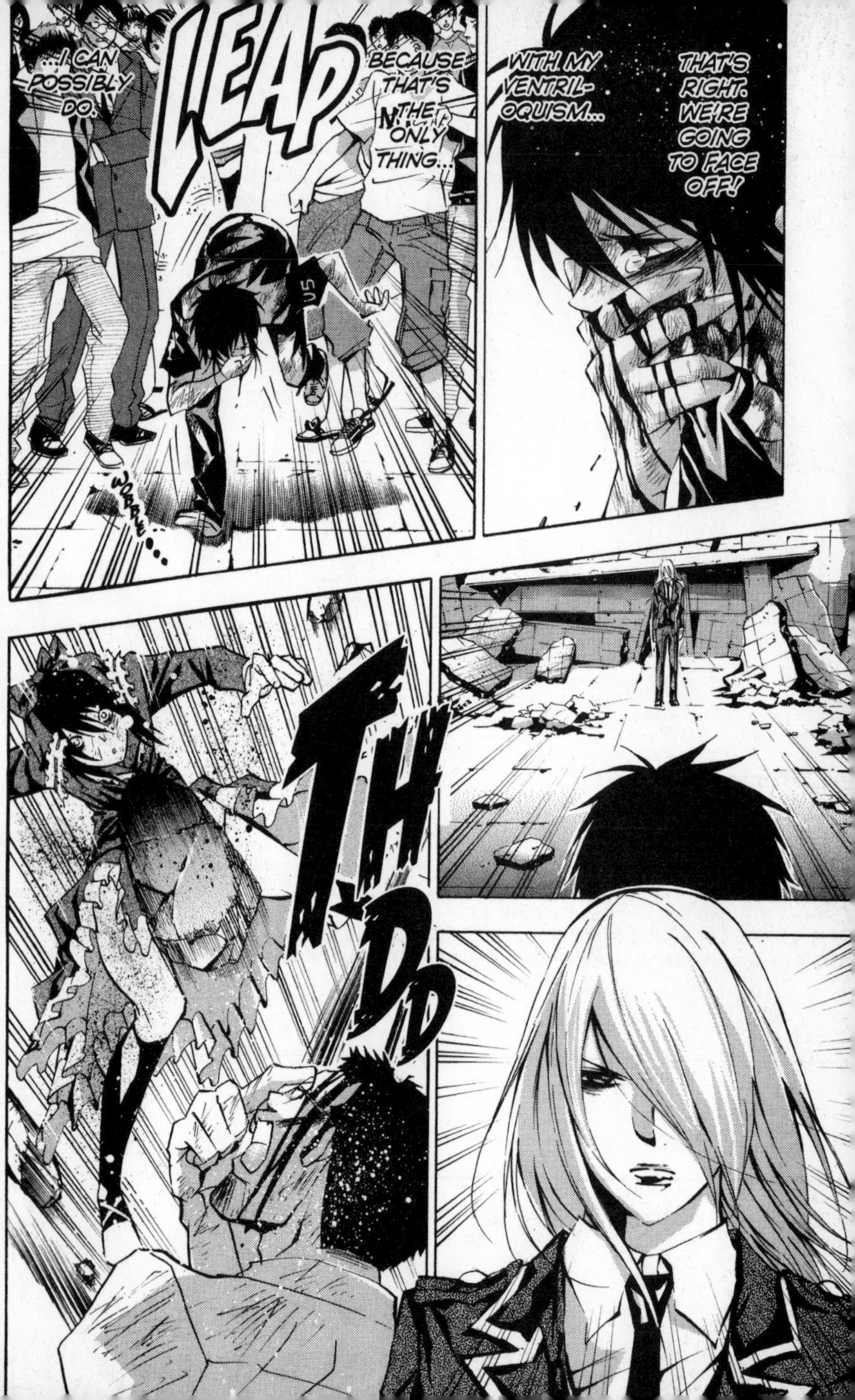
THAT'S RIGHT. WE'RE GOING TO FACE OFF!
WITH MY VENTRIL-OQUISM...
BECAUSE THAT'S THE ONLY THING...
...I CAN POSSIBLY DO.
LEAP
WOBBLE...
THD

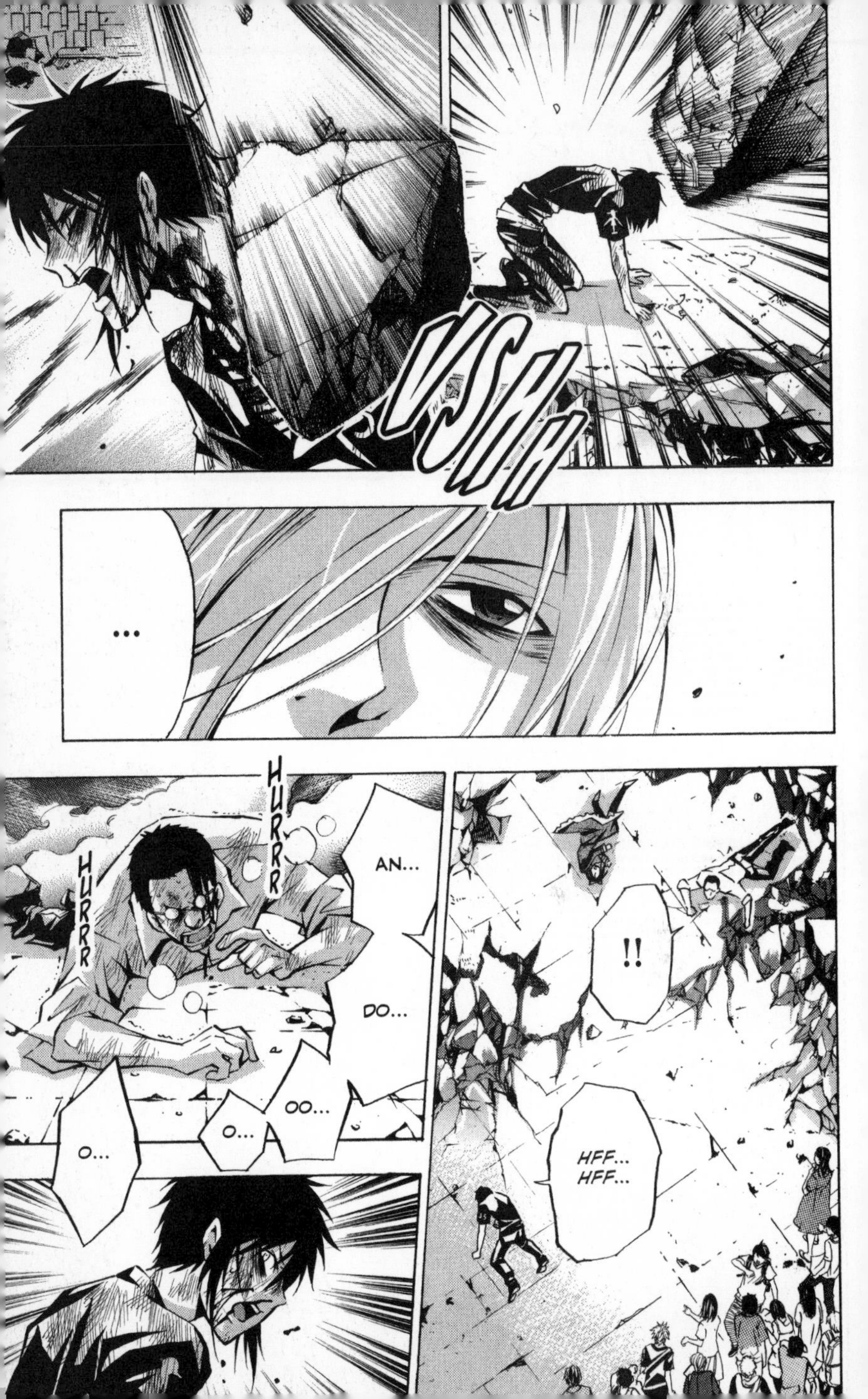
VSHH
...
!!
HFF...
HFF...
HURRR
HURRR
AN...
DO...
OO...
O...
O...

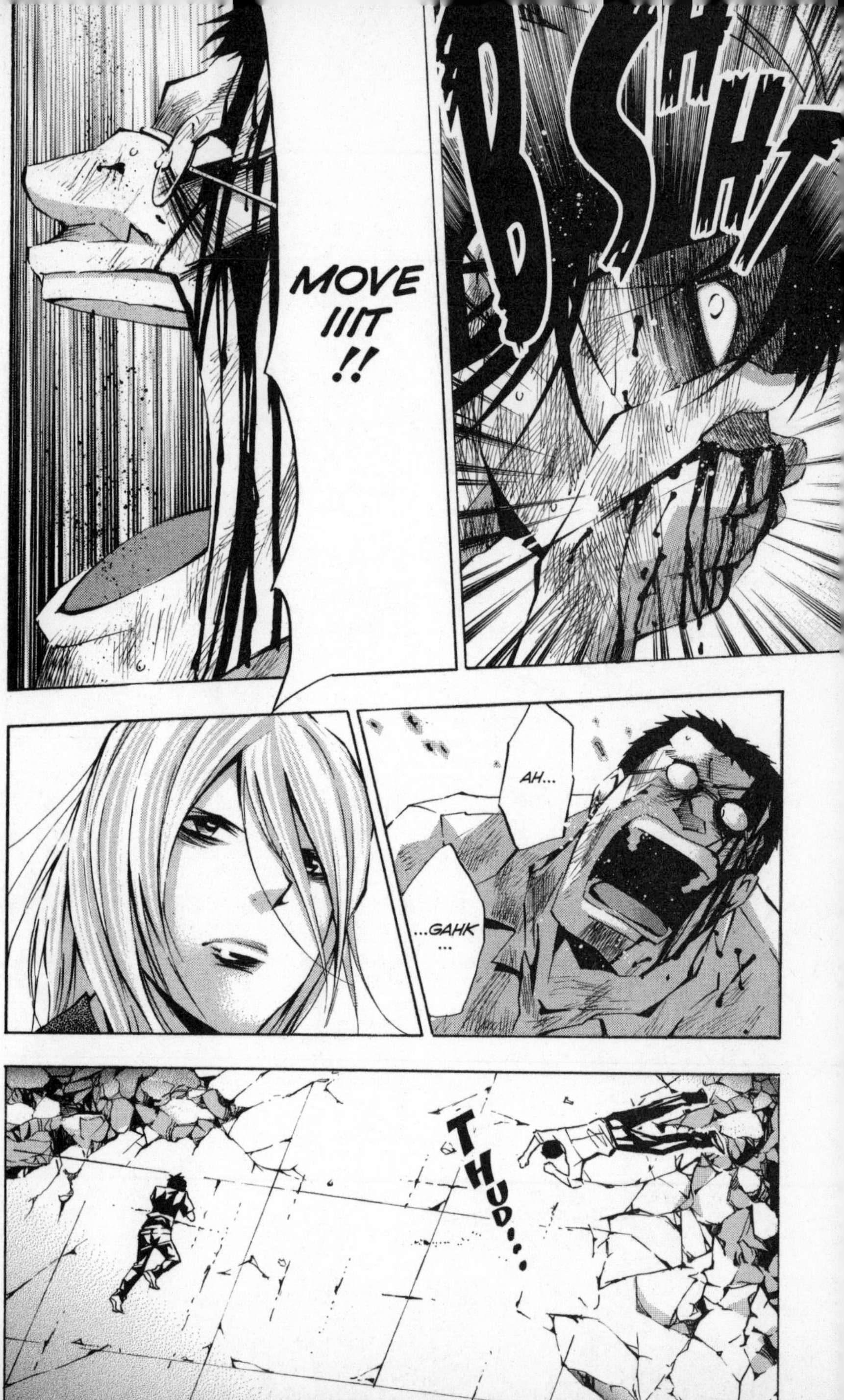
BSHT
MOVE IIIT !!
AH...
...GAHK ...
THUD...

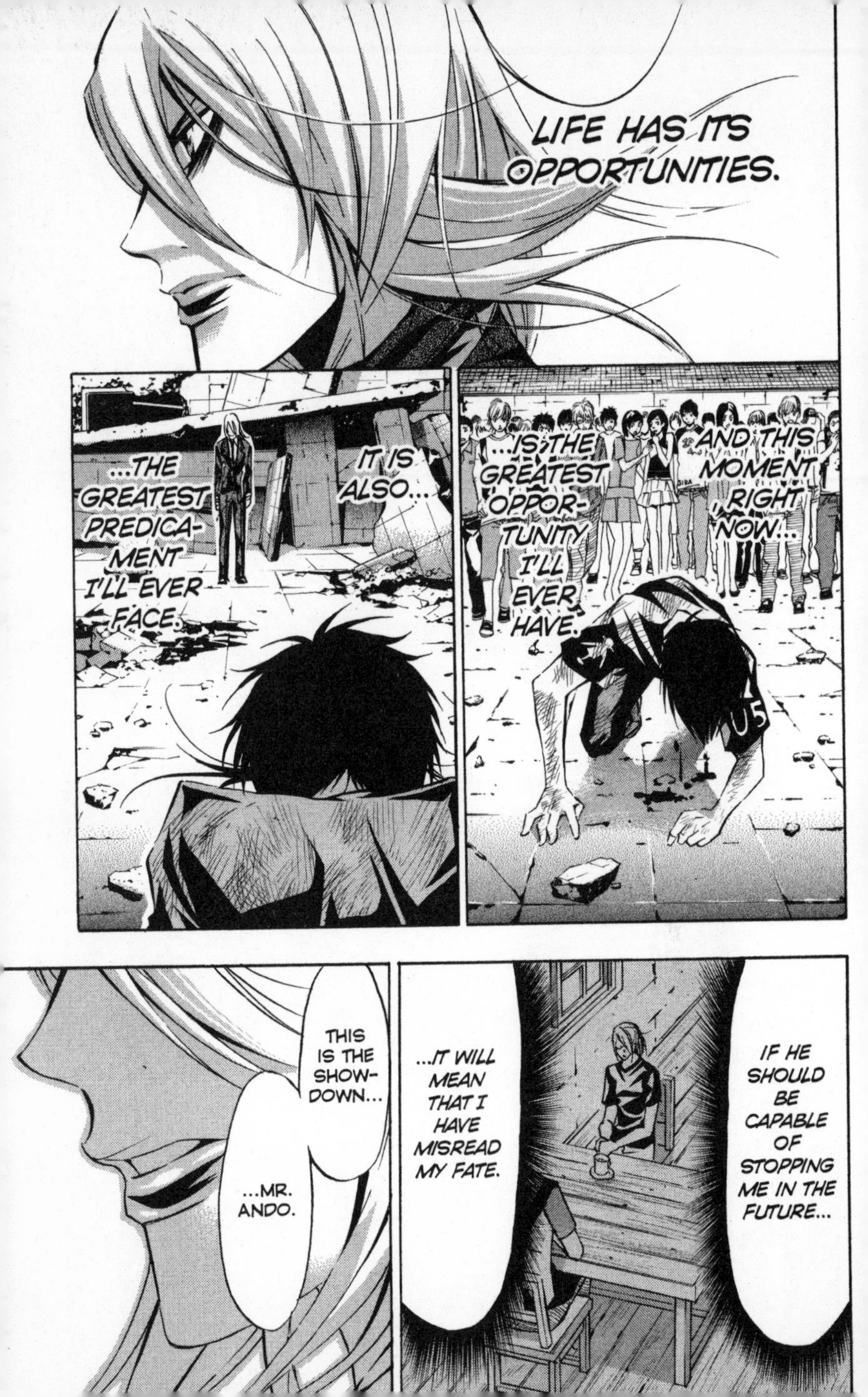
LIFE HAS ITS OPPORTUNITIES.
AND THIS MOMENT RIGHT NOW...
...IS THE GREATEST OPPORTUNITY I'LL EVER HAVE.
IT IS ALSO...
...THE GREATEST PREDICAMENT I'LL EVER FACE.
IF HE SHOULD BE CAPABLE OF STOPPING ME IN THE FUTURE...
...IT WILL MEAN THAT I HAVE MISREAD MY FATE.
THIS IS THE SHOWDOWN...
...MR. ANDO.

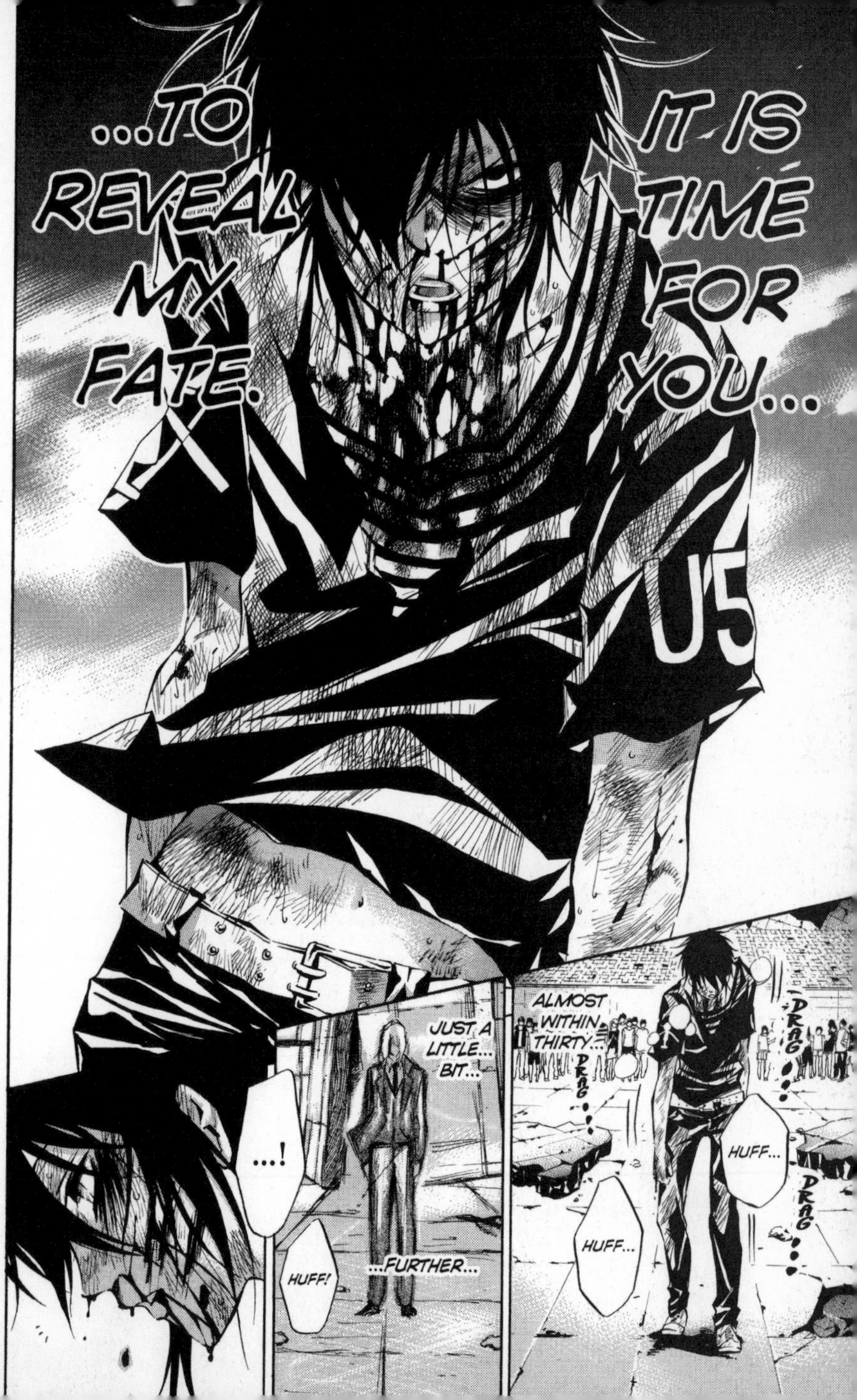
IT IS TIME FOR YOU...
...TO REVEAL MY FATE.
ALMOST WITHIN THIRTY...
DRAG
DRAG...
HUFF...
DRAG
HUFF...
JUST A LITTLE... BIT...
...FURTHER...
HUFF!
...!

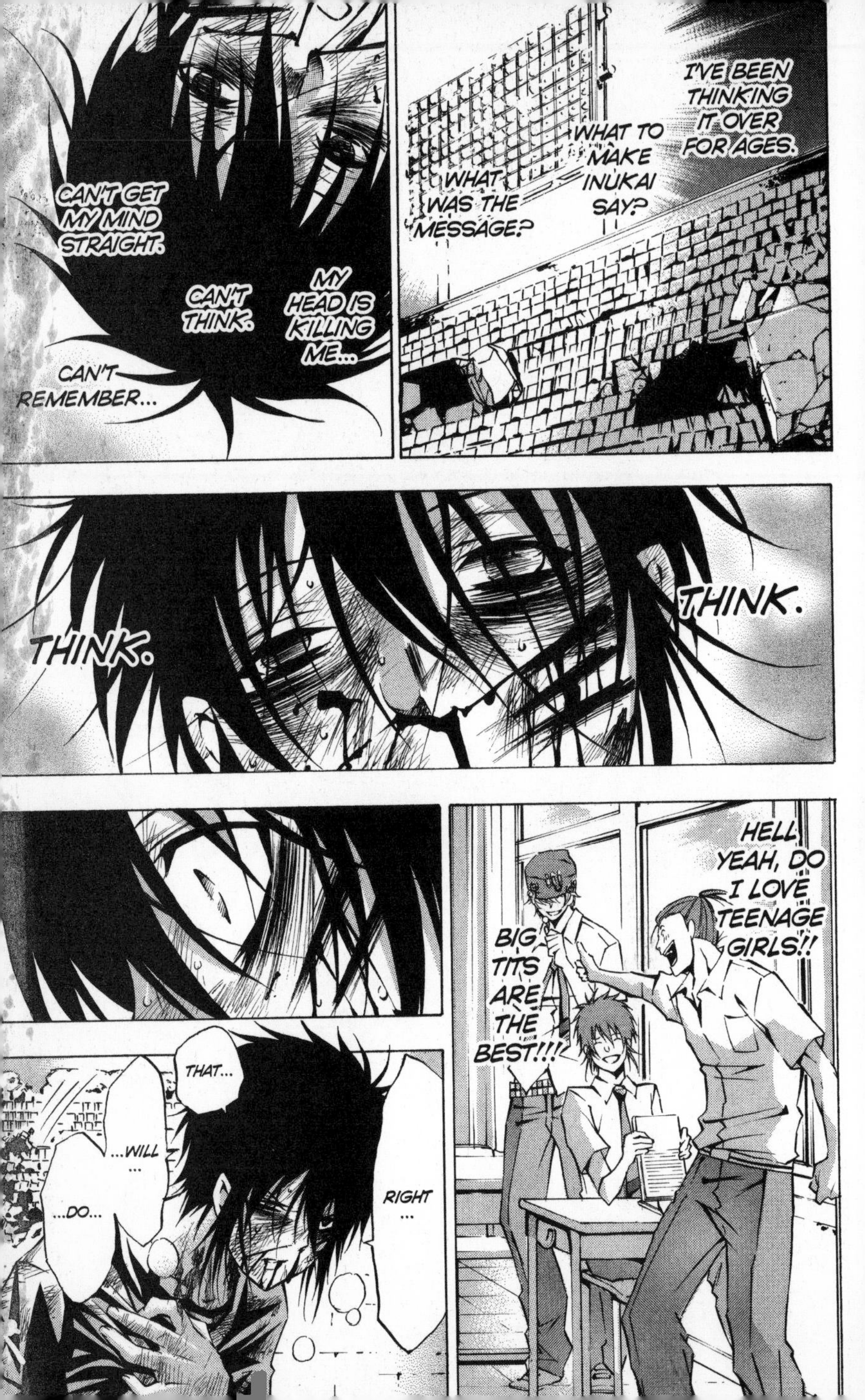

I'VE BEEN THINKING IT OVER FOR AGES.
WHAT TO MAKE INUKAI SAY?
WHAT WAS THE MESSAGE?
MY HEAD IS KILLING ME...
CAN'T THINK.
CAN'T GET MY MIND STRAIGHT.
CAN'T REMEMBER...
THINK.
THINK.
HELL YEAH, DO I LOVE TEENAGE GIRLS!!
BIG TITS ARE THE BEST!!!
RIGHT ...
THAT...
...WILL ...
...DO...

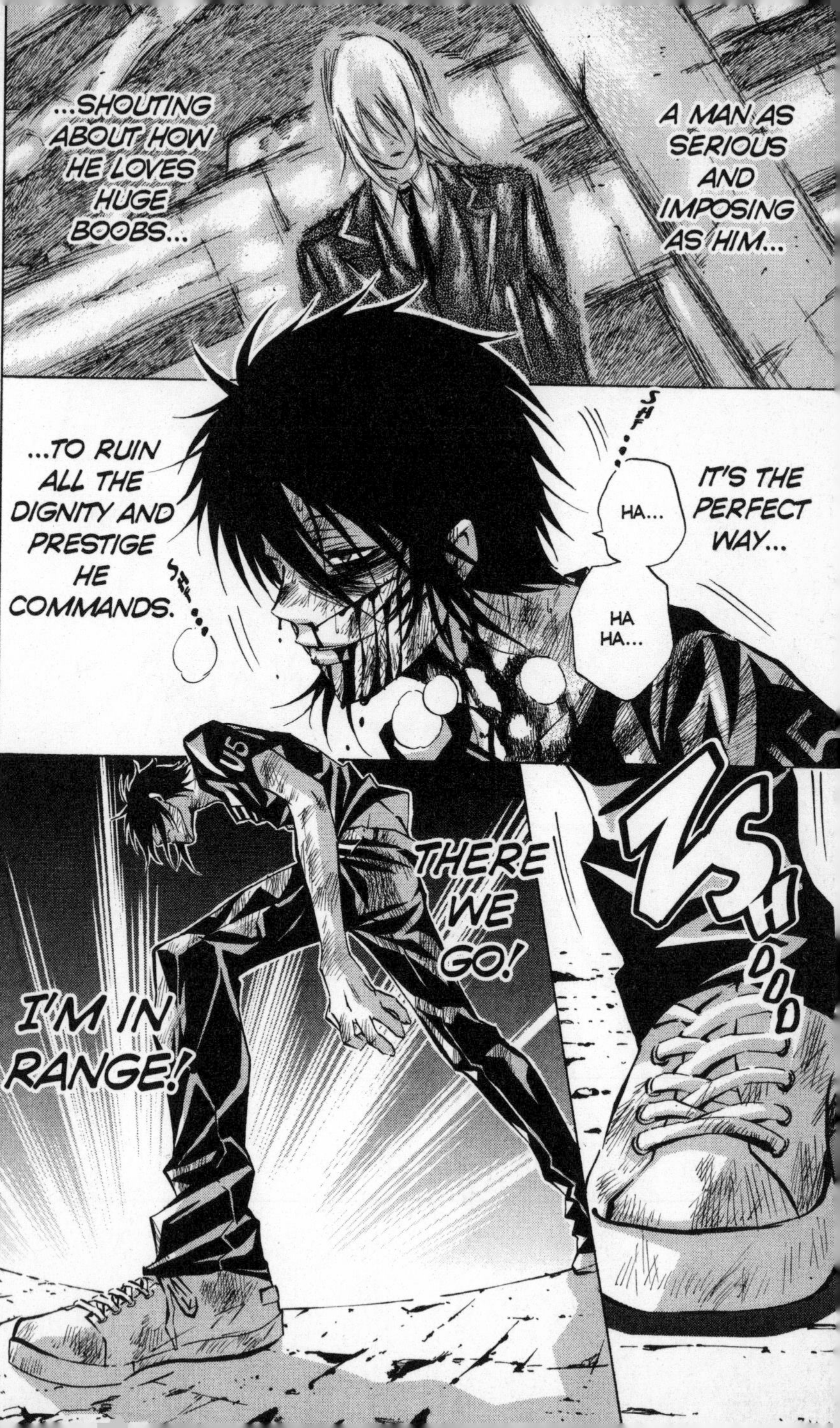
A MAN AS SERIOUS AND IMPOSING AS HIM...
...SHOUTING ABOUT HOW HE LOVES HUGE BOOBS...
IT'S THE PERFECT WAY...
HA...
HA HA...
...TO RUIN ALL THE DIGNITY AND PRESTIGE HE COMMANDS.
ZSHOOOO
THERE WE GO!
I'M IN RANGE!

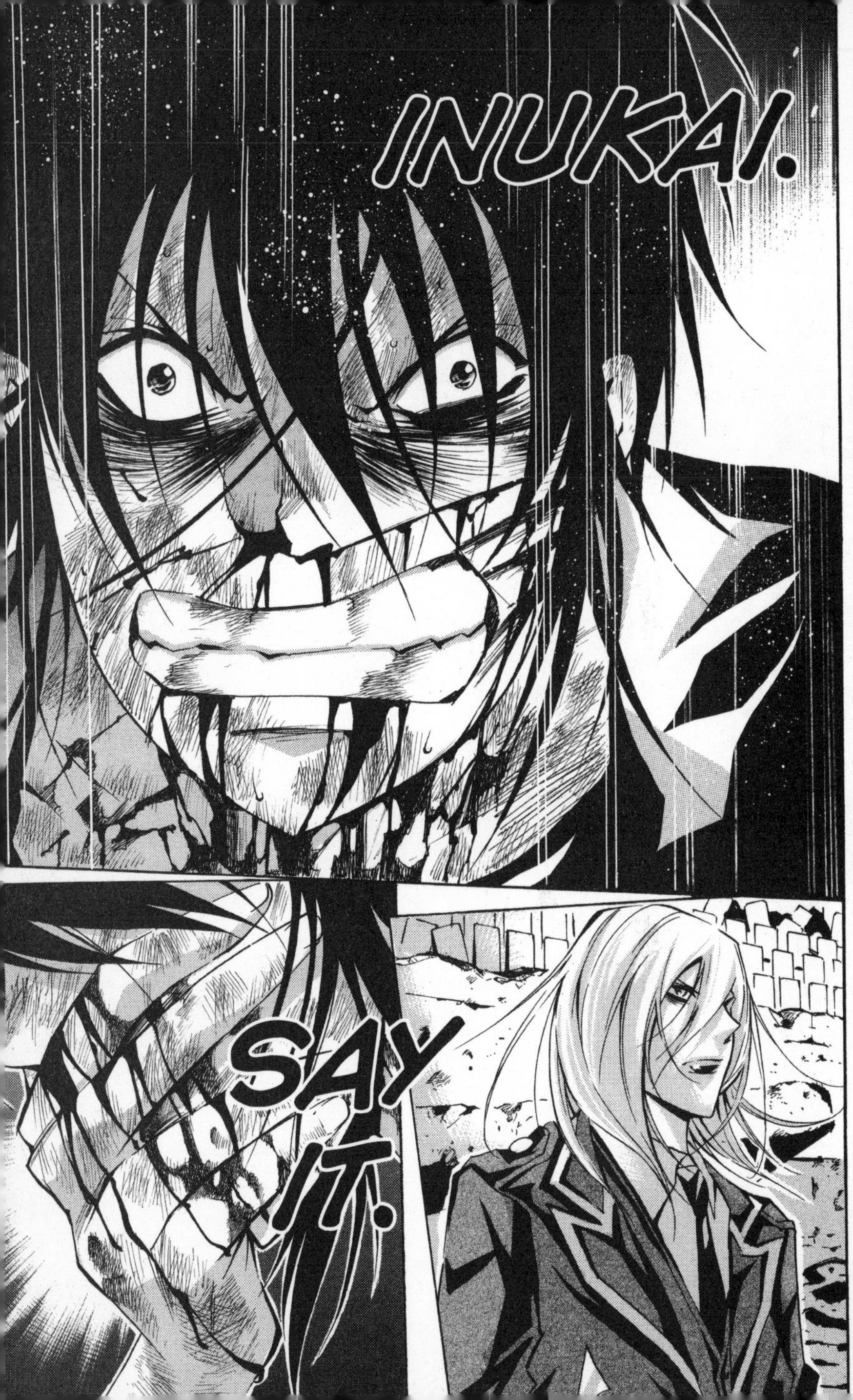
INUKAI.
SAY IT.

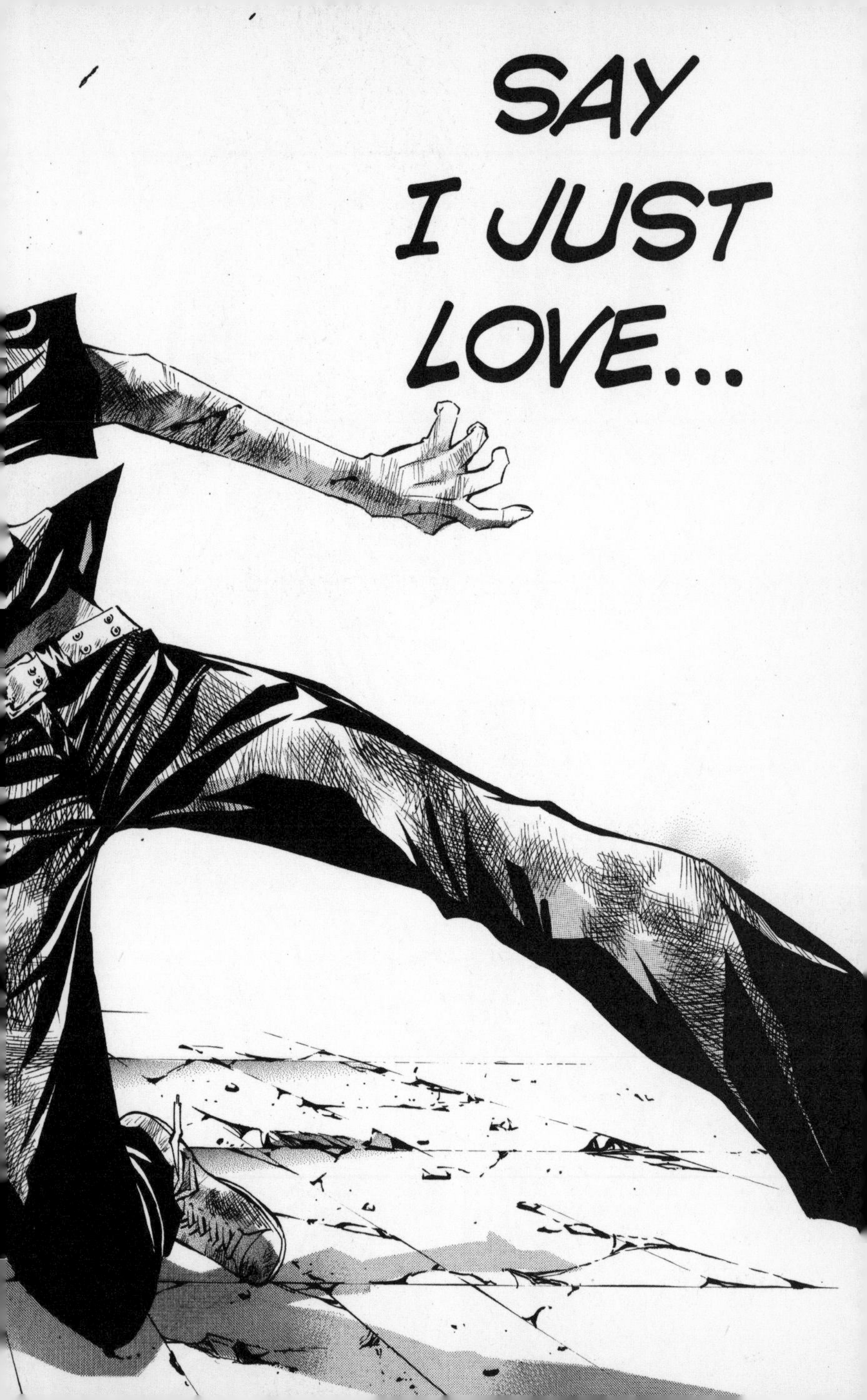
SAY I JUST LOVE...

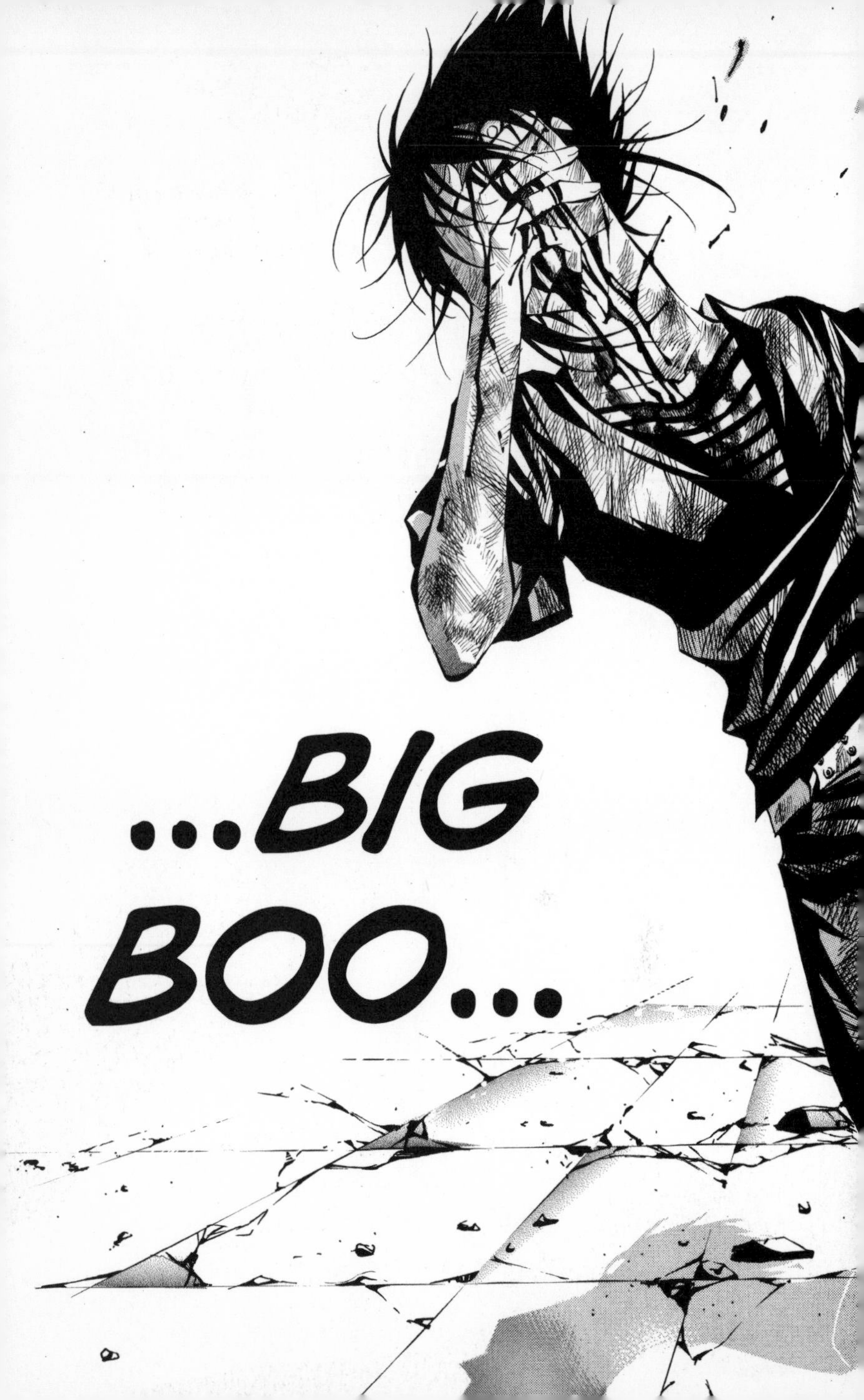
...BIG BOO...

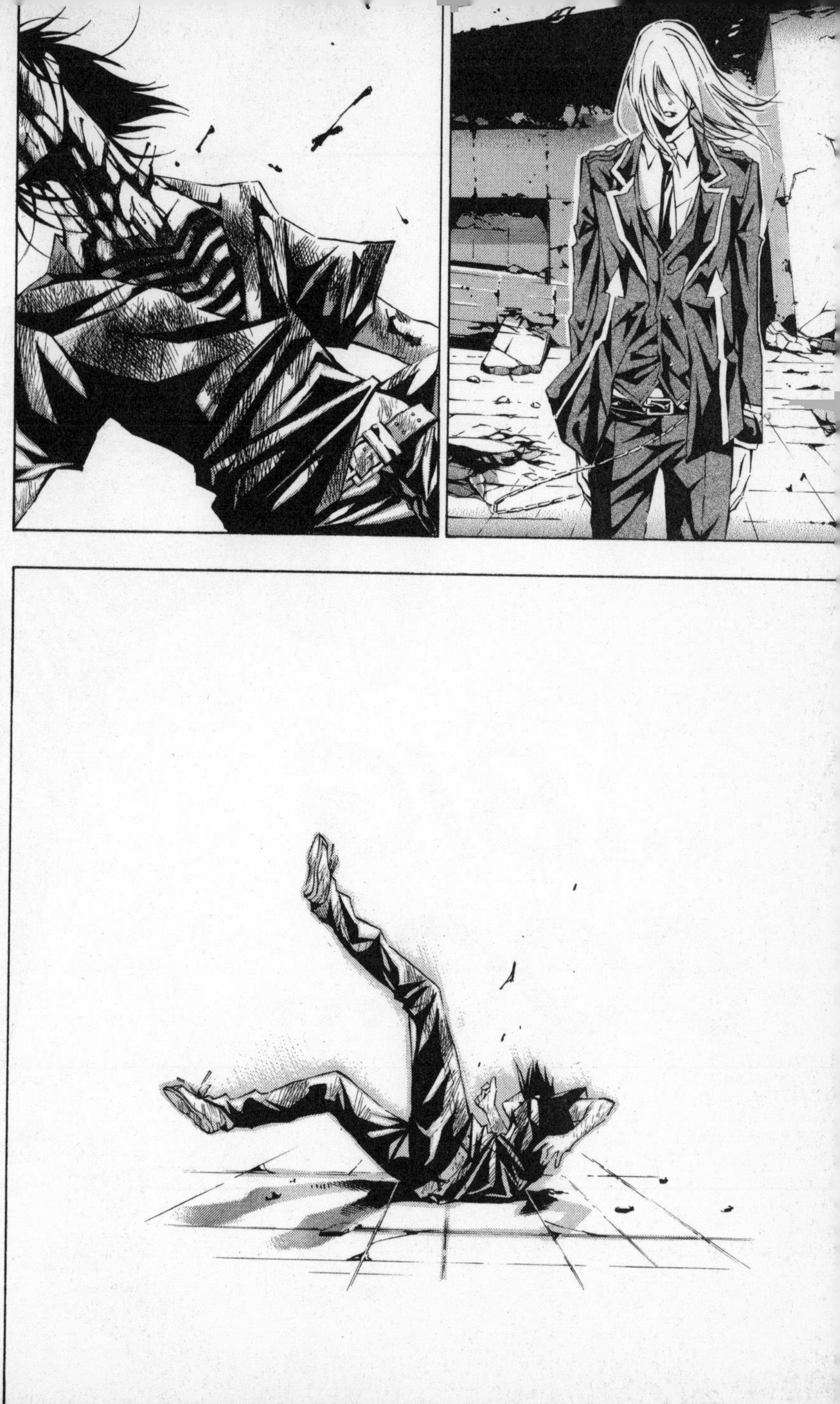

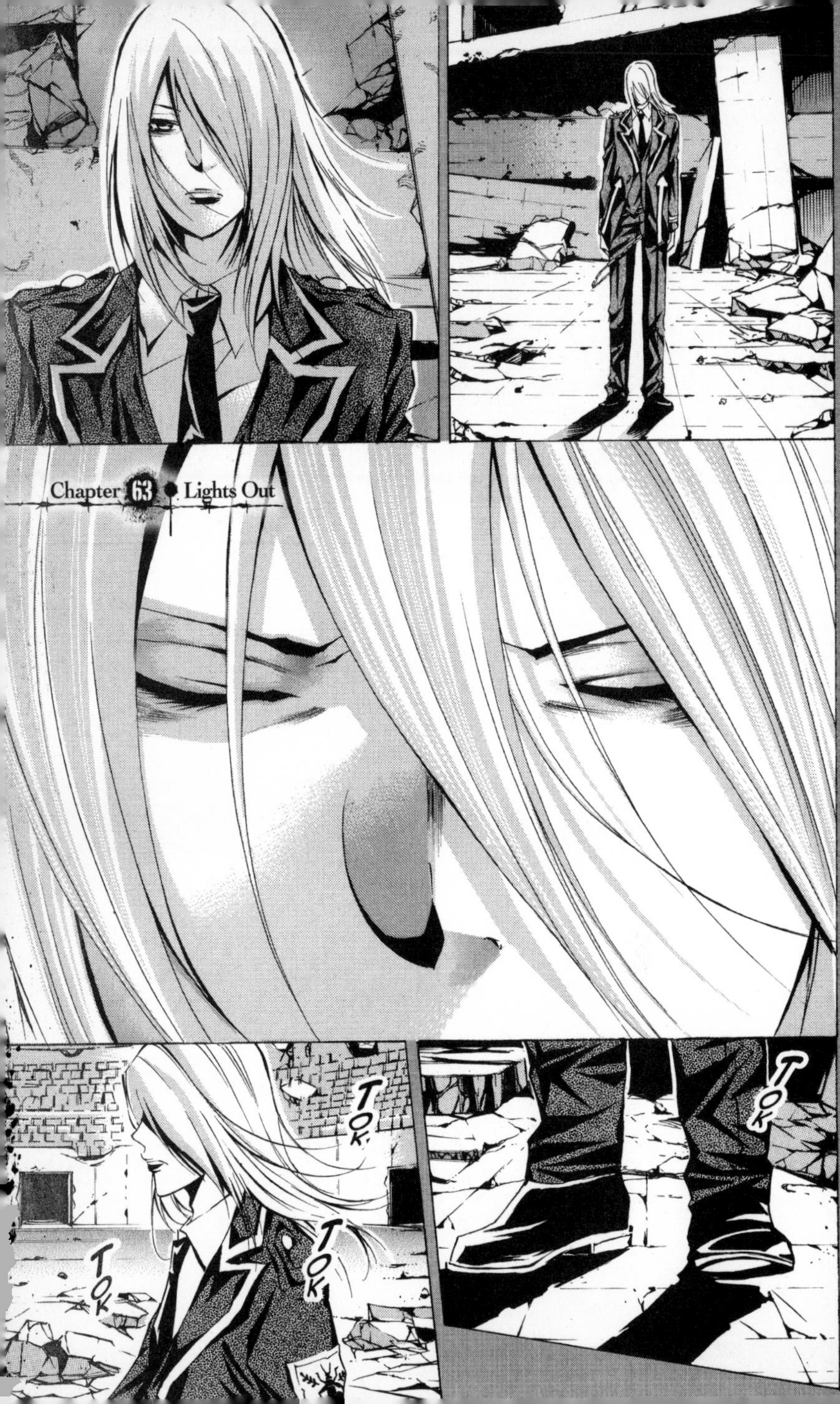
Chapter 63 Lights Out
TOK
TOK
TOK
TOK

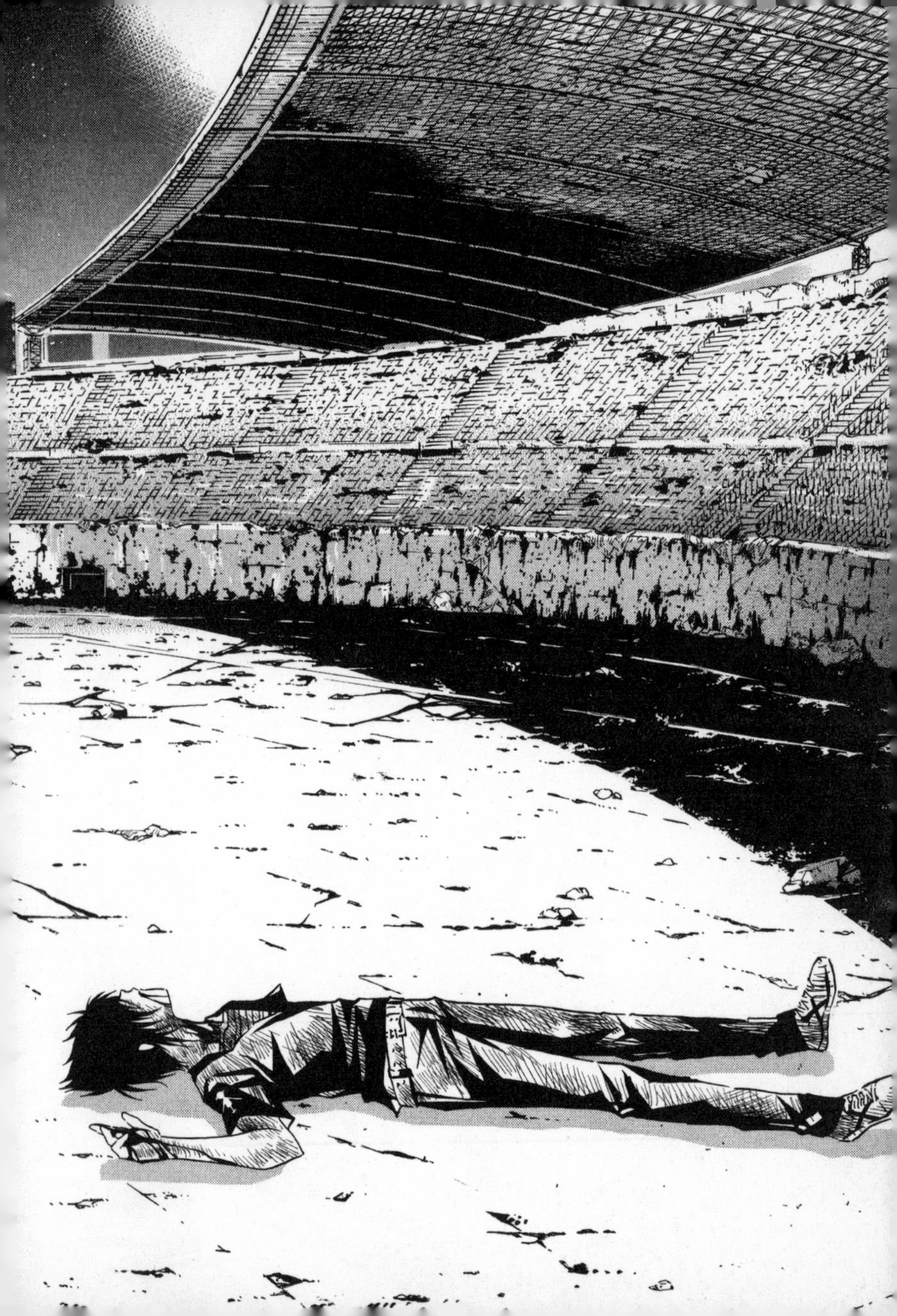

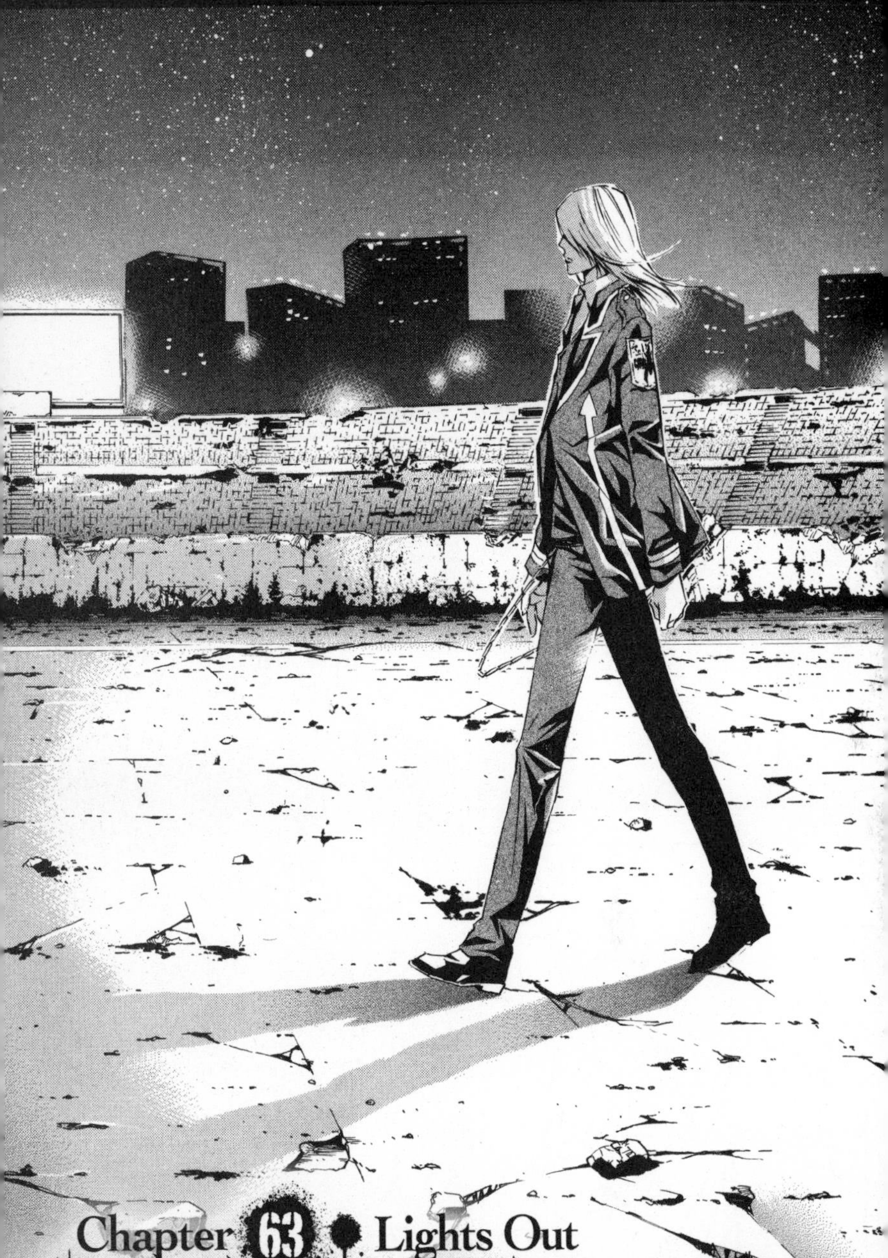
Chapter 63 Lights Out

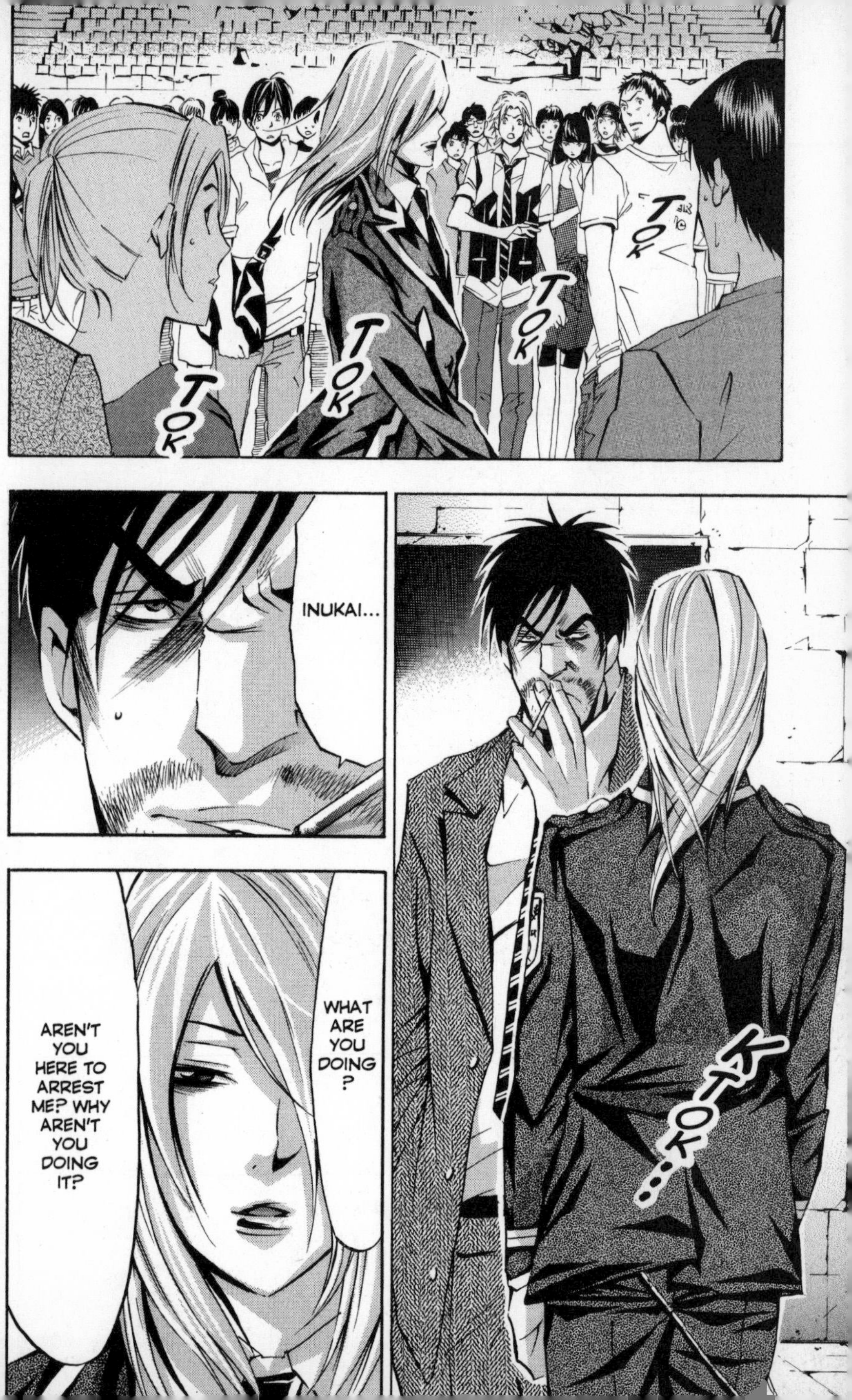
TOK
TOK
TOK
TOK
KATOK...
INUKAI...
WHAT ARE YOU DOING?
AREN'T YOU HERE TO ARREST ME? WHY AREN'T YOU DOING IT?

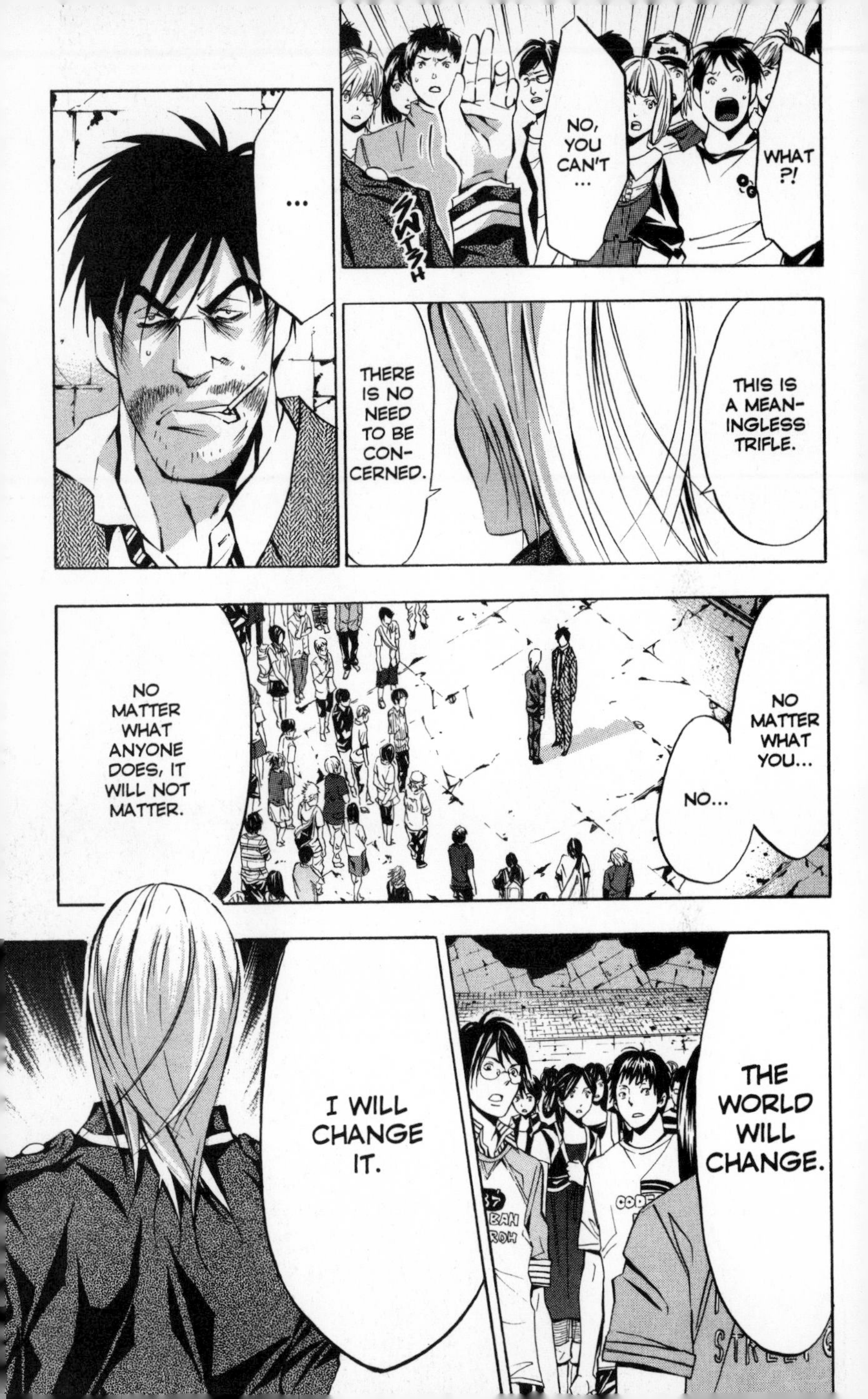
WHAT ?!
NO, YOU CAN'T ...
SWISH
THIS IS A MEAN-INGLESS TRIFLE.
THERE IS NO NEED TO BE CON-CERNED.
...
NO MATTER WHAT YOU...
NO...
NO MATTER WHAT ANYONE DOES, IT WILL NOT MATTER.
THE WORLD WILL CHANGE.
I WILL CHANGE IT.

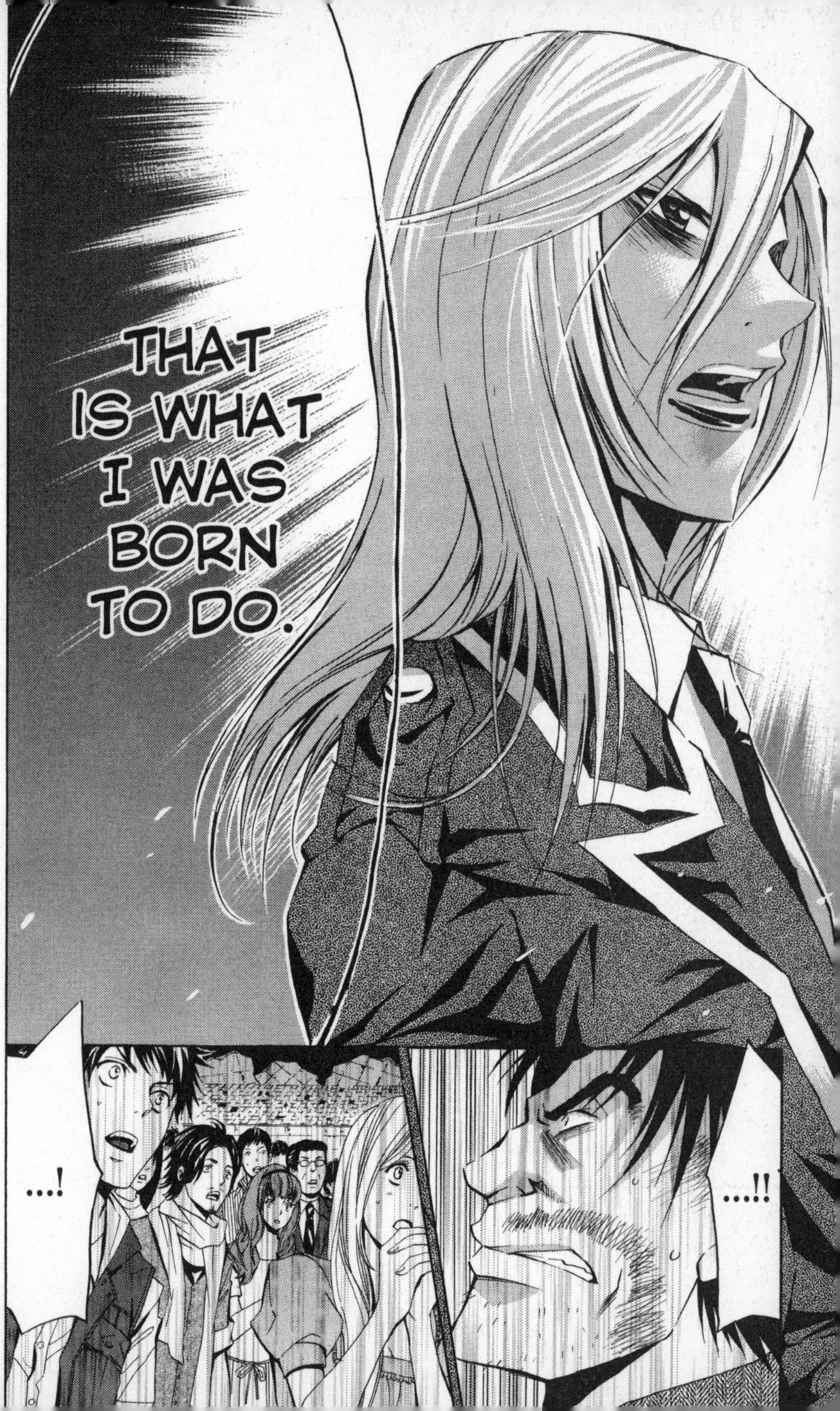
THAT IS WHAT I WAS BORN TO DO.
...!!
...!

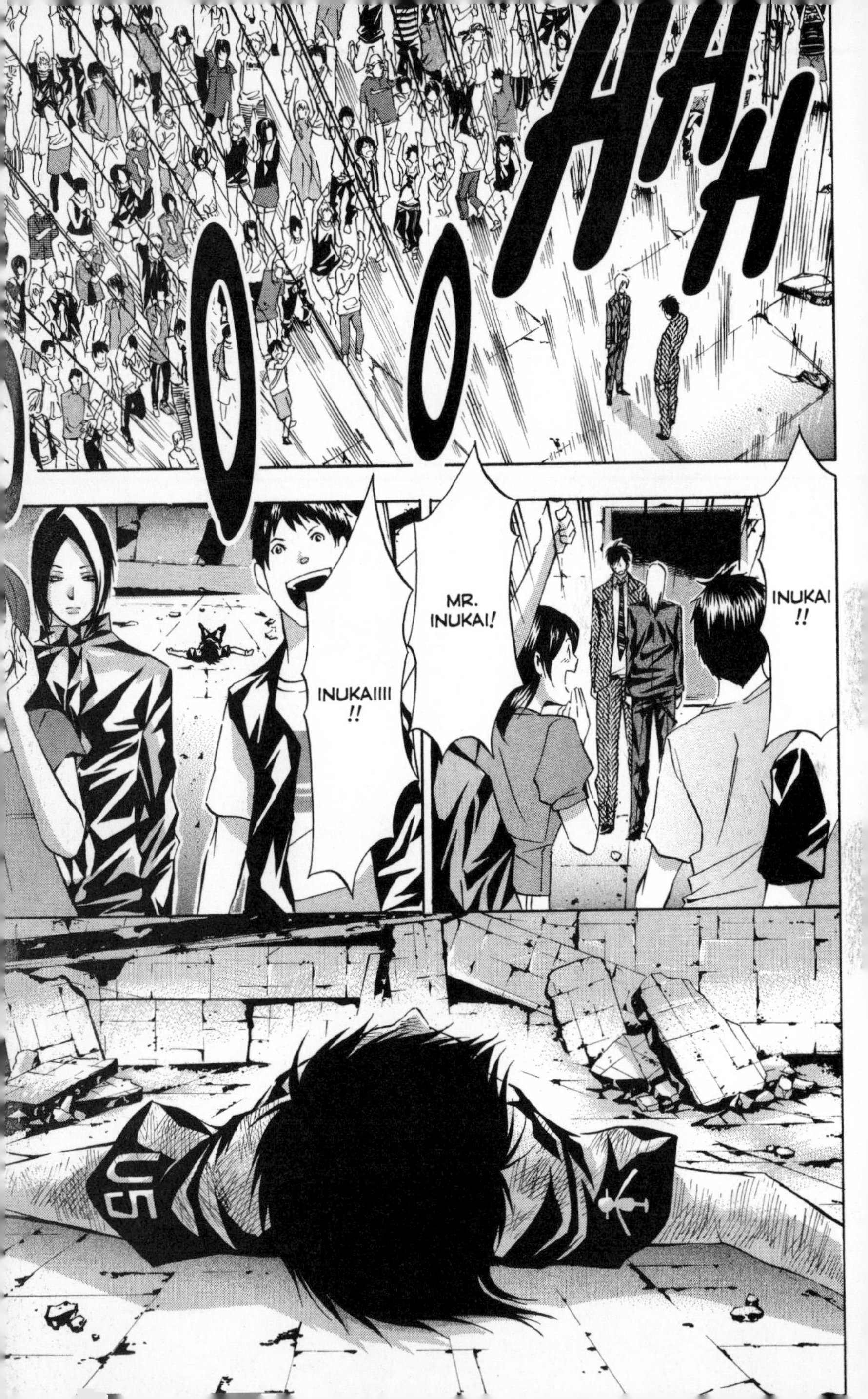

OOOHH
INUKAI !!
MR. INUKAI!
INUKAIIII !!

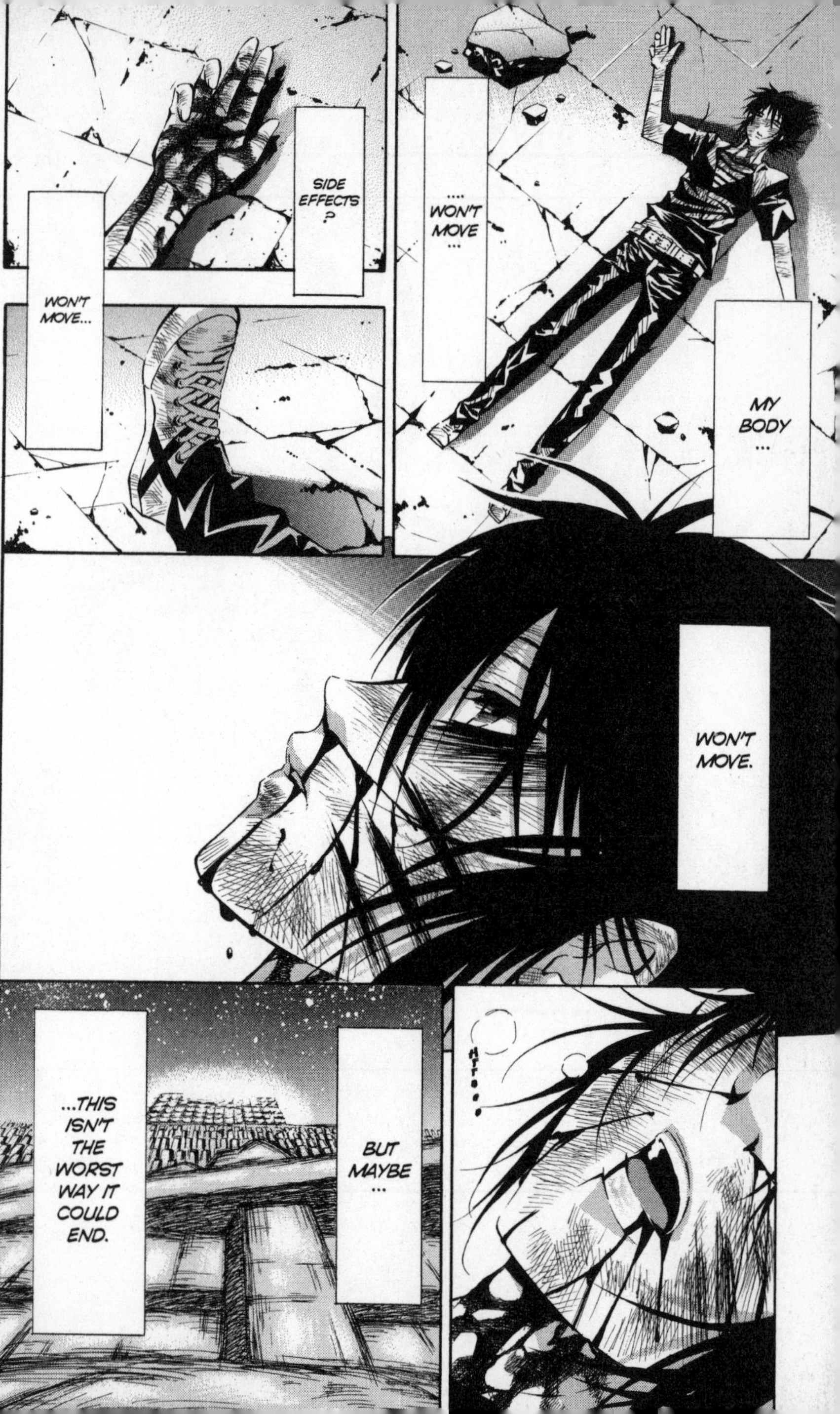
MY BODY ...
... WON'T MOVE ...
SIDE EFFECTS ?
WON'T MOVE...
WON'T MOVE.
BUT MAYBE ...
...THIS ISN'T THE WORST WAY IT COULD END.

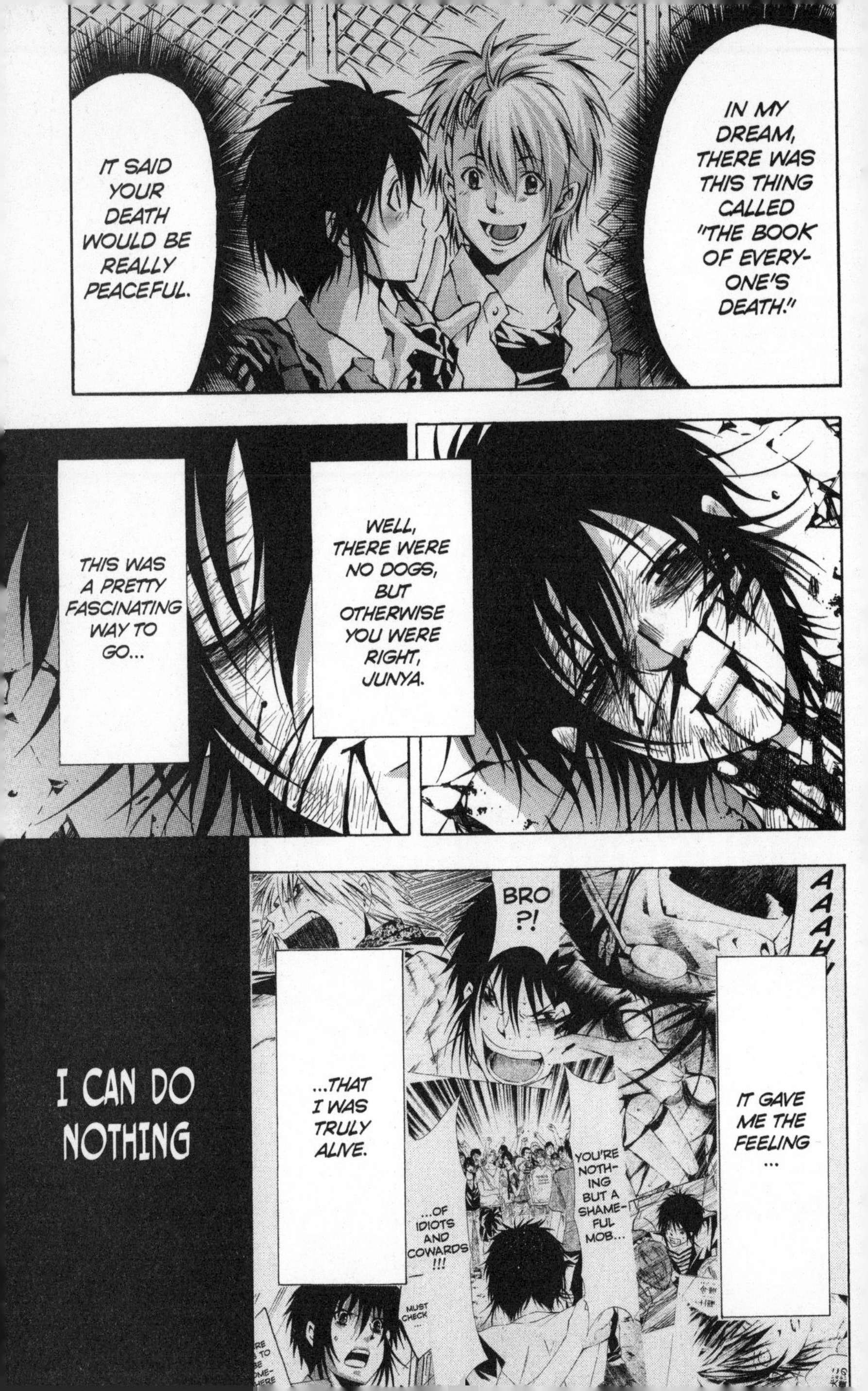
IN MY DREAM, THERE WAS THIS THING CALLED "THE BOOK OF EVERY-ONE'S DEATH."
IT SAID YOUR DEATH WOULD BE REALLY PEACEFUL.
WELL, THERE WERE NO DOGS, BUT OTHERWISE YOU WERE RIGHT, JUNYA.
THIS WAS A PRETTY FASCINATING WAY TO GO...
AAAH
BRO ?!
IT GAVE ME THE FEELING ...
...THAT I WAS TRULY ALIVE.
YOU'RE NOTHING BUT A SHAME-FUL MOB...
...OF IDIOTS AND COWARDS !!!
MUST CHECK ...
I CAN DO NOTHING

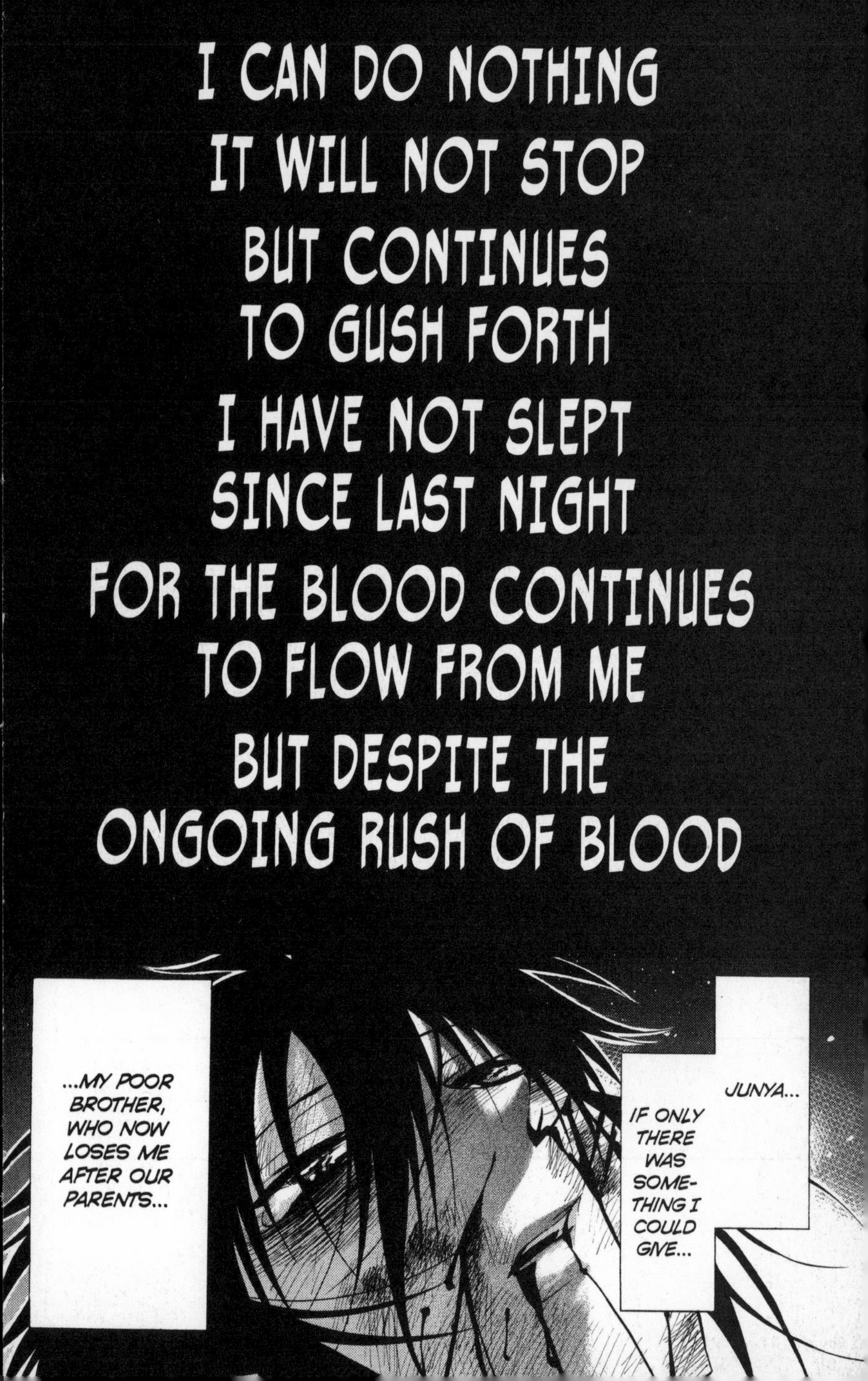
I CAN DO NOTHING
IT WILL NOT STOP
BUT CONTINUES
TO GUSH FORTH
I HAVE NOT SLEPT
SINCE LAST NIGHT
FOR THE BLOOD CONTINUES
TO FLOW FROM ME
BUT DESPITE THE
ONGOING RUSH OF BLOOD
JUNYA... IF ONLY THERE WAS SOME-THING I COULD GIVE...
...MY POOR BROTHER, WHO NOW LOSES ME AFTER OUR PARENTS...

I AM CALM AND
WITHOUT AGONY

A SIGN WITH MY SOUL
MUST BE SLIPPING FROM
THE MORTAL FRAME

THE WORST PART IS THAT
BECAUSE OF THIS BLOOD

I AM UNABLE TO TELL
ANYONE OF THIS FEELING

...GENTLE BROTHER.

IF ONLY THERE WAS SOMETHING I COULD LEAVE BEHIND FOR YOU...

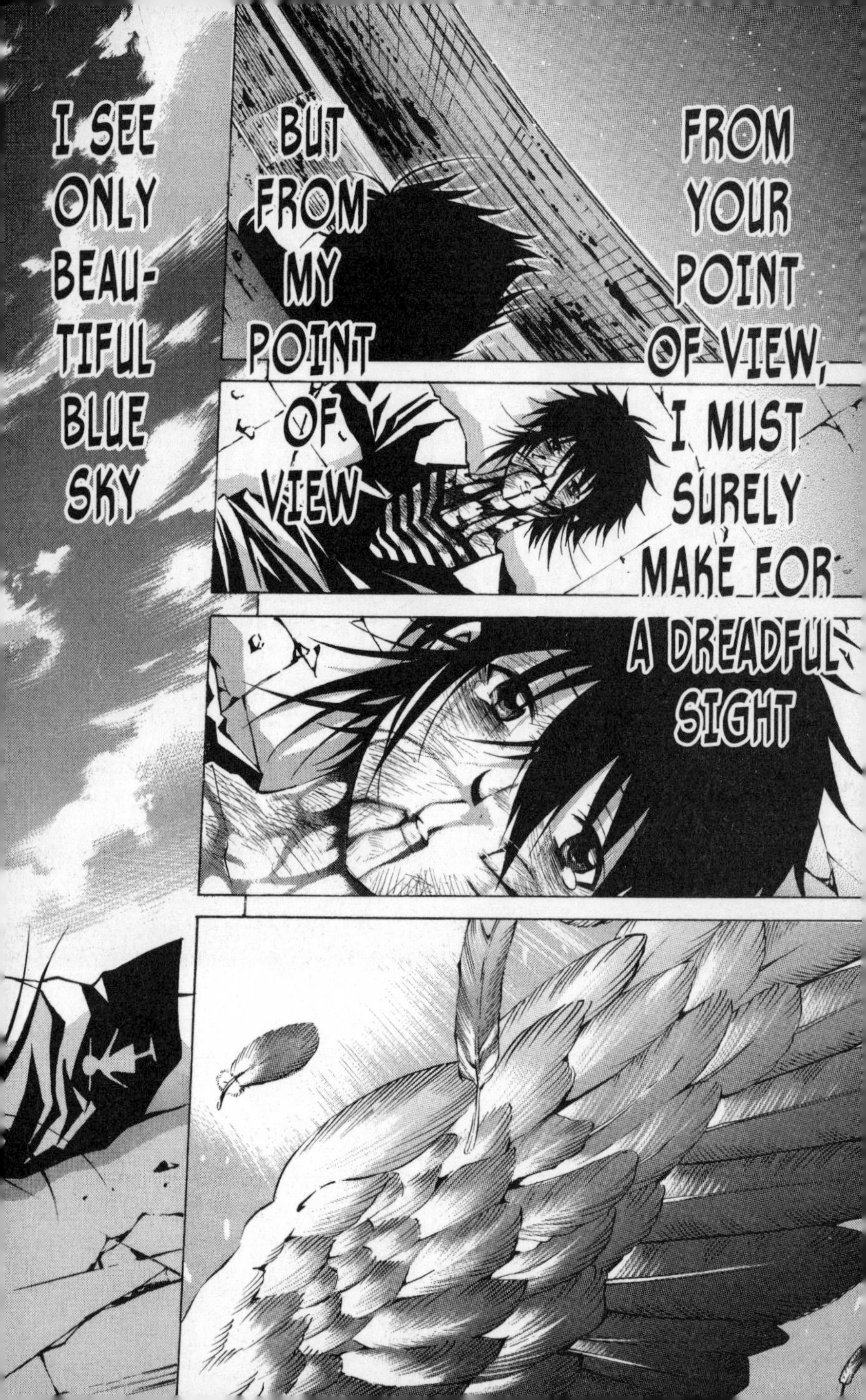
FROM YOUR POINT OF VIEW, I MUST SURELY MAKE FOR A DREADFUL SIGHT
BUT FROM MY POINT OF VIEW
I SEE ONLY BEAUTIFUL BLUE SKY

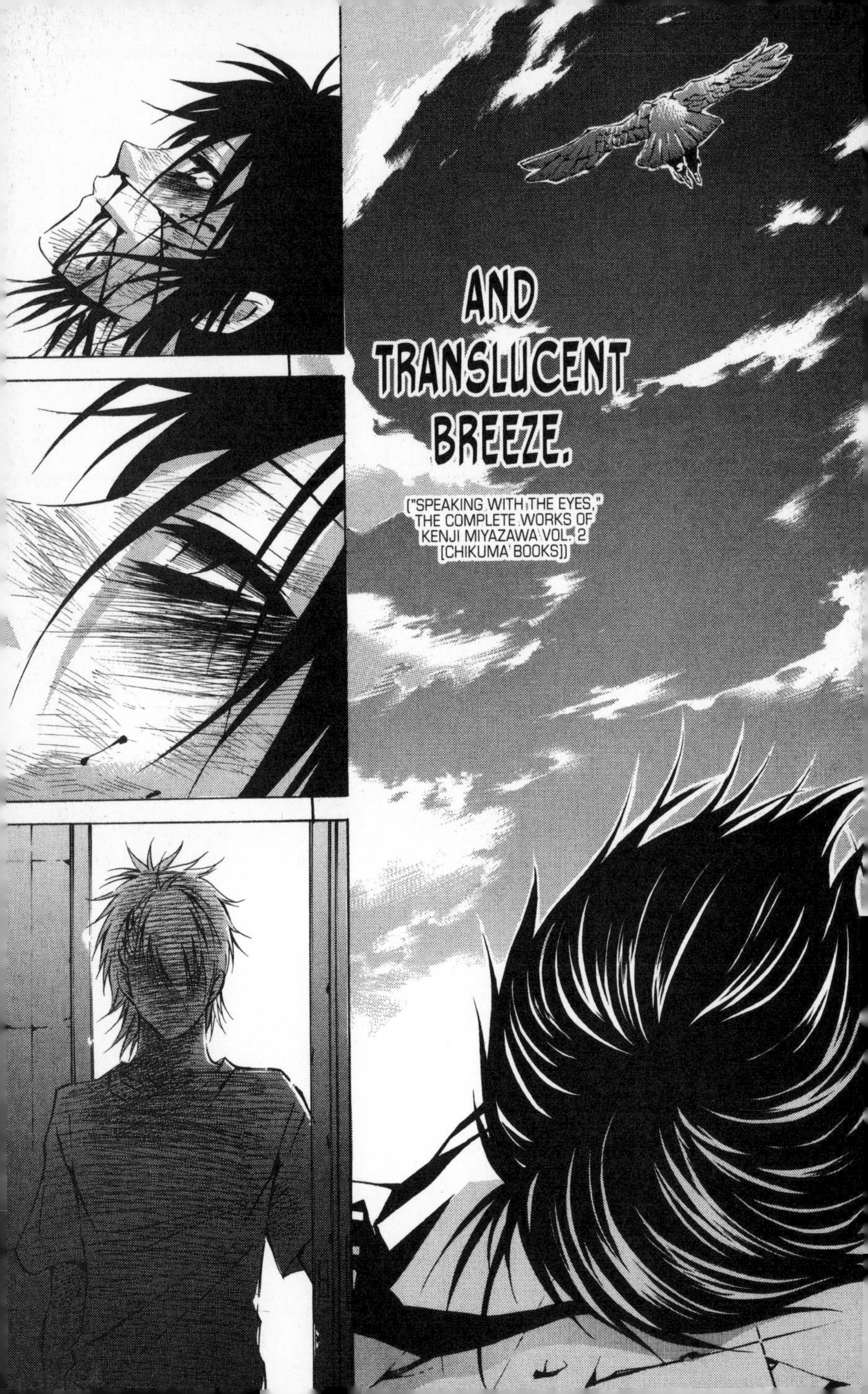
AND TRANSLUCENT BREEZE.
("SPEAKING WITH THE EYES," THE COMPLETE WORKS OF KENJI MIYAZAWA VOL. 2 [CHIKUMA BOOKS])

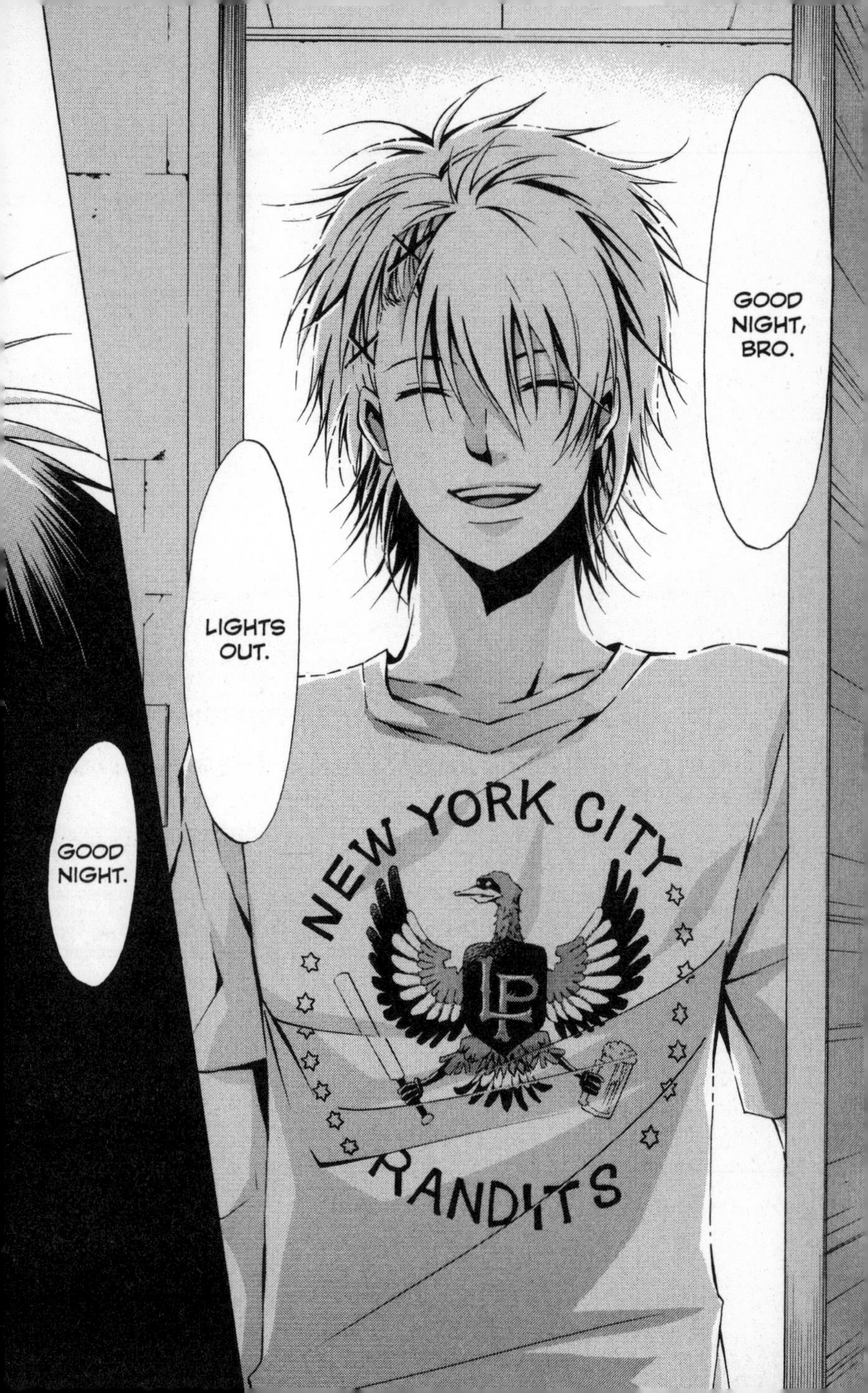
GOOD NIGHT, BRO.
LIGHTS OUT.
GOOD NIGHT.
NEW YORK CITY
RANDITS

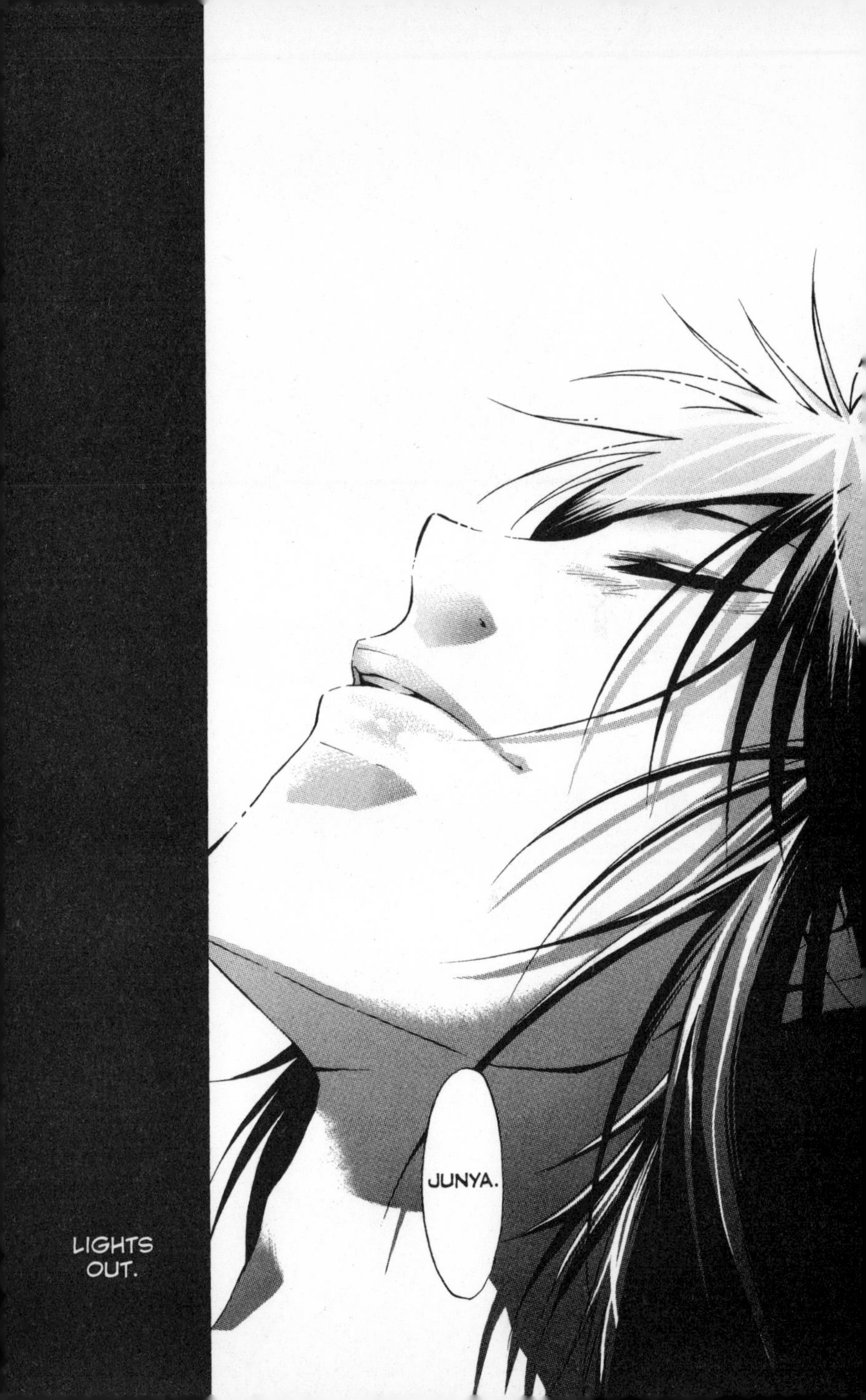
JUNYA.
LIGHTS OUT.

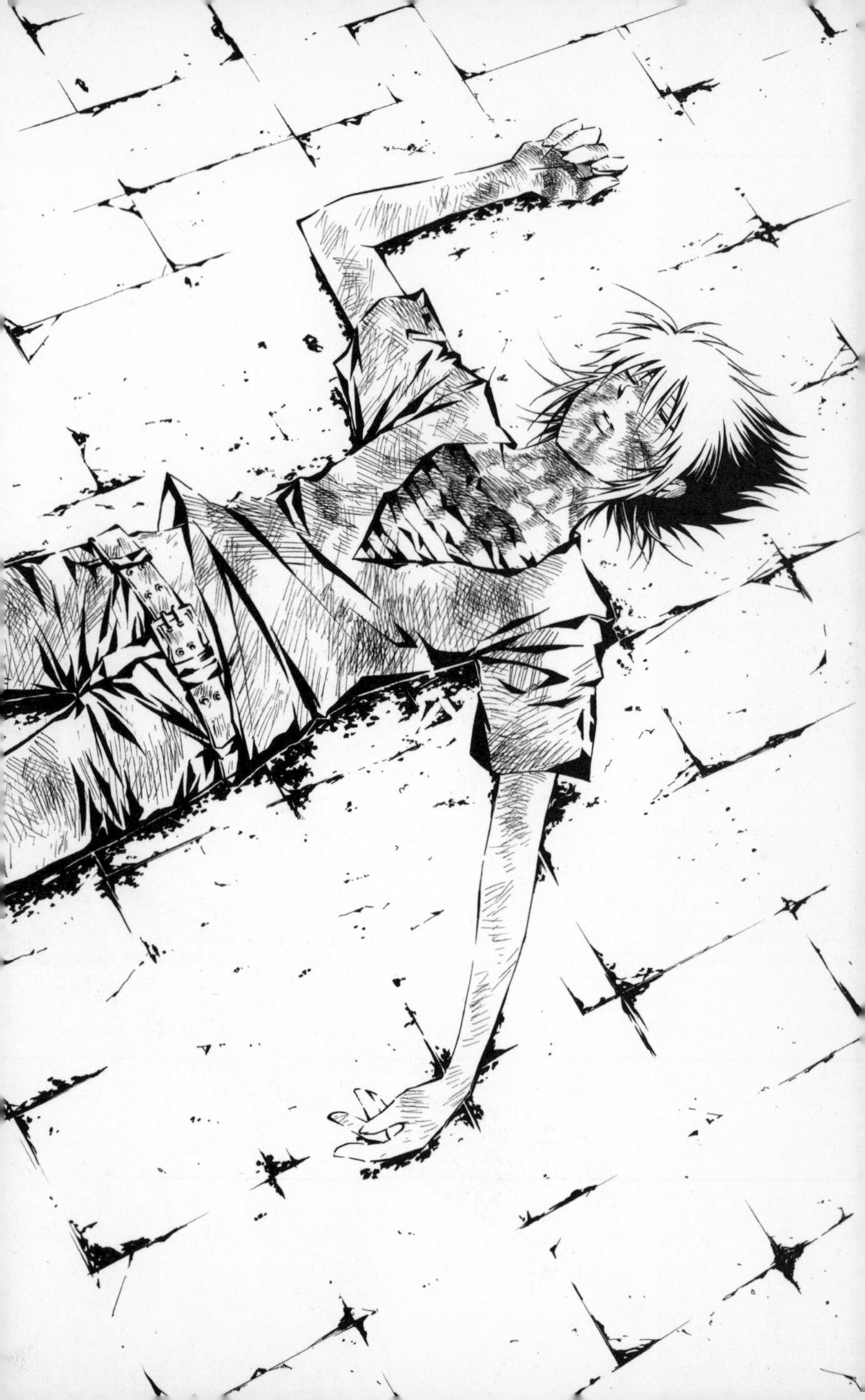

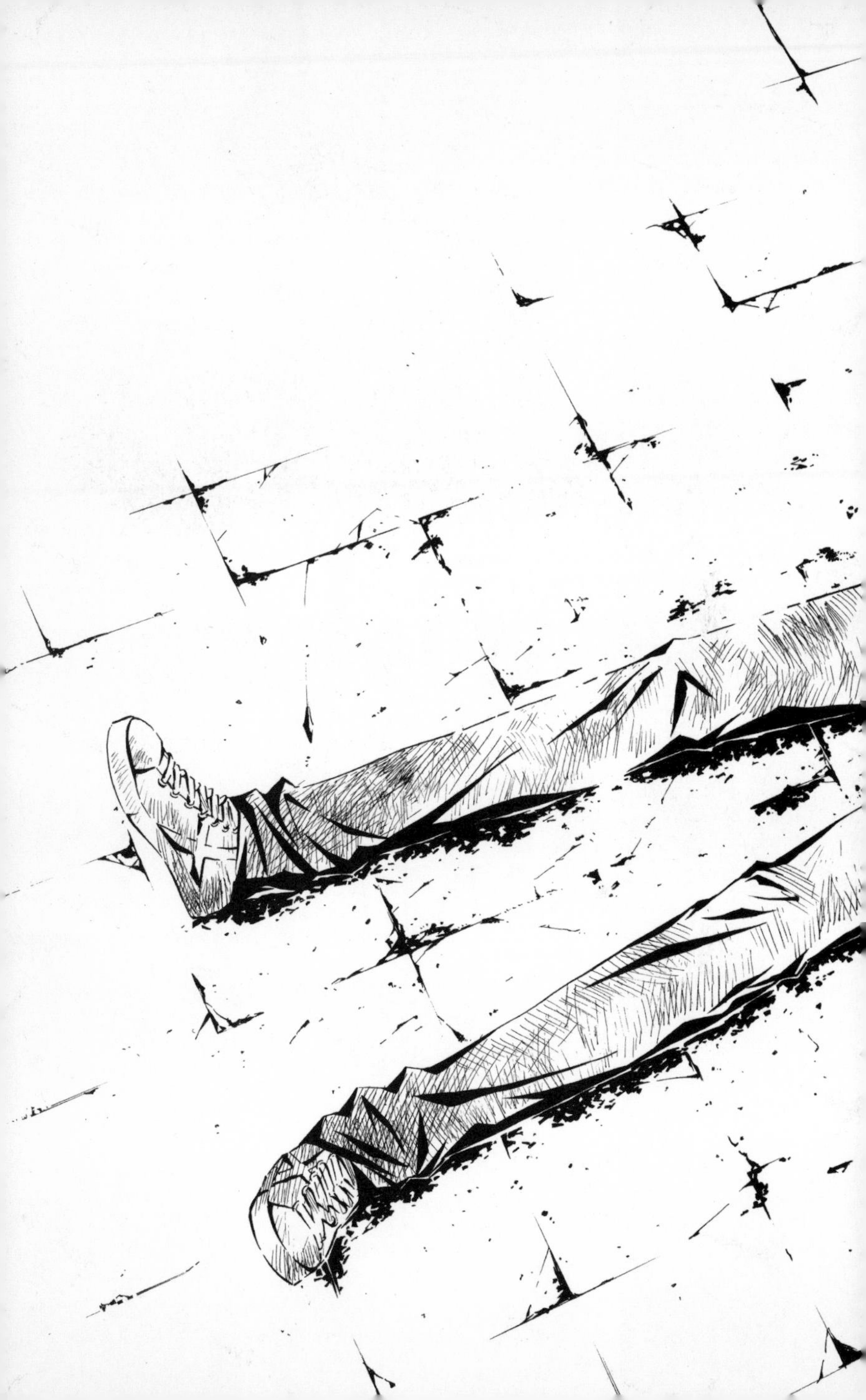

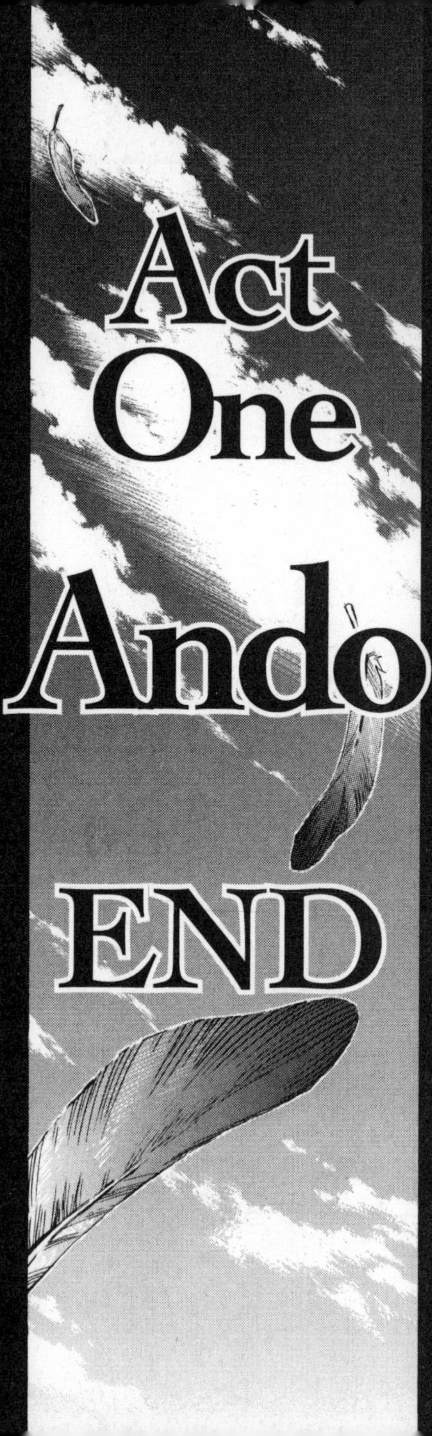
Act One
Ando
END

MAOH
JUVENILE REMIX

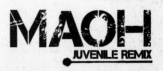

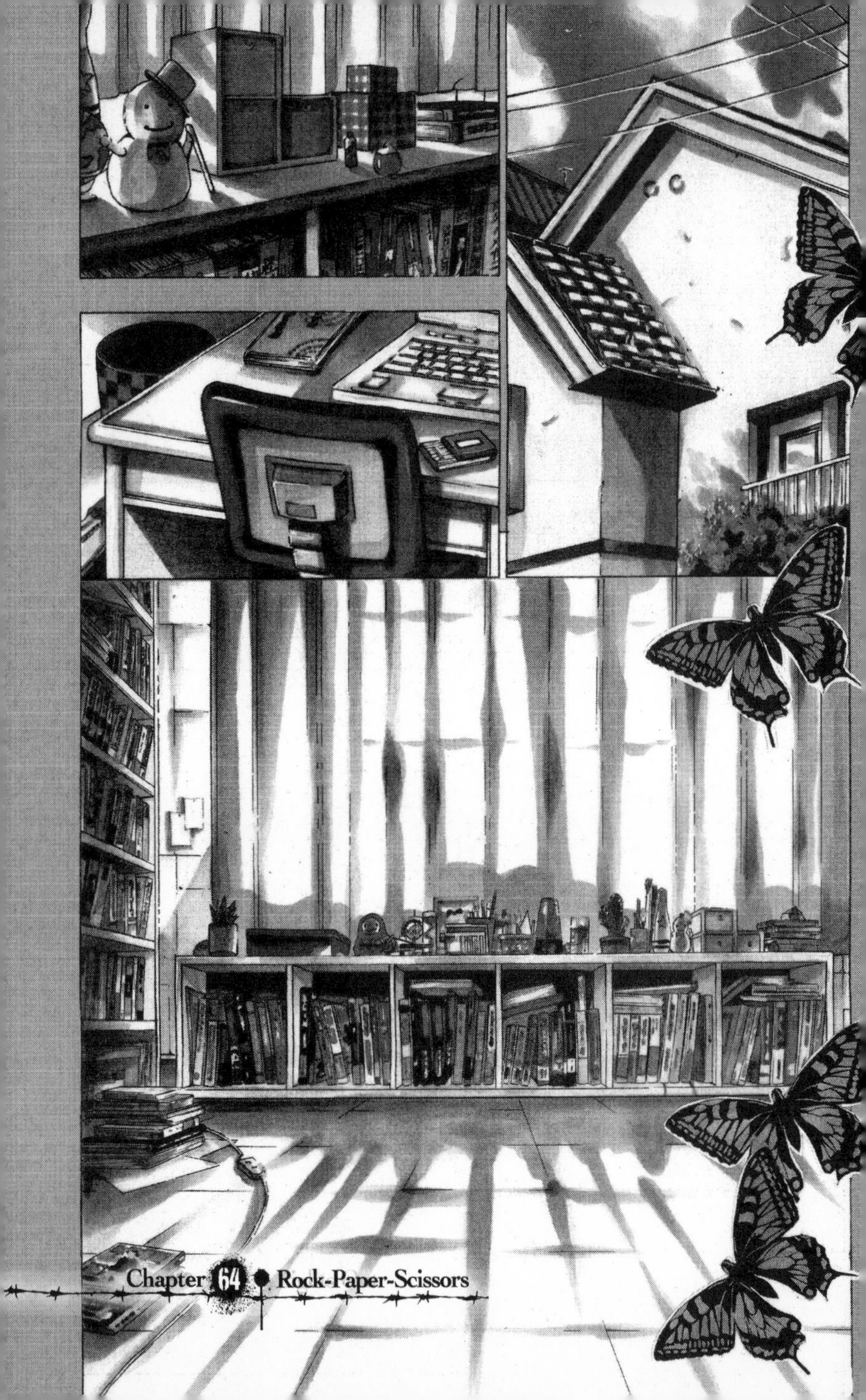
Chapter 64 Rock-Paper-Scissors

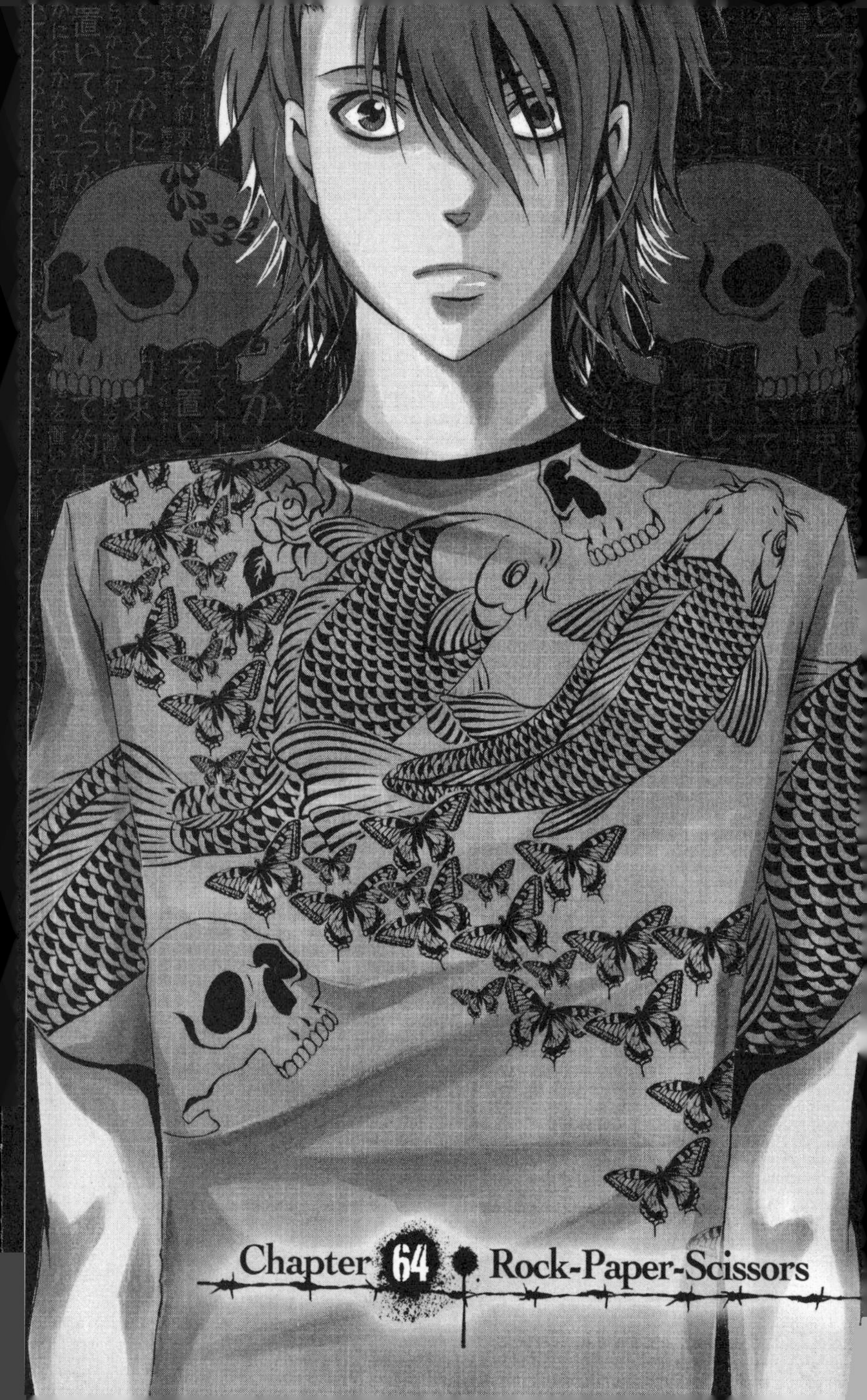

# Chapter 64 Rock-Paper-Scissors

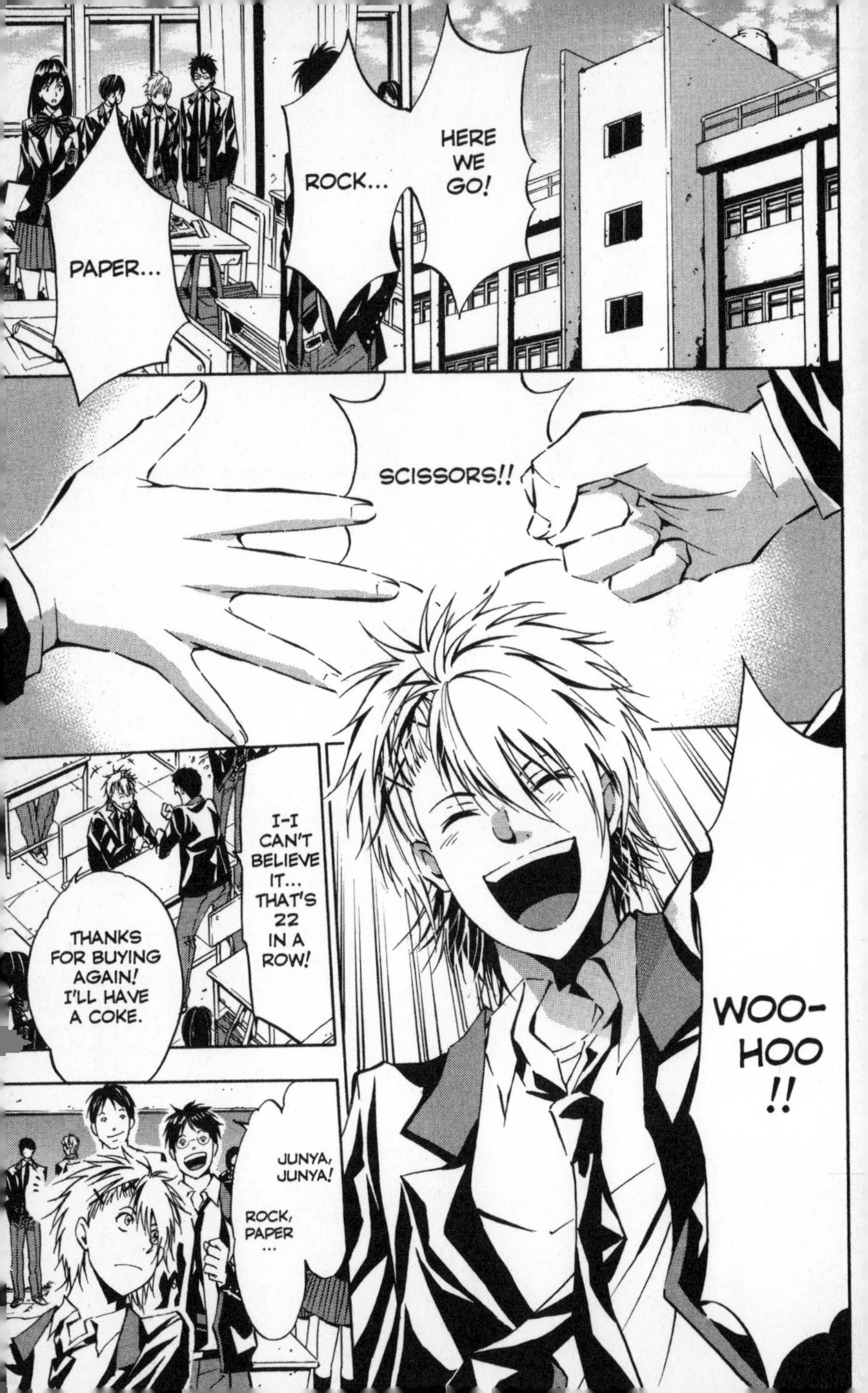
HERE WE GO!
ROCK...
PAPER...
SCISSORS!!
WOO-HOO!!
I-I CAN'T BELIEVE IT... THAT'S 22 IN A ROW!
THANKS FOR BUYING AGAIN! I'LL HAVE A COKE.
JUNYA, JUNYA!
ROCK, PAPER...

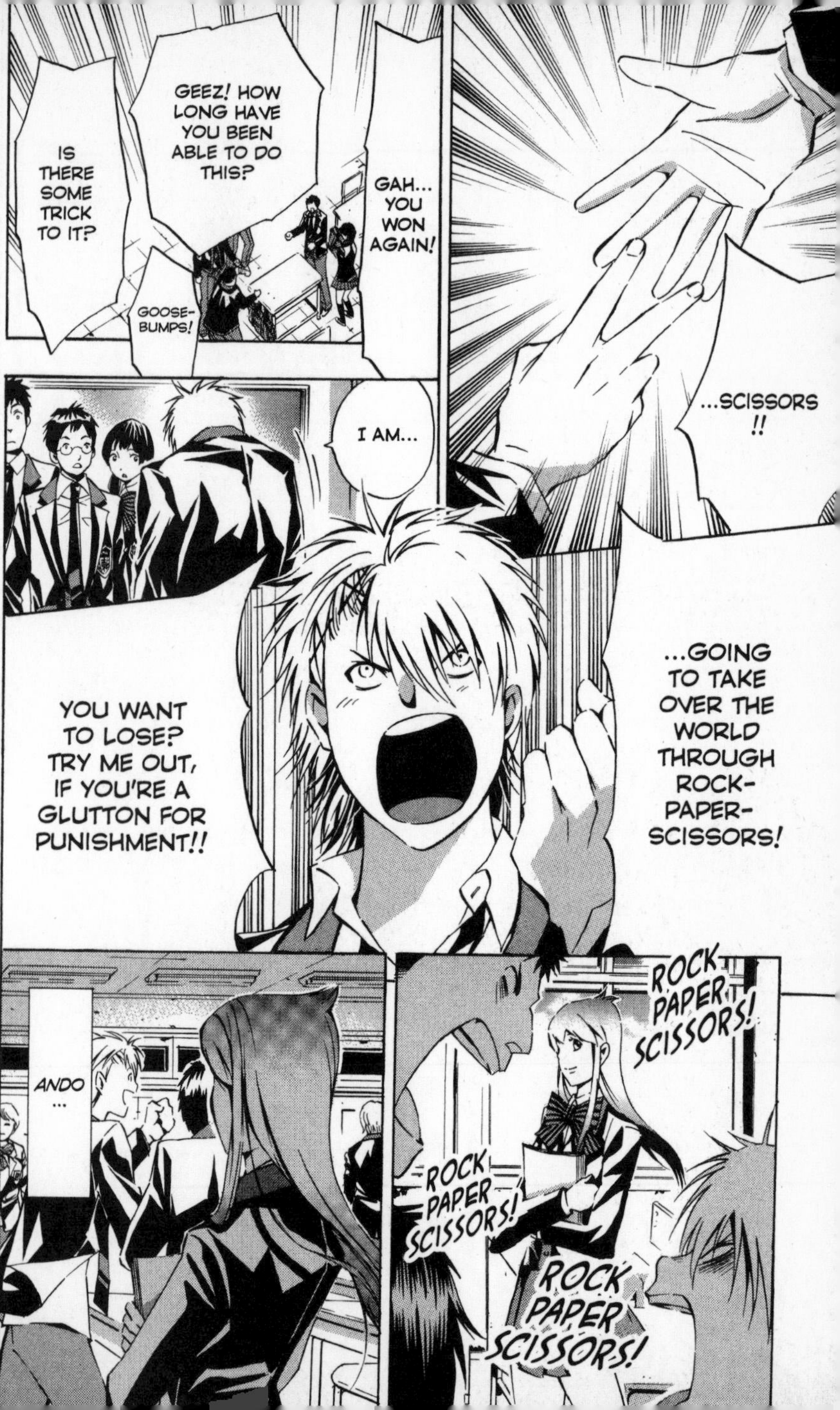
...SCISSORS !!
GAH... YOU WON AGAIN!
GEEZ! HOW LONG HAVE YOU BEEN ABLE TO DO THIS?
IS THERE SOME TRICK TO IT?
GOOSE-BUMPS!
I AM...
...GOING TO TAKE OVER THE WORLD THROUGH ROCK-PAPER-SCISSORS!
YOU WANT TO LOSE? TRY ME OUT, IF YOU'RE A GLUTTON FOR PUNISHMENT!!
ROCK PAPER SCISSORS!
ROCK PAPER SCISSORS!
ROCK PAPER SCISSORS!
ANDO ...

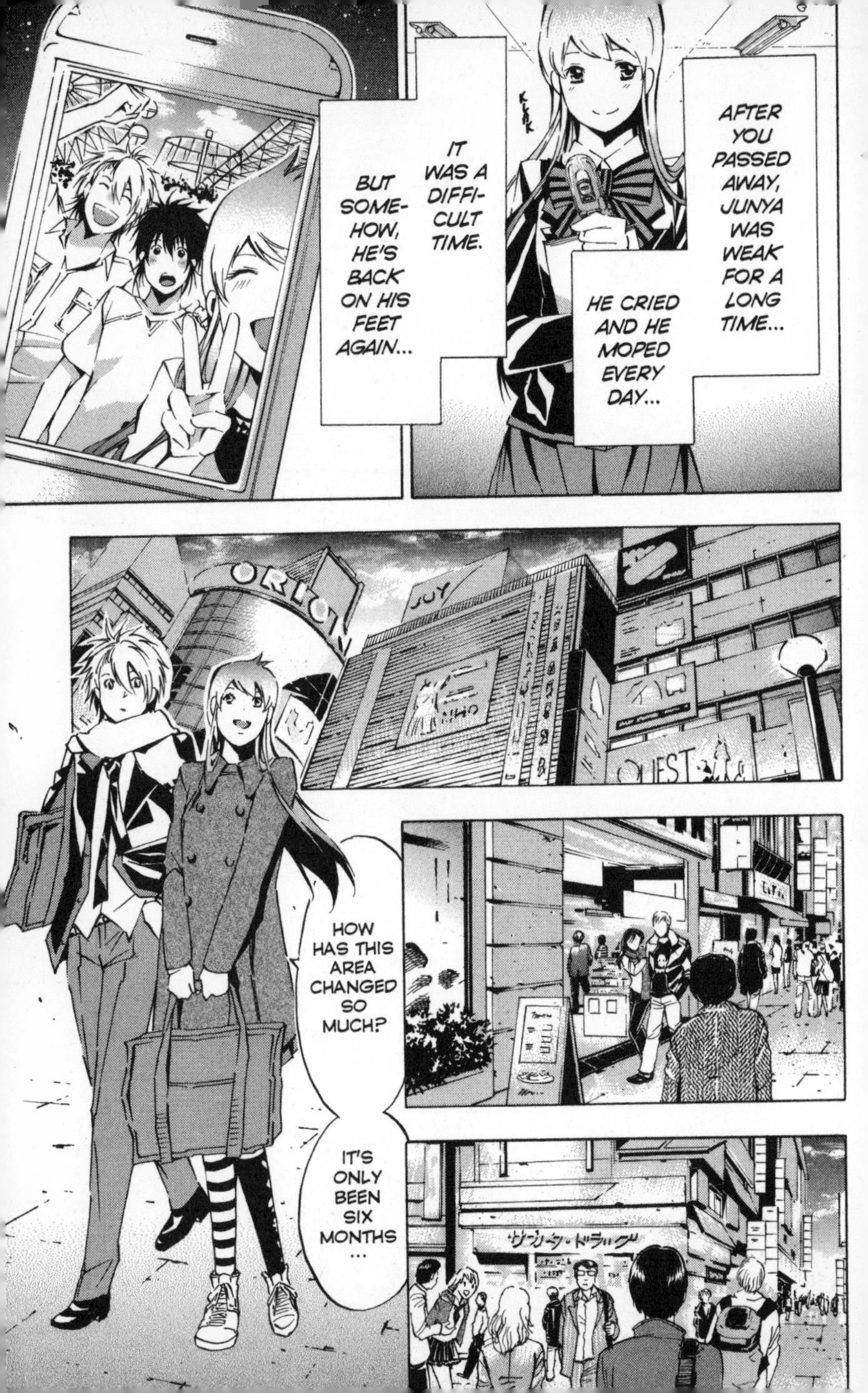
AFTER YOU PASSED AWAY, JUNYA WAS WEAK FOR A LONG TIME...
HE CRIED AND HE MOPED EVERY DAY...
IT WAS A DIFFICULT TIME.
BUT SOMEHOW, HE'S BACK ON HIS FEET AGAIN...
HOW HAS THIS AREA CHANGED SO MUCH?
IT'S ONLY BEEN SIX MONTHS...

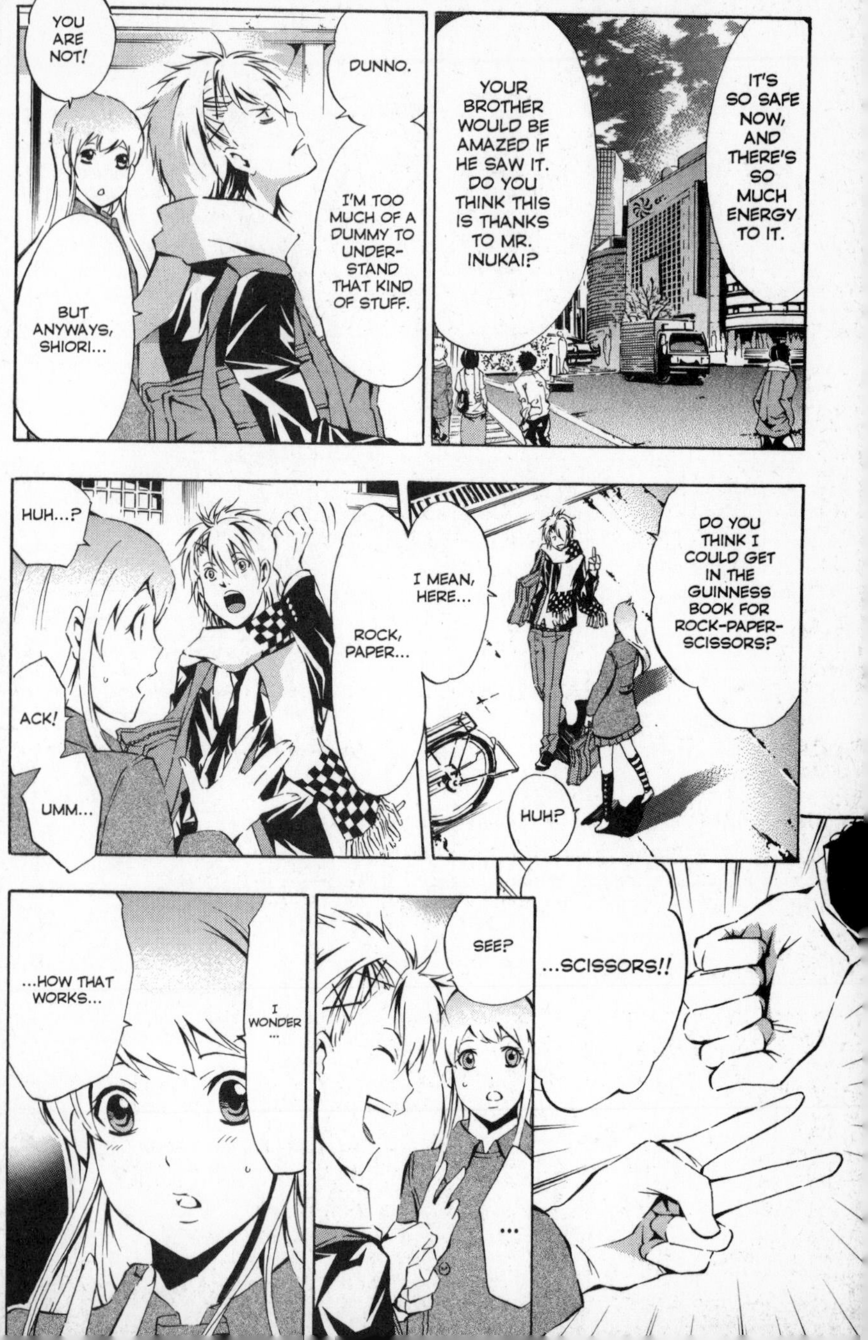
IT'S SO SAFE NOW, AND THERE'S SO MUCH ENERGY TO IT.
YOUR BROTHER WOULD BE AMAZED IF HE SAW IT. DO YOU THINK THIS IS THANKS TO MR. INUKAI?
DUNNO.
I'M TOO MUCH OF A DUMMY TO UNDER-STAND THAT KIND OF STUFF.
YOU ARE NOT!
BUT ANYWAYS, SHIORI...
DO YOU THINK I COULD GET IN THE GUINNESS BOOK FOR ROCK-PAPER-SCISSORS?
HUH?
I MEAN, HERE...
ROCK, PAPER...
HUH...?
ACK!
UMM...
...SCISSORS!!
SEE?
...
I WONDER...
...HOW THAT WORKS...

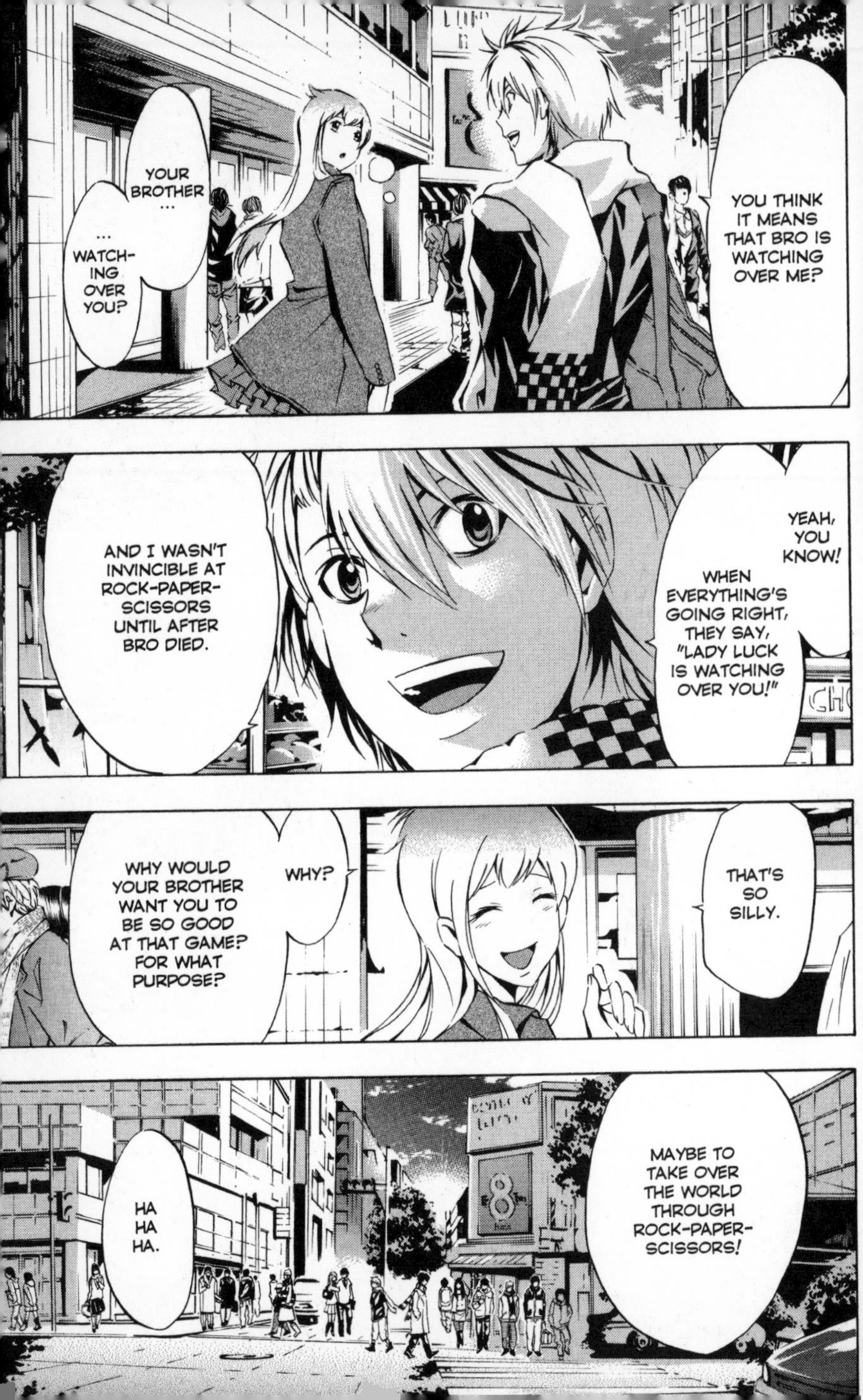
YOU THINK IT MEANS THAT BRO IS WATCHING OVER ME?
YOUR BROTHER ... ... WATCHING OVER YOU?
YEAH, YOU KNOW!
WHEN EVERYTHING'S GOING RIGHT, THEY SAY, "LADY LUCK IS WATCHING OVER YOU!"
AND I WASN'T INVINCIBLE AT ROCK-PAPER-SCISSORS UNTIL AFTER BRO DIED.
THAT'S SO SILLY.
WHY?
WHY WOULD YOUR BROTHER WANT YOU TO BE SO GOOD AT THAT GAME? FOR WHAT PURPOSE?
MAYBE TO TAKE OVER THE WORLD THROUGH ROCK-PAPER-SCISSORS!
HA HA HA.

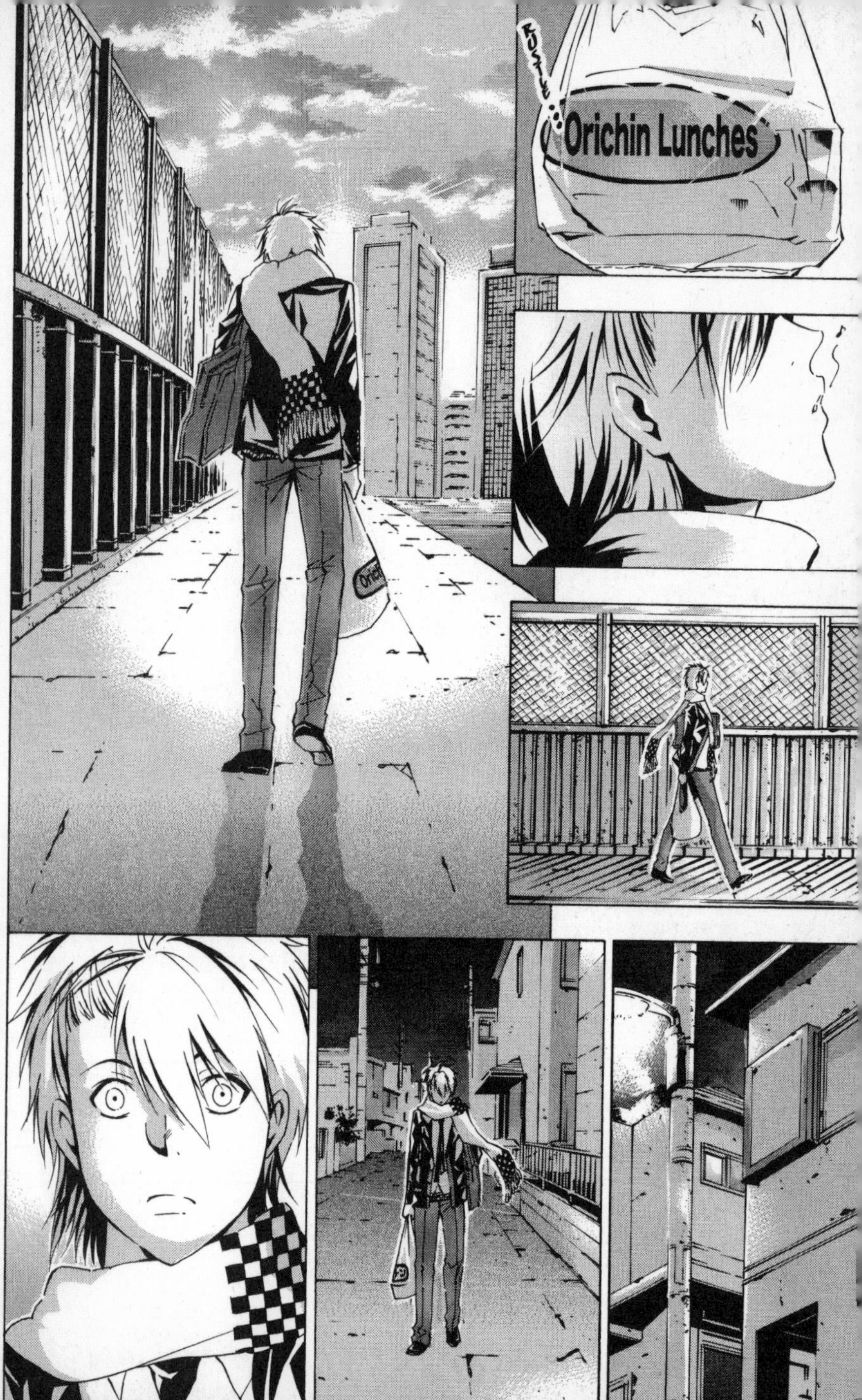
RUSTLE...
Orichin Lunches

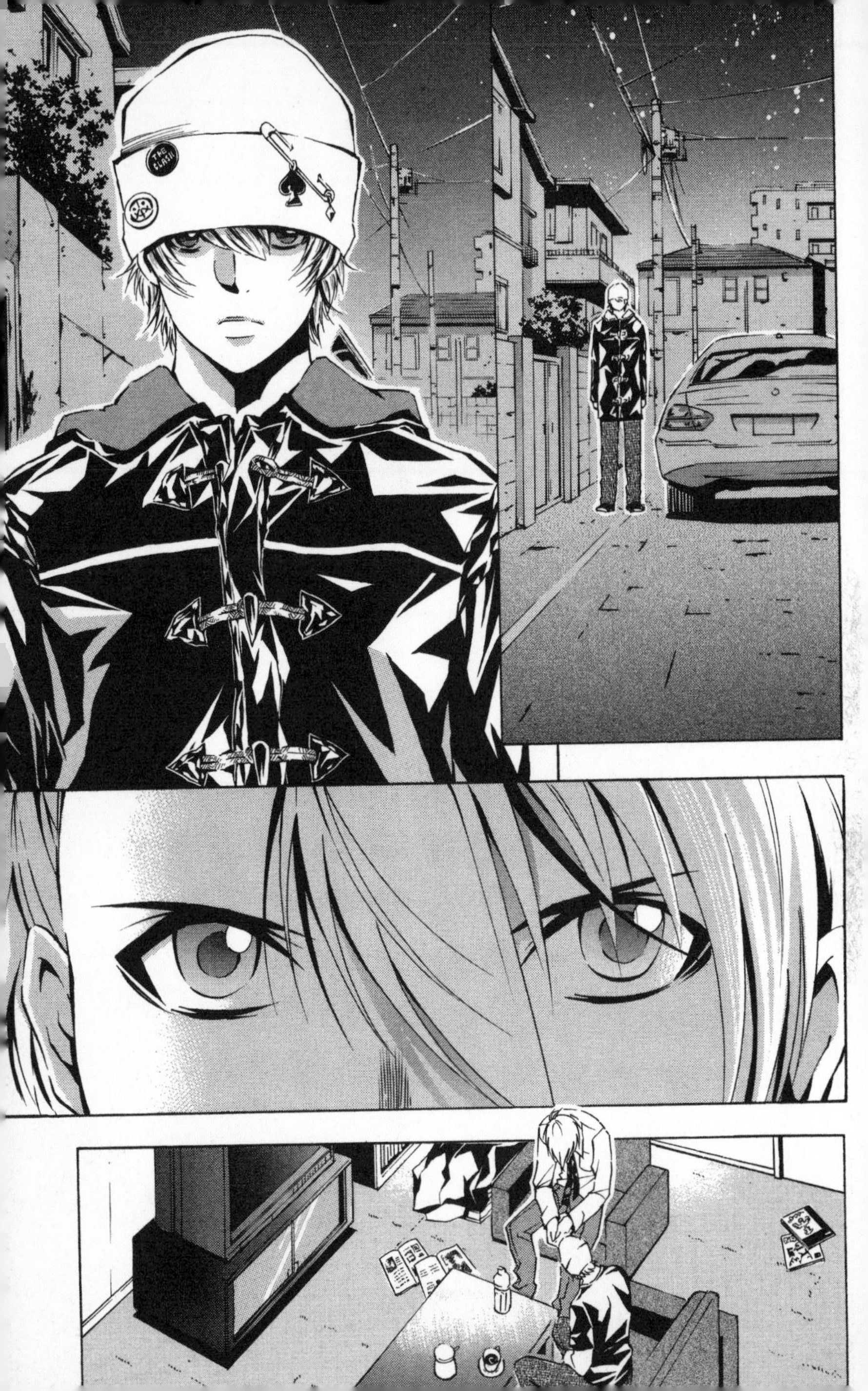
THE CLASH

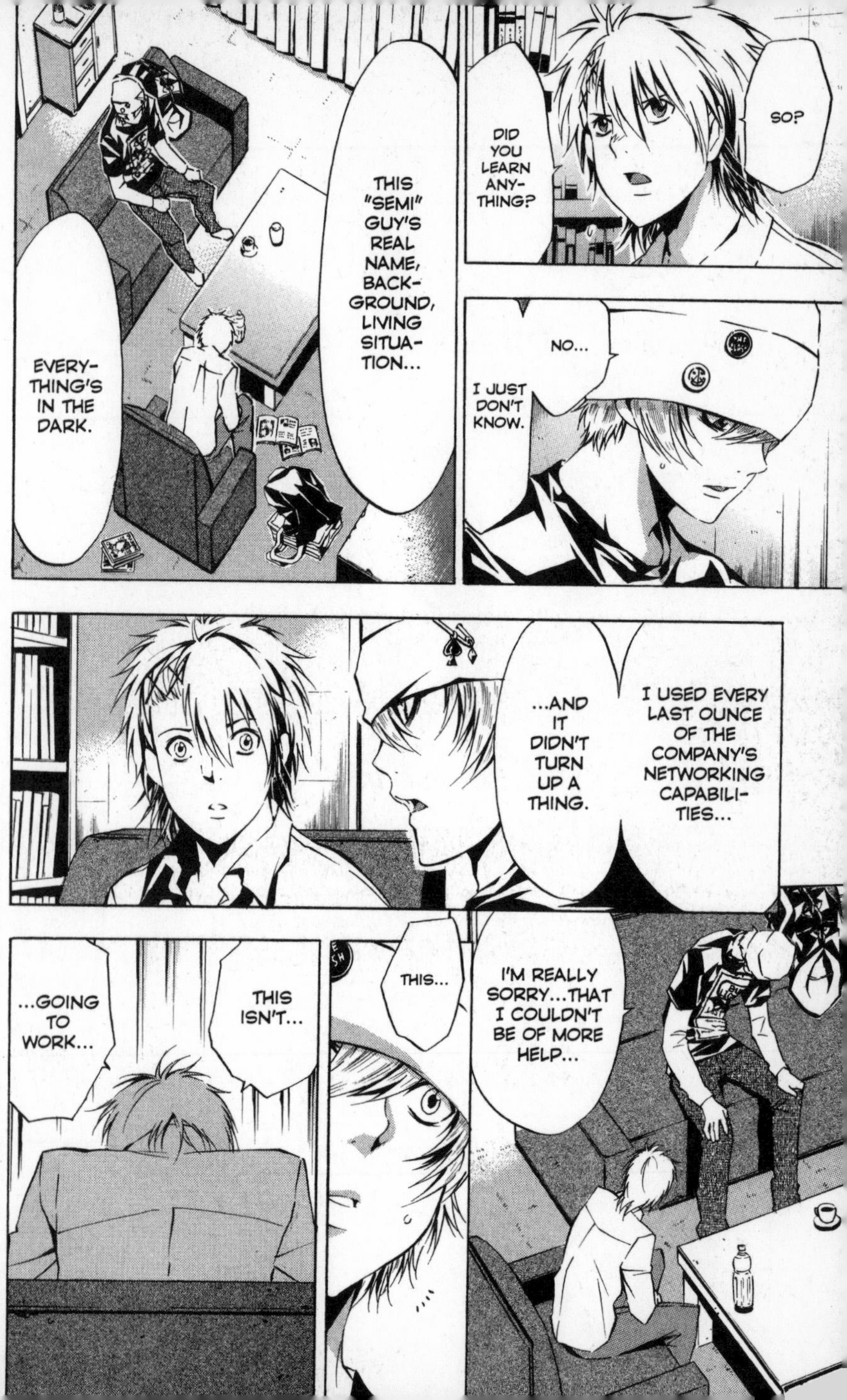

SO?
DID YOU LEARN ANYTHING?
NO...
I JUST DON'T KNOW.
THIS "SEMI" GUY'S REAL NAME, BACKGROUND, LIVING SITUATION...
EVERYTHING'S IN THE DARK.
I USED EVERY LAST OUNCE OF THE COMPANY'S NETWORKING CAPABILITIES...
...AND IT DIDN'T TURN UP A THING.
I'M REALLY SORRY...THAT I COULDN'T BE OF MORE HELP...
THIS...
THIS ISN'T...
...GOING TO WORK...

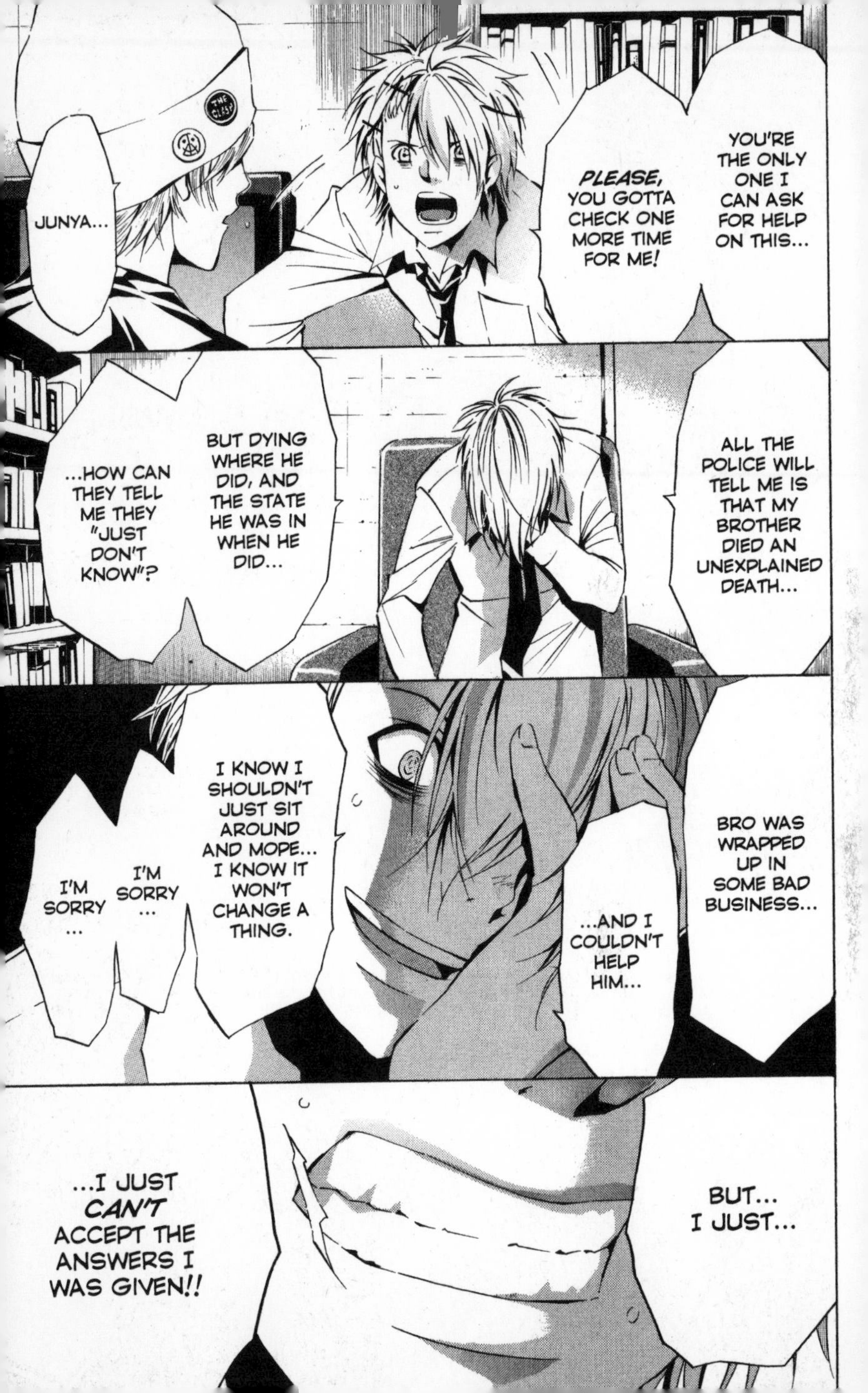
YOU'RE THE ONLY ONE I CAN ASK FOR HELP ON THIS...
*PLEASE,* YOU GOTTA CHECK ONE MORE TIME FOR ME!
JUNYA...
ALL THE POLICE WILL TELL ME IS THAT MY BROTHER DIED AN UNEXPLAINED DEATH...
BUT DYING WHERE HE DID, AND THE STATE HE WAS IN WHEN HE DID...
...HOW CAN THEY TELL ME THEY "JUST DON'T KNOW"?
BRO WAS WRAPPED UP IN SOME BAD BUSINESS...
...AND I COULDN'T HELP HIM...
I KNOW I SHOULDN'T JUST SIT AROUND AND MOPE... I KNOW IT WON'T CHANGE A THING.
I'M SORRY...
I'M SORRY...
BUT... I JUST...
...I JUST *CAN'T* ACCEPT THE ANSWERS I WAS GIVEN!!

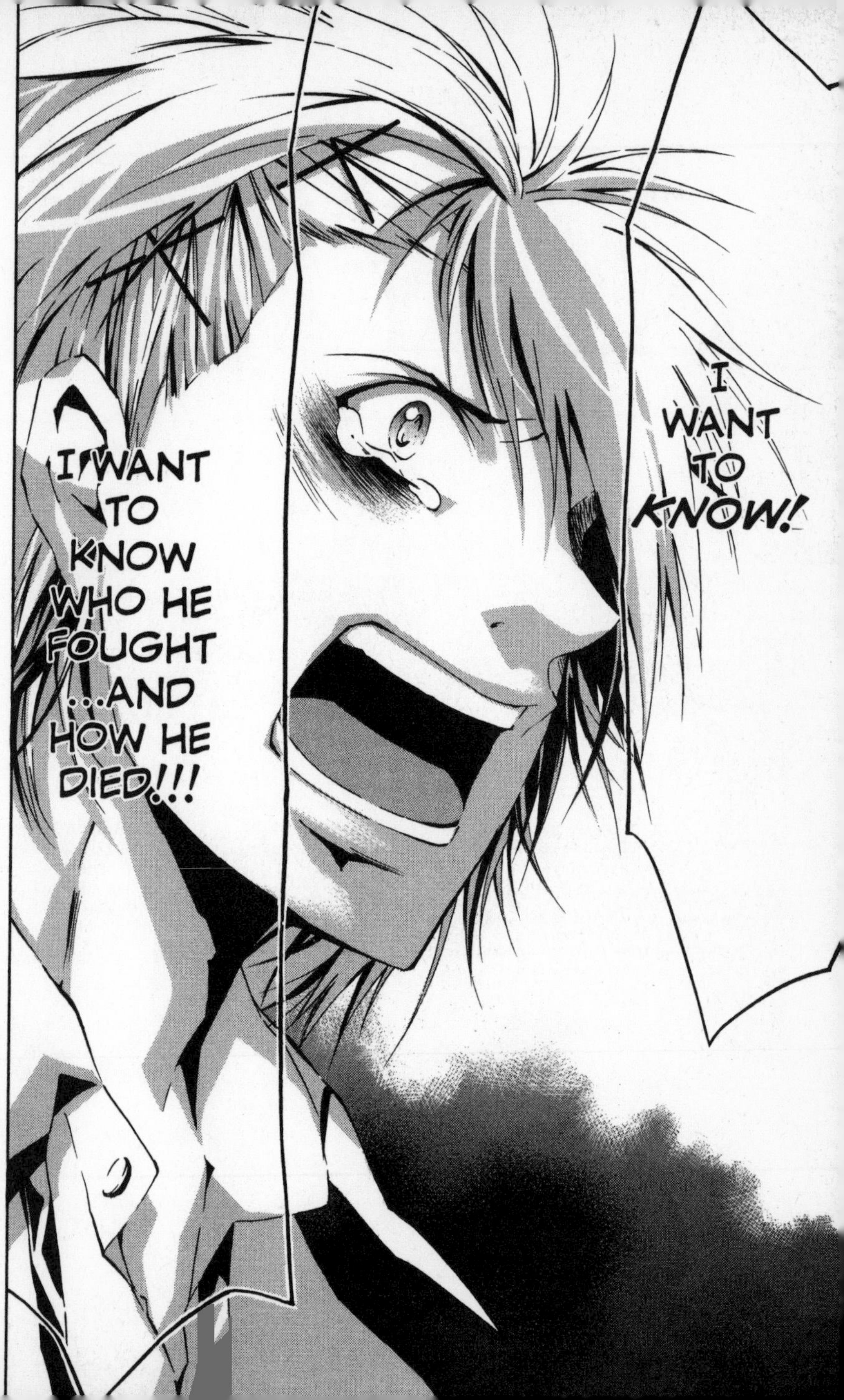
I WANT TO KNOW!
I WANT TO KNOW WHO HE FOUGHT ...AND HOW HE DIED!!!

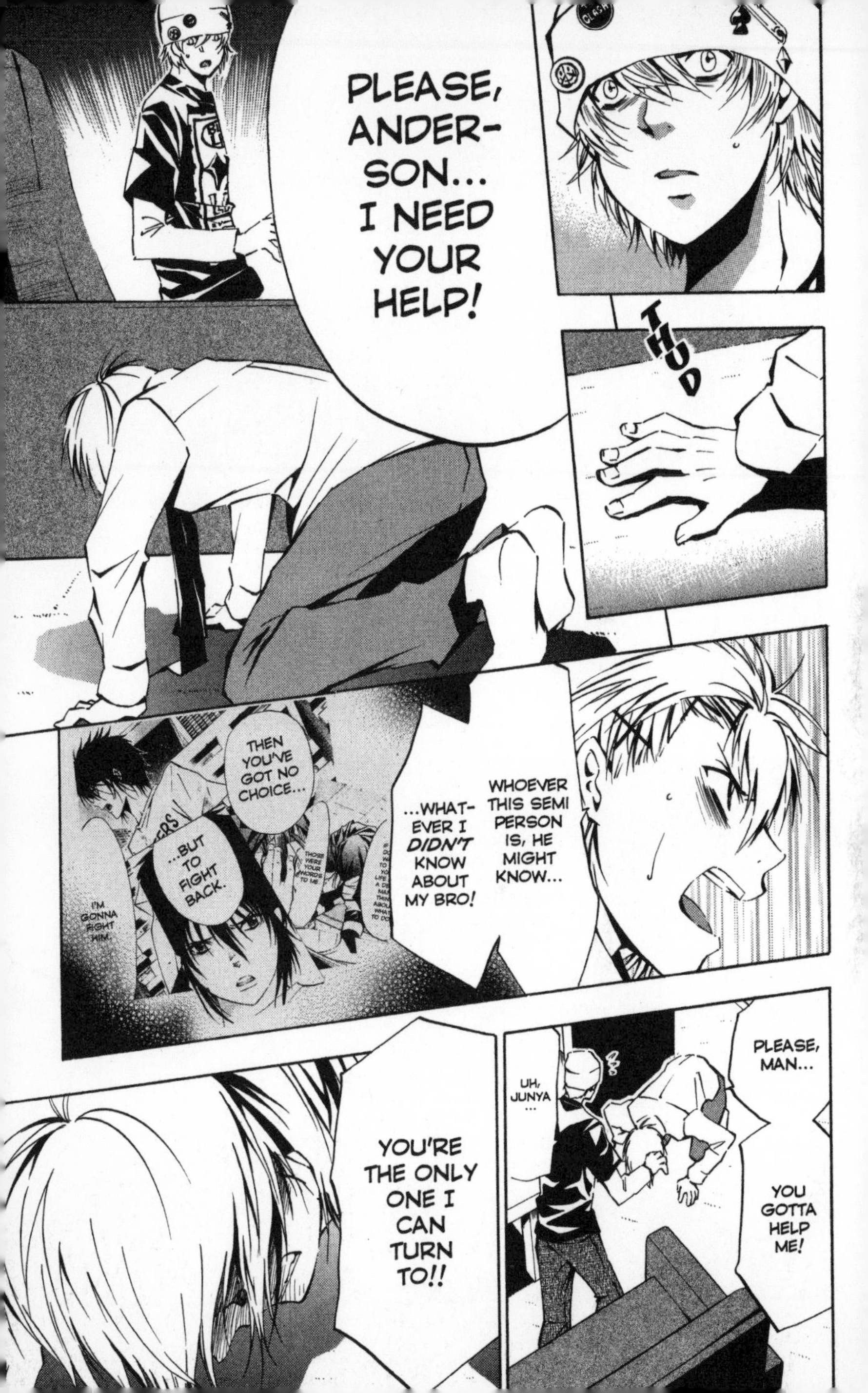
THUD
PLEASE, ANDER-SON... I NEED YOUR HELP!
WHOEVER THIS SEMI PERSON IS, HE MIGHT KNOW...
...WHAT-EVER I *DIDN'T* KNOW ABOUT MY BRO!
THEN YOU'VE GOT NO CHOICE...
...BUT TO FIGHT BACK.
THOSE WERE YOUR WORDS TO ME.
I'M GONNA FIGHT HIM.
PLEASE, MAN...
YOU GOTTA HELP ME!
UH, JUNYA...
YOU'RE THE ONLY ONE I CAN TURN TO!!

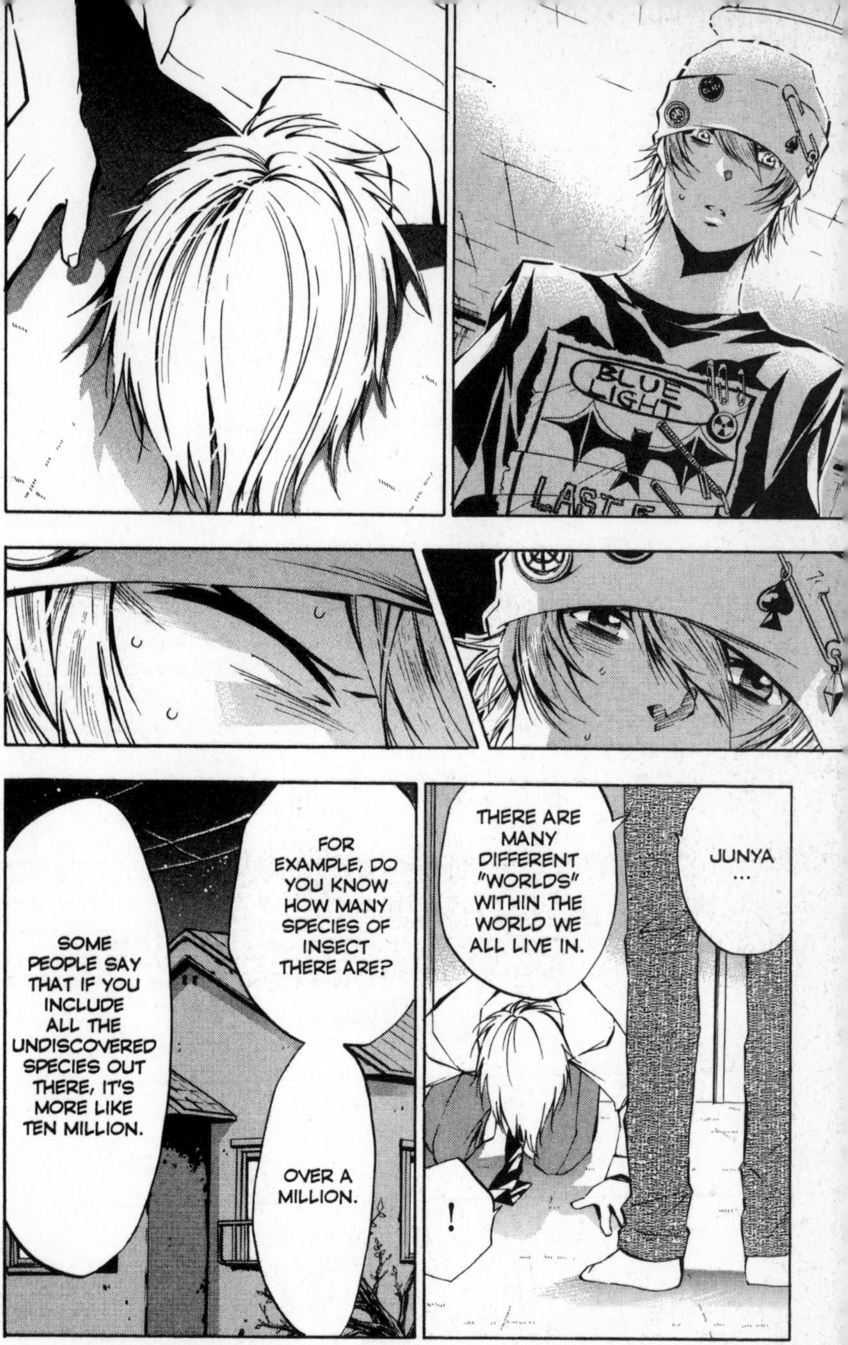
JUNYA ...
THERE ARE MANY DIFFERENT "WORLDS" WITHIN THE WORLD WE ALL LIVE IN.
!
FOR EXAMPLE, DO YOU KNOW HOW MANY SPECIES OF INSECT THERE ARE?
OVER A MILLION.
SOME PEOPLE SAY THAT IF YOU INCLUDE ALL THE UNDISCOVERED SPECIES OUT THERE, IT'S MORE LIKE TEN MILLION.

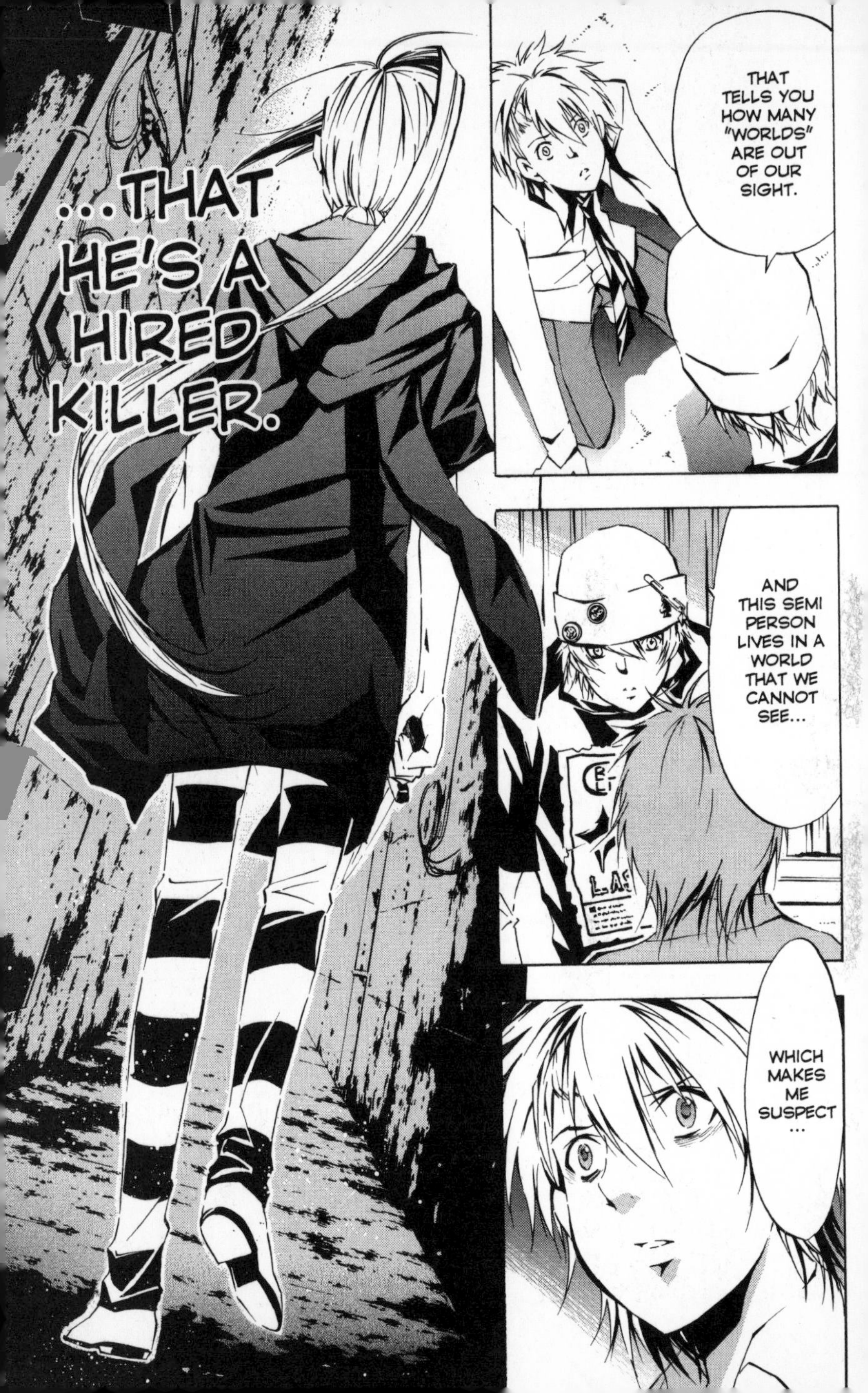
THAT TELLS YOU HOW MANY "WORLDS" ARE OUT OF OUR SIGHT.
AND THIS SEMI PERSON LIVES IN A WORLD THAT WE CANNOT SEE...
WHICH MAKES ME SUSPECT ...
...THAT HE'S A HIRED KILLER.

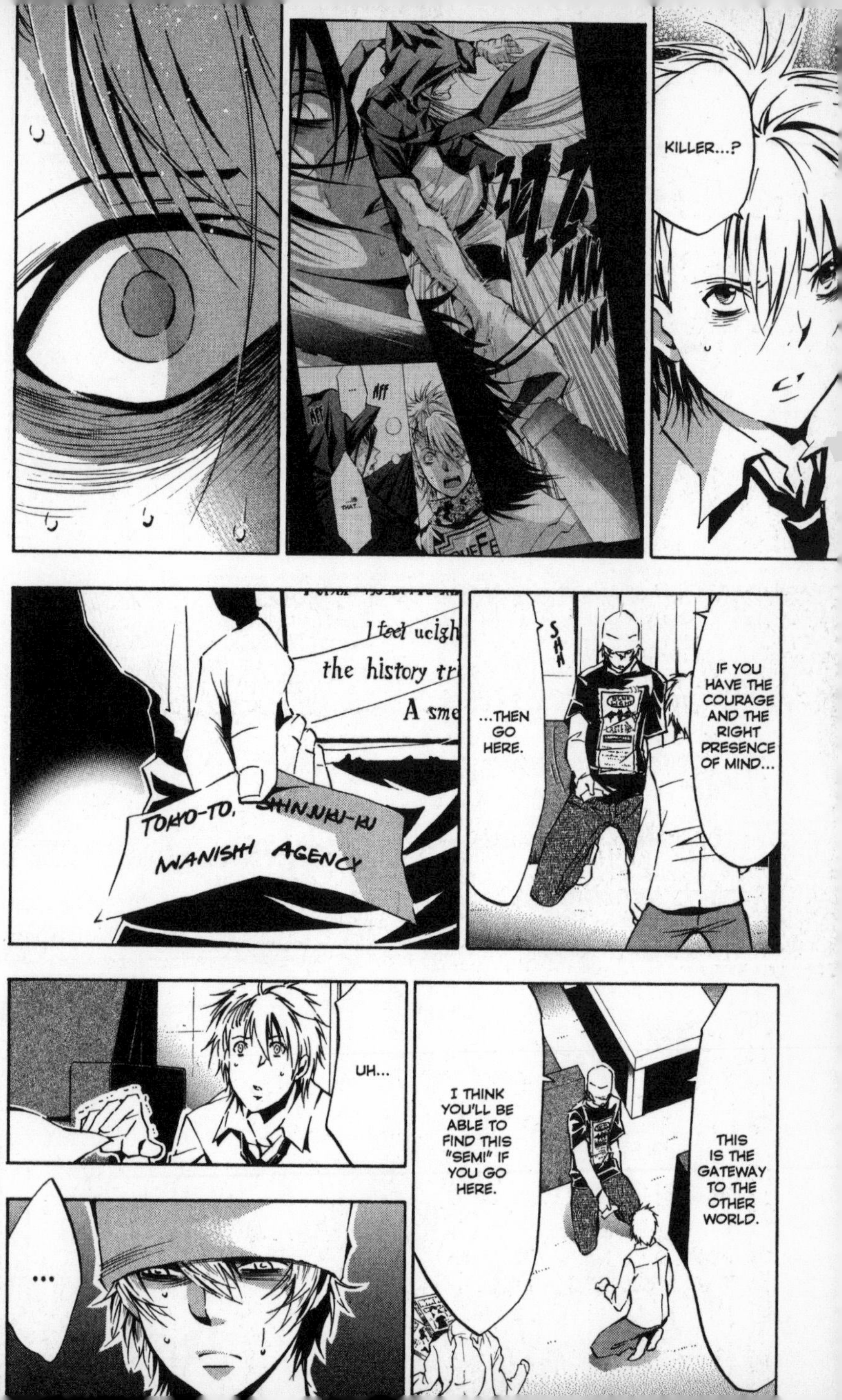
KILLER...?
IF YOU HAVE THE COURAGE AND THE RIGHT PRESENCE OF MIND...
...THEN GO HERE.
TOKYO-TO, SHINJUKU-KU
MANISHI AGENCY
THIS IS THE GATEWAY TO THE OTHER WORLD.
I THINK YOU'LL BE ABLE TO FIND THIS "SEMI" IF YOU GO HERE.
UH...
...

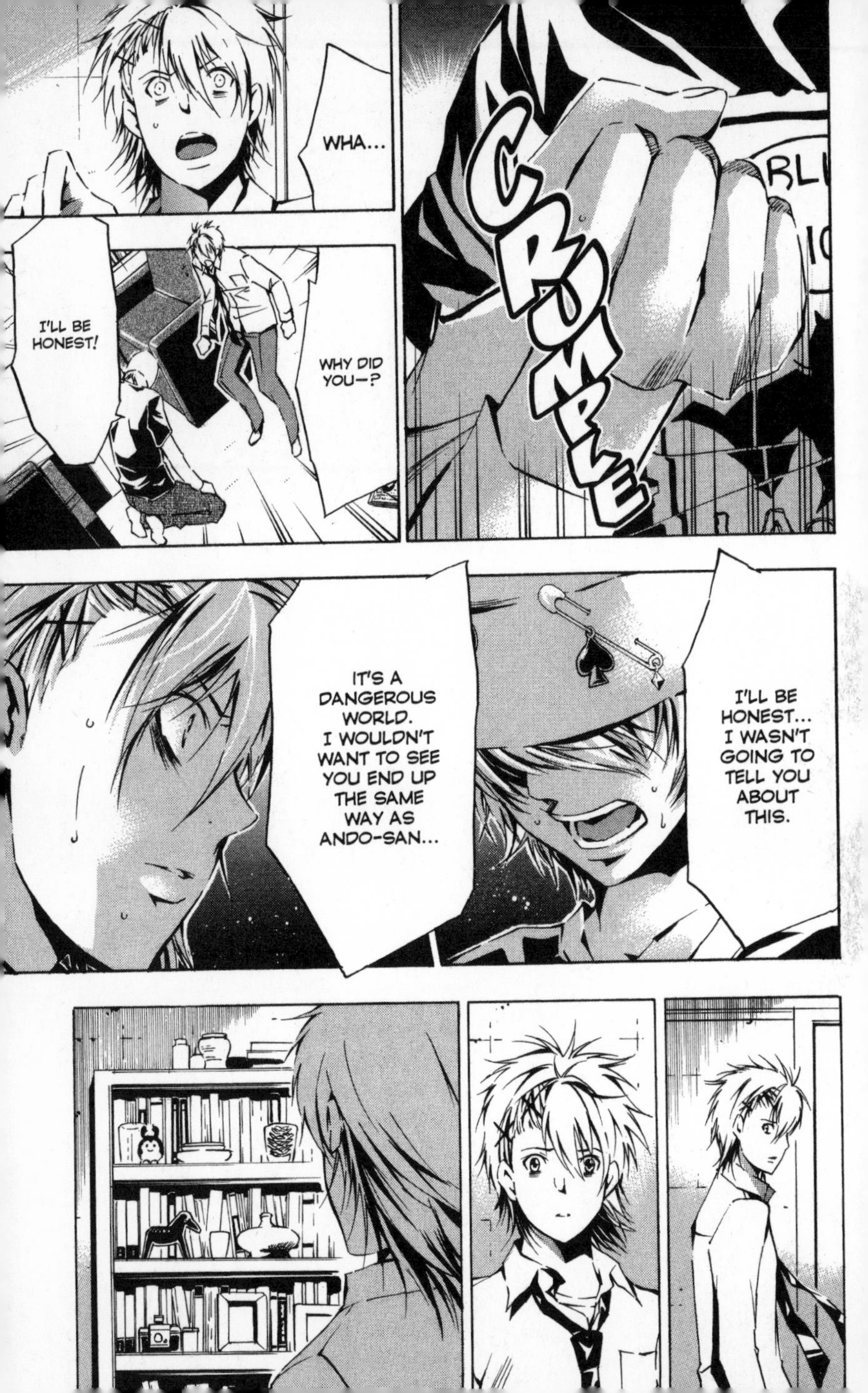
CRUMPLE
WHA...
WHY DID YOU—?
I'LL BE HONEST!
I'LL BE HONEST... I WASN'T GOING TO TELL YOU ABOUT THIS.
IT'S A DANGEROUS WORLD. I WOULDN'T WANT TO SEE YOU END UP THE SAME WAY AS ANDO-SAN...

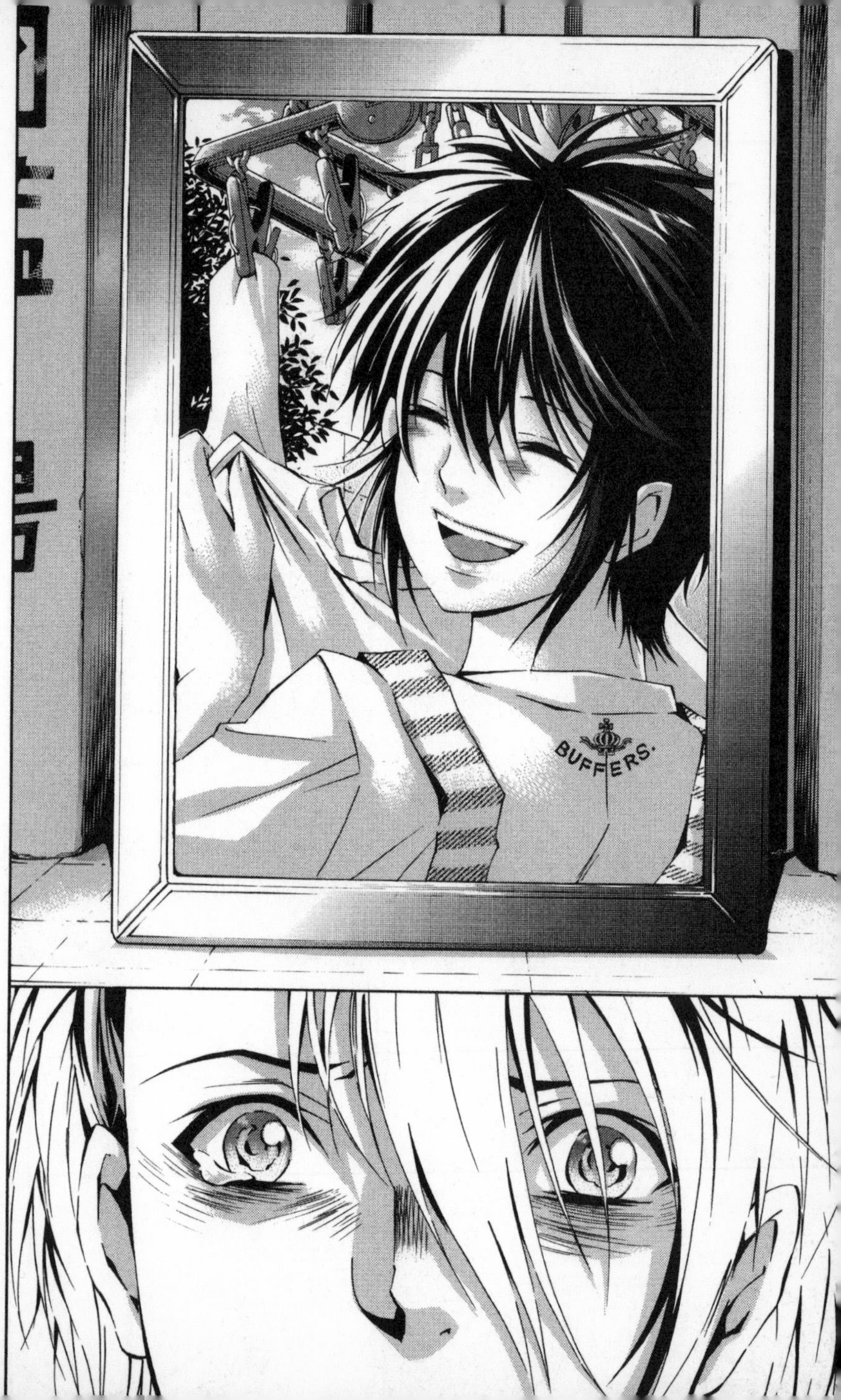
BUFFERS.

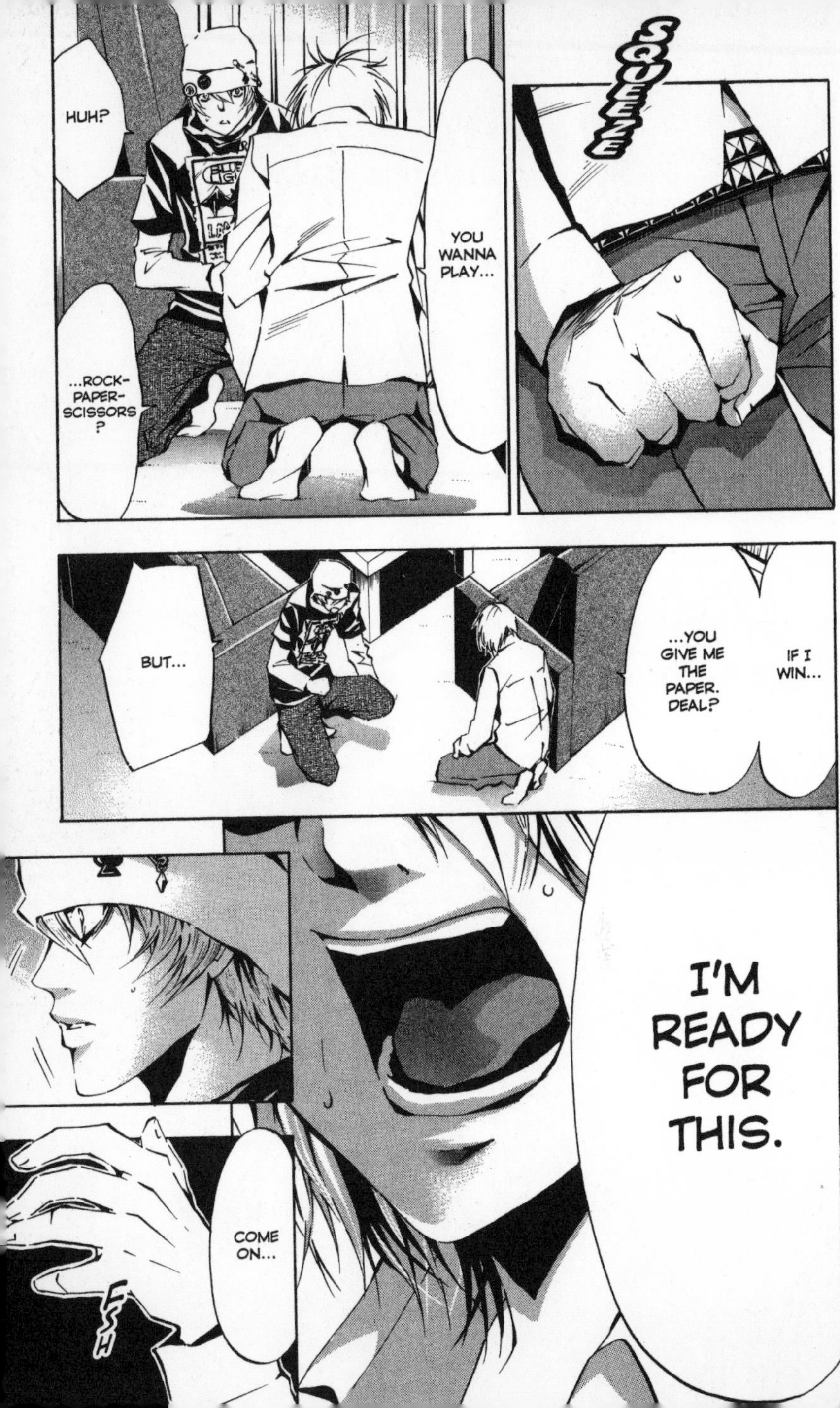
SQUEEZE
YOU WANNA PLAY...
HUH?
...ROCK-PAPER-SCISSORS?
IF I WIN...
...YOU GIVE ME THE PAPER. DEAL?
BUT...
I'M READY FOR THIS.
COME ON...

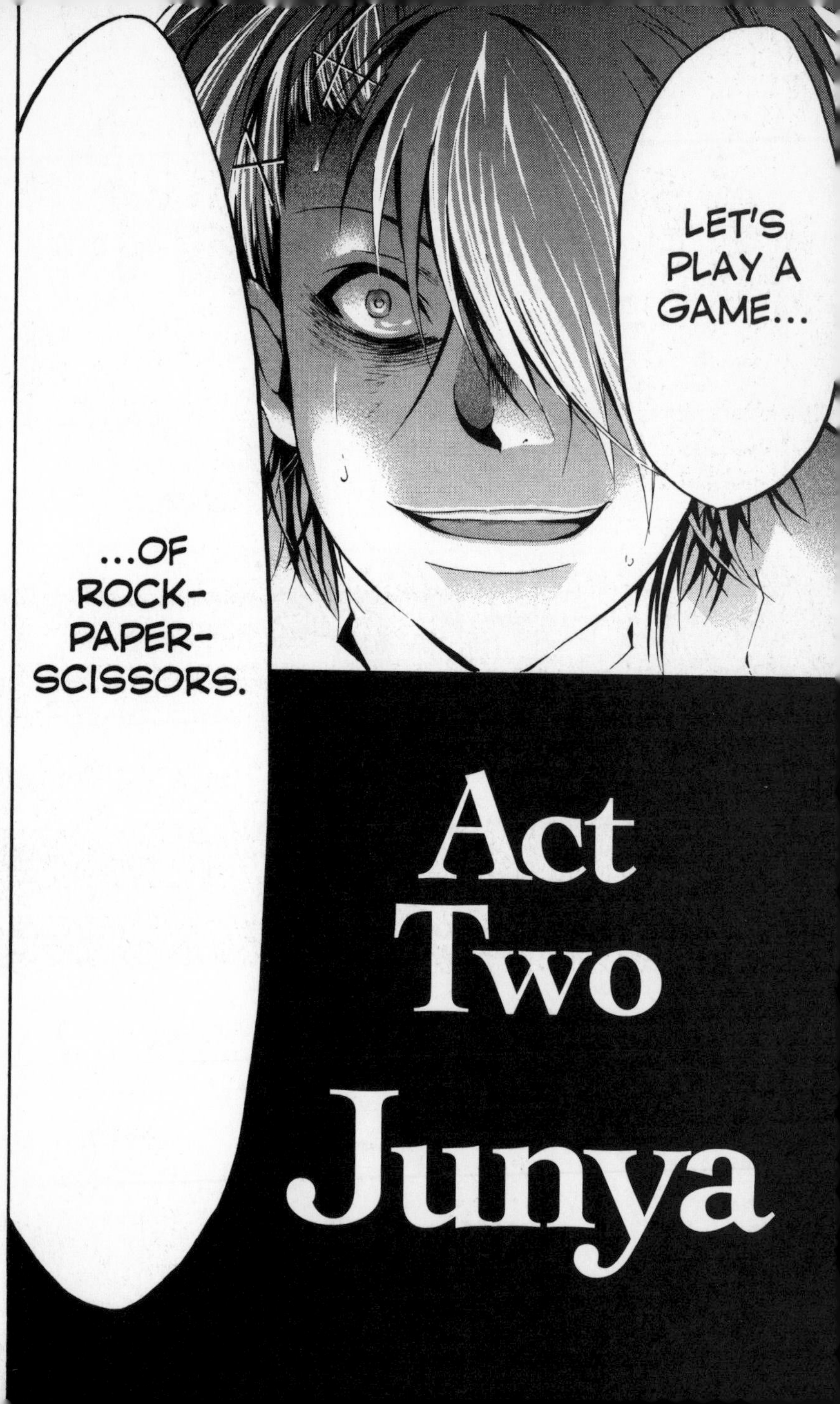
LET'S PLAY A GAME...
...OF ROCK-PAPER-SCISSORS.
Act Two
Junya

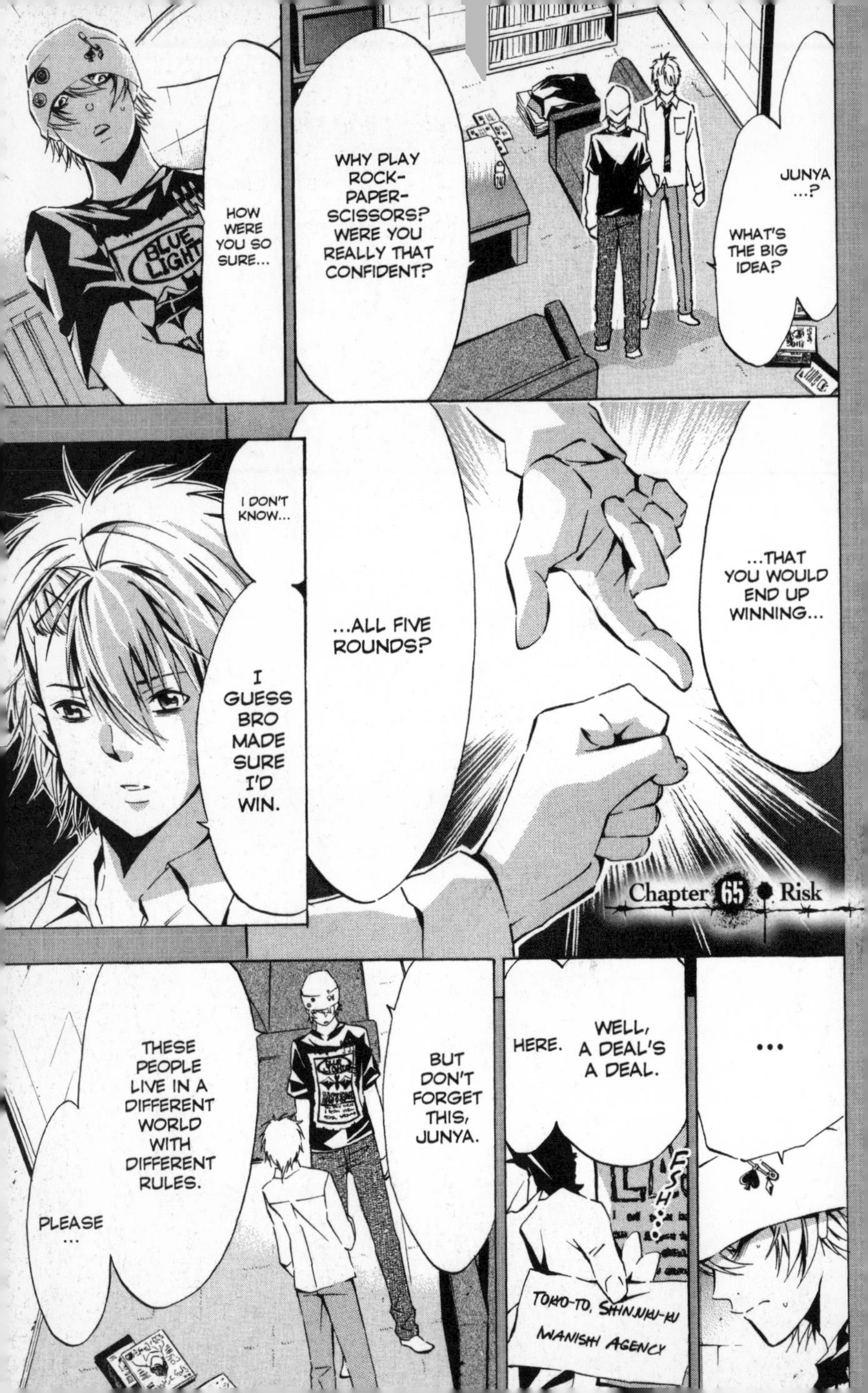
JUNYA ...?
WHAT'S THE BIG IDEA?
WHY PLAY ROCK-PAPER-SCISSORS? WERE YOU REALLY THAT CONFIDENT?
HOW WERE YOU SO SURE...
...THAT YOU WOULD END UP WINNING...
...ALL FIVE ROUNDS?
Chapter 65 Risk
I DON'T KNOW...
I GUESS BRO MADE SURE I'D WIN.
...
WELL, A DEAL'S A DEAL.
HERE.
TOKYO-TO, SHINJUKU-KU
IWANISHI AGENCY
BUT DON'T FORGET THIS, JUNYA.
THESE PEOPLE LIVE IN A DIFFERENT WORLD WITH DIFFERENT RULES.
PLEASE ...

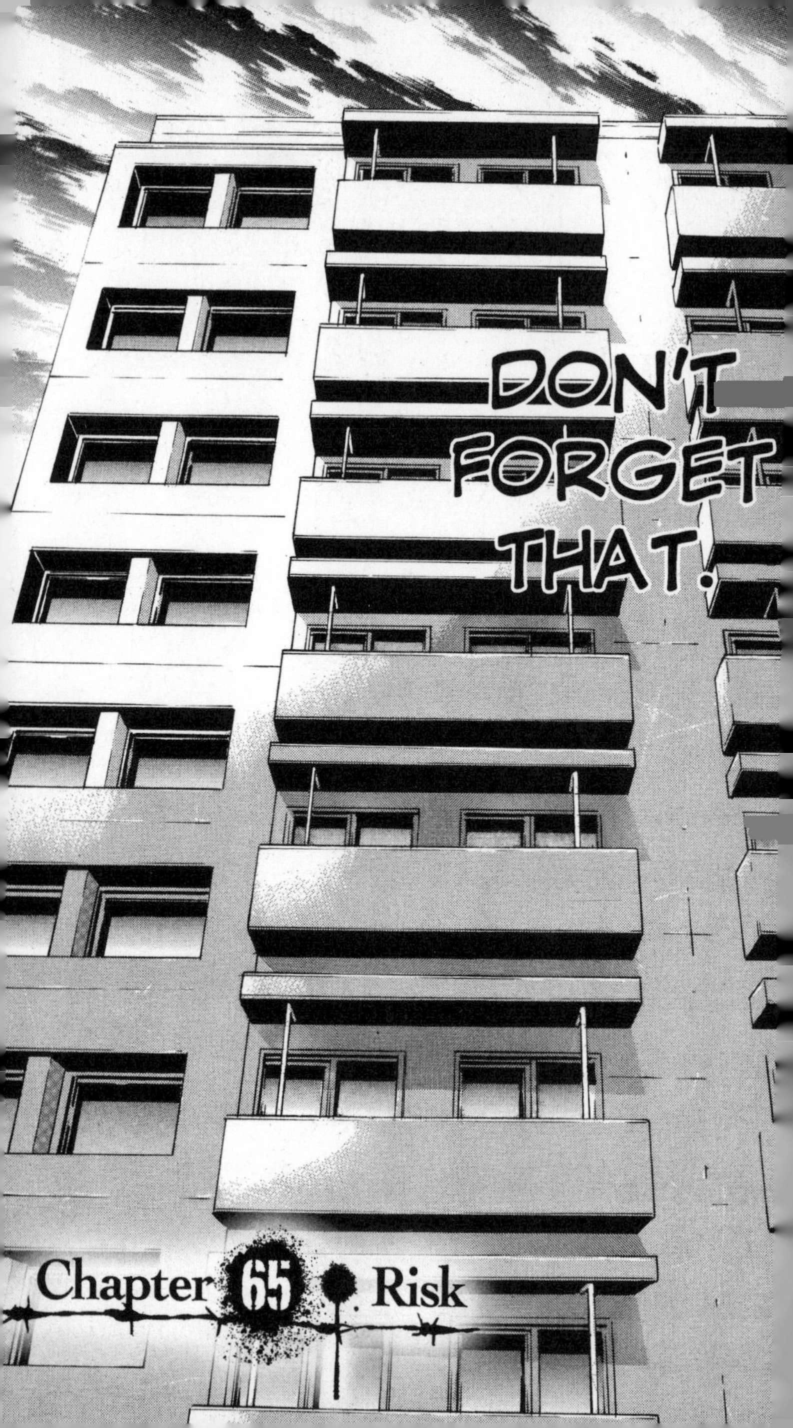
DON'T FORGET THAT!
Chapter 65 Risk

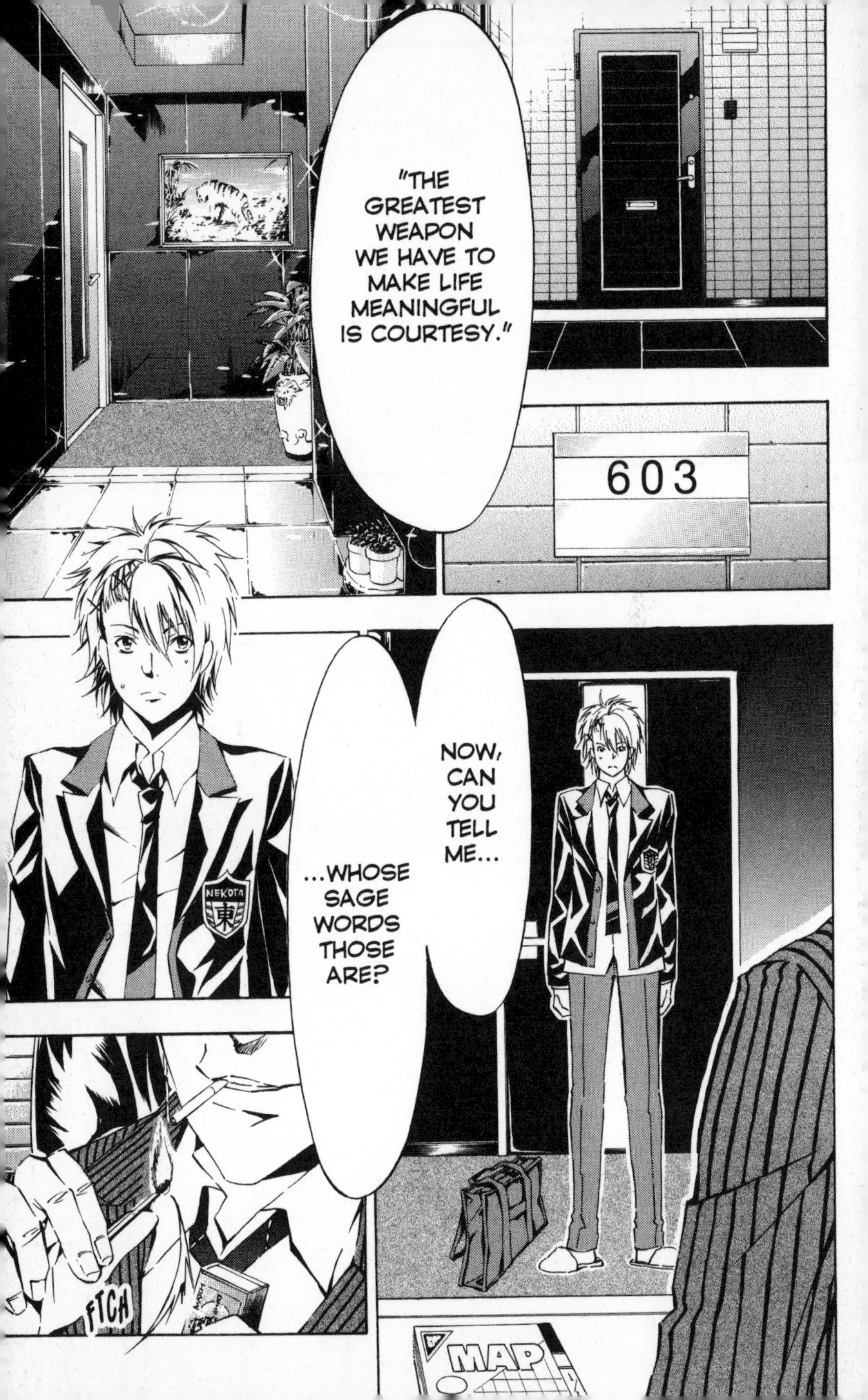
"THE GREATEST WEAPON WE HAVE TO MAKE LIFE MEANINGFUL IS COURTESY."
603
NOW, CAN YOU TELL ME...
...WHOSE SAGE WORDS THOSE ARE?
NEKOTA
FTCH
MAP

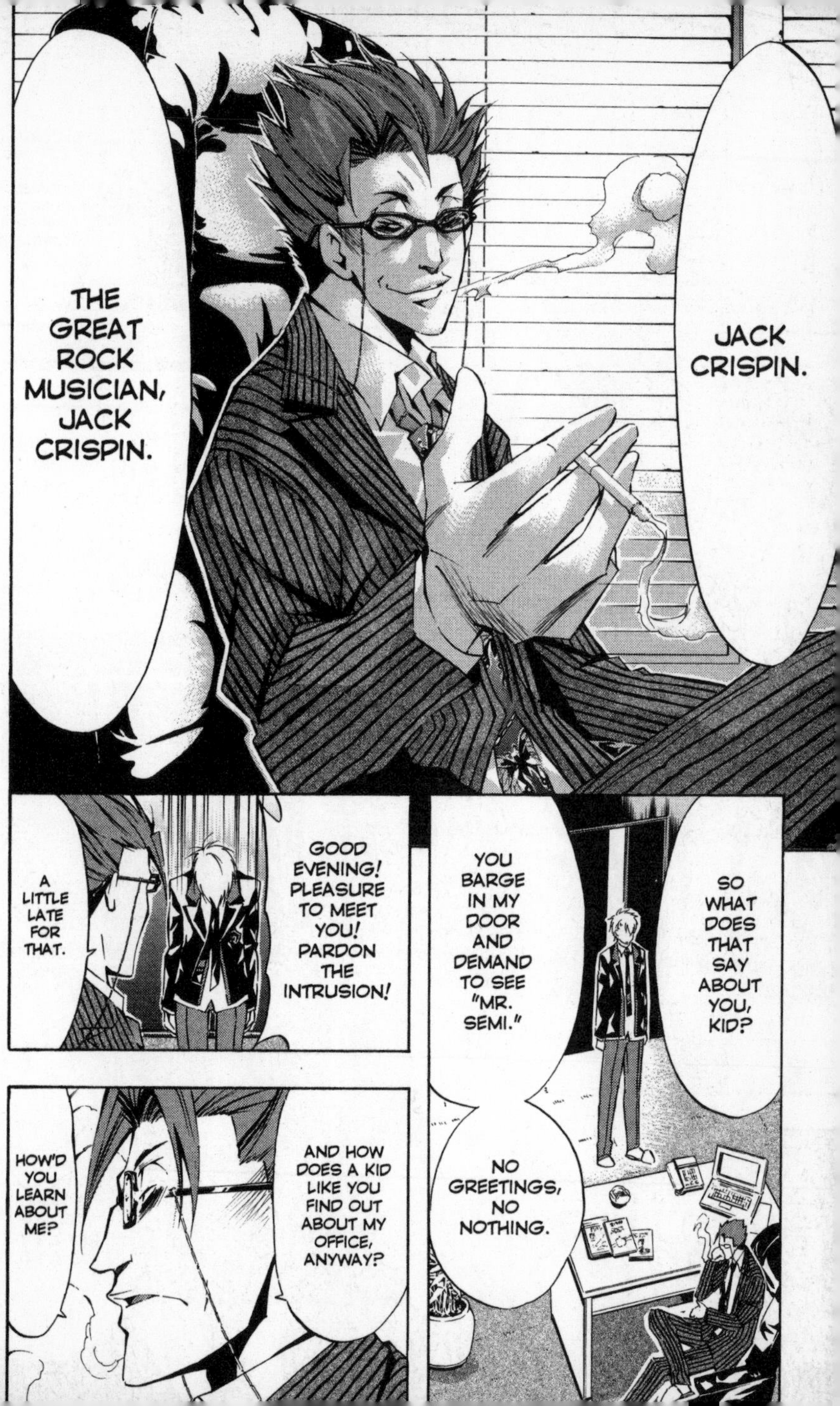
THE GREAT ROCK MUSICIAN, JACK CRISPIN.
JACK CRISPIN.
GOOD EVENING! PLEASURE TO MEET YOU! PARDON THE INTRUSION!
A LITTLE LATE FOR THAT.
YOU BARGE IN MY DOOR AND DEMAND TO SEE "MR. SEMI."
NO GREETINGS, NO NOTHING.
SO WHAT DOES THAT SAY ABOUT YOU, KID?
AND HOW DOES A KID LIKE YOU FIND OUT ABOUT MY OFFICE, ANYWAY?
HOW'D YOU LEARN ABOUT ME?

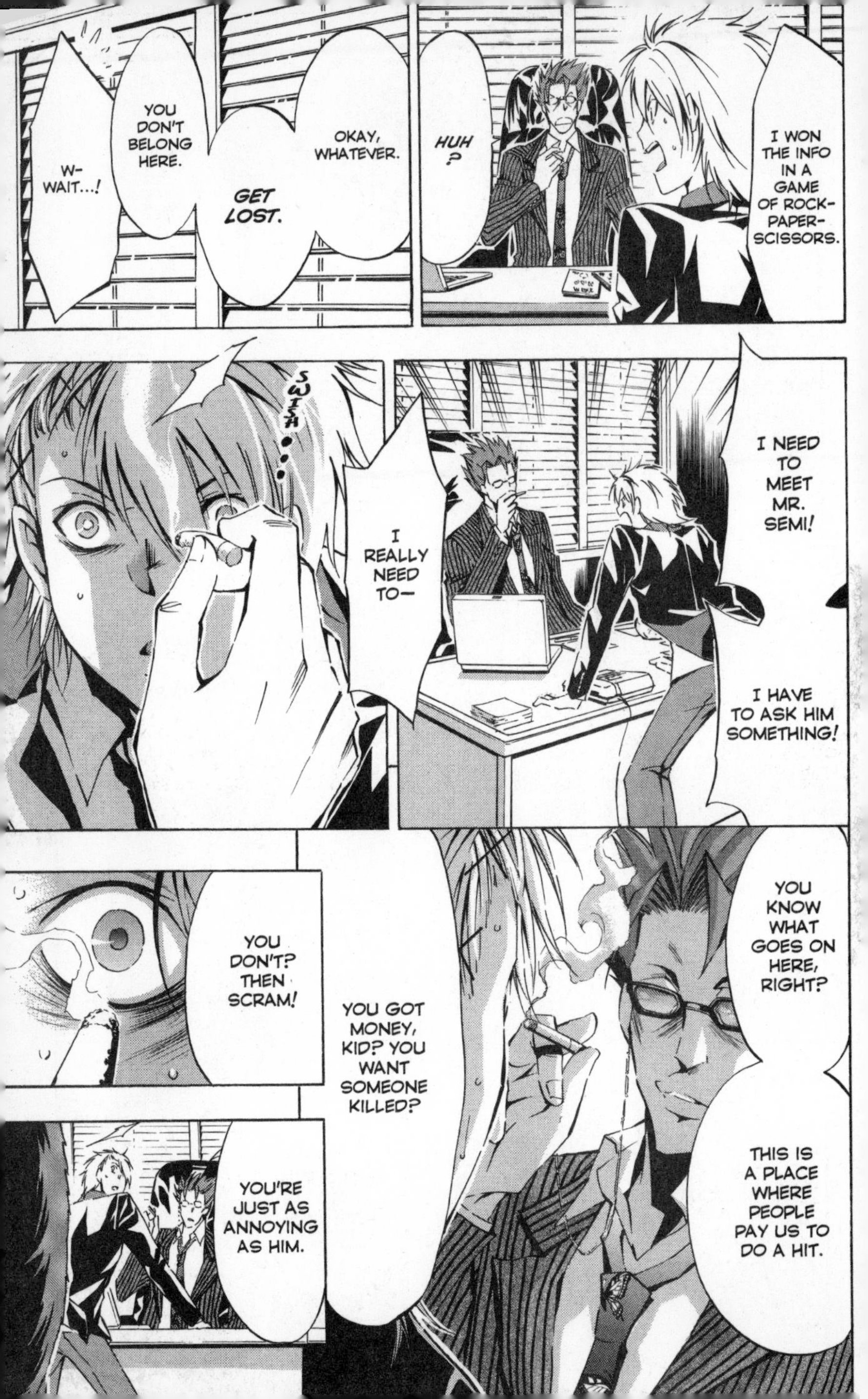
I WON THE INFO IN A GAME OF ROCK-PAPER-SCISSORS.
HUH?
OKAY, WHATEVER.
GET LOST.
YOU DON'T BELONG HERE.
W-WAIT...!
I NEED TO MEET MR. SEMI!
I HAVE TO ASK HIM SOMETHING!
I REALLY NEED TO—
SWISH...
YOU KNOW WHAT GOES ON HERE, RIGHT?
THIS IS A PLACE WHERE PEOPLE PAY US TO DO A HIT.
YOU GOT MONEY, KID? YOU WANT SOMEONE KILLED?
YOU DON'T? THEN SCRAM!
YOU'RE JUST AS ANNOYING AS HIM.

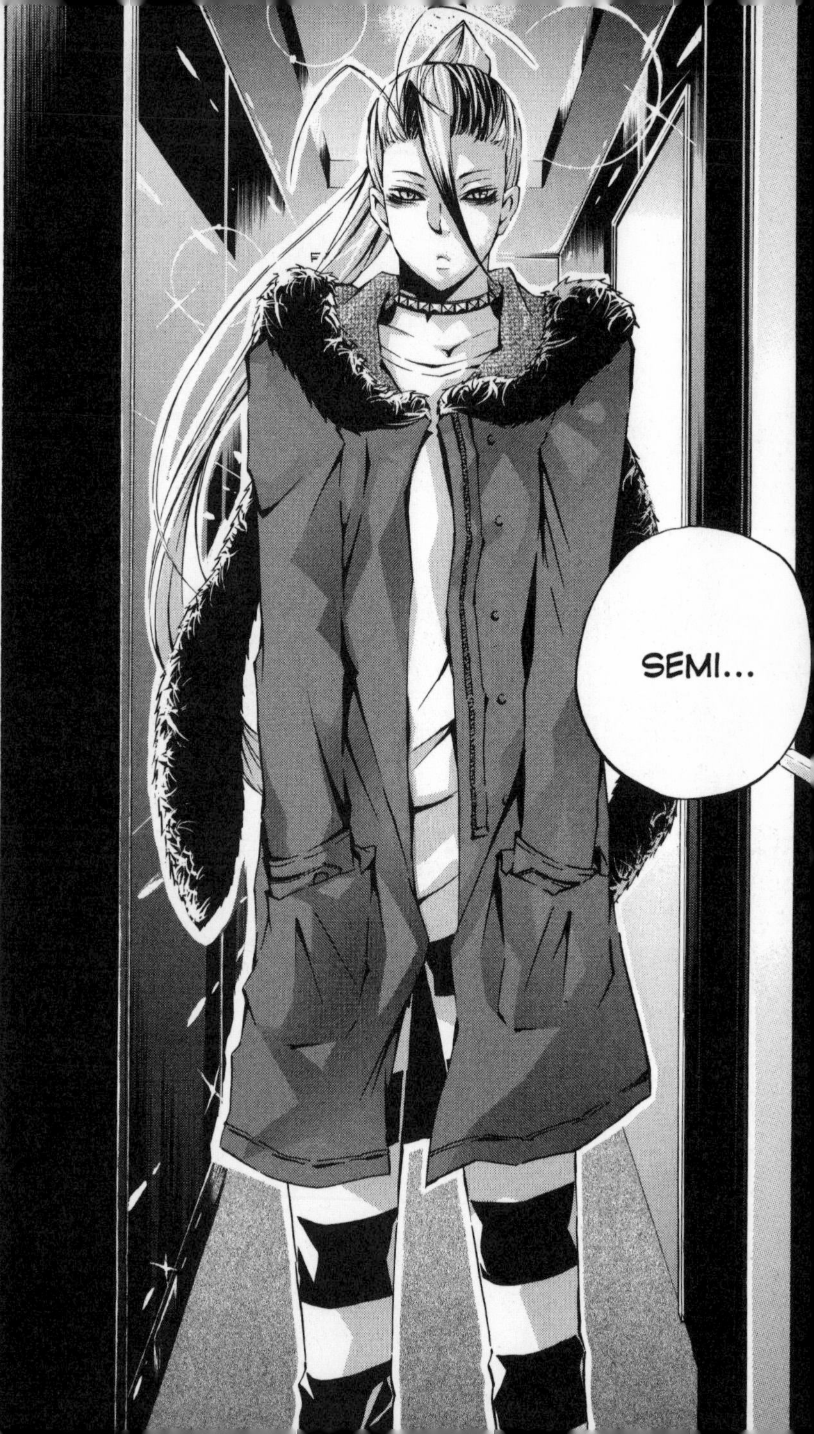
SEMI...

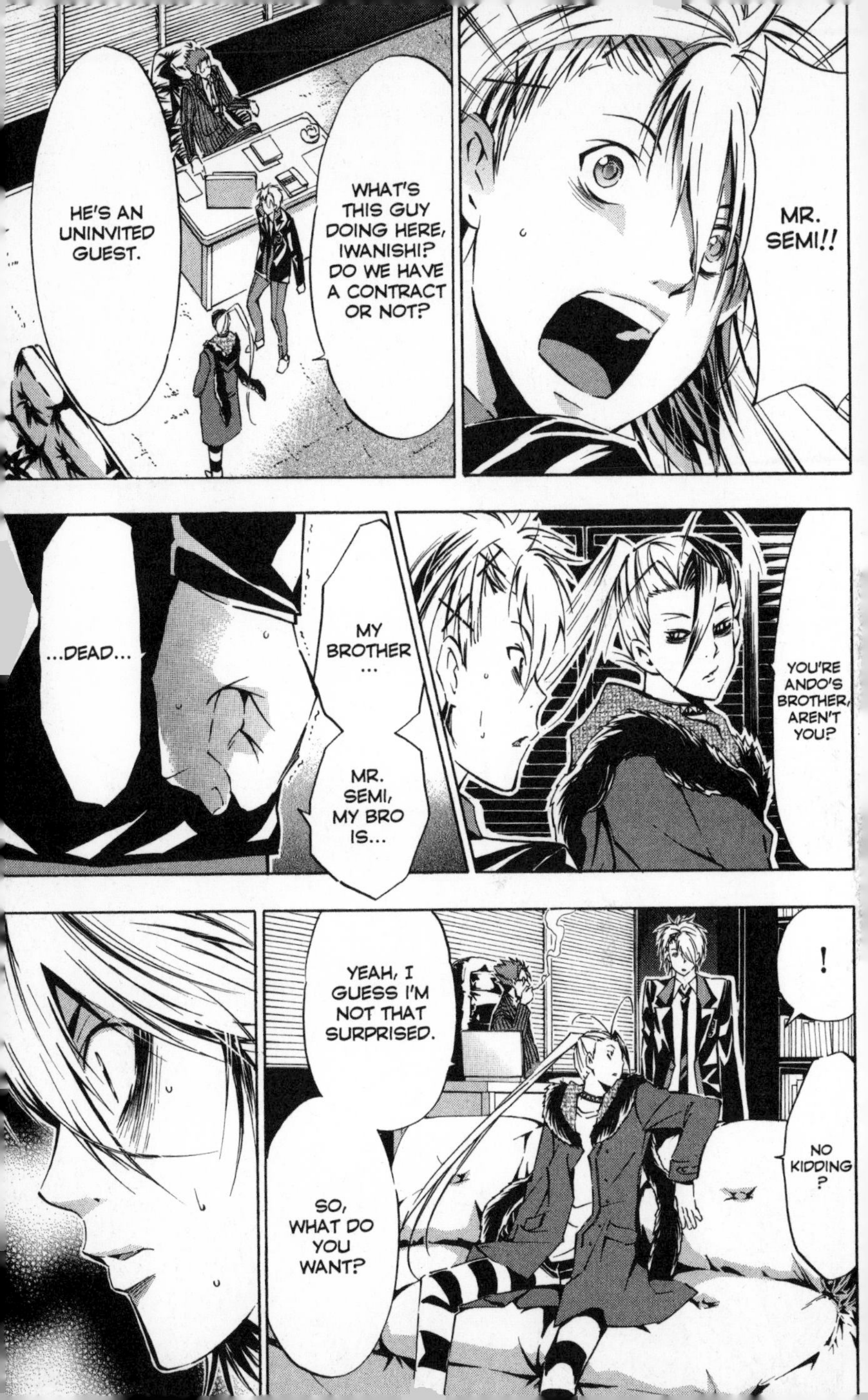
MR. SEMI!!
WHAT'S THIS GUY DOING HERE, IWANISHI? DO WE HAVE A CONTRACT OR NOT?
HE'S AN UNINVITED GUEST.
YOU'RE ANDO'S BROTHER, AREN'T YOU?
MY BROTHER ...
MR. SEMI, MY BRO IS...
...DEAD...
!
NO KIDDING?
YEAH, I GUESS I'M NOT THAT SURPRISED.
SO, WHAT DO YOU WANT?

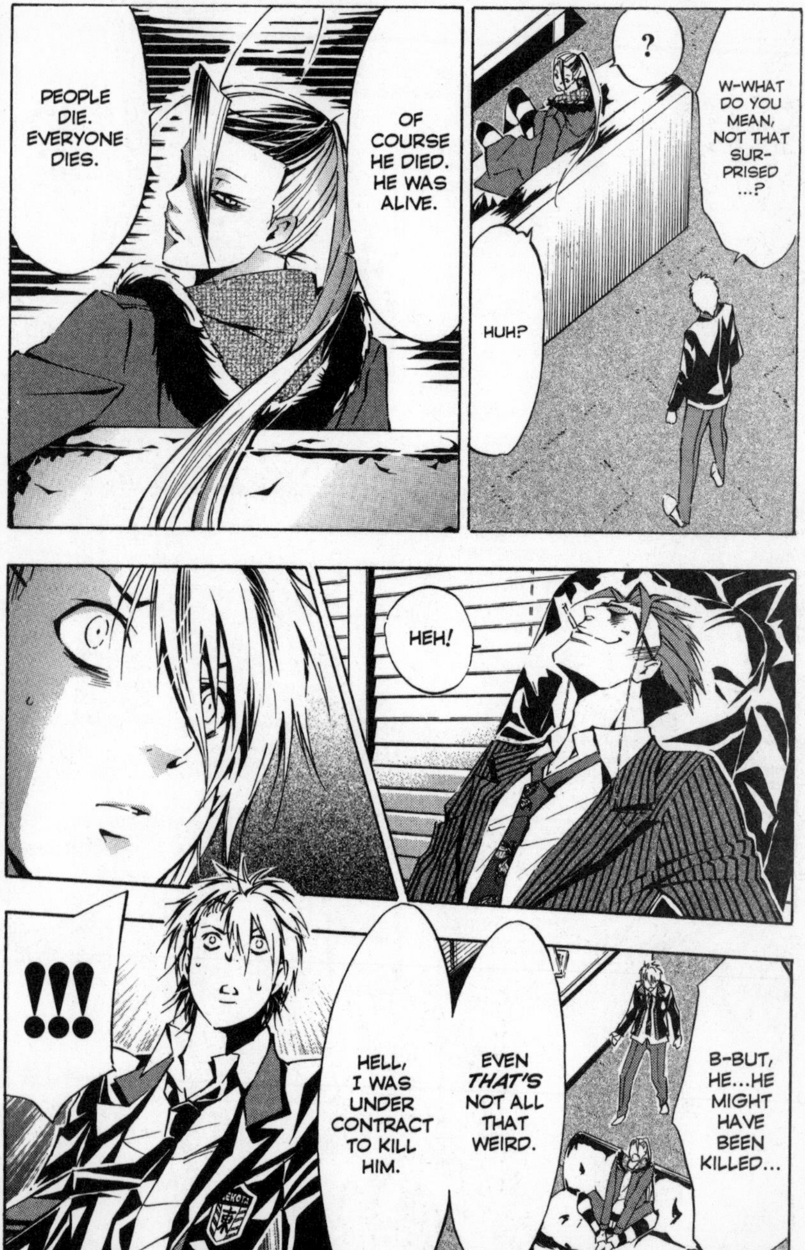
W-WHAT DO YOU MEAN, NOT THAT SUR-PRISED ...?
?
HUH?
OF COURSE HE DIED. HE WAS ALIVE.
PEOPLE DIE. EVERYONE DIES.
HEH!
B-BUT, HE...HE MIGHT HAVE BEEN KILLED...
EVEN *THAT'S* NOT ALL THAT WEIRD.
HELL, I WAS UNDER CONTRACT TO KILL HIM.
!!!

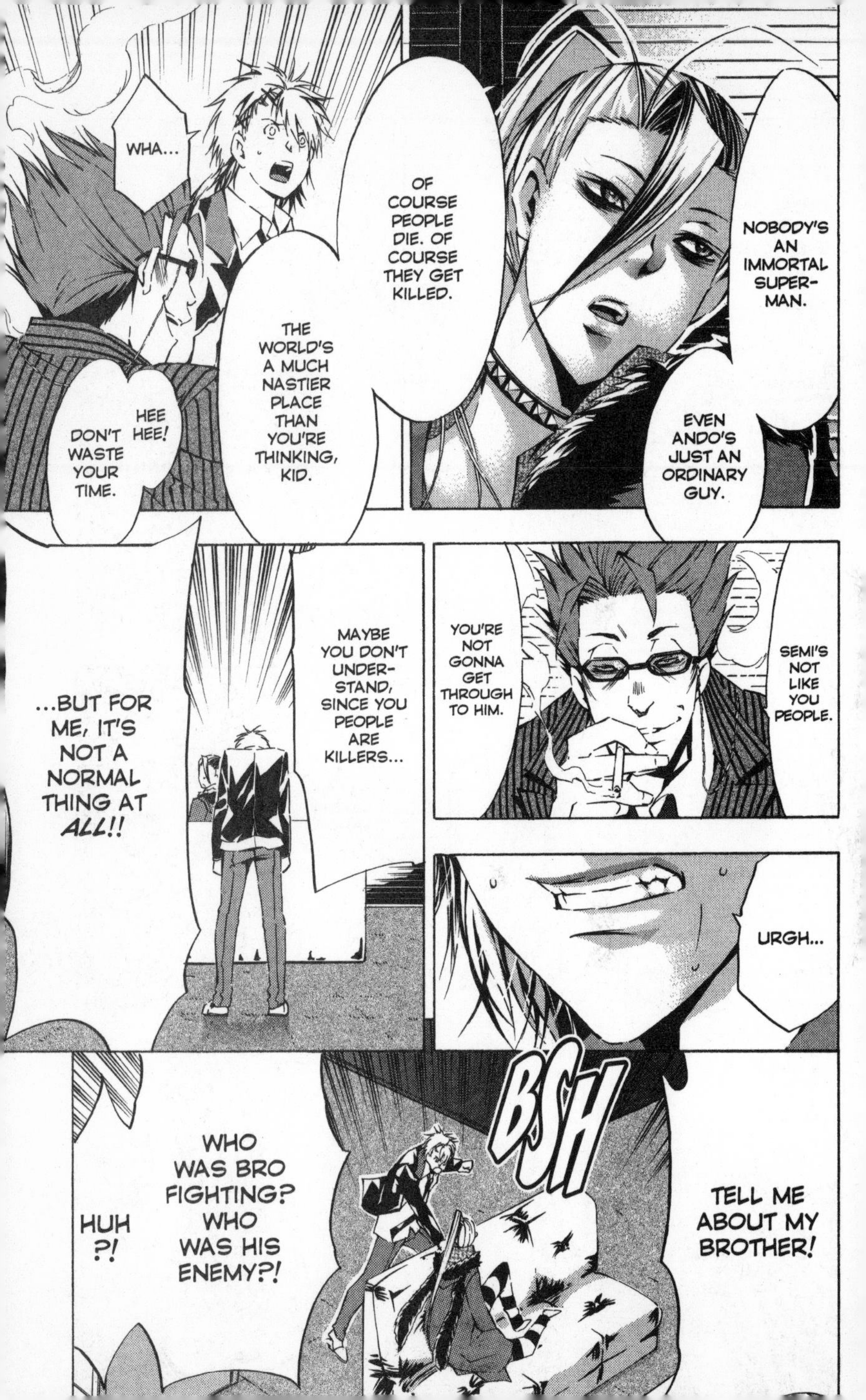
NOBODY'S AN IMMORTAL SUPER-MAN.
EVEN ANDO'S JUST AN ORDINARY GUY.
OF COURSE PEOPLE DIE. OF COURSE THEY GET KILLED.
THE WORLD'S A MUCH NASTIER PLACE THAN YOU'RE THINKING, KID.
WHA...
HEE HEE! DON'T WASTE YOUR TIME.
SEMI'S NOT LIKE YOU PEOPLE.
YOU'RE NOT GONNA GET THROUGH TO HIM.
URGH...
MAYBE YOU DON'T UNDER-STAND, SINCE YOU PEOPLE ARE KILLERS...
...BUT FOR ME, IT'S NOT A NORMAL THING AT ALL!!
TELL ME ABOUT MY BROTHER!
BSH
WHO WAS BRO FIGHTING? WHO WAS HIS ENEMY?!
HUH ?!

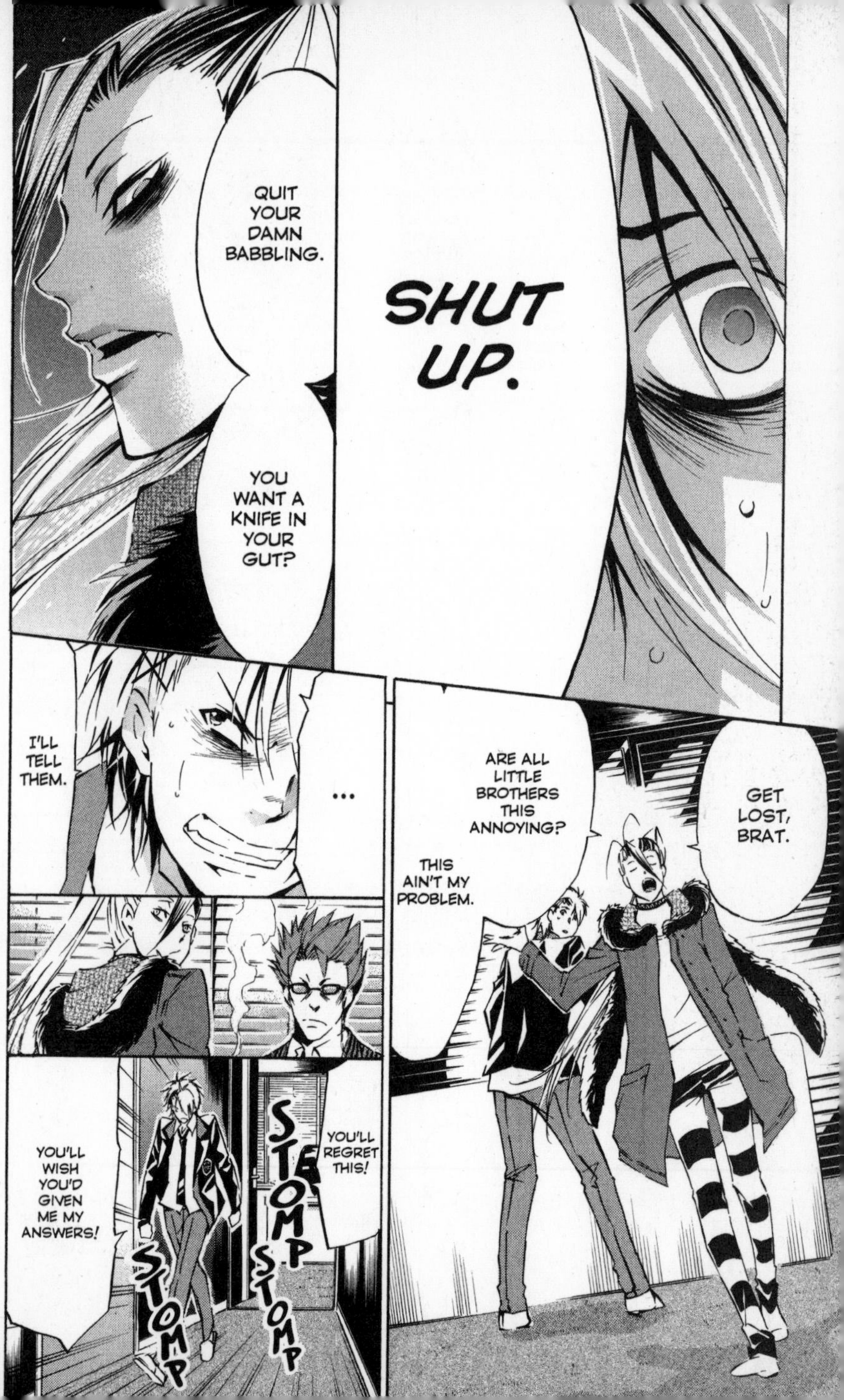
SHUT UP.
QUIT YOUR DAMN BABBLING.
YOU WANT A KNIFE IN YOUR GUT?
GET LOST, BRAT.
ARE ALL LITTLE BROTHERS THIS ANNOYING?
THIS AIN'T MY PROBLEM.
...
I'LL TELL THEM.
YOU'LL REGRET THIS!
STOMP
STOMP
YOU'LL WISH YOU'D GIVEN ME MY ANSWERS!
STOMP
STOMP

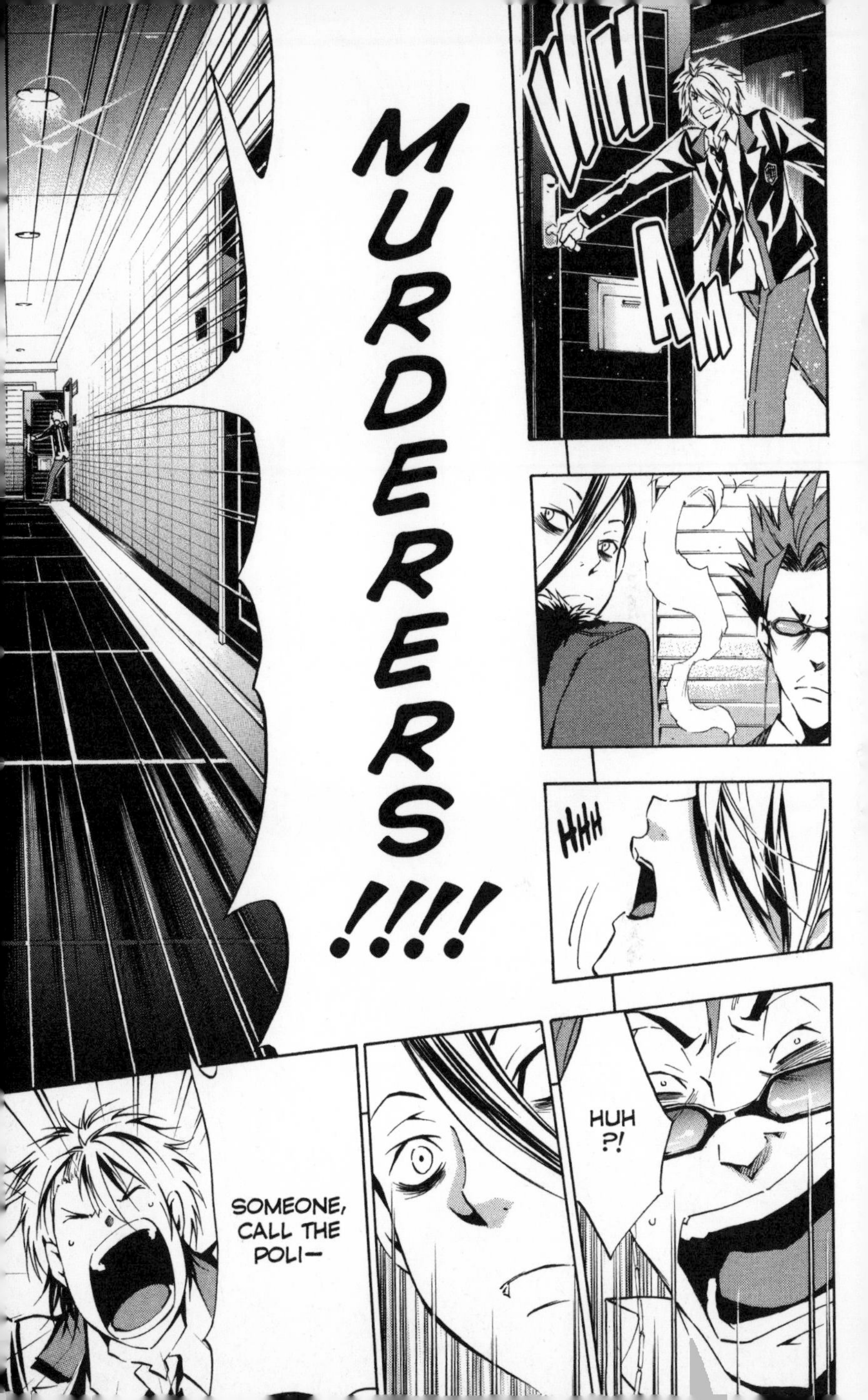
WHAM
HHH
MURDERERS!!!!
HUH ?!
SOMEONE, CALL THE POLI—

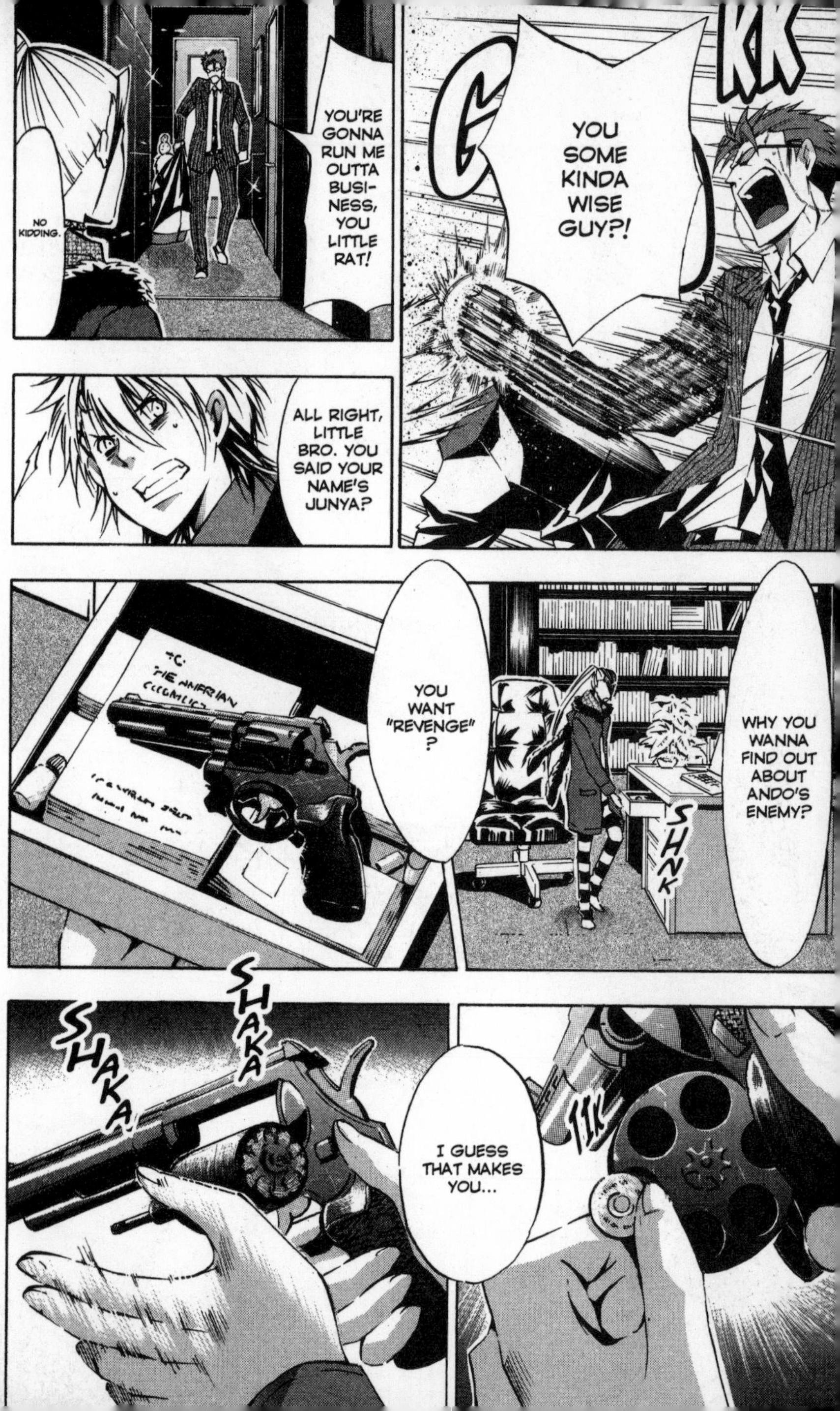

KK
YOU SOME KINDA WISE GUY?!
YOU'RE GONNA RUN ME OUTTA BUSI-NESS, YOU LITTLE RAT!
NO KIDDING.
ALL RIGHT, LITTLE BRO. YOU SAID YOUR NAME'S JUNYA?
WHY YOU WANNA FIND OUT ABOUT ANDO'S ENEMY?
SHNK
YOU WANT "REVENGE"?
I GUESS THAT MAKES YOU...
TIK
SHAKA
SHAKA

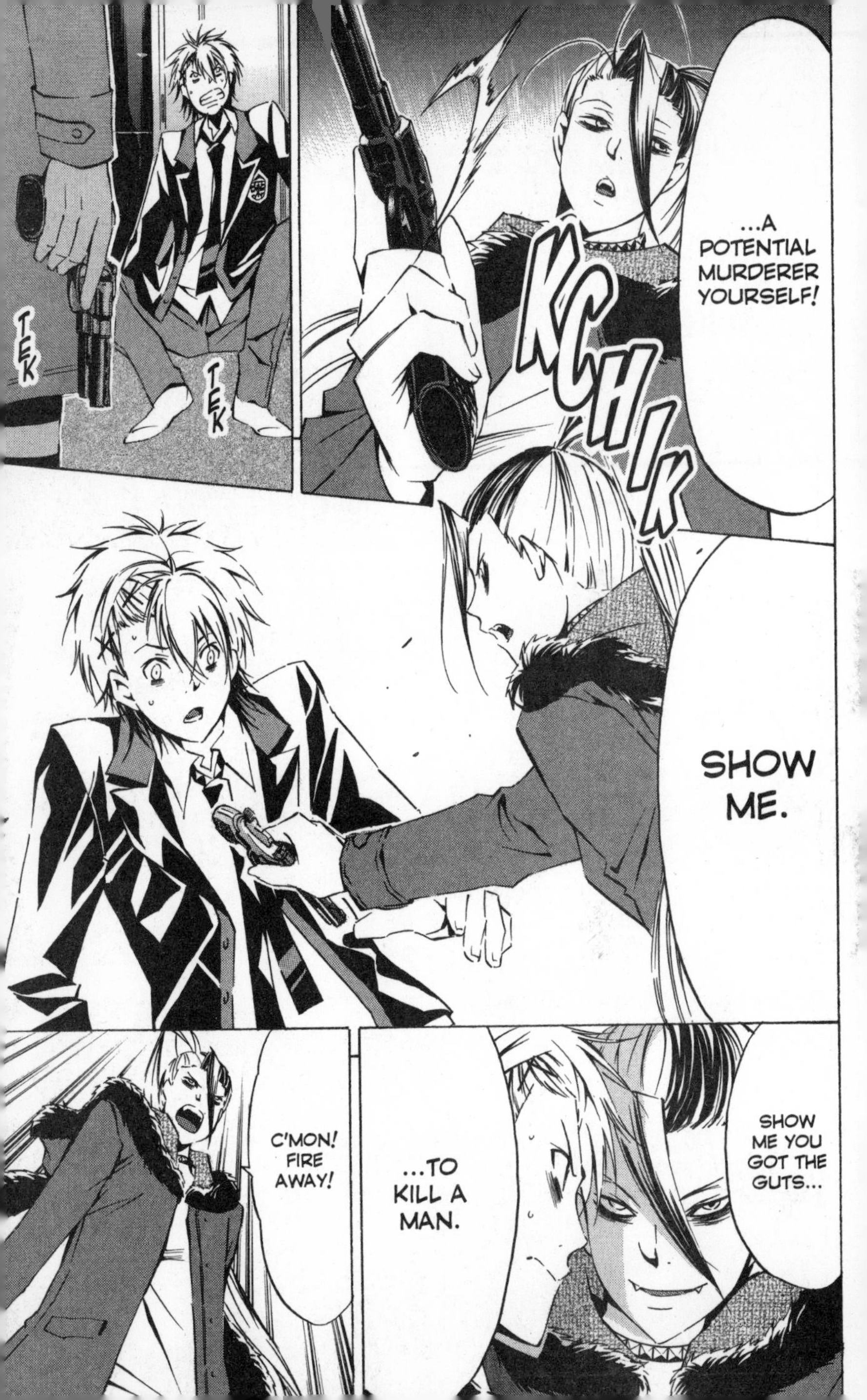
...A POTENTIAL MURDERER YOURSELF!
KCHIK
TEK
TEK
SHOW ME.
SHOW ME YOU GOT THE GUTS...
...TO KILL A MAN.
C'MON! FIRE AWAY!

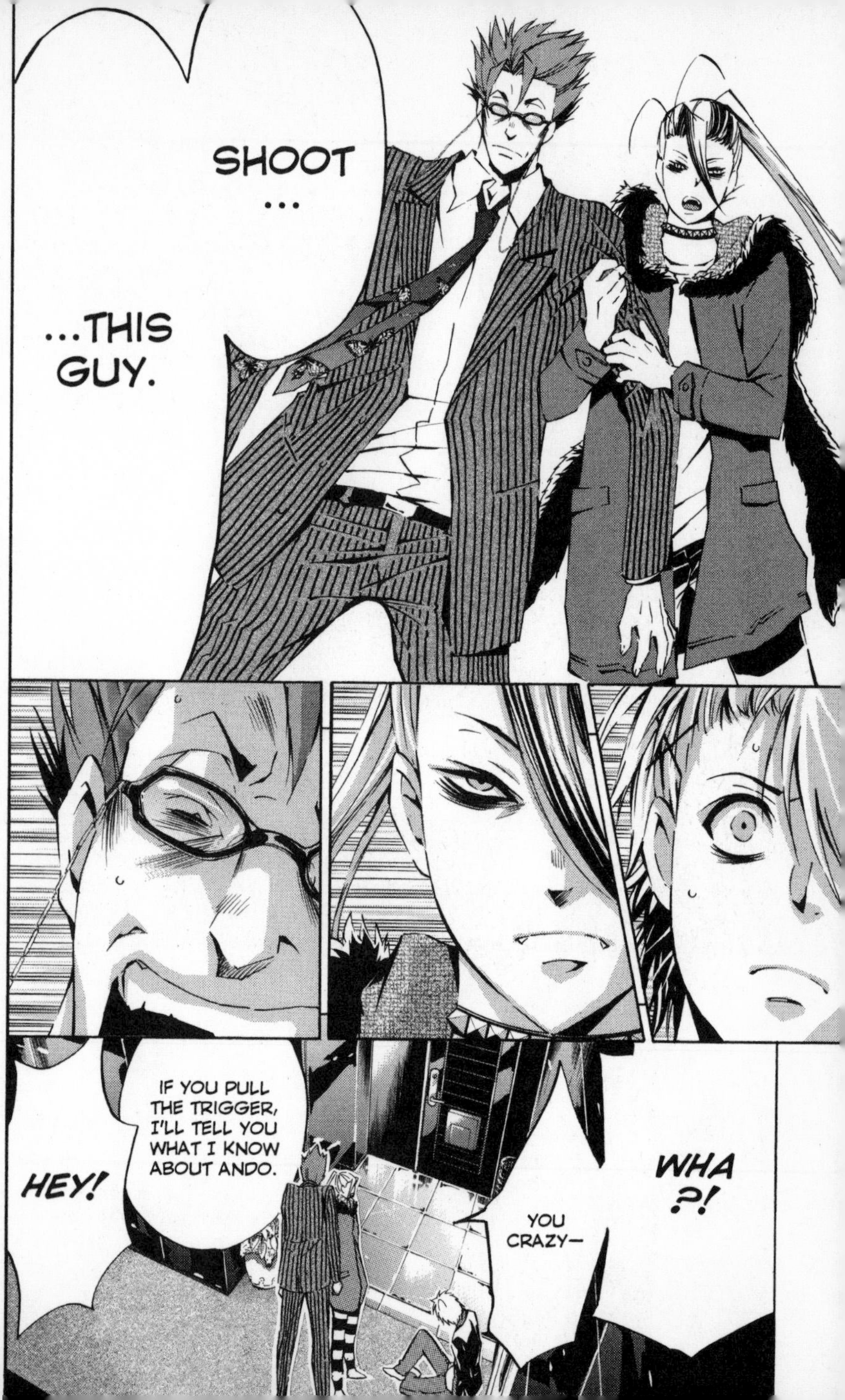
SHOOT ...
...THIS GUY.
WHA ?!
YOU CRAZY—
IF YOU PULL THE TRIGGER, I'LL TELL YOU WHAT I KNOW ABOUT ANDO.
HEY!

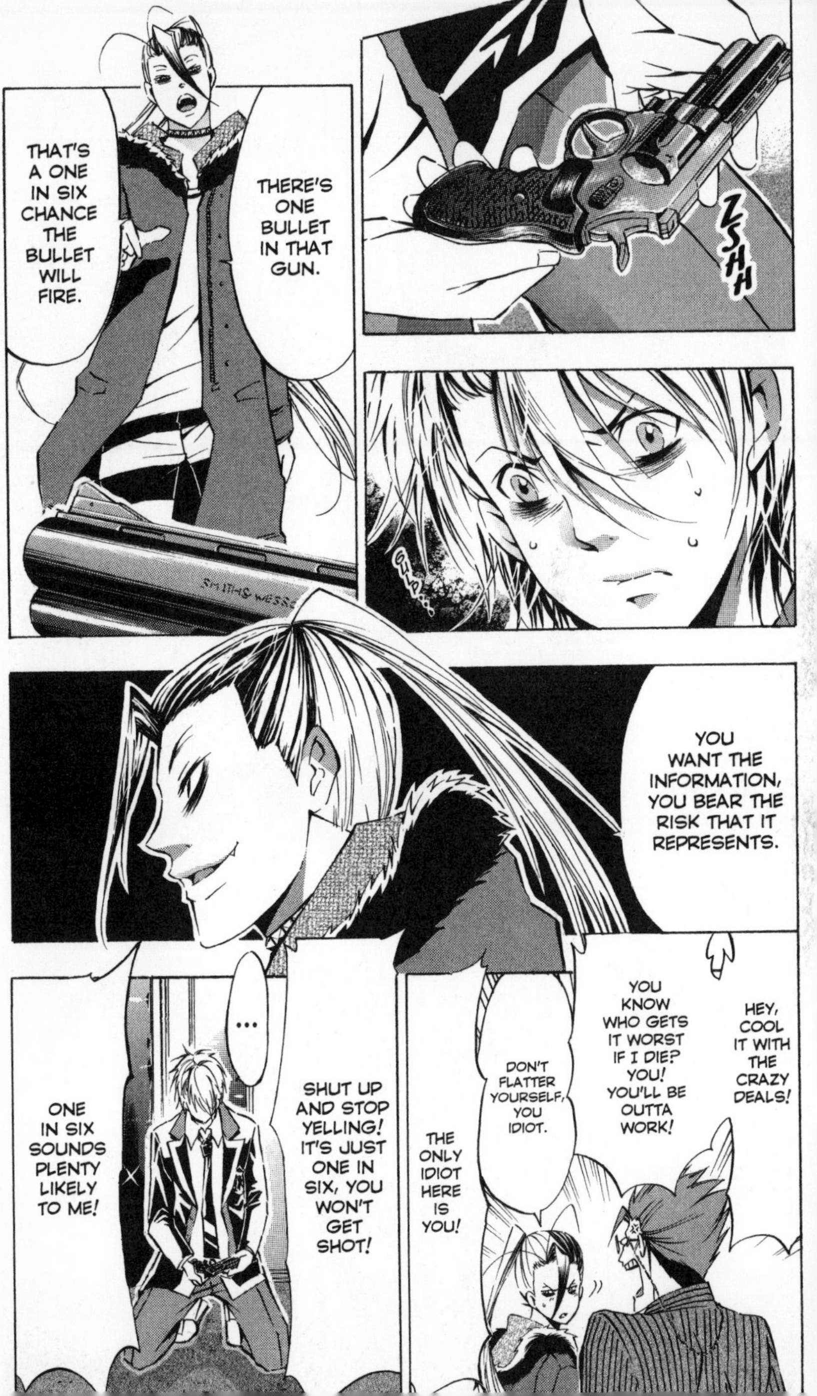
ZSHH
GULP...
THERE'S ONE BULLET IN THAT GUN.
THAT'S A ONE IN SIX CHANCE THE BULLET WILL FIRE.
YOU WANT THE INFORMATION, YOU BEAR THE RISK THAT IT REPRESENTS.
HEY, COOL IT WITH THE CRAZY DEALS!
YOU KNOW WHO GETS IT WORST IF I DIE? YOU! YOU'LL BE OUTTA WORK!
DON'T FLATTER YOURSELF, YOU IDIOT.
THE ONLY IDIOT HERE IS YOU!
SHUT UP AND STOP YELLING! IT'S JUST ONE IN SIX, YOU WON'T GET SHOT!
...
ONE IN SIX SOUNDS PLENTY LIKELY TO ME!

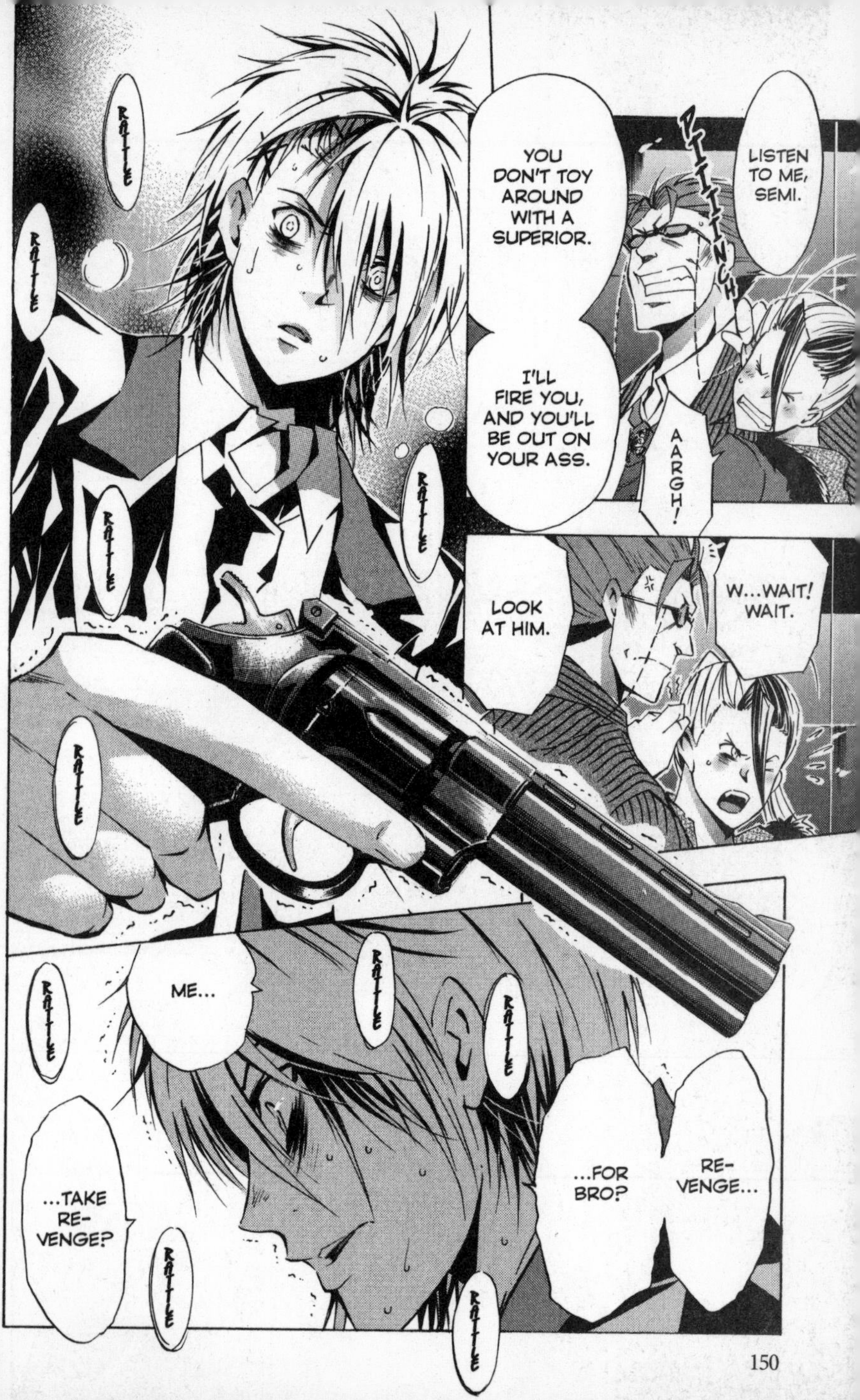
LISTEN TO ME, SEMI.
PIIIIINCH
YOU DON'T TOY AROUND WITH A SUPERIOR.
I'LL FIRE YOU, AND YOU'LL BE OUT ON YOUR ASS.
AARGH!
W...WAIT! WAIT.
LOOK AT HIM.
RATTLE
RATTLE
RATTLE
RATTLE
RATTLE
RATTLE
RE-VENGE...
...FOR BRO?
RATTLE
RATTLE
ME...
RATTLE
...TAKE RE-VENGE?
RATTLE
RATTLE

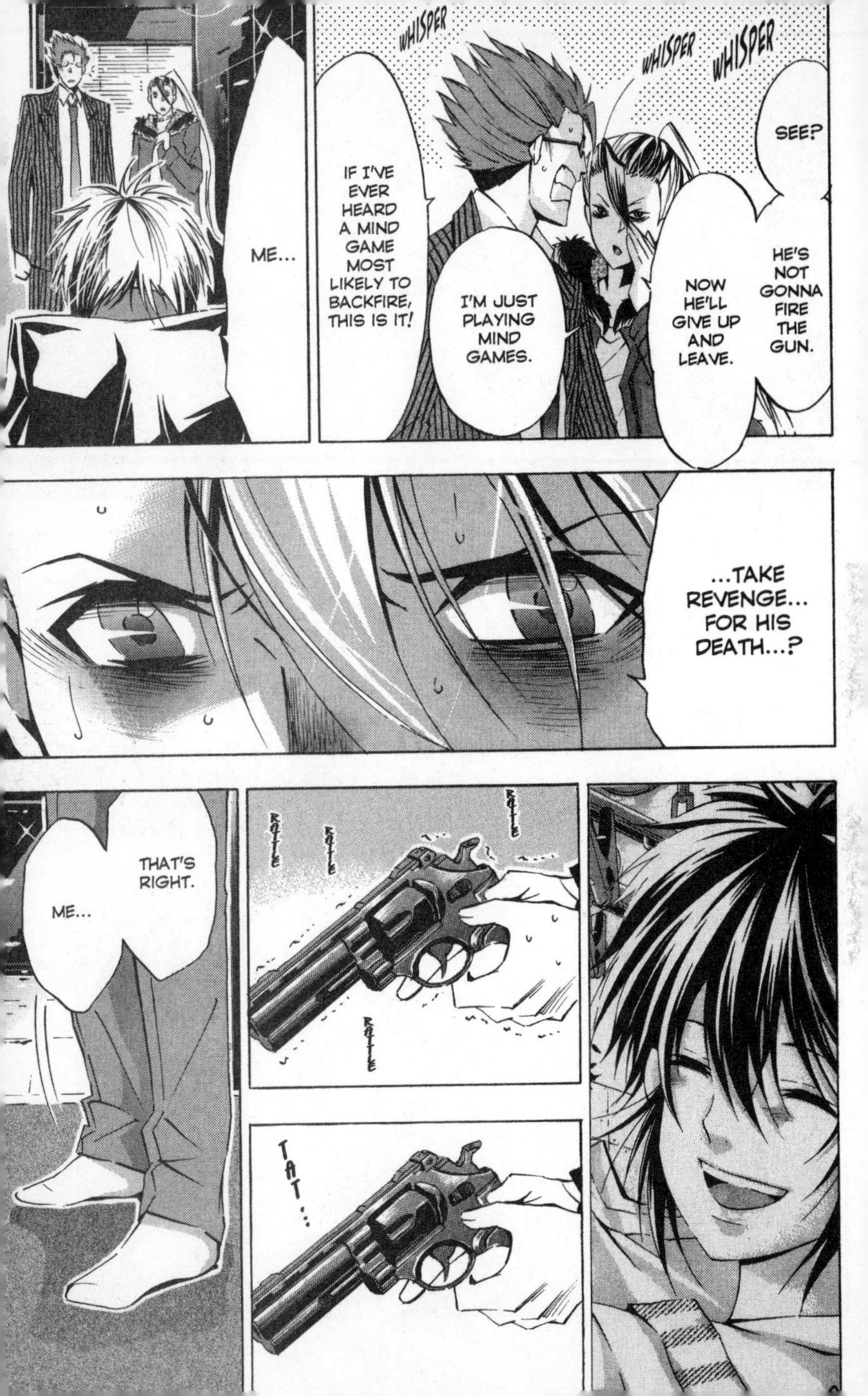
WHISPER
WHISPER
WHISPER
SEE?
HE'S NOT GONNA FIRE THE GUN.
NOW HE'LL GIVE UP AND LEAVE.
I'M JUST PLAYING MIND GAMES.
IF I'VE EVER HEARD A MIND GAME MOST LIKELY TO BACKFIRE, THIS IS IT!
ME...
...TAKE REVENGE... FOR HIS DEATH...?
RATTLE
RATTLE
RATTLE
RATTLE
TAT...
THAT'S RIGHT.
ME...

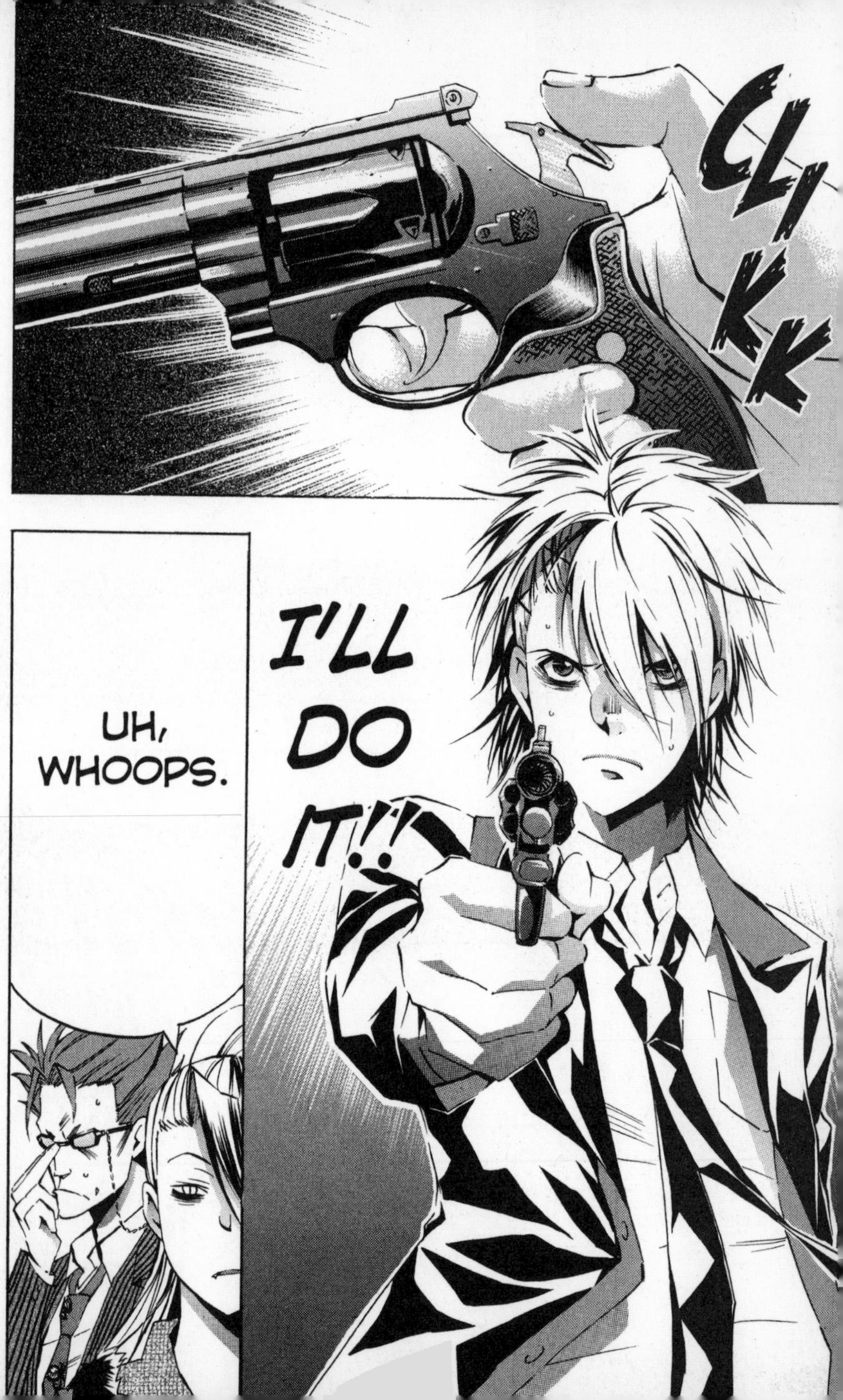
CLIKK
I'LL DO IT!!
UH, WHOOPS.

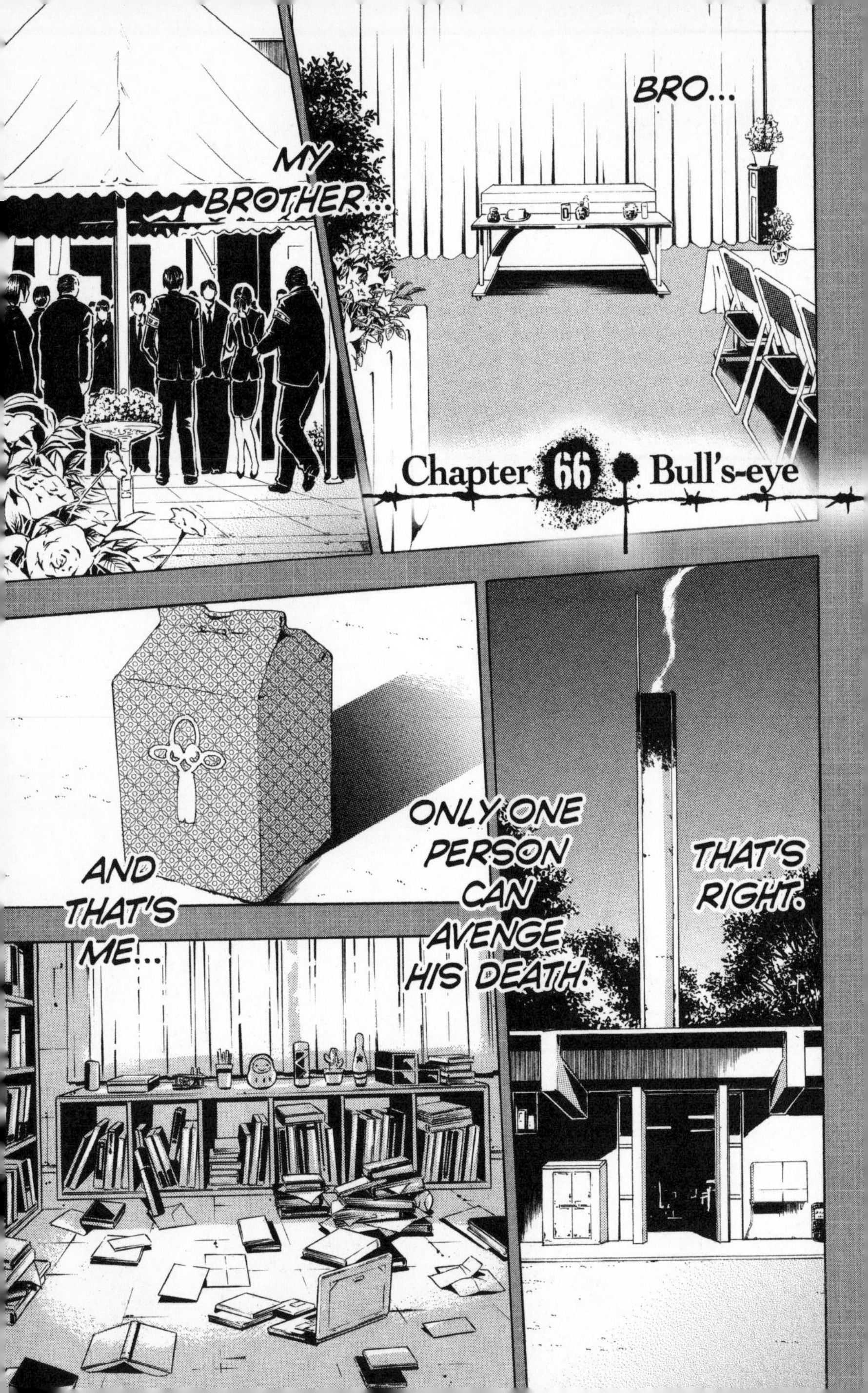
BRO...
Chapter 66 Bull's-eye
MY BROTHER...
THAT'S RIGHT.
ONLY ONE PERSON CAN AVENGE HIS DEATH.
AND THAT'S ME...

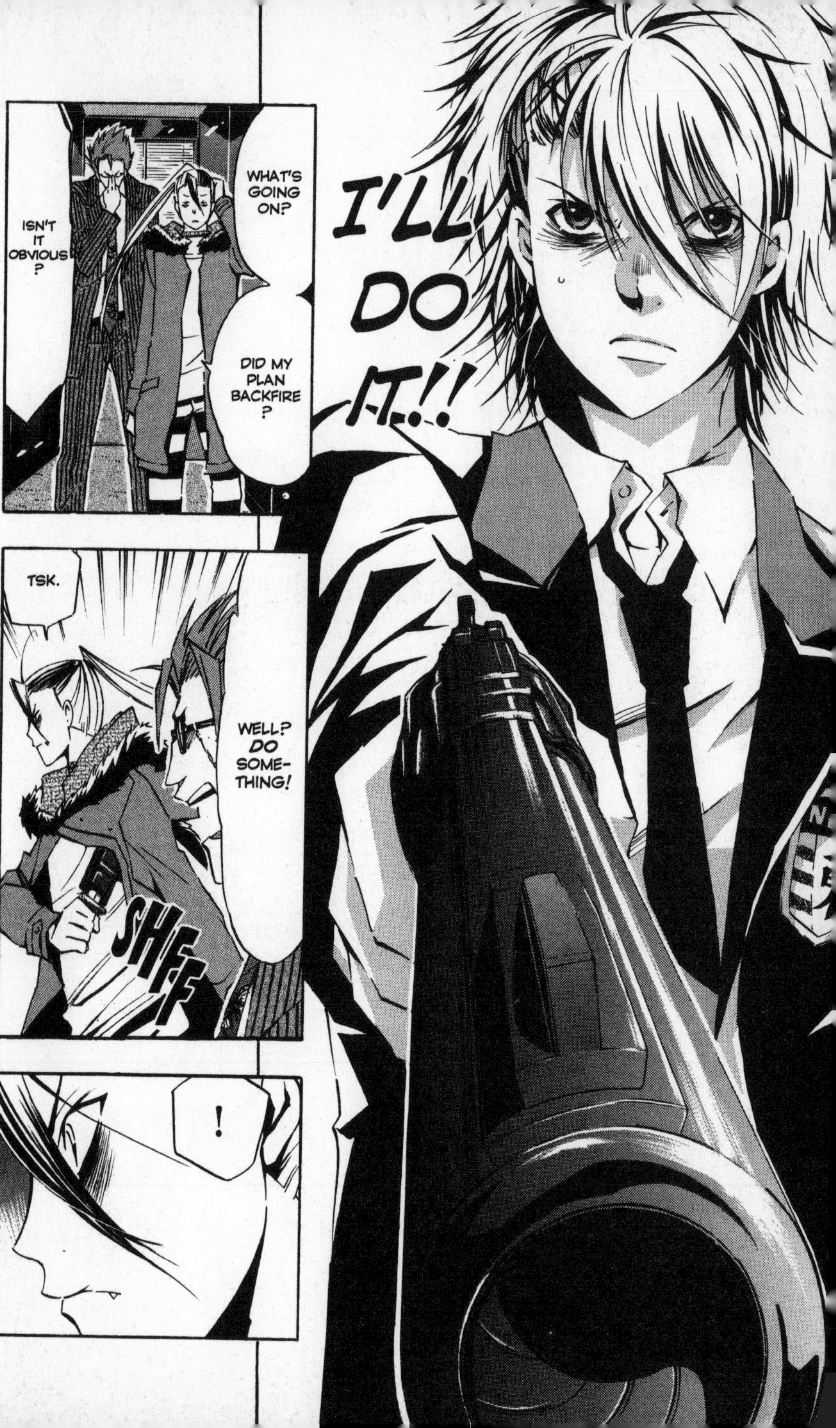
I'LL DO IT!!
WHAT'S GOING ON?
ISN'T IT OBVIOUS?
DID MY PLAN BACKFIRE?
WELL? DO SOMETHING!
TSK.
SHFF
!

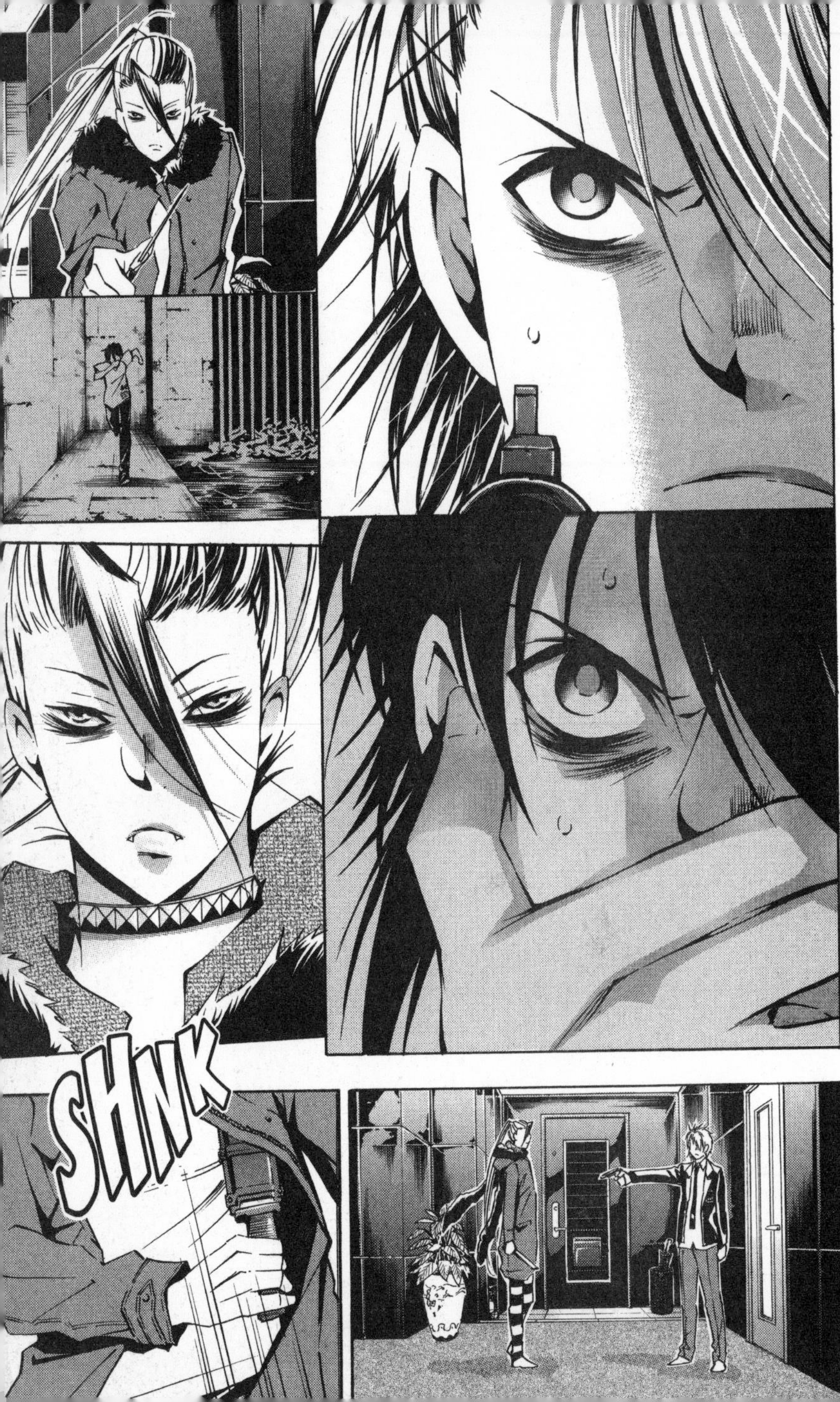
SHNK

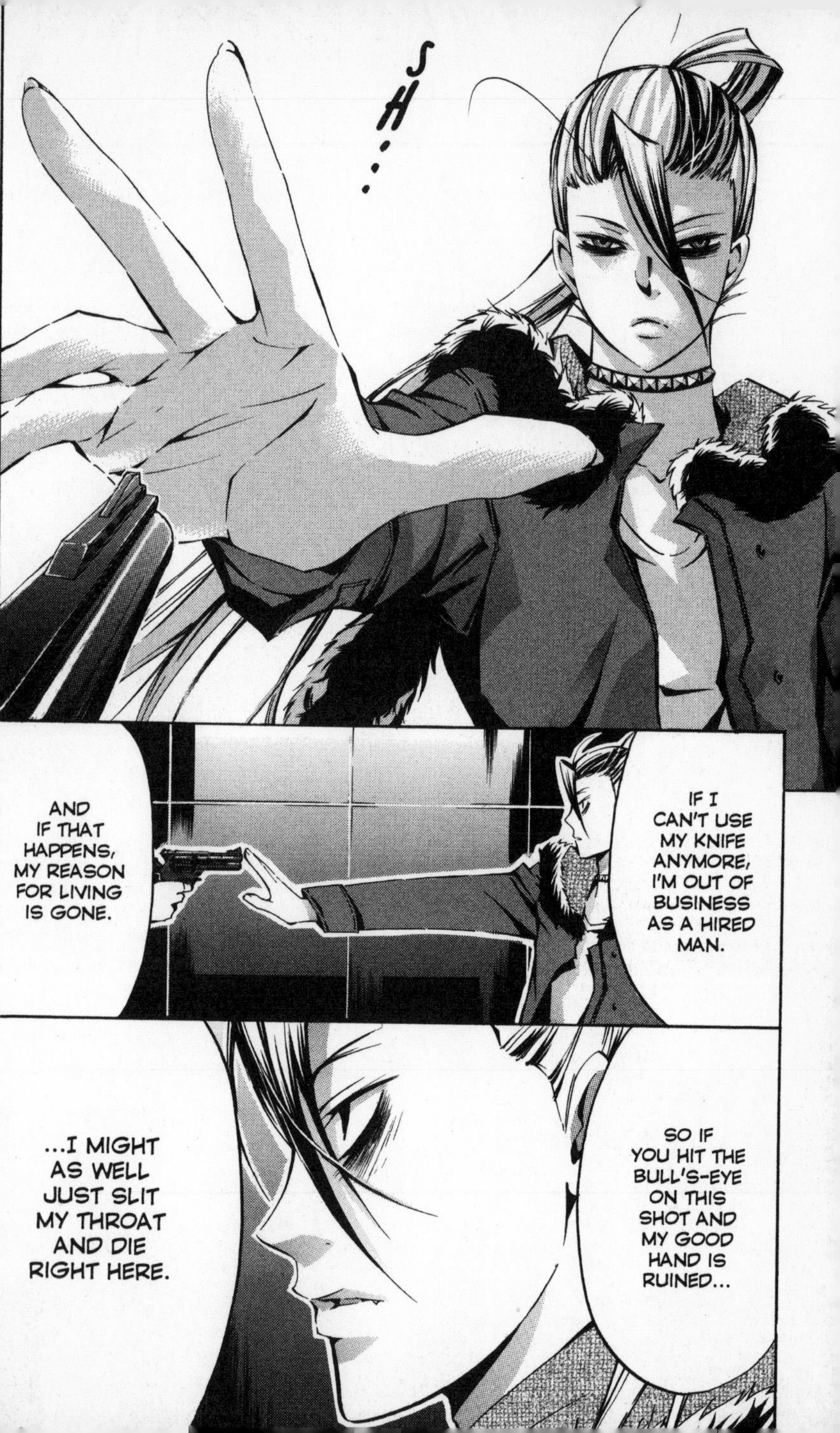
SH...
IF I CAN'T USE MY KNIFE ANYMORE, I'M OUT OF BUSINESS AS A HIRED MAN.
AND IF THAT HAPPENS, MY REASON FOR LIVING IS GONE.
SO IF YOU HIT THE BULL'S-EYE ON THIS SHOT AND MY GOOD HAND IS RUINED...
...I MIGHT AS WELL JUST SLIT MY THROAT AND DIE RIGHT HERE.

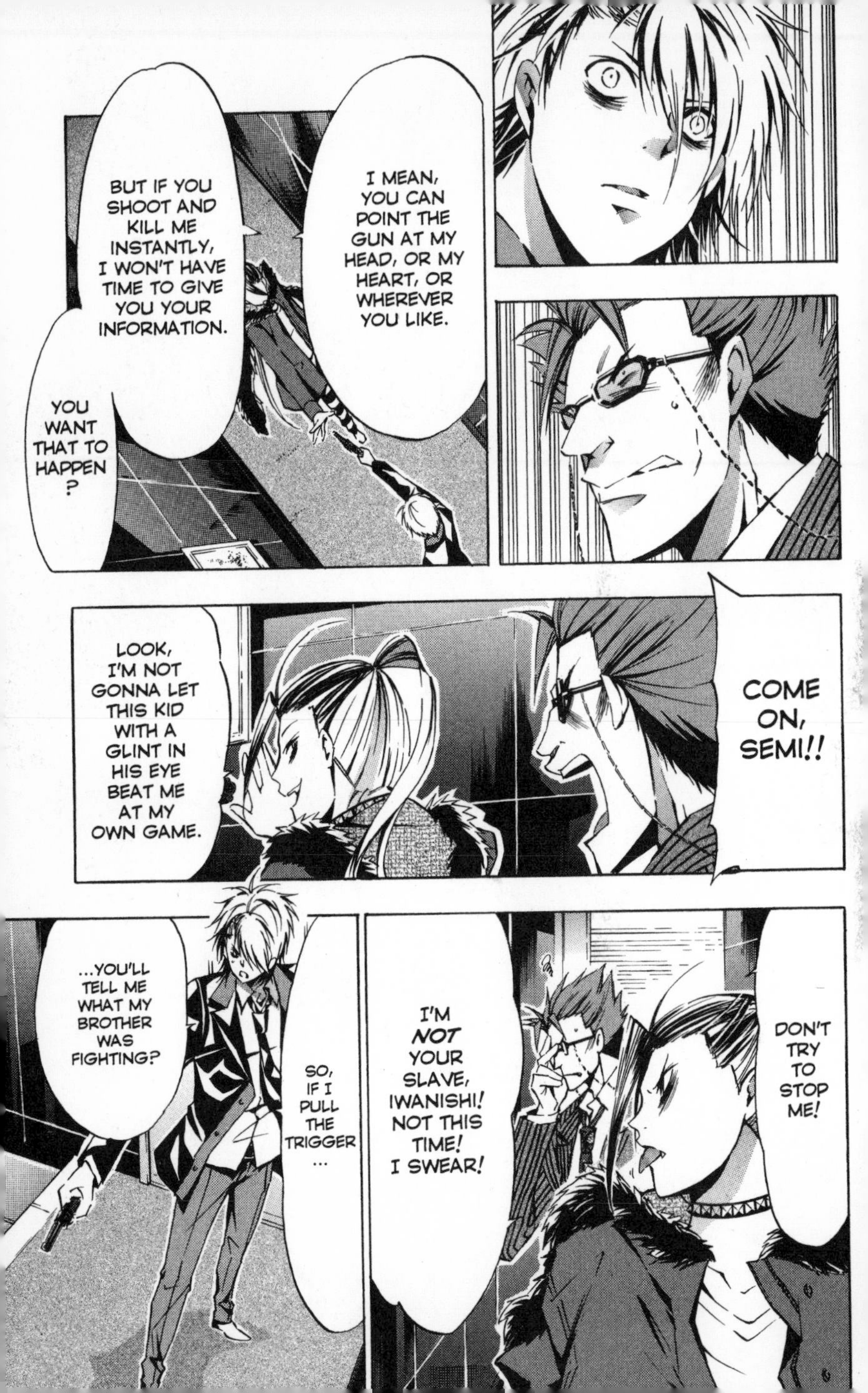
I MEAN, YOU CAN POINT THE GUN AT MY HEAD, OR MY HEART, OR WHEREVER YOU LIKE.
BUT IF YOU SHOOT AND KILL ME INSTANTLY, I WON'T HAVE TIME TO GIVE YOU YOUR INFORMATION.
YOU WANT THAT TO HAPPEN?
COME ON, SEMI!!
LOOK, I'M NOT GONNA LET THIS KID WITH A GLINT IN HIS EYE BEAT ME AT MY OWN GAME.
DON'T TRY TO STOP ME!
I'M *NOT* YOUR SLAVE, IWANISHI! NOT THIS TIME! I SWEAR!
SO, IF I PULL THE TRIGGER...
...YOU'LL TELL ME WHAT MY BROTHER WAS FIGHTING?

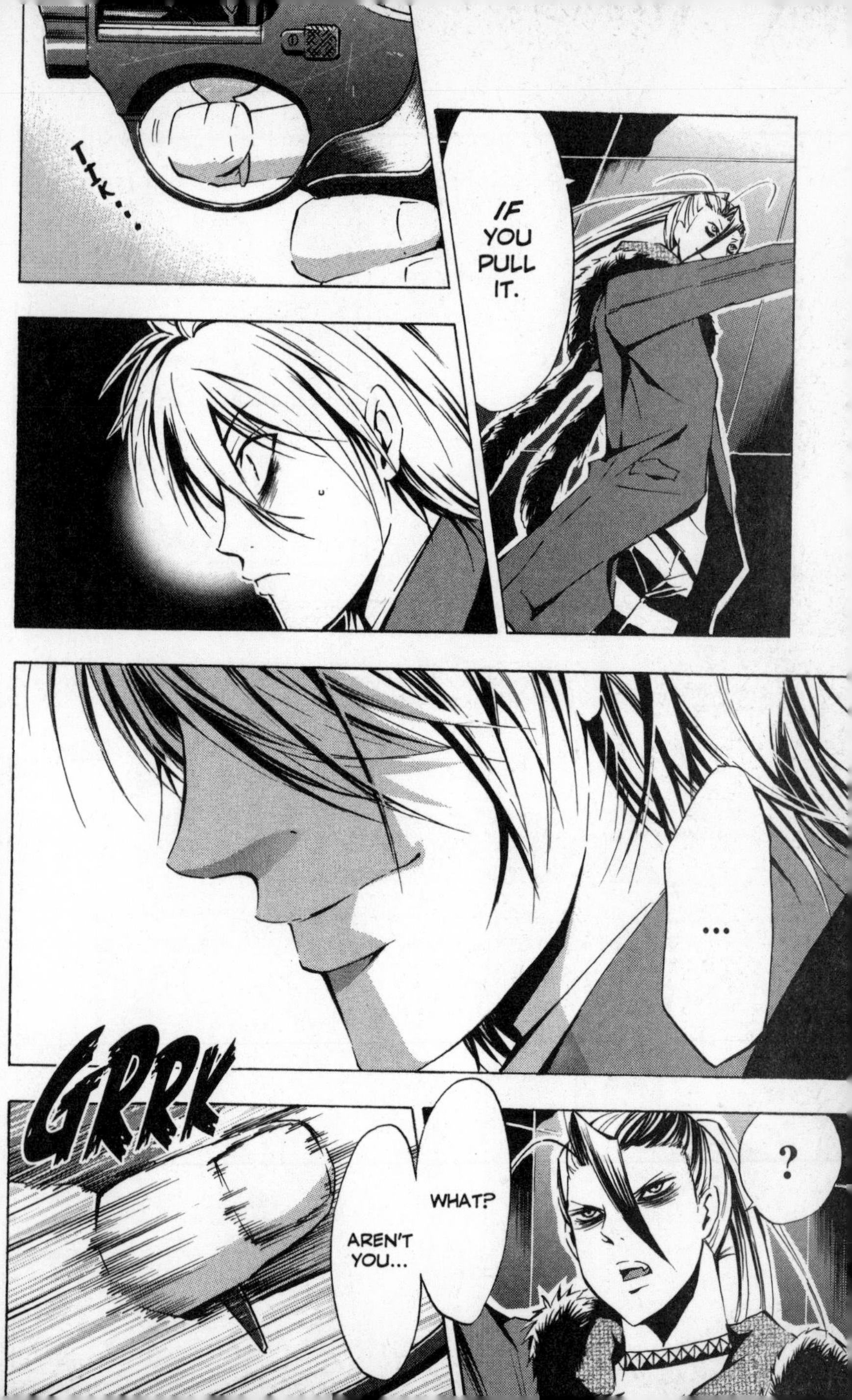
IF YOU PULL IT.
TIIK...
...
?
WHAT? AREN'T YOU...
GRRK

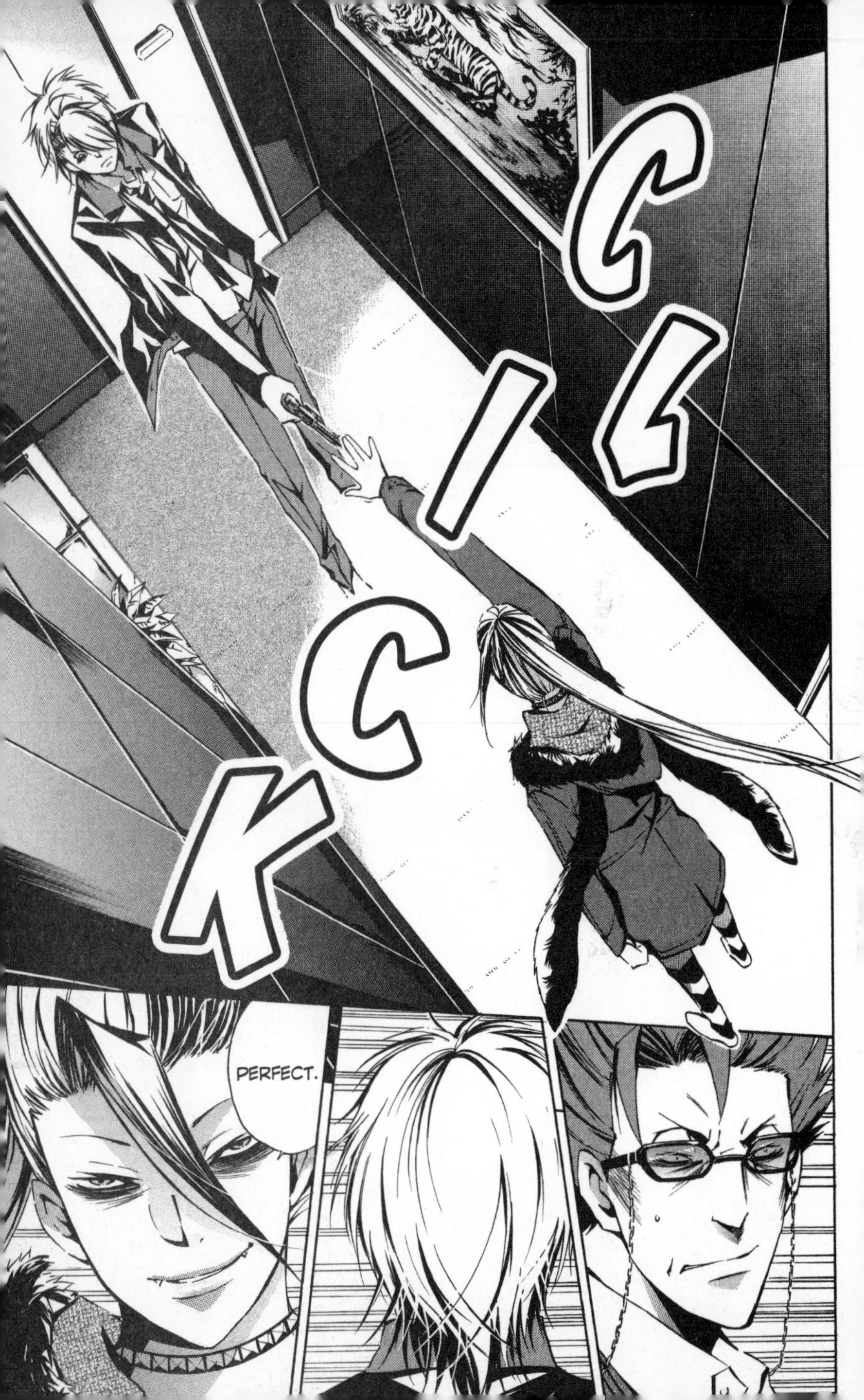
CLICK
PERFECT.

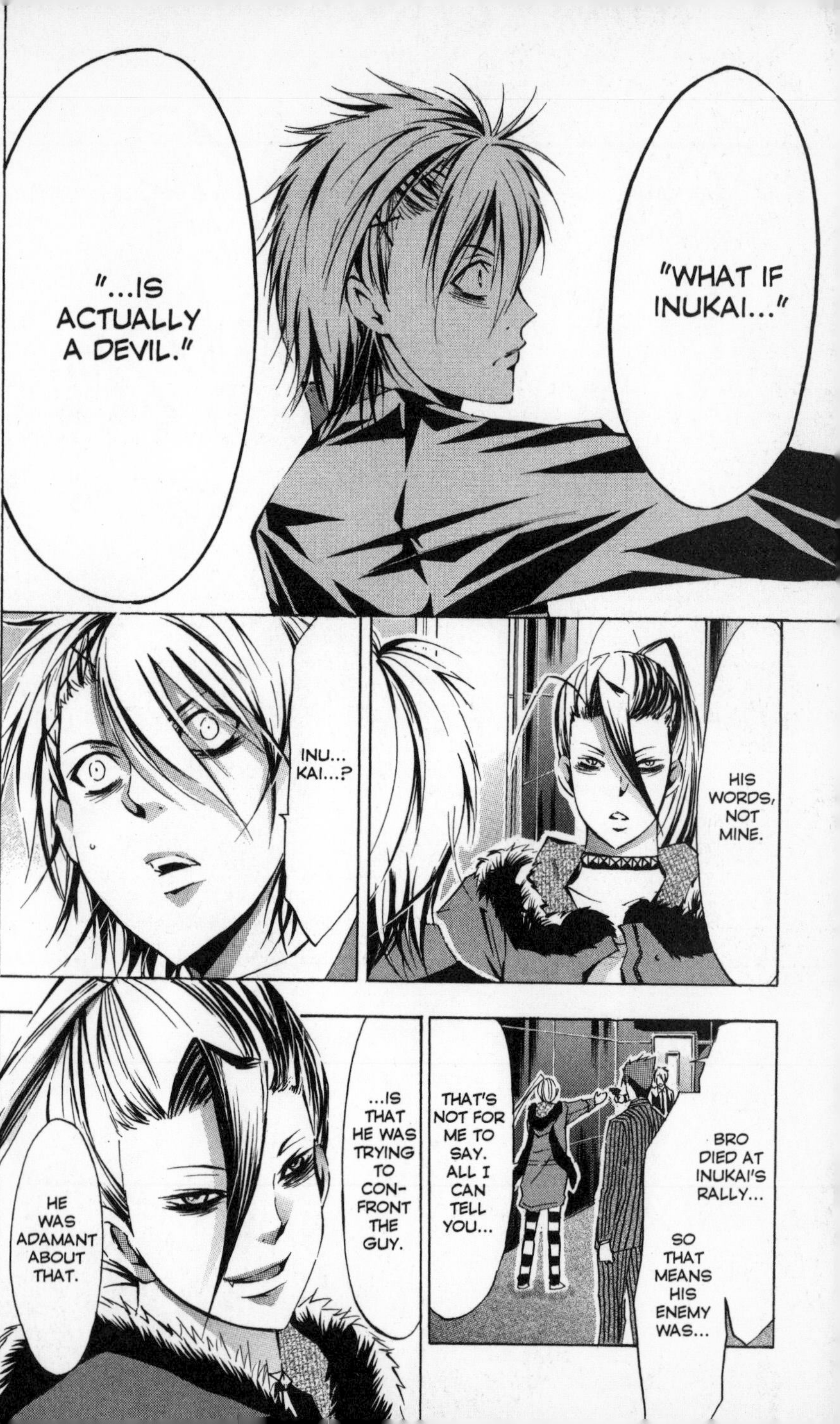
"WHAT IF INUKAI..."
"...IS ACTUALLY A DEVIL."
HIS WORDS, NOT MINE.
INU... KAI...?
BRO DIED AT INUKAI'S RALLY...
SO THAT MEANS HIS ENEMY WAS...
THAT'S NOT FOR ME TO SAY. ALL I CAN TELL YOU...
...IS THAT HE WAS TRYING TO CON-FRONT THE GUY.
HE WAS ADAMANT ABOUT THAT.

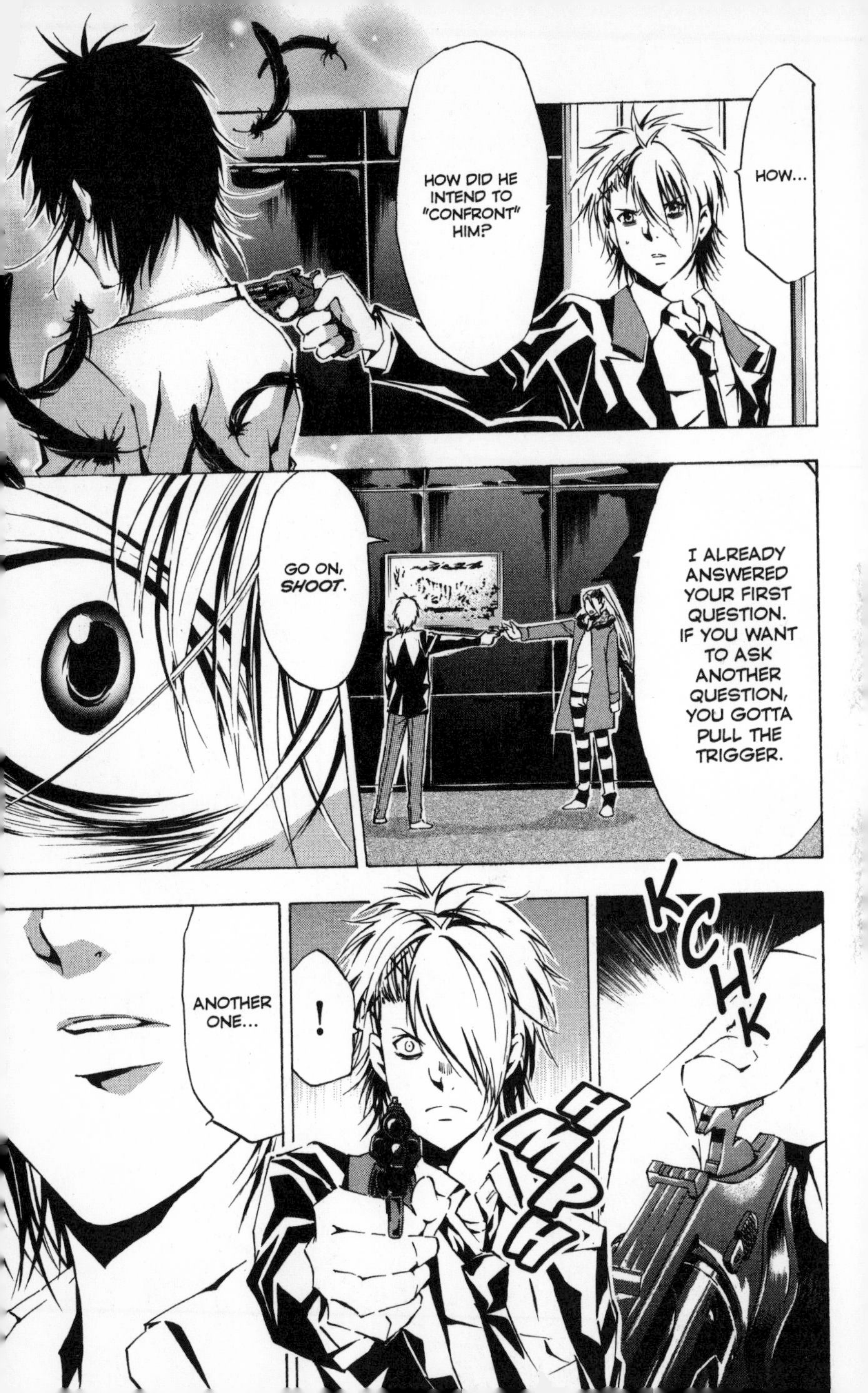
HOW...
HOW DID HE INTEND TO "CONFRONT" HIM?
I ALREADY ANSWERED YOUR FIRST QUESTION. IF YOU WANT TO ASK ANOTHER QUESTION, YOU GOTTA PULL THE TRIGGER.
GO ON, *SHOOT*.
KCHK
HMPH
!
ANOTHER ONE...

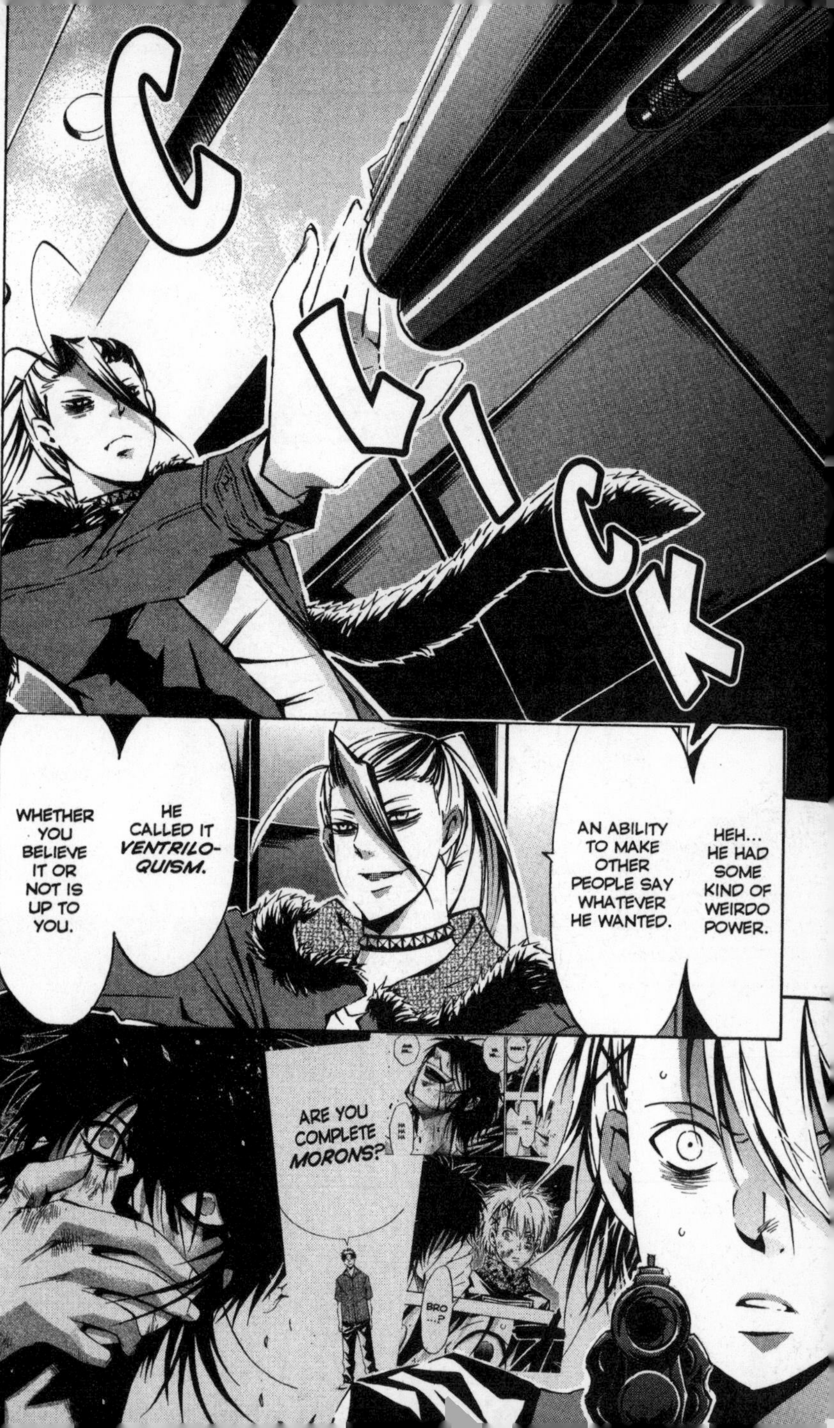
CLICK
HEH... HE HAD SOME KIND OF WEIRDO POWER.
AN ABILITY TO MAKE OTHER PEOPLE SAY WHATEVER HE WANTED.
HE CALLED IT *VENTRILOQUISM*.
WHETHER YOU BELIEVE IT OR NOT IS UP TO YOU.
ARE YOU COMPLETE *MORONS*?
BRO...?

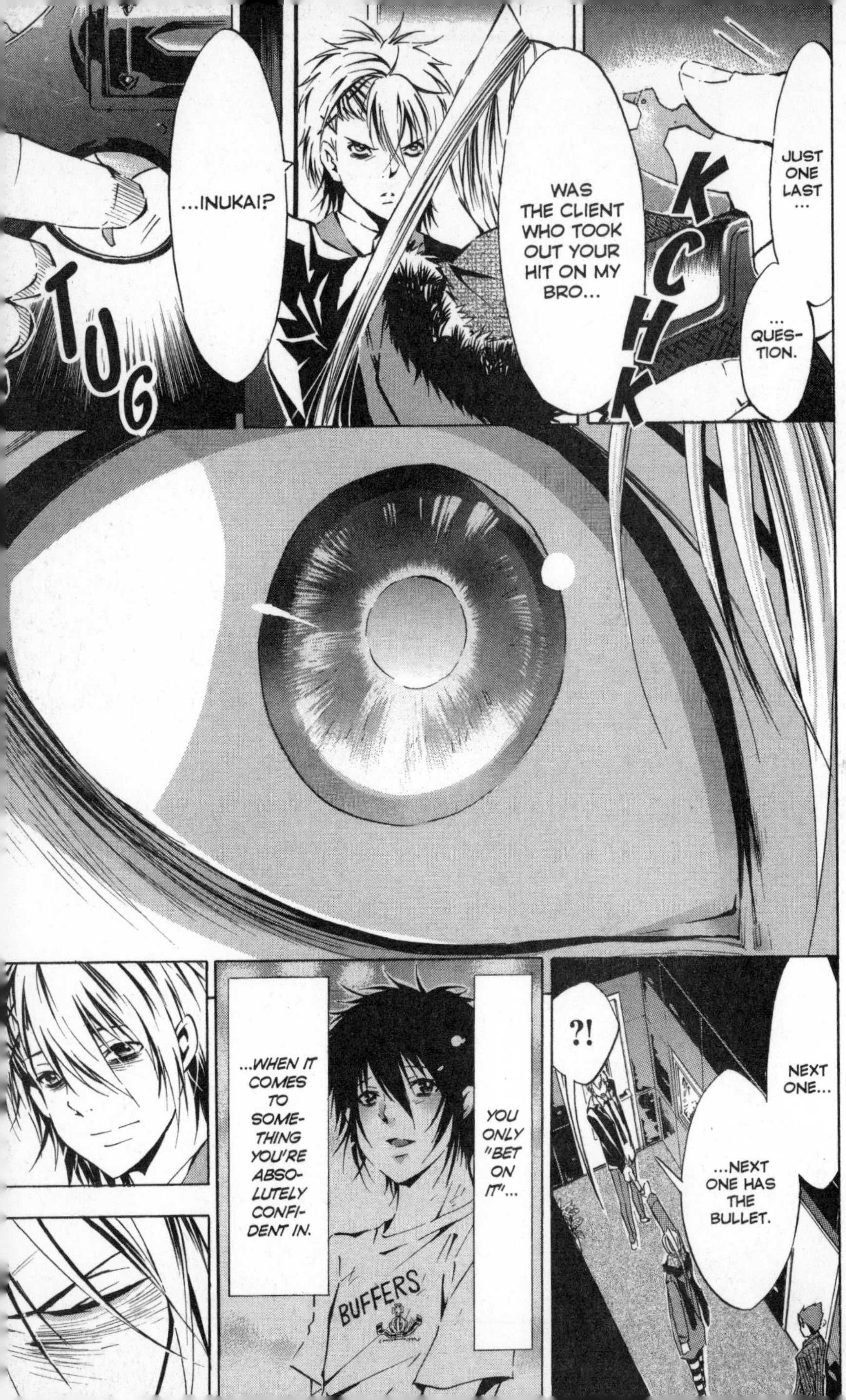
JUST ONE LAST...
KCHK
...QUESTION.
WAS THE CLIENT WHO TOOK OUT YOUR HIT ON MY BRO...
...INUKAI?
TUG
NEXT ONE...
...NEXT ONE HAS THE BULLET.
?!
YOU ONLY "BET ON IT"...
...WHEN IT COMES TO SOMETHING YOU'RE ABSOLUTELY CONFIDENT IN.
BUFFERS

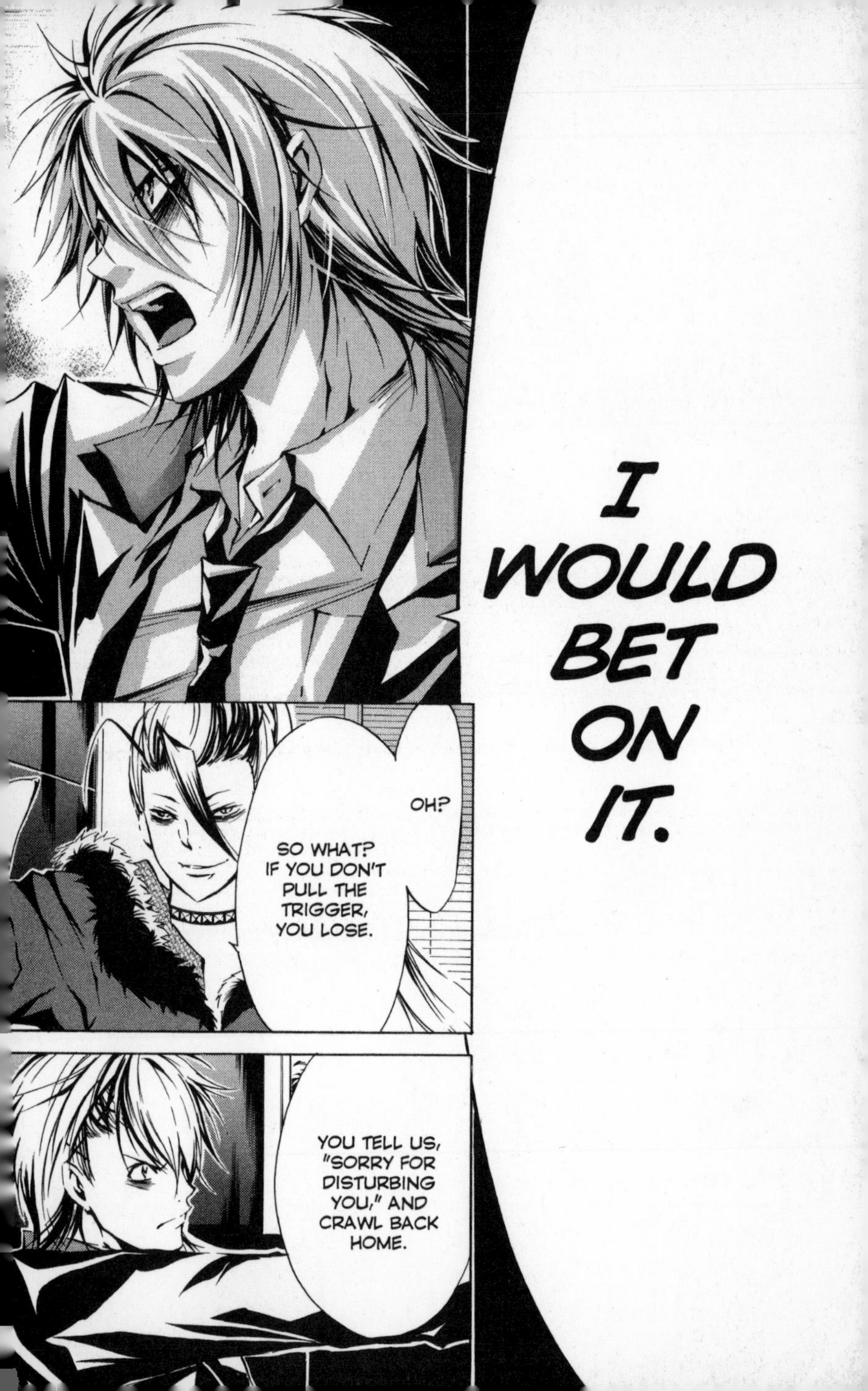
I WOULD BET ON IT.
OH?
SO WHAT? IF YOU DON'T PULL THE TRIGGER, YOU LOSE.
YOU TELL US, "SORRY FOR DISTURBING YOU," AND CRAWL BACK HOME.

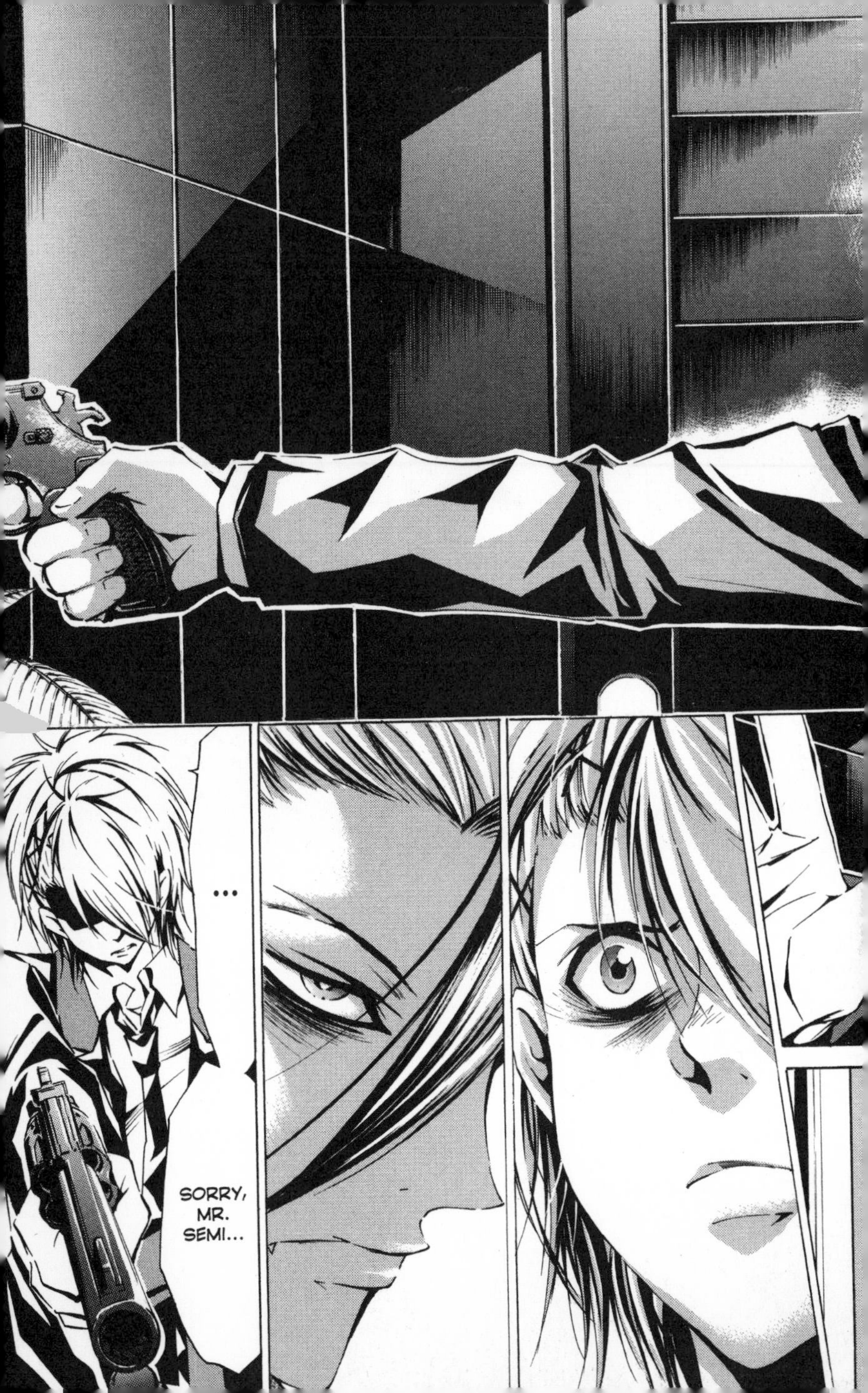
...
SORRY, MR. SEMI...

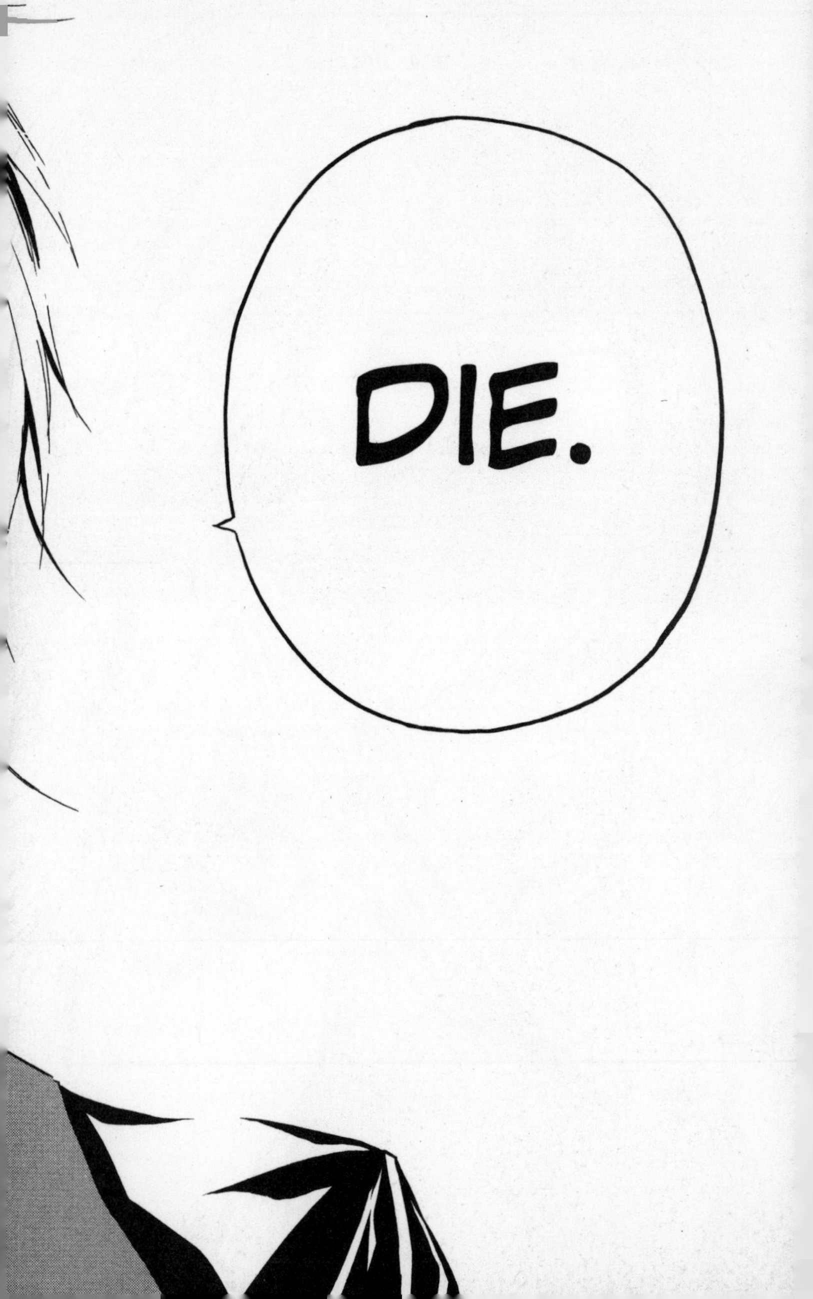
DIE.

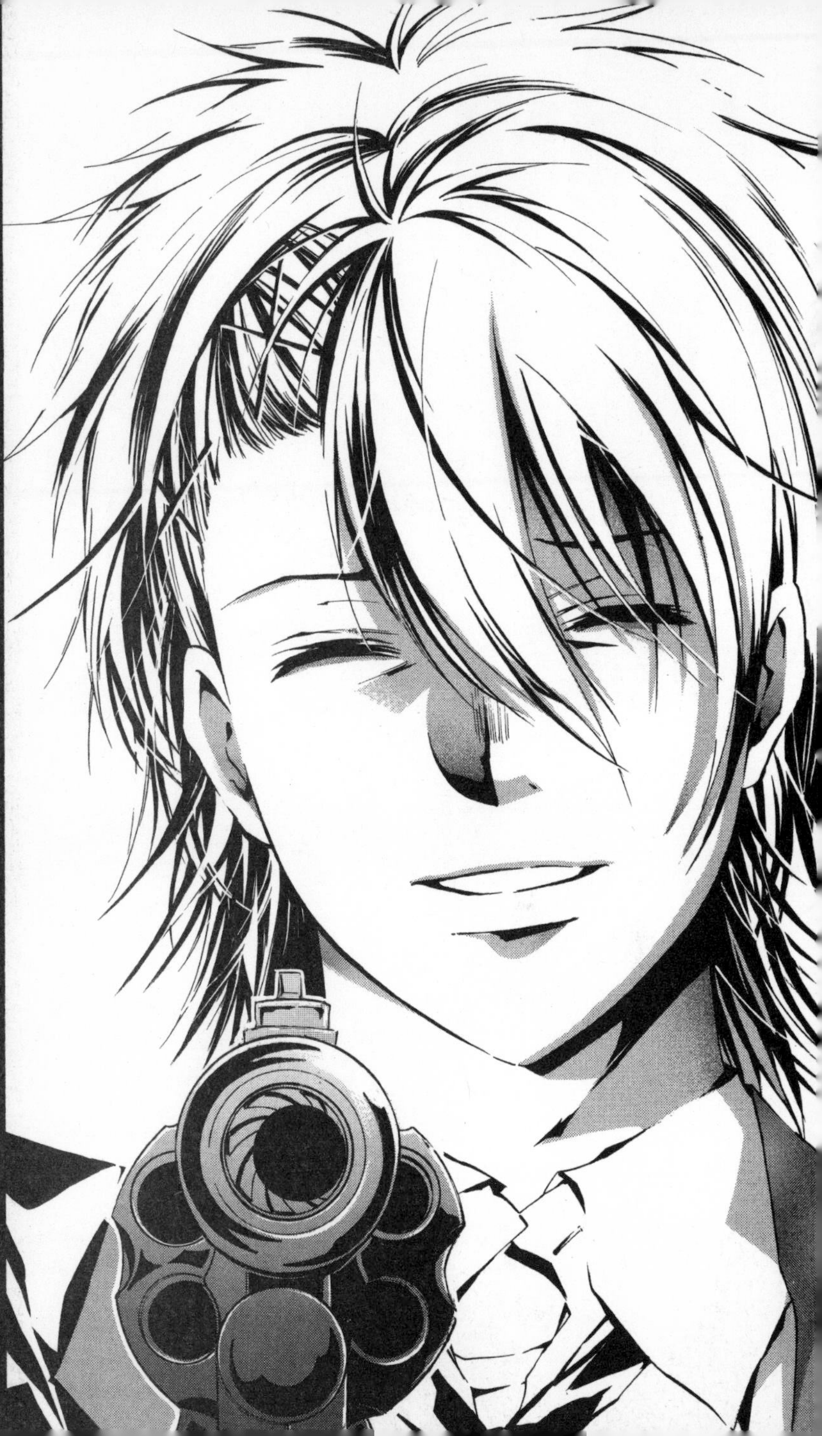

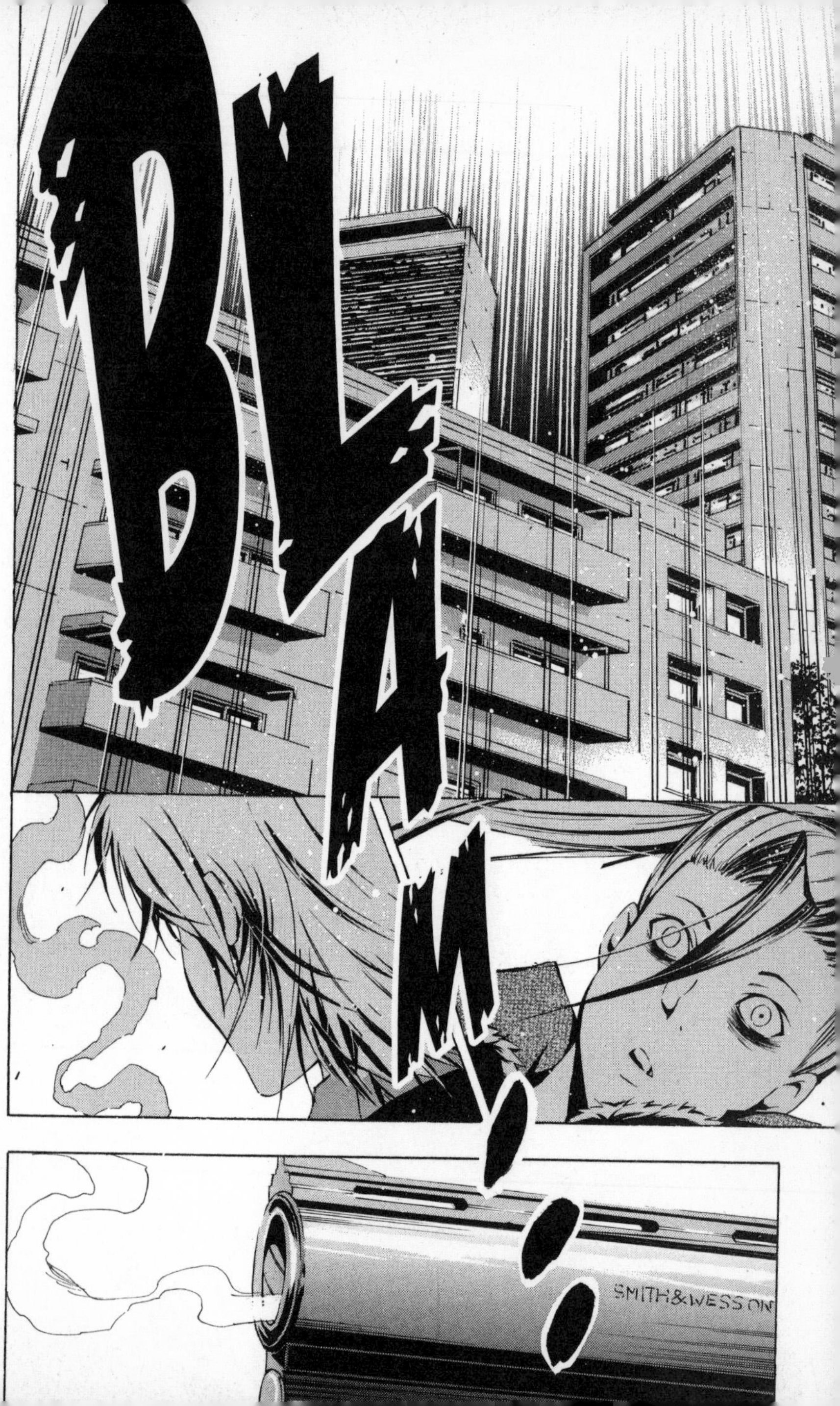
BLAM!
SMITH&WESSON

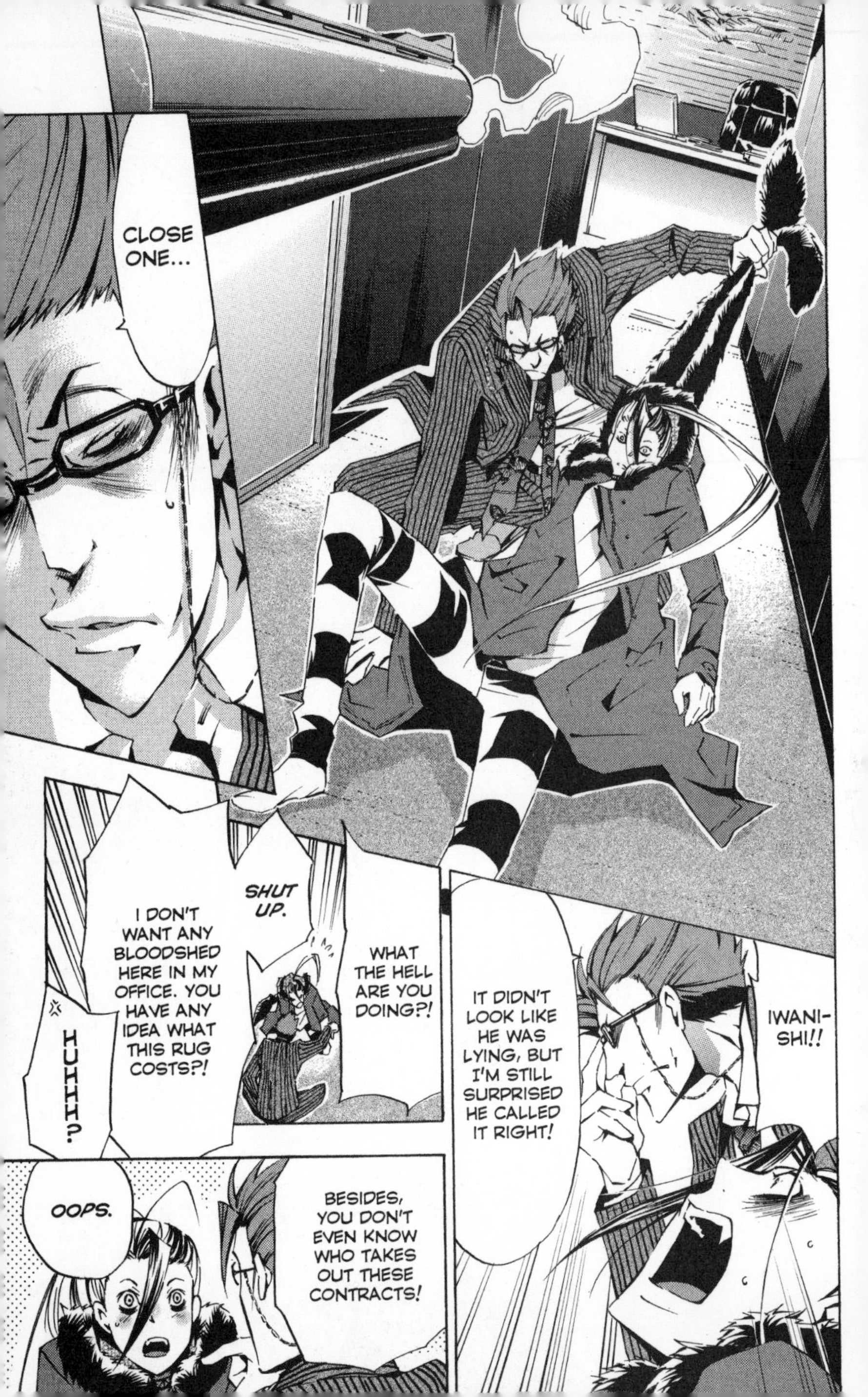
CLOSE ONE...
IWANI-SHI!!
IT DIDN'T LOOK LIKE HE WAS LYING, BUT I'M STILL SURPRISED HE CALLED IT RIGHT!
WHAT THE HELL ARE YOU DOING?!
SHUT UP.
I DON'T WANT ANY BLOODSHED HERE IN MY OFFICE. YOU HAVE ANY IDEA WHAT THIS RUG COSTS?!
HUHHH?
BESIDES, YOU DON'T EVEN KNOW WHO TAKES OUT THESE CONTRACTS!
OOPS.

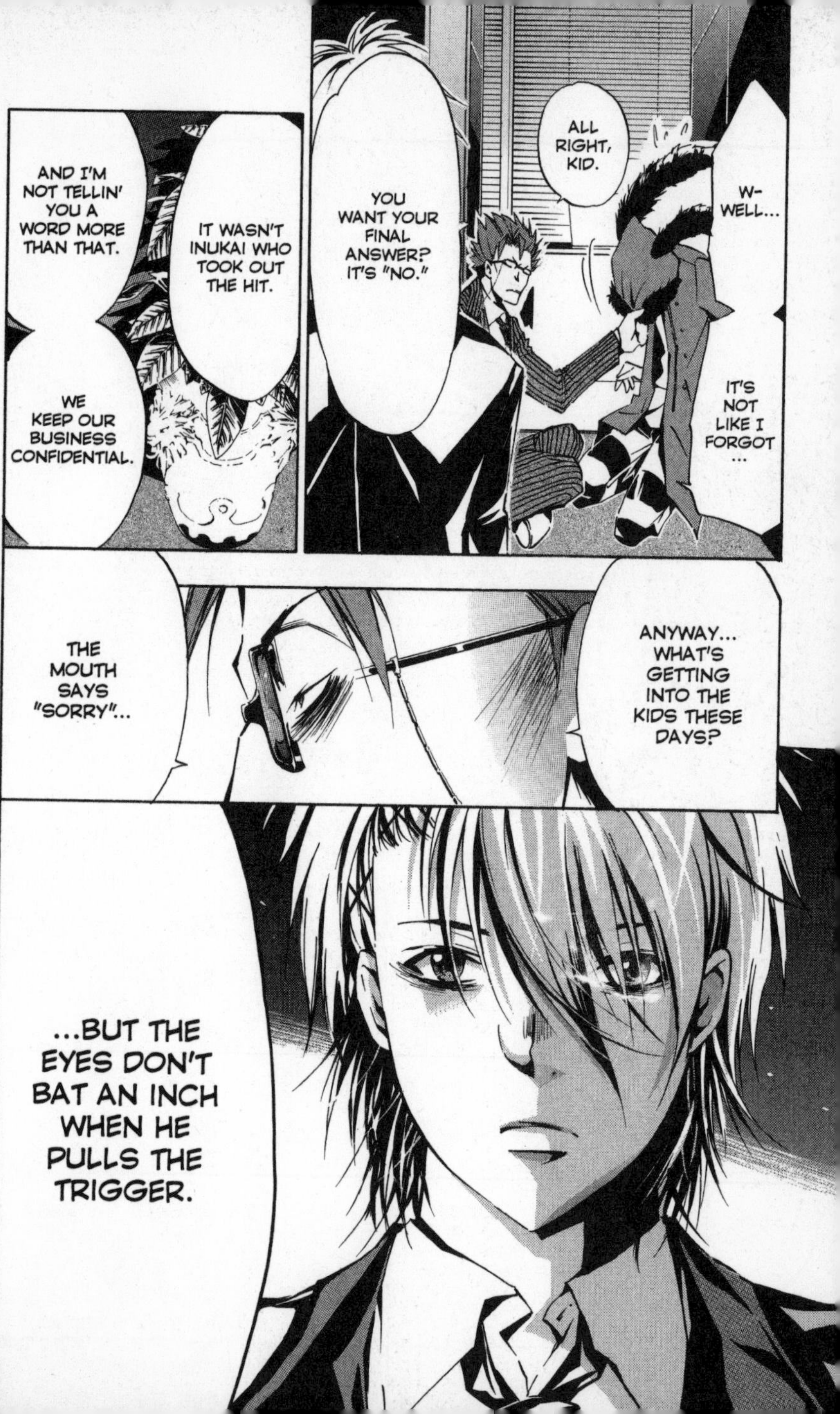
W-WELL...
IT'S NOT LIKE I FORGOT...
ALL RIGHT, KID.
YOU WANT YOUR FINAL ANSWER? IT'S "NO."
IT WASN'T INUKAI WHO TOOK OUT THE HIT.
AND I'M NOT TELLIN' YOU A WORD MORE THAN THAT.
WE KEEP OUR BUSINESS CONFIDENTIAL.
ANYWAY... WHAT'S GETTING INTO THE KIDS THESE DAYS?
THE MOUTH SAYS "SORRY"...
...BUT THE EYES DON'T BAT AN INCH WHEN HE PULLS THE TRIGGER.

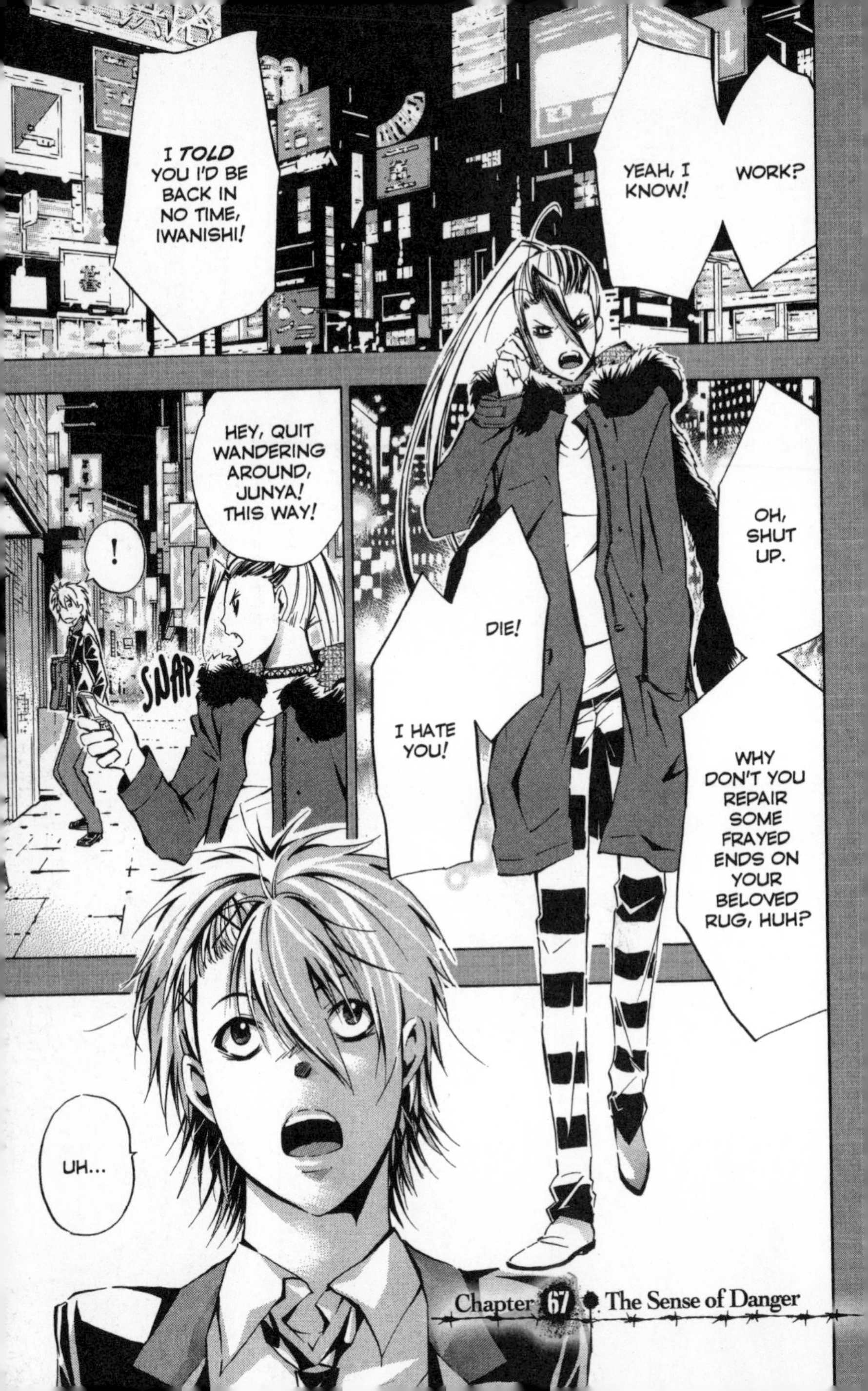
WORK?
YEAH, I KNOW!
I TOLD YOU I'D BE BACK IN NO TIME, IWANISHI!
OH, SHUT UP.
WHY DON'T YOU REPAIR SOME FRAYED ENDS ON YOUR BELOVED RUG, HUH?
DIE!
I HATE YOU!
HEY, QUIT WANDERING AROUND, JUNYA! THIS WAY!
!
SNAP
UH...

## Chapter 67 The Sense of Danger

# Chapter 67 The Sense of Danger

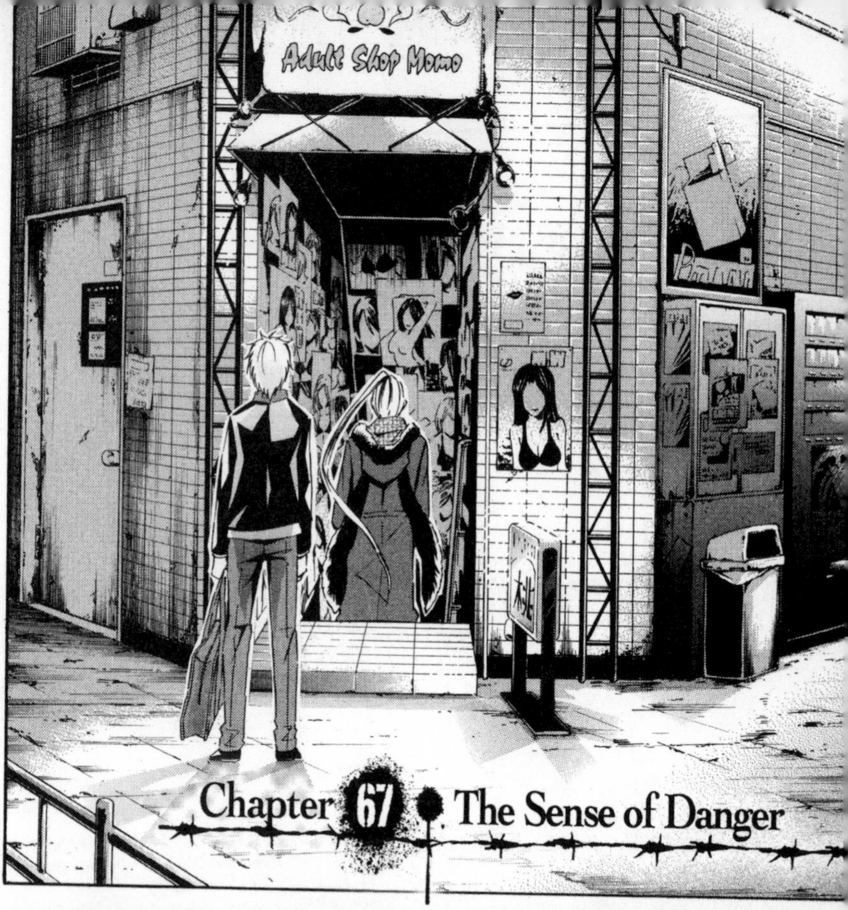
Adult Shop Momo

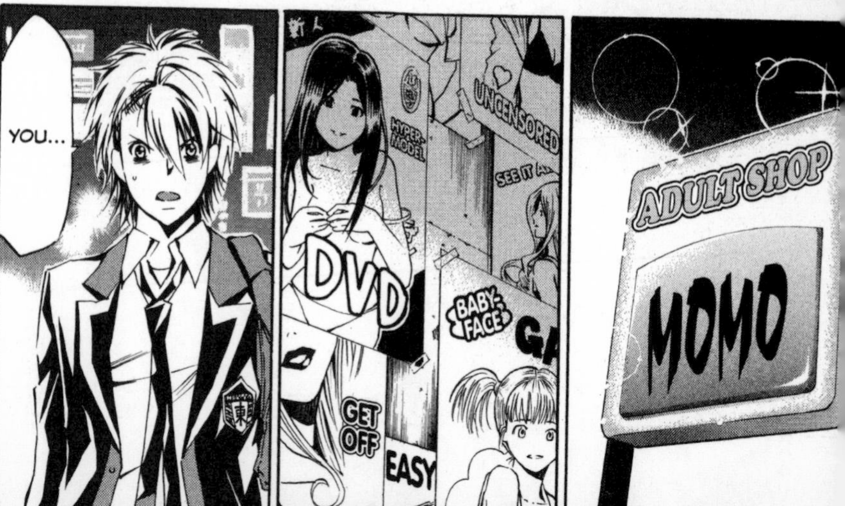
ADULT SHOP
MOMO
UNCENSORED
HYPER-MODEL
DVD
BABY-FACE
GET OFF
EASY
YOU...

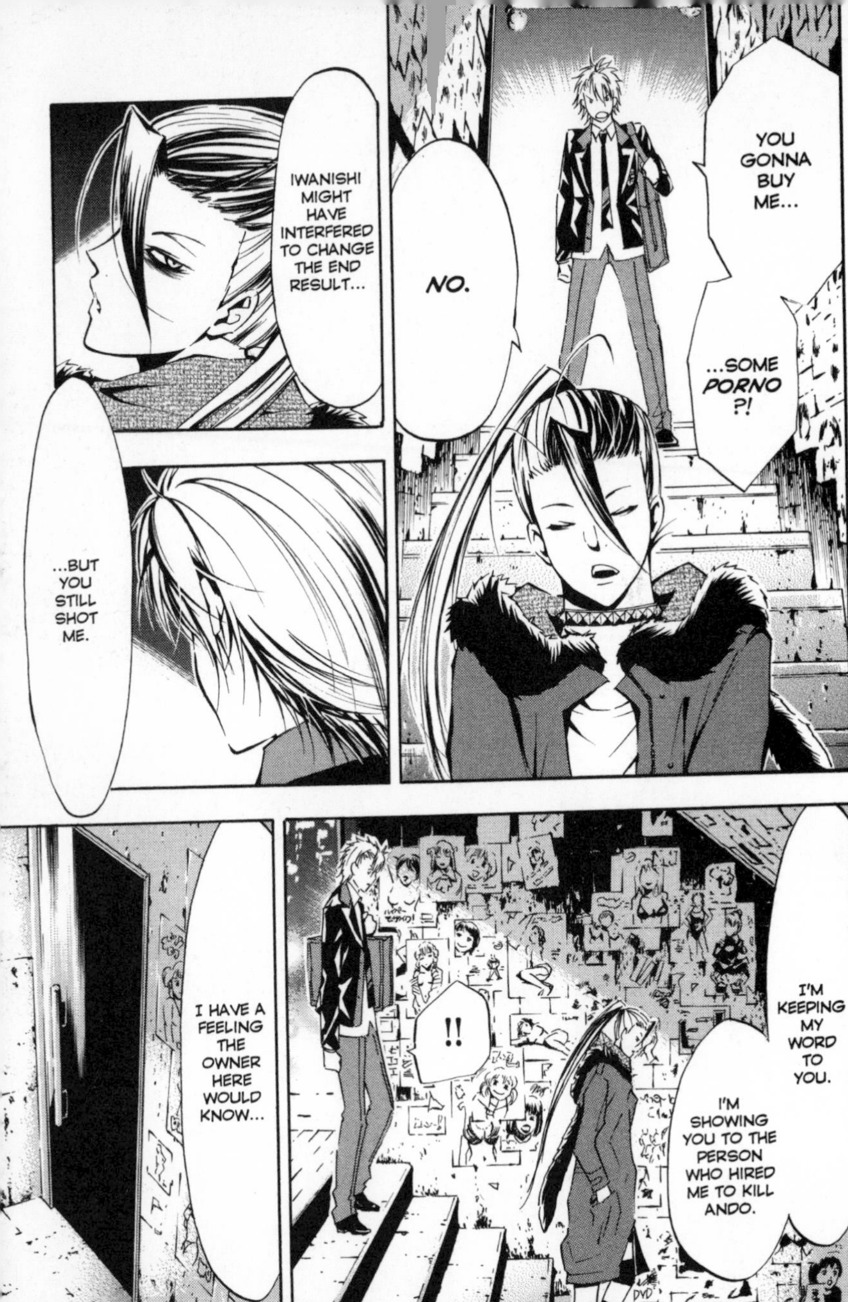
YOU GONNA BUY ME...
...SOME *PORNO* ?!
*NO.*
IWANISHI MIGHT HAVE INTERFERED TO CHANGE THE END RESULT...
...BUT YOU STILL SHOT ME.
I'M KEEPING MY WORD TO YOU.
I'M SHOWING YOU TO THE PERSON WHO HIRED ME TO KILL ANDO.
!!
I HAVE A FEELING THE OWNER HERE WOULD KNOW...

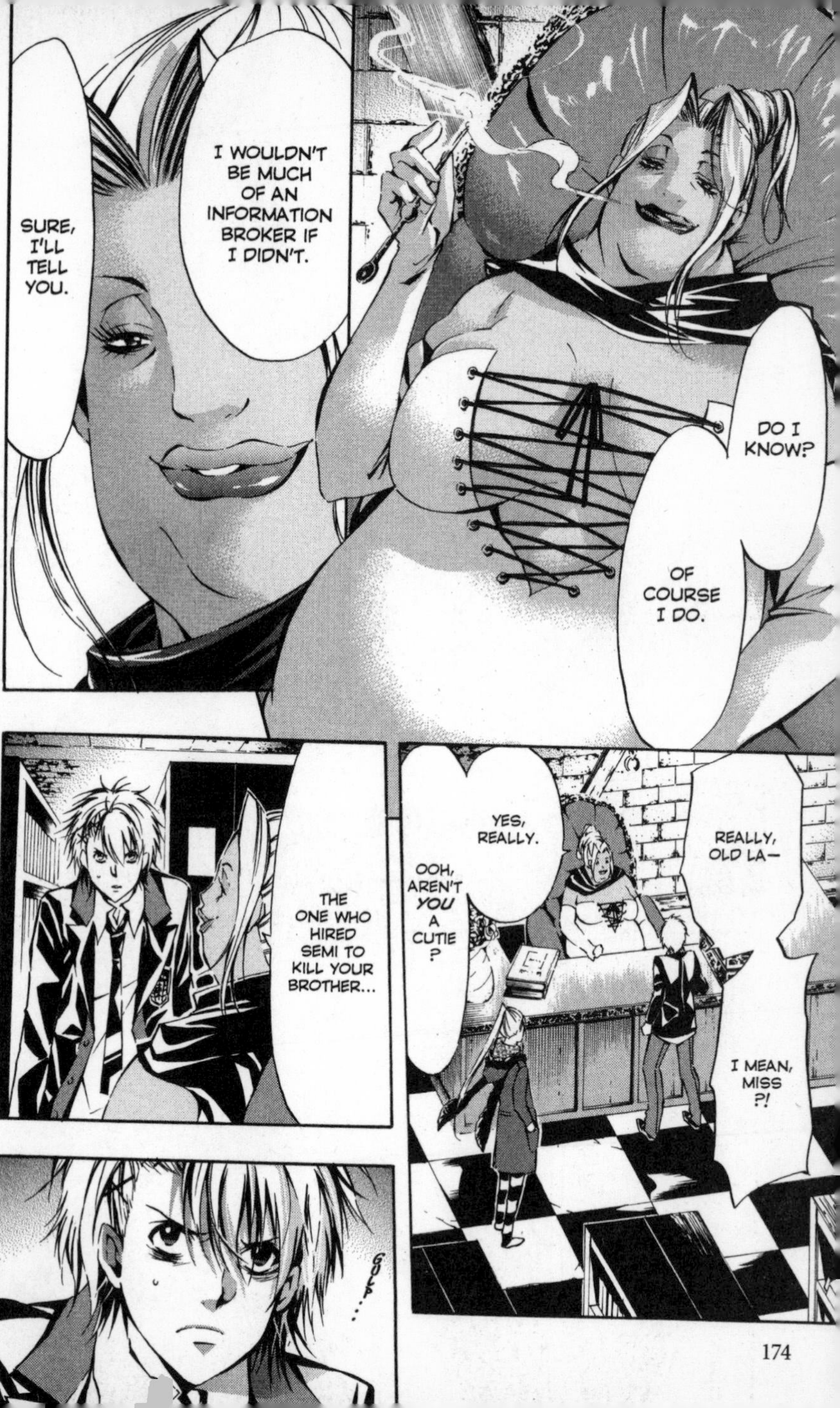
DO I KNOW?
OF COURSE I DO.
I WOULDN'T BE MUCH OF AN INFORMATION BROKER IF I DIDN'T.
SURE, I'LL TELL YOU.
REALLY, OLD LA—
I MEAN, MISS?!
YES, REALLY.
OOH, AREN'T *YOU* A CUTIE?
THE ONE WHO HIRED SEMI TO KILL YOUR BROTHER...
GULP...

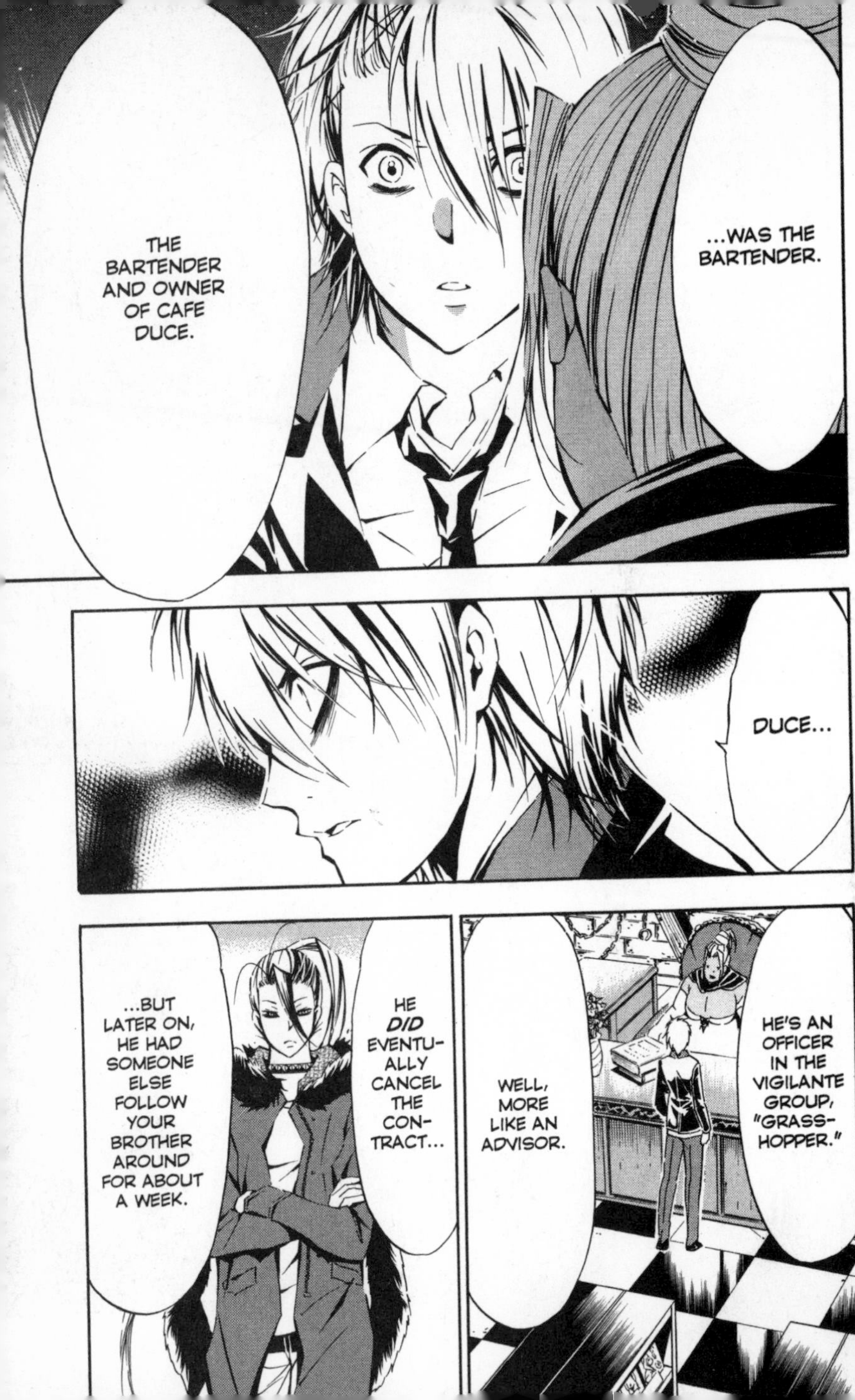
...WAS THE BARTENDER.
THE BARTENDER AND OWNER OF CAFE DUCE.
DUCE...
HE'S AN OFFICER IN THE VIGILANTE GROUP, "GRASSHOPPER."
WELL, MORE LIKE AN ADVISOR.
HE *DID* EVENTUALLY CANCEL THE CONTRACT...
...BUT LATER ON, HE HAD SOMEONE ELSE FOLLOW YOUR BROTHER AROUND FOR ABOUT A WEEK.

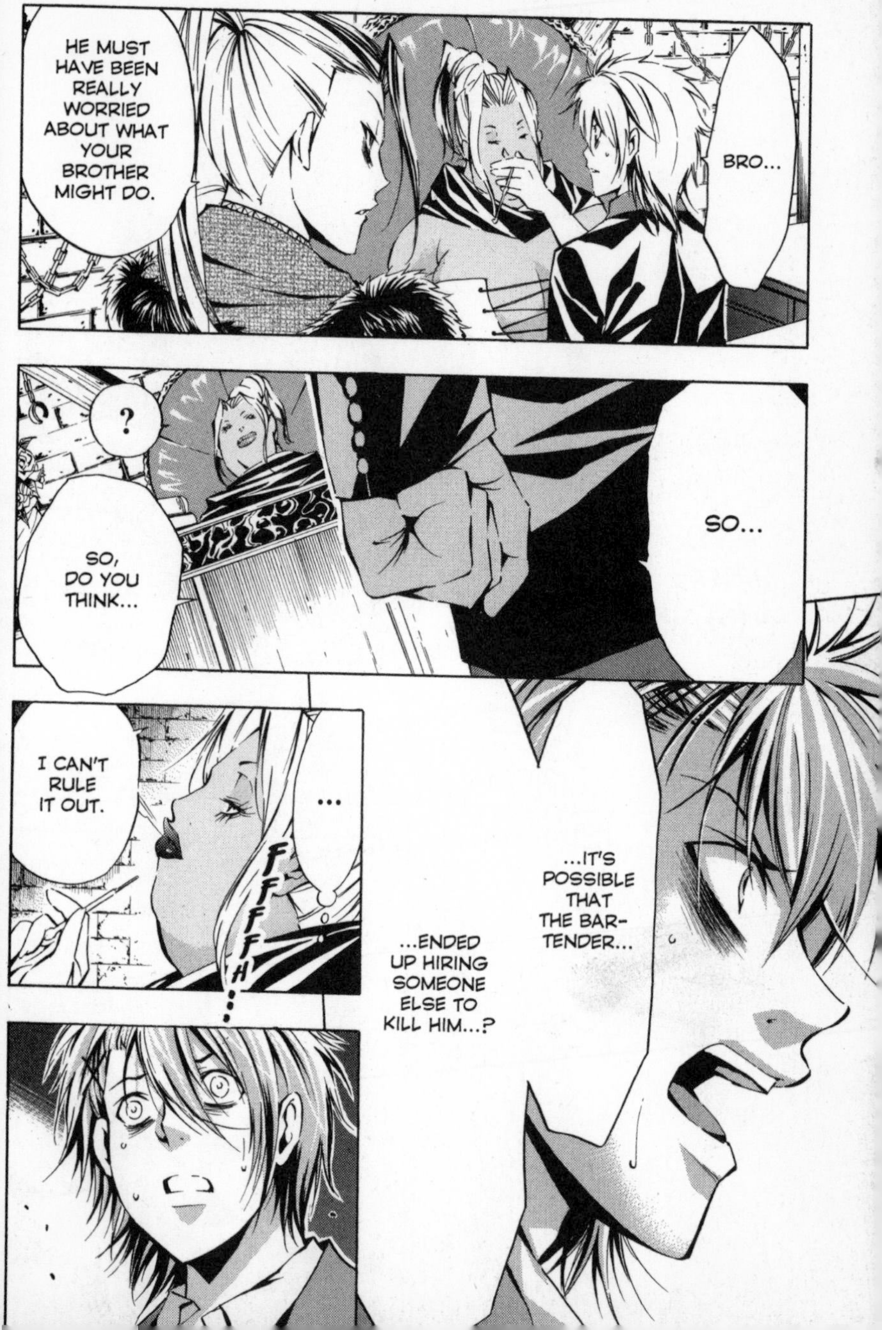
BRO...
HE MUST HAVE BEEN REALLY WORRIED ABOUT WHAT YOUR BROTHER MIGHT DO.
SO...
?
SO, DO YOU THINK...
...IT'S POSSIBLE THAT THE BAR-TENDER...
...ENDED UP HIRING SOMEONE ELSE TO KILL HIM...?
...
I CAN'T RULE IT OUT.
FFFFFH...

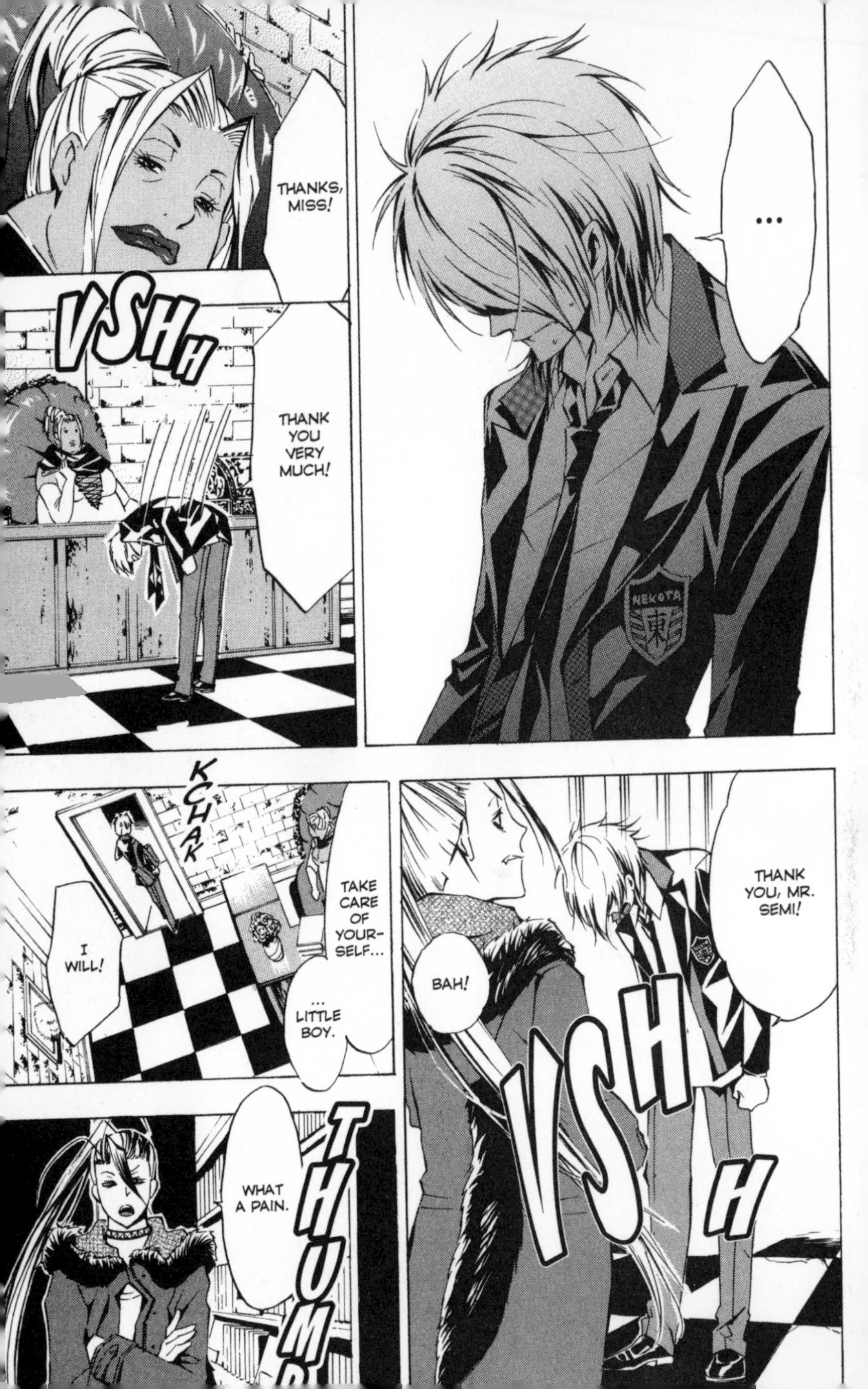
...
THANKS, MISS!
VSHH
THANK YOU VERY MUCH!
THANK YOU, MR. SEMI!
BAH!
VSHH
KCHAK
TAKE CARE OF YOUR-SELF...
... LITTLE BOY.
I WILL!
THUMP
WHAT A PAIN.

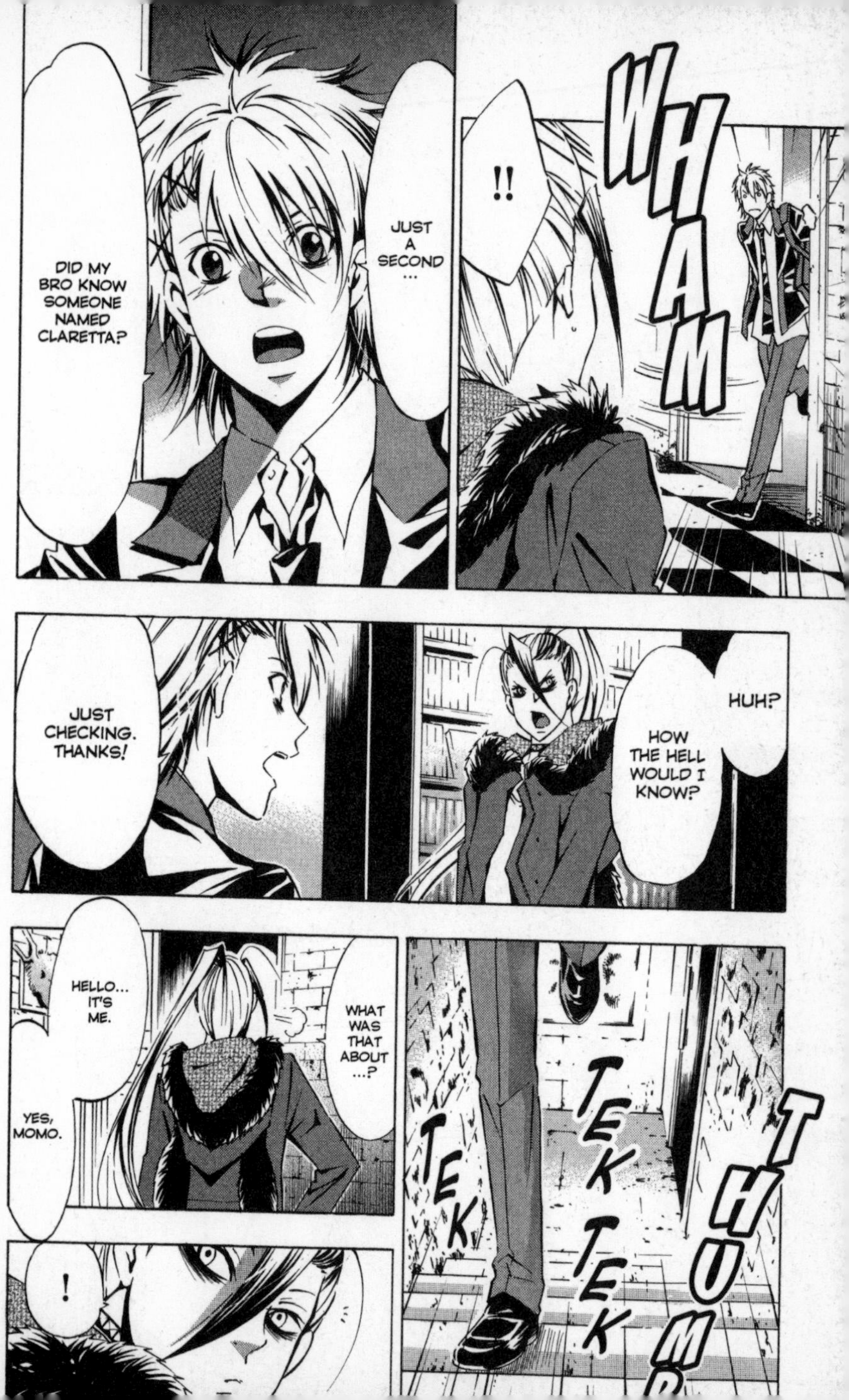
WHAM
!!
JUST A SECOND...
DID MY BRO KNOW SOMEONE NAMED CLARETTA?
HUH?
HOW THE HELL WOULD I KNOW?
JUST CHECKING. THANKS!
THUM
TEK TEK
TEK
WHAT WAS THAT ABOUT...?
HELLO... IT'S ME.
YES, MOMO.
!

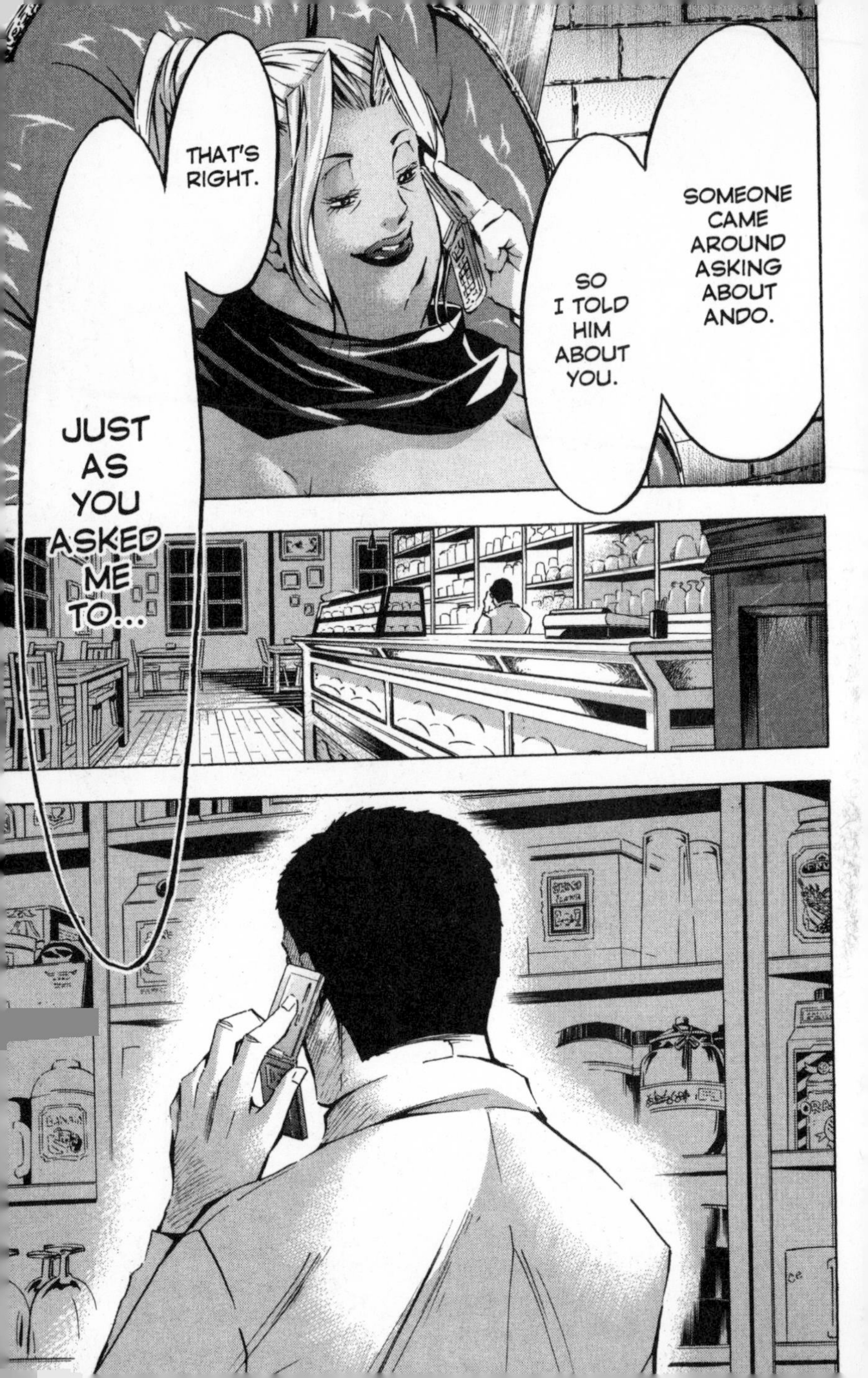
SOMEONE CAME AROUND ASKING ABOUT ANDO.
SO I TOLD HIM ABOUT YOU.
THAT'S RIGHT.
JUST AS YOU ASKED ME TO...

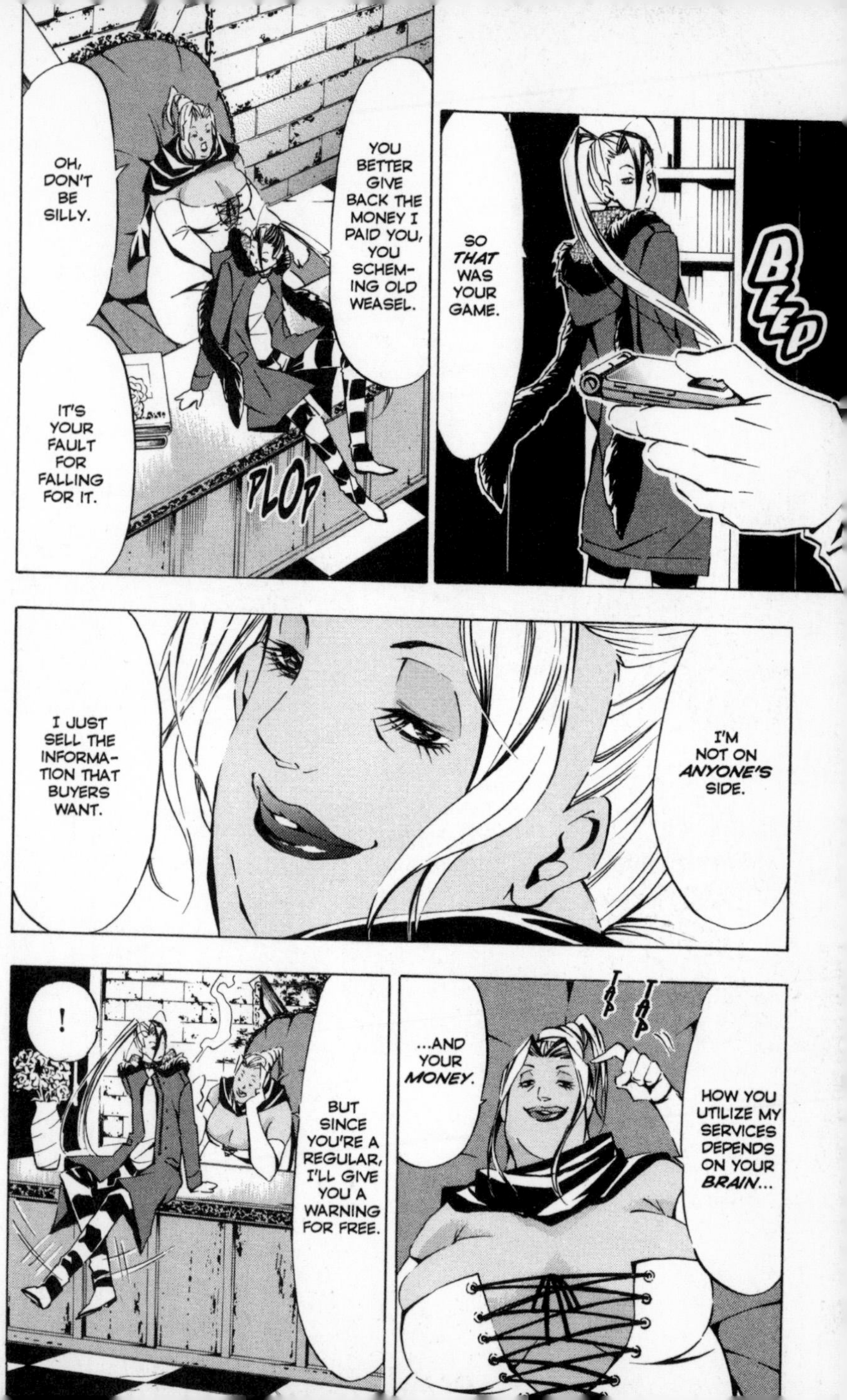
BEEP
SO *THAT* WAS YOUR GAME.
YOU BETTER GIVE BACK THE MONEY I PAID YOU, YOU SCHEMING OLD WEASEL.
OH, DON'T BE SILLY.
IT'S YOUR FAULT FOR FALLING FOR IT.
PLOP
I'M NOT ON *ANYONE'S* SIDE.
I JUST SELL THE INFORMATION THAT BUYERS WANT.
HOW YOU UTILIZE MY SERVICES DEPENDS ON YOUR *BRAIN*...
TAP TAP
...AND YOUR *MONEY*.
!
BUT SINCE YOU'RE A REGULAR, I'LL GIVE YOU A WARNING FOR FREE.

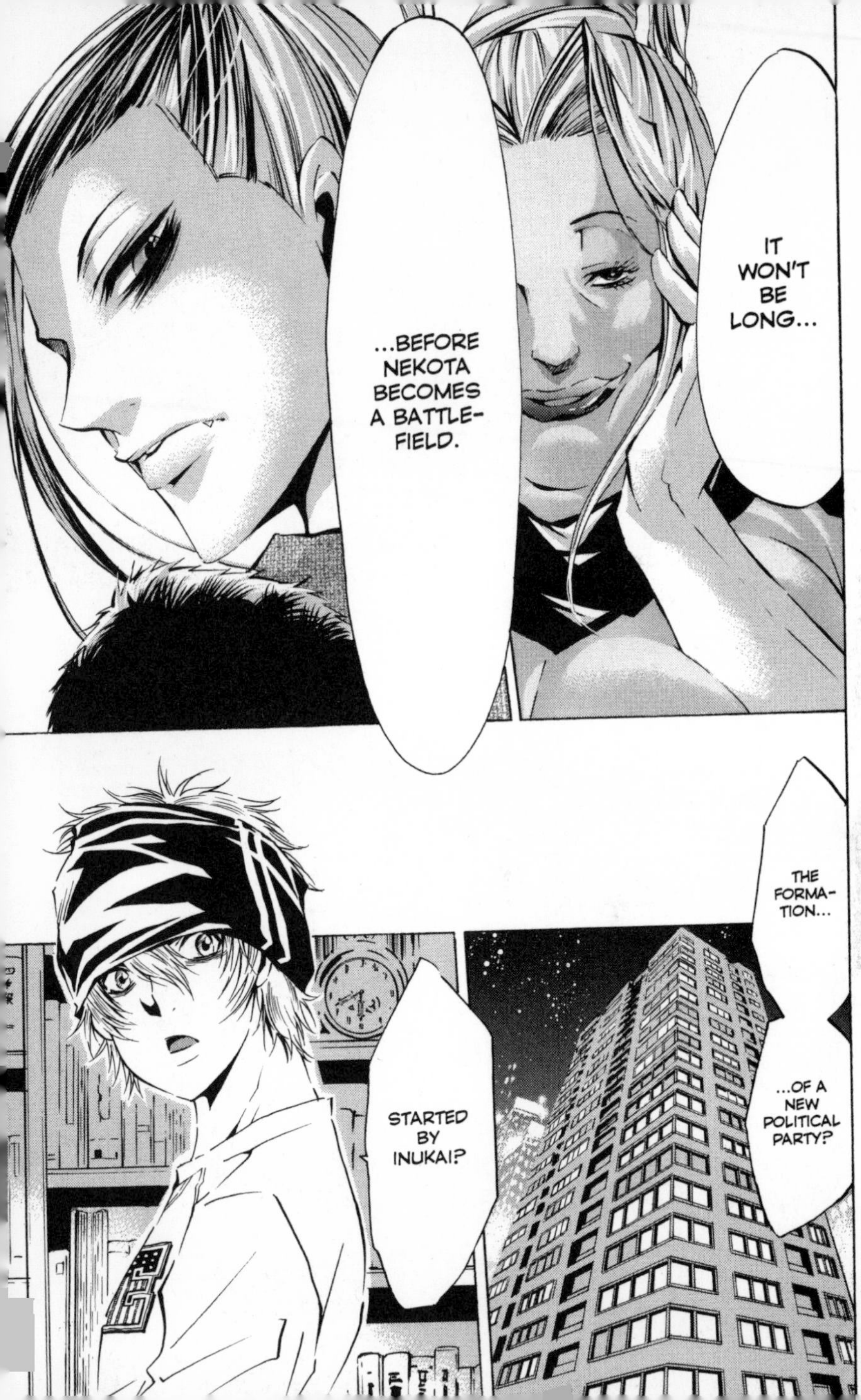
IT WON'T BE LONG...
...BEFORE NEKOTA BECOMES A BATTLE-FIELD.
THE FORMA-TION...
...OF A NEW POLITICAL PARTY?
STARTED BY INUKAI?

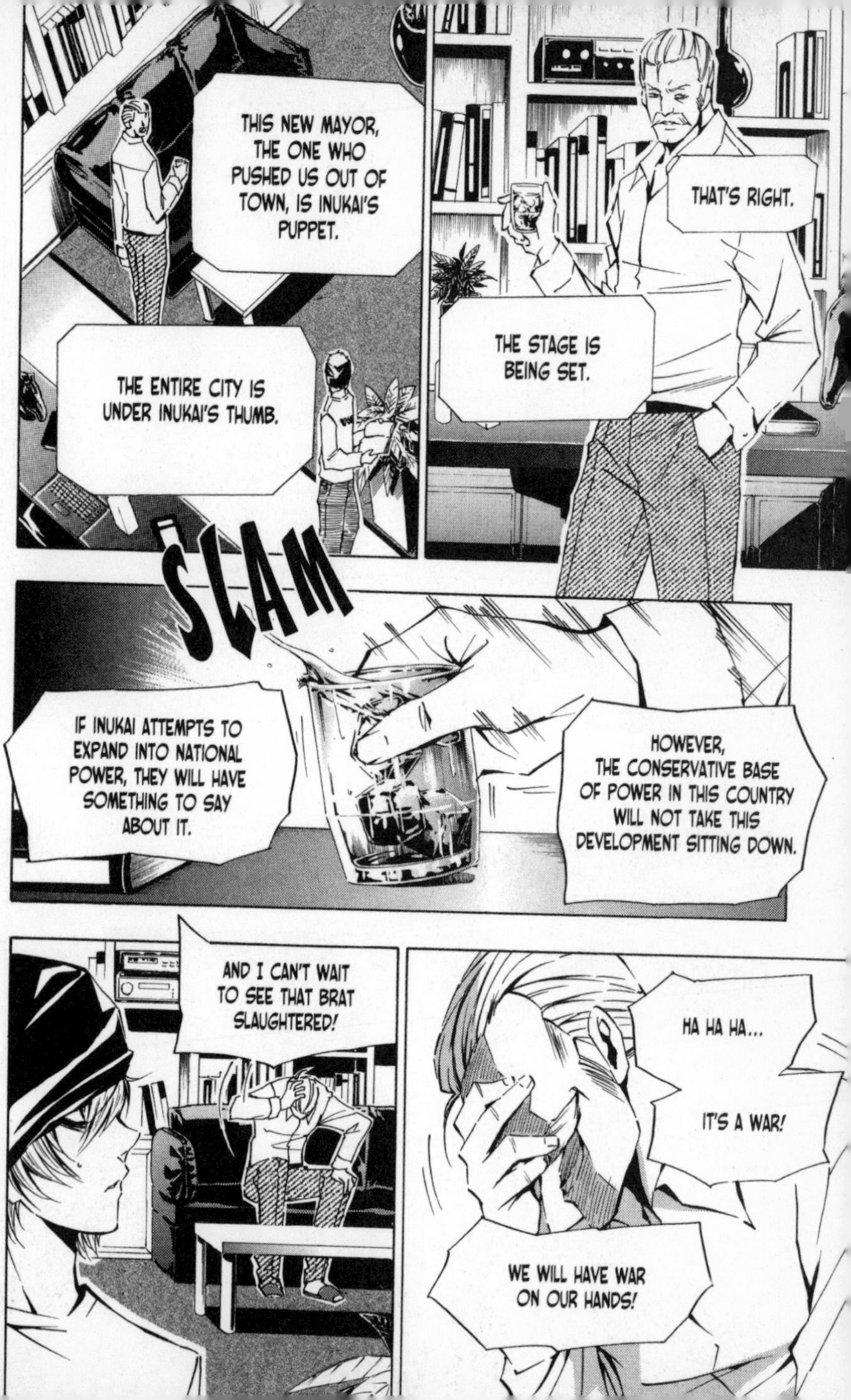
THAT'S RIGHT.
THE STAGE IS BEING SET.
THIS NEW MAYOR, THE ONE WHO PUSHED US OUT OF TOWN, IS INUKAI'S PUPPET.
THE ENTIRE CITY IS UNDER INUKAI'S THUMB.
SLAM
HOWEVER, THE CONSERVATIVE BASE OF POWER IN THIS COUNTRY WILL NOT TAKE THIS DEVELOPMENT SITTING DOWN.
IF INUKAI ATTEMPTS TO EXPAND INTO NATIONAL POWER, THEY WILL HAVE SOMETHING TO SAY ABOUT IT.
HA HA HA...
IT'S A WAR!
WE WILL HAVE WAR ON OUR HANDS!
AND I CAN'T WAIT TO SEE THAT BRAT SLAUGHTERED!

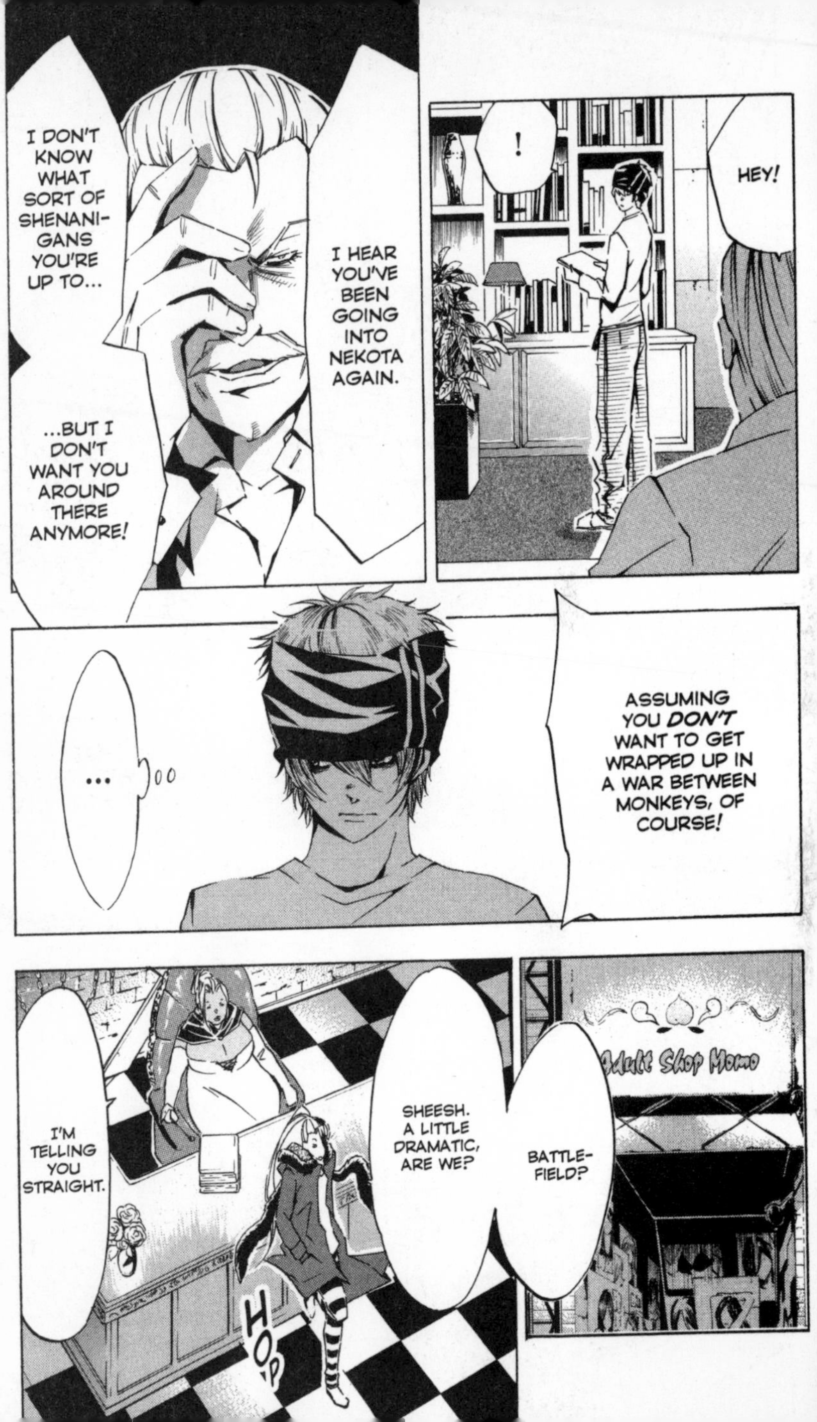
HEY!
!
I HEAR YOU'VE BEEN GOING INTO NEKOTA AGAIN.
I DON'T KNOW WHAT SORT OF SHENANI-GANS YOU'RE UP TO...
...BUT I DON'T WANT YOU AROUND THERE ANYMORE!
ASSUMING YOU ***DON'T*** WANT TO GET WRAPPED UP IN A WAR BETWEEN MONKEYS, OF COURSE!
...
Adult Shop Momo
BATTLE-FIELD?
SHEESH. A LITTLE DRAMATIC, ARE WE?
I'M TELLING YOU STRAIGHT.
HOP

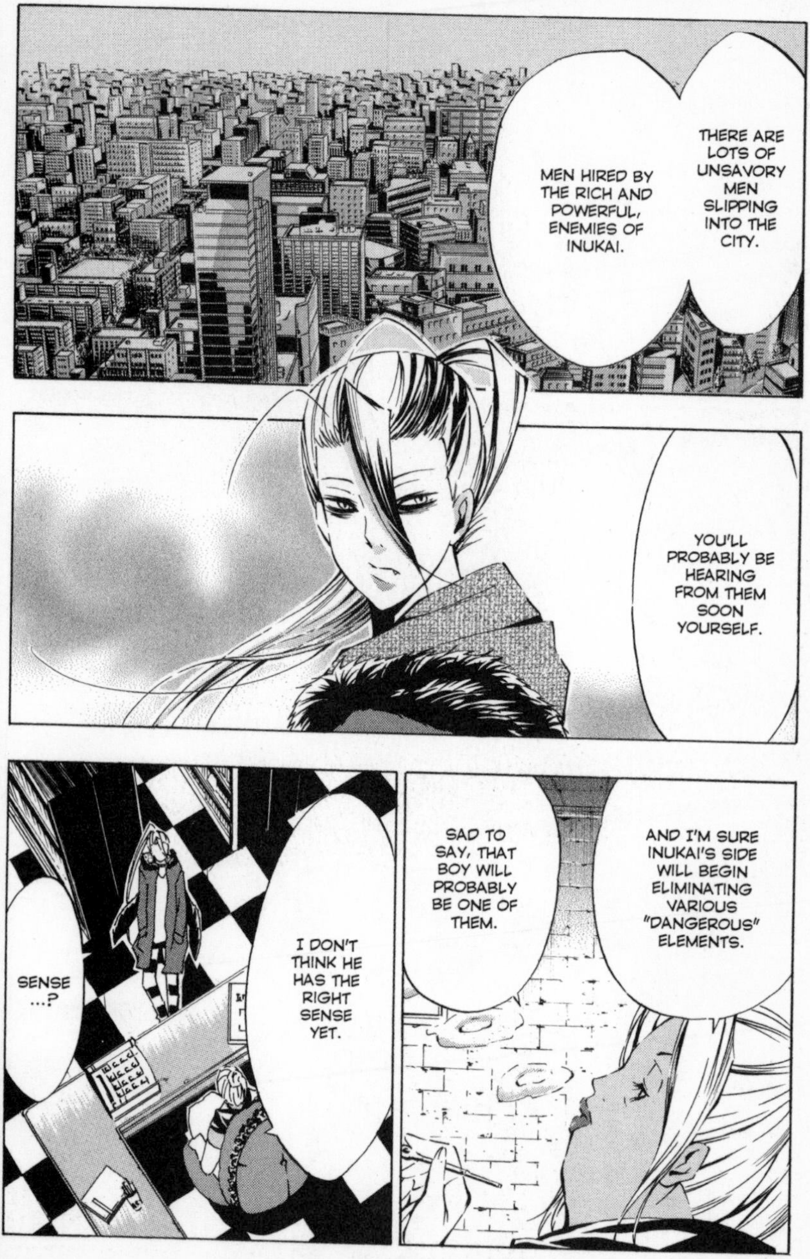
THERE ARE LOTS OF UNSAVORY MEN SLIPPING INTO THE CITY.
MEN HIRED BY THE RICH AND POWERFUL, ENEMIES OF INUKAI.
YOU'LL PROBABLY BE HEARING FROM THEM SOON YOURSELF.
AND I'M SURE INUKAI'S SIDE WILL BEGIN ELIMINATING VARIOUS "DANGEROUS" ELEMENTS.
SAD TO SAY, THAT BOY WILL PROBABLY BE ONE OF THEM.
I DON'T THINK HE HAS THE RIGHT SENSE YET.
SENSE ...?

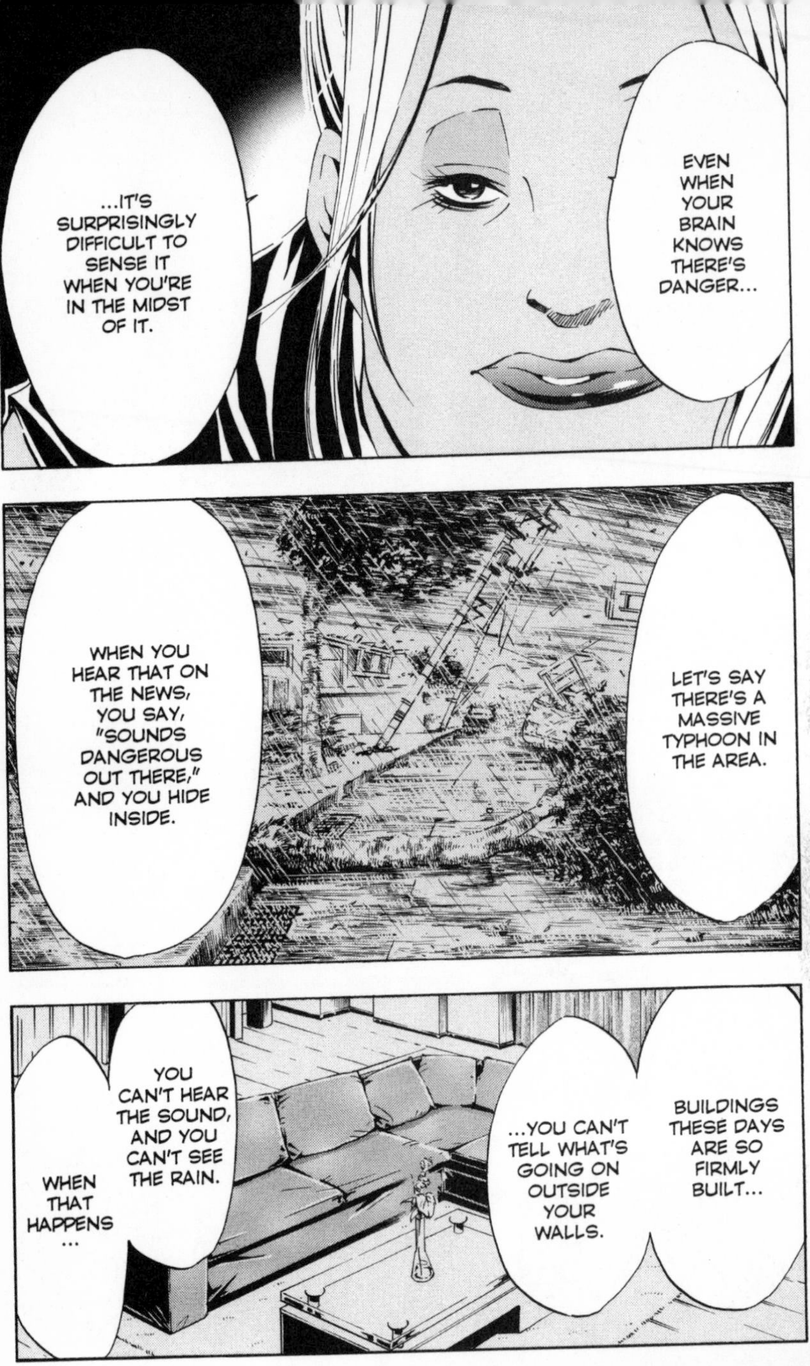
EVEN WHEN YOUR BRAIN KNOWS THERE'S DANGER...
...IT'S SURPRISINGLY DIFFICULT TO SENSE IT WHEN YOU'RE IN THE MIDST OF IT.
LET'S SAY THERE'S A MASSIVE TYPHOON IN THE AREA.
WHEN YOU HEAR THAT ON THE NEWS, YOU SAY, "SOUNDS DANGEROUS OUT THERE," AND YOU HIDE INSIDE.
BUILDINGS THESE DAYS ARE SO FIRMLY BUILT...
...YOU CAN'T TELL WHAT'S GOING ON OUTSIDE YOUR WALLS.
YOU CAN'T HEAR THE SOUND, AND YOU CAN'T SEE THE RAIN.
WHEN THAT HAPPENS ...

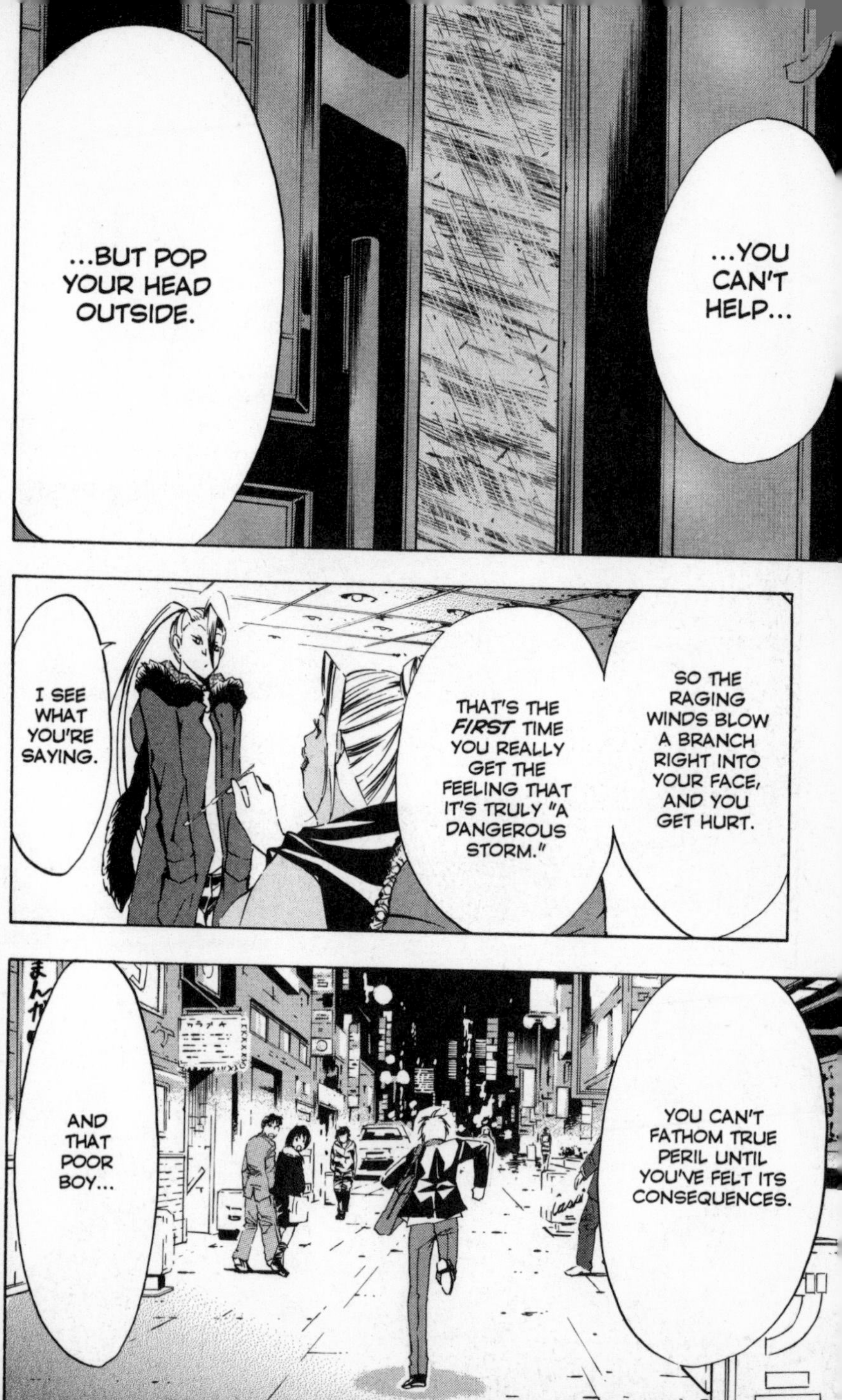
...YOU CAN'T HELP...
...BUT POP YOUR HEAD OUTSIDE.
SO THE RAGING WINDS BLOW A BRANCH RIGHT INTO YOUR FACE, AND YOU GET HURT.
THAT'S THE *FIRST* TIME YOU REALLY GET THE FEELING THAT IT'S TRULY "A DANGEROUS STORM."
I SEE WHAT YOU'RE SAYING.
YOU CAN'T FATHOM TRUE PERIL UNTIL YOU'VE FELT ITS CONSEQUENCES.
AND THAT POOR BOY...

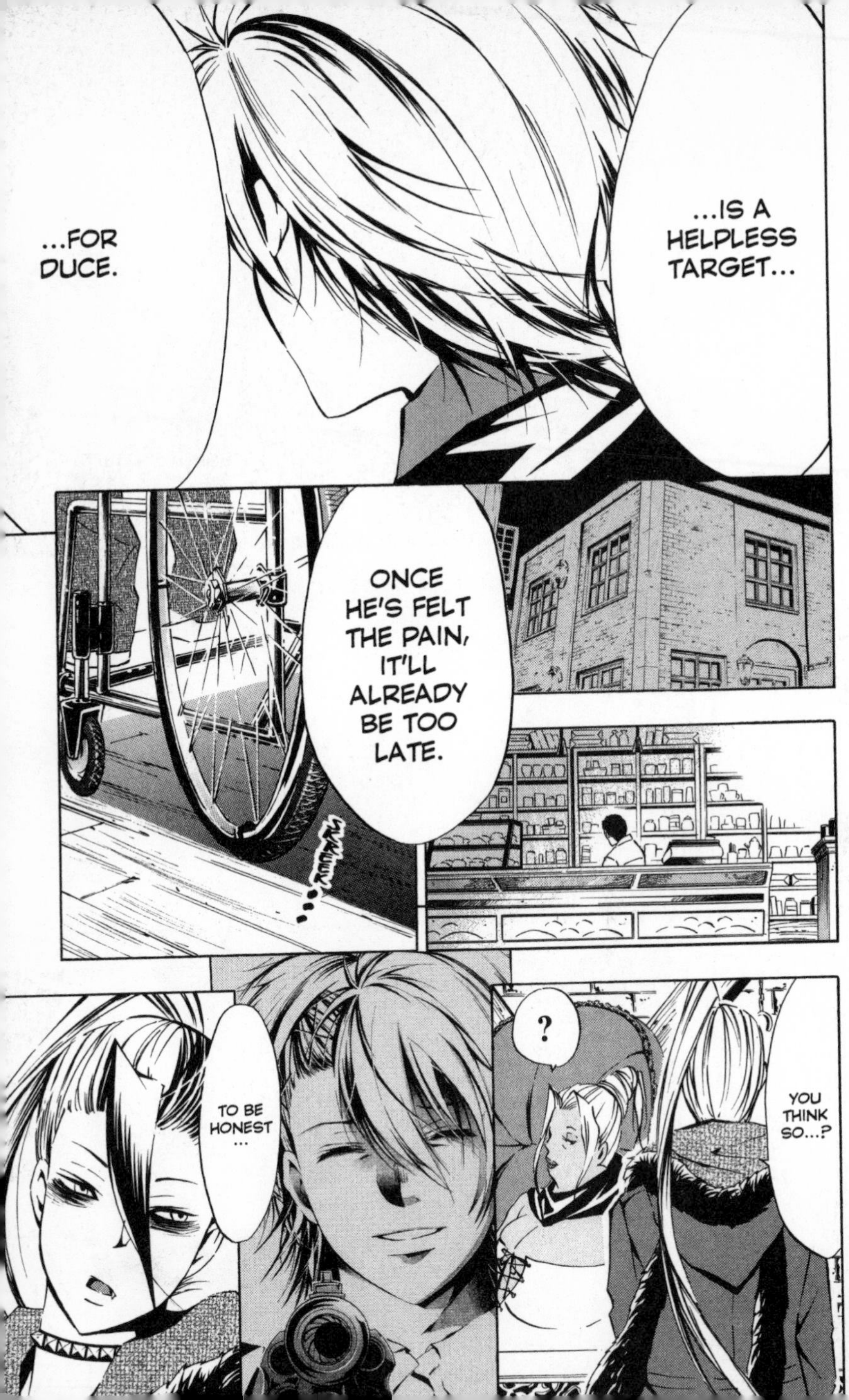
...IS A HELPLESS TARGET...
...FOR DUCE.
ONCE HE'S FELT THE PAIN, IT'LL ALREADY BE TOO LATE.
SKREEK...
YOU THINK SO...?
?
TO BE HONEST...

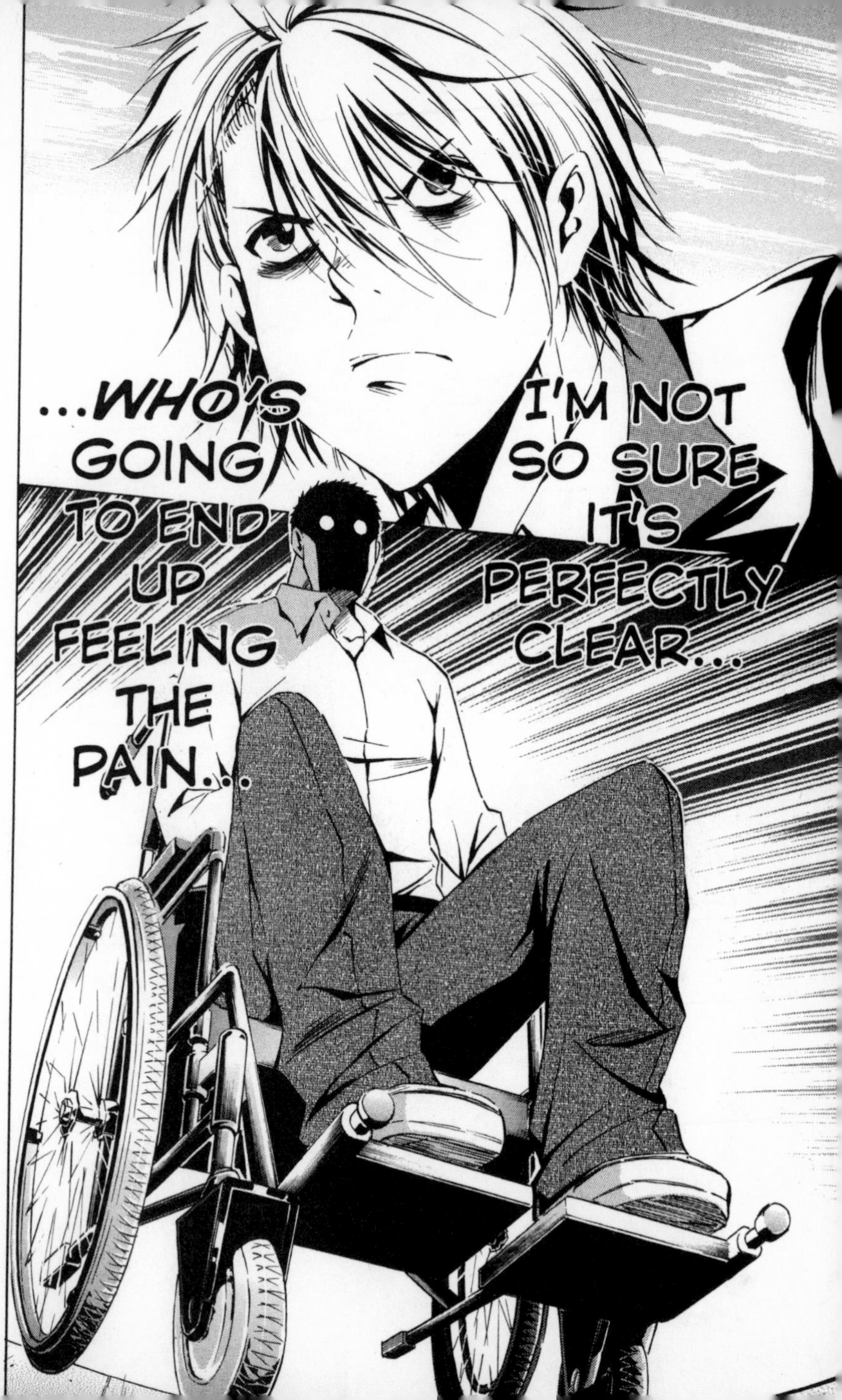
I'M NOT SO SURE IT'S PERFECTLY CLEAR...
...WHO'S GOING TO END UP FEELING THE PAIN...

IT CONTINUES IN Vol.08

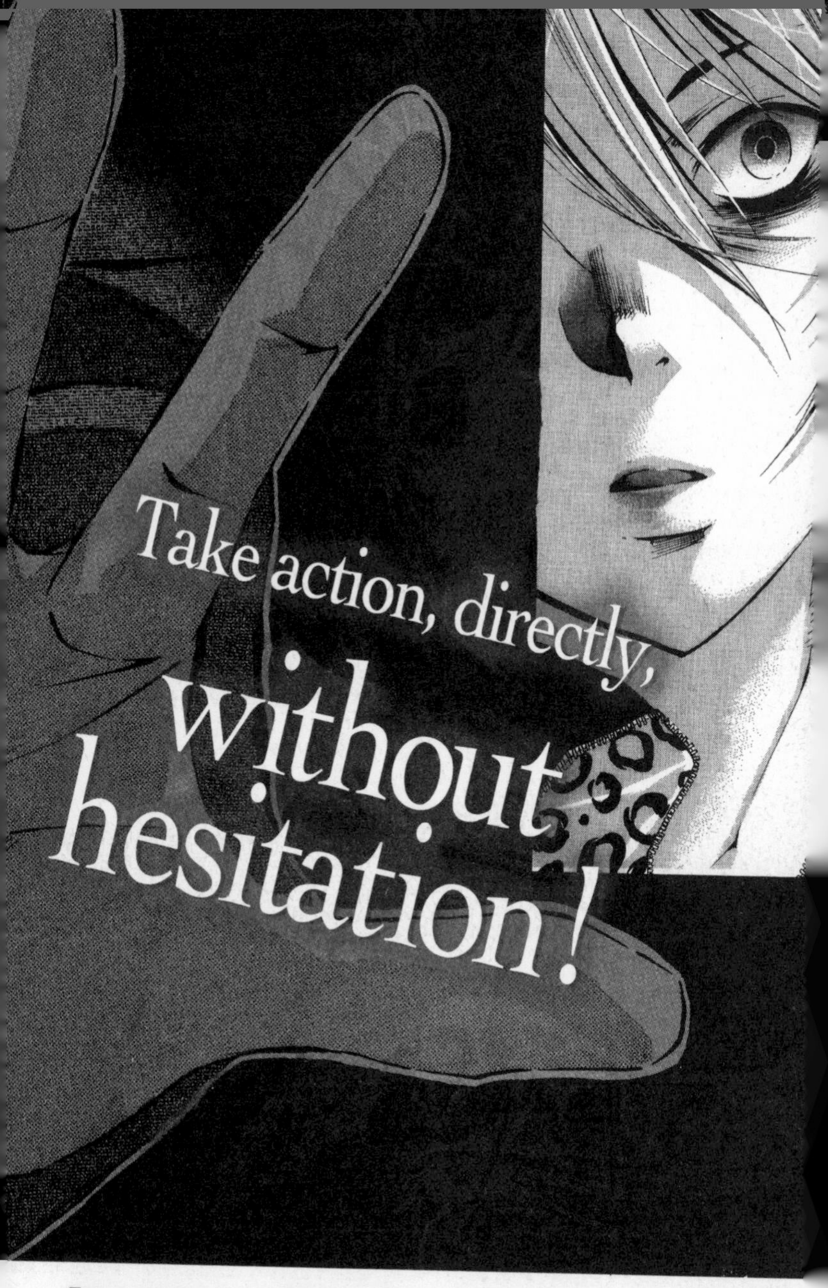
Take action, directly, without hesitation!

JUVENILE REMIX, COMING SOON!!

And then, Junya has
a fateful meeting...
With the **greatest**
**killer** in the business...
**Shock** after **shock**!
Act Two continues
in a blaze!
Look no further
for the highest level
of entertainment!

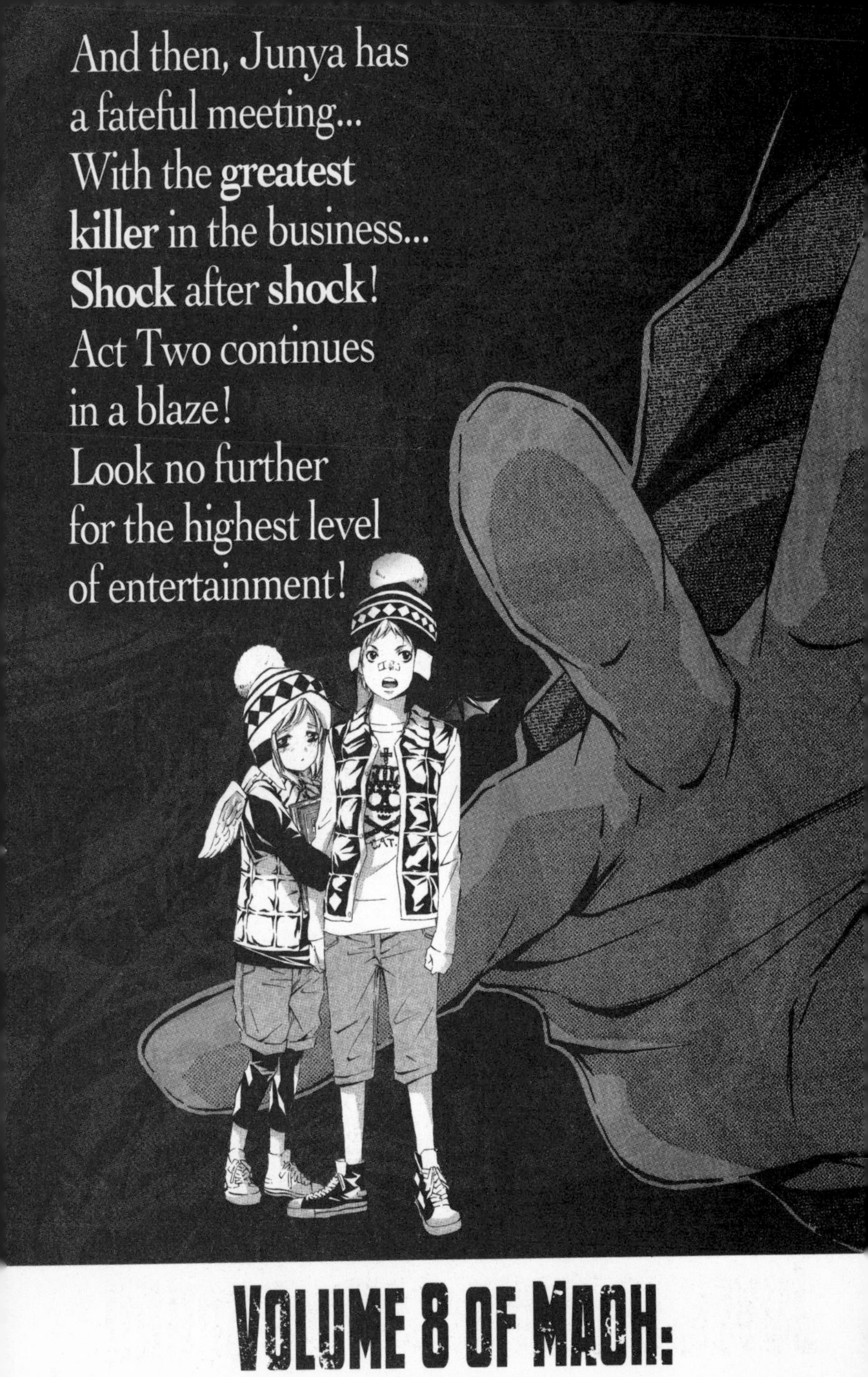

# VOLUME 8 OF MAOH:

## MEGUMI OSUGA

WE HAVE AN INCREDIBLE CONSUMPTION RATE OF CURRY BREAD IN THE STUDIO. EVERYONE'S EATING CURRY BREAD ALL THE TIME. EVEN I'M EATING THE STUFF. WHEN DID THINGS GET THIS WAY...?

ALSO, I HAVE A WONDERFUL BUT TOTALLY IRRELEVANT ANNOUNCEMENT TO MAKE. LATELY I'VE SWITCHED OVER FROM MASHED SWEET BEAN PASTE TO WHOLE SWEET BEANS. THE TEXTURE'S PRETTY ADDICTING, AFTER ALL.

### MEGUMI OSUGA

BORN DECEMBER 21 IN CHIBA PREFECTURE, MEGUMI OSUGA MADE HER DEBUT WITH *TONPACHI*, WHICH RAN IN *SHONEN SUNDAY R*, AND HAD A SHORT SERIES IN *SHONEN SUNDAY SUPER* CALLED *HONOU NO ANA NO YOMI*. IN 2007, HER SERIALIZATION OF *MAOH: JUVENILE REMIX* STARTED IN *SHONEN SUNDAY*.

### KOTARO ISAKA

BORN IN 1971 IN CHIBA PREFECTURE, KOTARO ISAKA IS ONE OF THE MOST POPULAR JAPANESE NOVELISTS AND HAS RECEIVED NUMEROUS AWARDS. HE HAS MANY TITLES UNDER HIS BELT, MOST OF WHICH HAVE BEEN TURNED INTO LIVE-ACTION MOVIES.

# MAOH: JUVENILE REMIX
## Volume 07

### Shonen Sunday Edition

Original Story by **KOTARO ISAKA**
Story and Art by **MEGUMI OSUGA**

© 2007 Kotaro ISAKA, Megumi OSUGA/Shogakukan
All rights reserved.
Original Japanese edition "MAOH JUVENILE REMIX" published by SHOGAKUKAN Inc.

Logo and cover design created by Isao YOSHIMURA & Bay Bridge Studio.

Translation/Stephen Paul
Touch-up Art & Lettering/James Dashiell
Design/Sam Elzway
Editor/Alexis Kirsch

Printed in the U.S.A.

Published by VIZ Media, LLC
P.O. Box 77010
San Francisco, CA 94107

10 9 8 7 6 5 4 3 2 1
First printing, October 2011

www.viz.com

MANGA STARTS ON SUNDAY

www.shonensunday.com

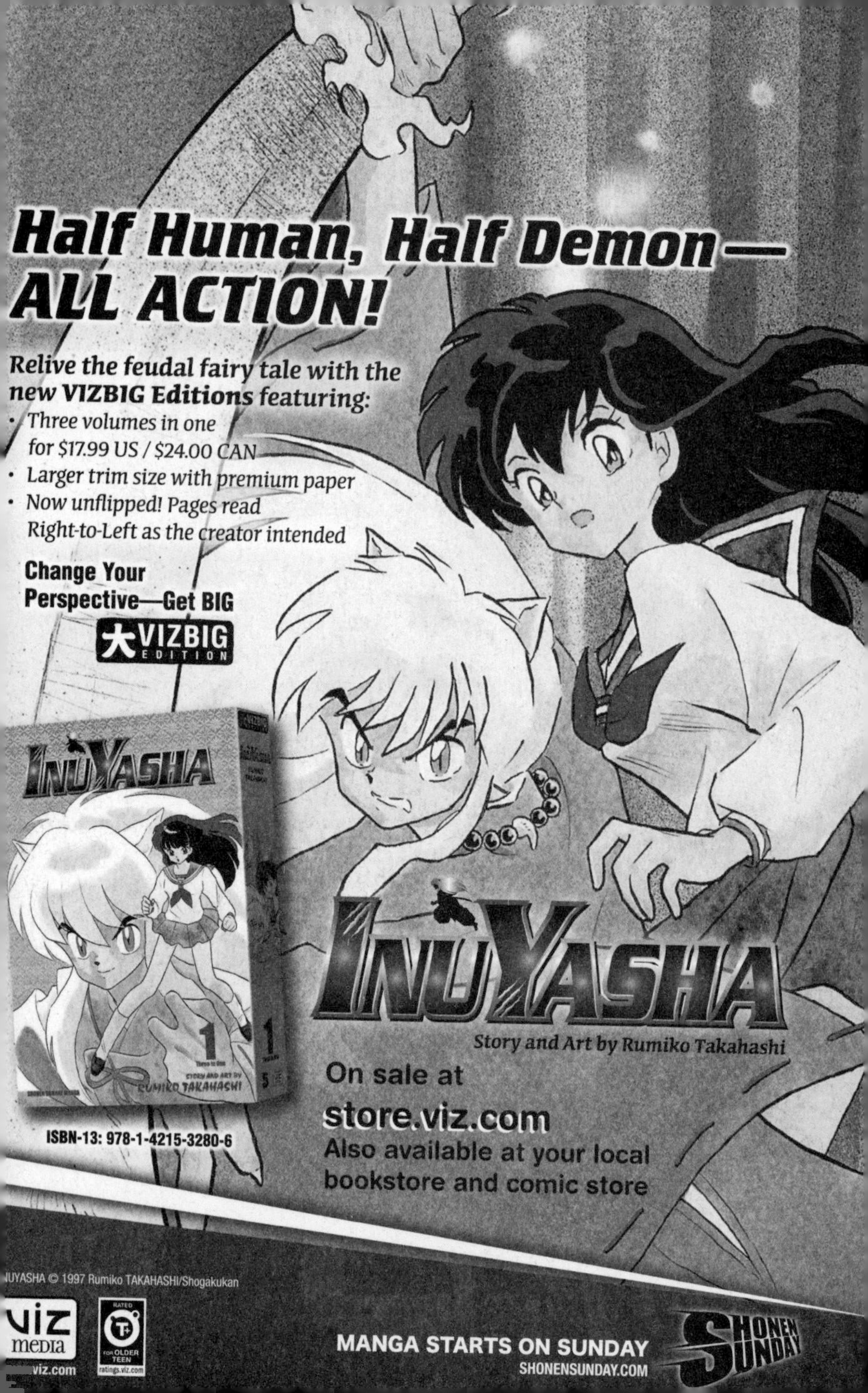
Half Human, Half Demon—
ALL ACTION!
Relive the feudal fairy tale with the new VIZBIG Editions featuring:
• Three volumes in one for $17.99 US / $24.00 CAN
• Larger trim size with premium paper
• Now unflipped! Pages read Right-to-Left as the creator intended
Change Your Perspective—Get BIG
大 VIZBIG EDITION
INUYASHA
1
STORY AND ART BY RUMIKO TAKAHASHI
ISBN-13: 978-1-4215-3280-6
INUYASHA
Story and Art by Rumiko Takahashi
On sale at
store.viz.com
Also available at your local bookstore and comic store
INUYASHA © 1997 Rumiko TAKAHASHI/Shogakukan
viz media
viz.com
RATED T+ FOR OLDER TEEN
ratings.viz.com
MANGA STARTS ON SUNDAY
SHONENSUNDAY.COM
SHONEN SUNDAY

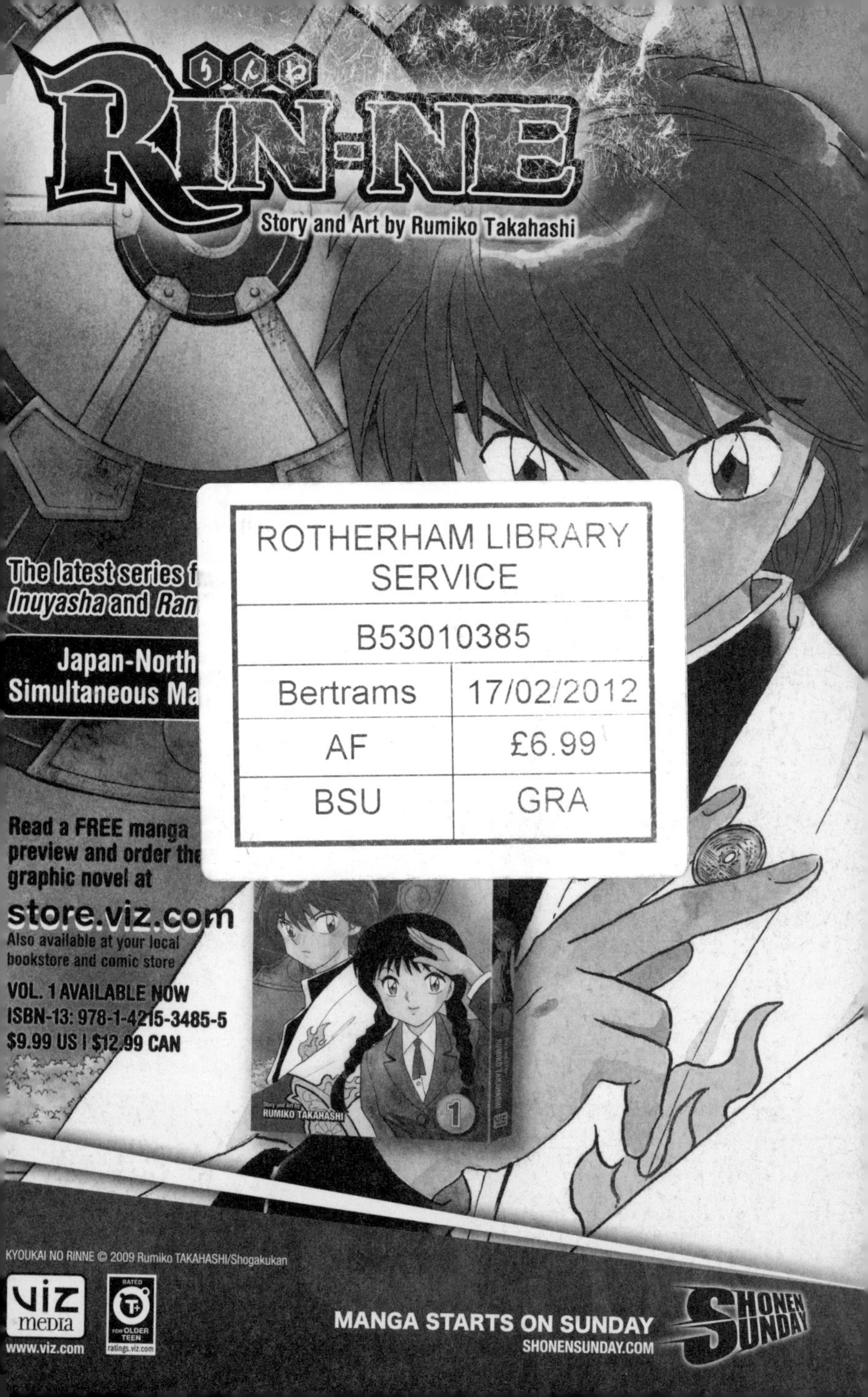
らんね
RIN-NE
Story and Art by Rumiko Takahashi
The latest series
Inuyasha and
Japan-North
Simultaneous
Read a FREE manga
preview and order the
graphic novel at
store.viz.com
Also available at your local
bookstore and comic store
VOL. 1 AVAILABLE NOW
ISBN-13: 978-1-4215-3485-5
$9.99 US | $12.99 CAN
Story and Art by
RUMIKO TAKAHASHI
1
KYOUKAI NO RINNE © 2009 Rumiko TAKAHASHI/Shogakukan
viz media
www.viz.com
RATED T+ FOR OLDER TEEN
ratings.viz.com
MANGA STARTS ON SUNDAY
SHONENSUNDAY.COM
SHONEN SUNDAY

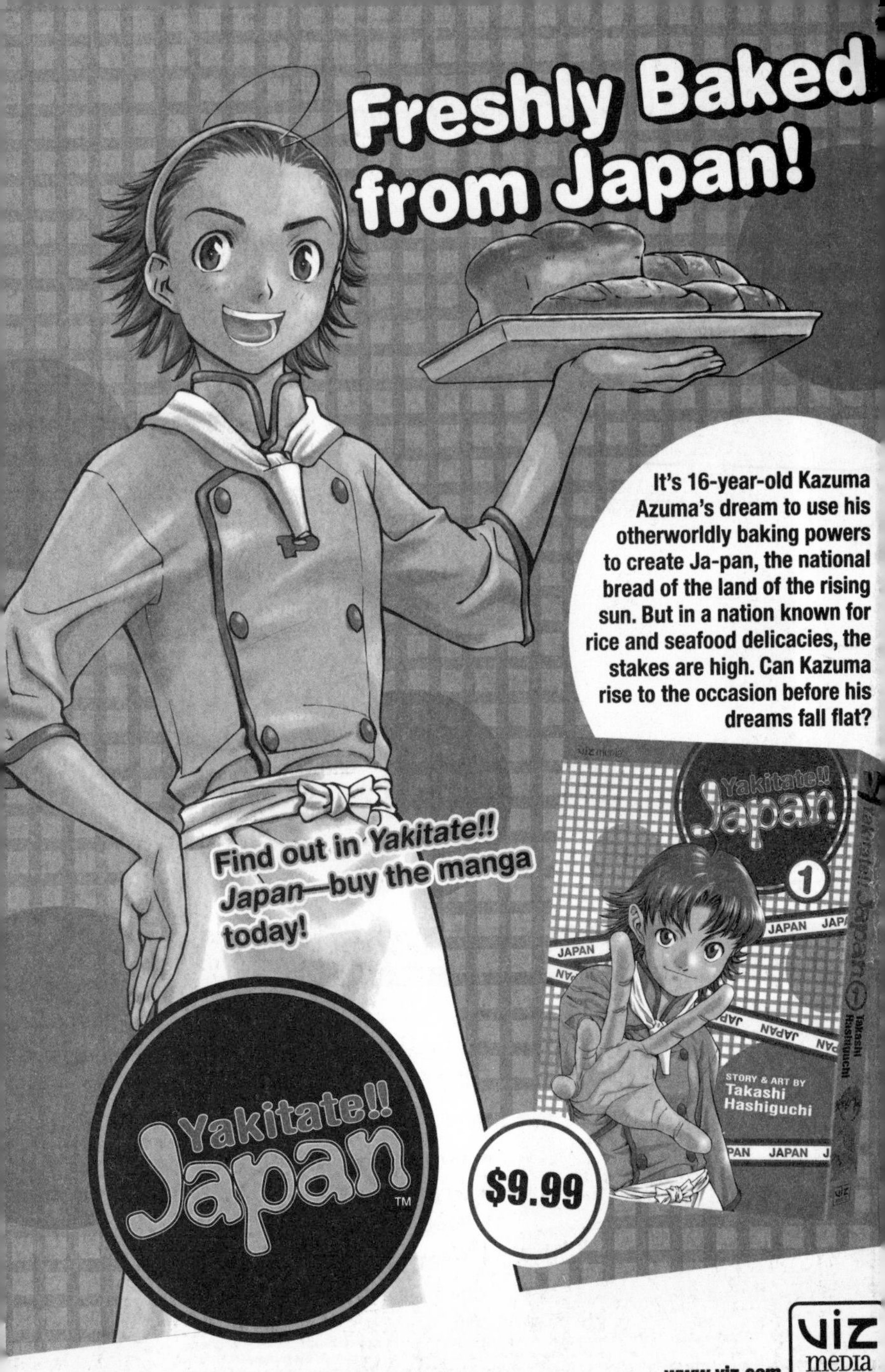

Freshly Baked from Japan!
It's 16-year-old Kazuma Azuma's dream to use his otherworldly baking powers to create Ja-pan, the national bread of the land of the rising sun. But in a nation known for rice and seafood delicacies, the stakes are high. Can Kazuma rise to the occasion before his dreams fall flat?
Find out in *Yakitate!! Japan*—buy the manga today!
Yakitate!! Japan™
$9.99
Yakitate!! Japan 1
STORY & ART BY Takashi Hashiguchi
viz media
www.viz.com

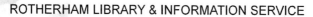
DEATH NOTE © 2003 by Tsugumi Ohba, Takeshi Obata/SHUEISHA Inc.    viz.com/25years